In Quest of the Buddha

A Journey on The Silk Road

In Quest of the Buddha

A Journey on The Silk Road

With Best Compliments from:

Mahuaa Media Private Limited. New Delhi

Published 2009 by
Rupa & Co
7/16, Ansari Road, Daryaganj,
New Delhi 110 002

Sales Centres:
Allahabad Bangalooru Chandigarh Chennai
Hyderabad Jaipur Kathmandu
Kolkata Mumbai

Typeset in 12pt Goudy old style
Designed by Arrt Creations
45 Nehru Apartments, Kalkaji
New Delhi 110 019

Printed in India by
Gopsons Paper Ltd.
Noida 201301

This book is sponsored by
Mahuaa Media Pvt Ltd., New Delhi

pg ii: The grand image of Bodhisattva Avalokitesvara inside the main Buddha Hall of the renowned Sera monastery in Lhasa.

pg xlii: Silk banner recovered in 1907 by Aurel Stein from Dunhuang, dated AD tenth century portrays the most popular theme of 'Buddhist Paradise' – the 'Pure Land' of Heavenly bliss.

Dedication

For you, dear Rakesh
Who walked hand in hand with me
along the enchanting Silk Road,
peeping into caves, jumping along rivers,
climbing snowy hills and dunes in the desert,
always by my side.
In my hours of despair
when I could not take another step
you told me to go ahead
fearlessly
and look for the great Buddha
in every crevice, dust and particle
of the Silk Road.
Without you my dreams
would have remained only that.

Contents

Acknowledgements

I express heartfelt gratitude to the renowned scholar of Tibetan, Mongolian and Sino-Japanese Buddhism, the eminent Prof Lokesh Chandra for his gracious Foreword.

This book would never have been possible without the tremendous work done by scholars, historians, translators, travellers and pilgrims since ancient times. I have referred to them time and again to the best of my ability and to them I owe this book. I seek their forgiveness wherever I may have faulted.

To my publisher for publishing the book, to my editor, Sanjana Roy Choudhury, for undertaking the gruelling task of editing and Ritu Topa for her work in designing the book.

My acknowledgements to the great Chinese travellers and adventurers Zhang Qian, Fa Hien, Xuanzang whose record of their travels has inspired me to undertake the long and adventurous journey on the Silk Road and gather information regarding the ancient sites. To the great travellers Marco Polo and Ibn Batuta from whom I drew courage and who enlightened me by the account of their journey. To Leonardo Olschki, for his famous book on Marco Polo viz. *Marco Polo's Asia* and Henry Yule and Henri Cordier for *The Book of Ser Marco Polo*.

I owe my research to the books by Xinru Liu, Joseph Needham, Jonathan Tucker, Zhang Yiping, Zheng Lixin, B.N. Puri, P.C. Bagchi, M.A. Stein, Sven Hedin, Francis Younghusband, William Woodville Rockhill, Thomas H. Holdich, David Butler and Keith Miles.

I have read with great interest Susan Whitfield's *Life Along the Silk Road* and Peter Hopkirk's *The Great Game* and *Foreign Devils On The Silk Road* which helped me in gaining information on the great Asian highway. To the great Tibetan Lama Taranath for his valuable *History of Buddhism in India*. To Lama Chimpa and Alaka Chattopadhyay for a translation from Tibetan of Lama Taranath's book.

Edward Conze and Kala Acharya from whom I gained better understanding of Buddhism and Buddhist terminology. T.W. Rhys David for providing information about Buddhist ascendancy in ancient India in his famous book *Buddhist India*.

Samuel Beal for his invaluable translation of the *Si Yu Ki* from Chinese of Xuanzang (Hieun Tsiang) and *The Life History of Hieun Tsiang* by Shaman Hwui Li.

To Radha Banerji of the Indira Gandhi National Centre of Arts and Anand Banerji of Abha Prakashan for providing me a rare copy of Dr P. Banerji's illuminating works *New Light on Central Asian Art and Iconography* and *Central Asian Art-New Revelations from Xinjiang* to which I have referred in Chapter seventeen 'Gallery of Avalokitesvara'. Dr P. Banerji, a leading exponent of Indian and Central Asian Art served the National Museum, Delhi for twenty years in various capacities.

To D.C. Ahir for giving detailed information on the 'Dhamma Vijay' campaign of emperor Asoka in *Asoka The Great*.

To Romesh Bhattacharji for helping me with the maps especially with regards to routes into Tibet from Leh and North-East India.

To *Lonely Planet* for helping me trace many a Buddhist sites along the Silk Road.

My deepest obligation to all writers, translators and publishers who have carried the accounts of pilgrims and travellers on the Silk Road to the people. But for them few would have read the accounts.

To Zhang Jianshan, Liu Yunshi and Li Yuming whose *The Anxi Yulin Grottoes* helped me better understand the paintings inside the Anxi caves.Two paintings belonging to Cave 25—one of the village scene which was given to me by the Yulin grottoes staff and another of Bodhisattva Manjusri seated on a lion taken from the above book have been used by me. For this I express gratitude to the Yulin grottoes staff, chief editor Zhang Jianshan of the book and the Gansu Peoples Fine Arts Publishing House.

To World Heritage, Patrimoine Mundial, Deng Jinhui (former editor) and Ru Suichu (photo compiler) Wang Baoping, Xia Juxian and Guo Yan, whose pictorial book on Xian helped me to have a better copy of the terracotta warriors and the royal chariot found in the pit of Chinese emperor Qin shihuangdi and which were used by me in the book. To Wu Zhengke, Xue Qinxue and Zhang Minlin for their book *Probing Into the History of Dafosi Temple* and photo of the Reclining Buddha at Dafosi.

To the China Intercontinental Press, the State Council Information Office and Gansu People's Publishing House for providing valuable photographs and information on historical sites.

To the authorities at Famen, Wild Goose Pagoda, Dafosi, Labrang, Jiaohe, Gaochang, Subashi, Wenshuyan, Jewel Light Pagoda, Chengdu Daci, Longhua, Jade Buddha, Jokhang, Potala Palace, Drepung, Ramoche, Sera, Lamaling. Kashgar mosque, Chinibagh.

Grottoes authorities at Majishan, Binglingsi, Magao, Anxi-Yulin, Bezeklik, Kizil, Western Thousand Buddha, Dazu- Beishan and Baodingshan.

Museums at Banpo, Xian, Anxi, Dunhuang, Urumqi, Turfan, Khotan, Sanpula, Jiayuguan Fort, Dazu Park Carvings, Lhasa.

I would like to thank the China Tourism Department for providing site literature, study material and for allowing me to photograph the sites; the Dunhuang Research Academy, Xinjiang Institute of Archaeology and Xinjiang Kucha Institute of Caves for providing important photographic slides for use in this book and also excellent English speaking guides to provide commentary on the grottoes. To the Beijing Slides Publishing Company and the Dunhuang Slides Publishing Company for providing slides of statues and paintings inside the Magao grottoes. Young and enthusiastic Chinese guides Xingxiaochun, Xengxing, Habibullah, Gorbustan, Hasan and Zhu Ya (Juliet) who led me to difficult sites on the Silk Road and suffered hardships along with me. Without them I could not have reached the Buddhist sites. To Lama Jamyoung for taking me on a tour of the Labrang Monasteryin Xiahe.

I thank the Chinese Embassy and Yang Shuying, Press Attache, for including me in the Indian press delegation going to Tibet, for providing various information regarding the sites and important photographs of the opening ceremony of the Nathu la border.

My friend Li Hubing for providing me important photos of the train to Lhasa.

I thank the singers Abdullah and Arken who gave me company and livened up the long journeys through the Pamir mountains and the Gobi and the Taklamakan desert.

The workers who poured their blood and sweat in laying a metalled road through thousands of kilometers of difficult terrain of icy mountains peaks and the flaming deserts of China. They made it possible for millions of travellers to trace the ancient Silk Road through China.

The China Travel International for making excellent arrangements for my travels along the Silk Road.

Liu Chang, Chinese student of Delhi University and Ji Lili of the Culture department, Chinese Embassy, New Delhi, for helping in English translations from Chinese.

To the Government of India, Ministry of Culture and the National Museum, New Delhi, for providing me important photographs of the Central Asian antiquities. Dr K.K. Chakravarty (ex-director-general), Dr R.R.S. Chauhan, (director-exhibition and PR), J.C. Grover, (assistant curator, National Museum) and Binoy Sahai, assistant curator of the Central Asian Antiquities section for their help in procuring the photographs.

To Pratibha Parashar for permitting me to use the National Museum library.

The Indira Gandhi National Centre for Arts (IGNCA) for providing me a copy of Prof Duan Wenjie's most valuable *Dunhuang Art Through the Eyes of Duan Wenjie* edited by Prof Tan Chung.

The staff of Indian Council for Historical Research (ICHR) who have painstakingly helped me in digging out research material on the Silk Road.

My dear friend Preeti Lal Verma for providing a critical appraisal of the draft manuscript. My friend Salina Sen for patiently reading the draft and pointing out the errors that kept creeping in.

Balbir Singh and Dinesh Sharma who helped me in putting together the pages of this book.

My mother Saraswati Devi for teaching me to never lose hope in life.

My father-in-law Surendra Narayan Dwivedi and mother-in-law Shashi Dwivedi, whose blessings are always with me.

My husband Rakesh, for taking time off from his busy schedule and accompanying me on my travels and videographing the sites.

My children Jyotsna, Divya and Eklavya for always encouraging me to complete my work and for looking after themselves while I was always away on long journeys.

I am solely responsible for any errors that may have crept into my writing by way of inadvertently missing and faulty references, dates or historical facts. I claim no scholarly endeavour, only a fascination for travelling of which this travelogue is a humble account.

Prologue

Buddha is surely one of the three most influential persons in world history, the others being Jesus Christ and the Prophet Mohammad. Between them they continue to influence around half the population of the entire planet, and their presence is by no means confined to the country of their birth but has spread to the four corners of the world. The journey of Buddhism from the plains of Central India all the way to the nations of South and South-East Asia is a fascinating story. There were two routes for this, the land route which is known as the Silk Route, and the ocean route. It is also important to remember that along with Buddhism, Hinduism also travelled to South and South Asia, the most dramatic example of which is the fabulous Angkor Wat temple in Cambodia, the largest place of worship in the world.

The journey of the Silk Route is one of the most fascinating in human history, and has been the subject of a large number of memoirs and books by Indian, Chinese and European scholars. The present book with its learned Forword by the eminent Buddhist scholar Dr. Lokesh Chandra represents yet another significant addition to literature in this area. Sunita Dwivedi has researched the whole field extensively and has produced a volume which combines historical narrative with a contemporary travelogue. The illustrations are well chosen and give the reader a graphic picture of the varied cultural background of the countries to which Buddhism has spread.

In an age still torn with conflict, war and tension, the message of the Buddha remains even more significant than it was when he first delivered it 2-1/2 millennia ago. As it moved from India to different cultures and regions, Buddhism developed special forms and qualities so that where on the one hand we have somewhat rigid Hinayana tradition in Sri Lanka, in Japan thousands of miles away Buddhism has flourished in the form of Zen which itself is based on the Sanskrit word *Dhyan*. Similarly, the great mountain monasteries of Ladakh and Tibet have their own distinctive architecture compared with the magnificent Borobodour in Indonesia, based on the Sanskrit *Bhadra Vihar*. The whole area is full of fascinating cultural, linguistic, architectural and social facets, and I am sure this book will be of interest to students of Buddhism and of Asian culture around the world. I warmly commend the author for the energy and scholarship that she has put into the creation of this book.

1 September. 2009

(Karan Singh)
Member of Parliament
(Rajya Sabha)

Bezeklik, Temple no.9.
Pranidhi scene.
Sanskrit inscription on top.

Foreword

The free-flowing vademecum of a journey across the mindscape of the Tathagata in the heartland of the Han, in Central Asia and in Tibet emanates from the quartets of the life, spirituality, wanderlust, and writing genius of Sunita Dwivedi. Her temporal solidarity and loyalty with her birthplace of Kushinagara flows in a continuous stream in this delightful narrative. Kushinagara is one of the four most sacred places associated with the Buddha, the others being the place of his birth, of his enlightenment and of his first sermon. It was the capital of the Mallas. Malla means a hero. Like them the heroic author has undertaken the arduous trail where once trod scholars, generals, merchants, and envoys. The living sancta and weeping ruins can be visualised in the majestic radiance of the mind.

Crossing the Hiranyavati, or the Golden River, Lord Buddha had entered Kushinagara. This narrative too is golden like the Hiranyavati where the glory and majesty of Buddha's message burst into bloom. She opens up a time capsule that has preserved a marvellous slice of art and thought across two millennia, and continues to illumine the way for millions today.

The author commences her journey with a visit to the Famen monastery hallowed by Lord Buddha's relic and in tune with her intentions appropriately termed Gateway (*men*) to Dharma (*fa*). The octagonal pagoda represents the eight directions of space and the eight petals of the frail cup of a lotus. The mind is the eight-petalled lotus where blossoms the fire of the Spirit. Like the Vedic seers, she seeks the Agni born in an eight-petalled lotus. The frail lotus and the fiery luminosity of the mind are the powerful coordinates of the deep silence of the octagonal stupa.

The author speaks of the blue sky covering the Wild Goose Pagoda of Xuanzang. Blue is the colour of meditation in Buddhism or thought luminous by nature. What a strange coincidence that she should be fascinated by the blue sky before visiting the stupa dedicated to the great yogin Xuanzang. Wild Goose (or Great Goose) is a misunderstanding of the Sanskrit *parama-hamsa* who is an ascetic of the highest order and has attained the fourth or the supreme stage in abstract meditation. Xuanzang was accorded this honour by his teachers in India. *Hamsa* is swan and not goose. It is time that the nomenclature of the stupa to one of the greatest masters of Chinese Buddhism is corrected and its meditative symbolism restored. The author gives an absorbing account of the cultural relics that Xuanzang brought to China.

The author describes in vivid terms the mausoleum of the Chinese emperor Qin Shihuangdi (221-8 BC). As early as his reign, Yueh-chi Buddhist monks brought a number of Sutras to his court, but he did not accept the Dharma. These monks Sanskritised his dynastic name Qin (pronounced Chin) to *Cheena*, which travelled from India to South-east Asia, from

Malay to European languages and now it is the international name. China is a Sanskrit name given to the Middle Kingdom by the Yueh-chih.

Emperor Qin Shihuangdi had all the Confucian classics burnt all over China, and so Chinese scholars have professed a thorough contempt for the Qin dynasty. They freely call themselves 'Han people' after the Han dynasty which collected the Confucian classics and made them the central philosophy of Chinese life. The Qin emperor joined the different sections of the Great Wall of China and gave rise to Sinocentrism with China as the Central Kingdom and barbarians around to be conquered. The inner certitude of China arises in this rapture of their psychosphere to this day. The billboard at the entrance of Jichuan, the Space City of China, has enormous Chinese characters in scarlet, and interestingly enough their translation in English: 'Without Haste. Without Fear. We conquer the world'.

What a sensitive choice of the author, namely the city of Xian, to commence her pilgrimage to China's living and extinct symbols of glory and transcendence. It was the metropolis of the golden period of Chinese history under the Tang dynasty. The supreme power of the Tang was represented by the Thousand-armed Avalokitesvara who was painted by an Indian monk as early as 618-26. As recently as 8 August 2008, the World Olympic Games commenced with a dance of the Thousand-armed Avalokitesvara with a thousand girls dancing and singing his Sanskrit hymn in Chinese pronunciation. It was the Buddhist heritage of China followed by a recitation of the Confucian Classics by three thousand young men from 'bamboo books' used in the days of Confucius. The resounding resonance, the profound depth of time and the numbing number of thousands were to remind the visiting 'barbarians' of the might of the Confucian Land.

Away from the neolithic village of Banpo, the author speaks of Lady Yang Kweifei whose beauty mesmerized the emperor Xuanzong (r. 712-56). She became the heroine of his countless stage-plays, as well as the misfortune that marked the end of his reign. When An Lushan captured Chang-an in 756, the emperor fled and Lady Yang had to be offered for hanging. The emperor's fascination for her led to the neglect of the Central Asian states when they sought help from China. In 751, the Arabs gained victory over the Chinese in the Talas Valley and the Buddhist kingdoms of Central Asia were gradually taken over by the Islamic armies. It was not only an emperor's grief, however, the grief of the 'second blossoming of T'ang culture' and of a millenarian Buddhist culture.

The author's description of the Maijishan Caves arising out of the earth like a gigantic stupa and its environs is so vivid that we are there in its scenic charm and seclusion. The mountain derives its name *maiji* from its shape which resembles sheaves of grain. It recalls the great Indian monastery of Dhanya-kataka 'heap of grain', mentioned in the *Manjusri-mula-kalpa*. Dhanya-kataka 'shaped like a heap of grain' is one of the six conventional shapes of stupas in Sri Lanka. Maijishan was a holy site as early as the beginning of the fifth century. The works in the Cave of the Seven Buddhas are a transitional style between the early art of Yun-kang and Lung-men and the full Sui-Tang styles. The stiff hieratical style is replaced by naturalistic representations. The human foot is carved in the round with a shapely ankle and natural toes. The faces undergo a re-humanising process. Sexless deities become modest maidens, with a frank and worldly look, the archaic smile ends in dimples. The Four Guardians of Directions breathe martial vigour. Elegant flowing drapery surrounds mature goddesses, like an enjewelled *prima donna* with the 'majestic indolence of a sultana' (Grousset). The monumental Sung figures in the Maijishan caves come close to portraiture. The apostle Kasyapa in Cave 90 represents an Indian monk, and though imaginary, it carries naturalism in sculpture to a degree unknown in earlier times. These caves opened a completely new approach to sculpture.

As the author delineates the murals on the ceilings, the images of Buddhas and bodhisattvas, Arhats/ Lohan or apostles of Lord Buddha, or the kalavinka bird, in the long cave galleries, she takes the readers into the caves themselves by her evocative diction. She draws us into these splendid caverns to stir the eye and the spirit to their depths. They are symbolic tangents of what took place in the secret of human hearts for a millennium. Here time falls into the timeless, in the silence and solitude of meditation.

The author in her gripping life-like narrative is on a speedboat to the Binglingsi caves dominated by a twenty-seven metre high Maitreya or Future Buddha. The sculptures in these caves show a direct impact of Indian art as the expression of sophisticated worldly life when the bodies become more delicate and lithe. The sculptors give their deities relaxed and natural rhythms. A new elegance and sensitivity appears in these figures with an imposing majesty. The Indian style is acting directly and is being assimilated to serve the humanising tendencies in Buddhist sculpture, contradistinguished from the immobile and heavy figures of the Han dynasty, which resurfaced in the Ming period. The lovely sculpture of Amitabha accompanied by two Bodhisattvas and two Guardian kings in niche 51 of Binglingsi shows restyling in the graceful and dignified Indian mode, with the comparative slimness of the hips which Chinese sculptors felt to be a profane feature of Indian prototypes. The Bodhisattva on the left is Avalokitesvara who stands in an emphatic tribhanga. The sculpture displays all the vernal freshness and animation of pose, as distinct a rooted Chinese immobility of posture. Another stone image of Avalokitesvara in niche 50 stands in marked tribhanga, with the dhoti closely moulded to the body.

The author reaches the Labrang Monastery the first Tibetan monastery in her itinerary. It has been preserved in its original glory and its courses in Buddhist philosophy are in full depth of traditional learning.

On her way to Dafosi, the author saw the stupa of Kumarajiva who was the son of Kumarayana of Kashmir and Princess Jiva of Kucha. His translation of the *Lotus Sutra* is the major scripture of East Asia which is enjoying a vibrant renaissance in the Soka Gakkai movement of creating values. It is the first enunciation of the Peace, Harmony and Bliss of humanity. Kumarajiva is the only Indian whose Chinese diction has been hailed over the centuries by Chinese men of letters. He was self-sacrificing and humane, strikingly handsome, intellectually brilliant and hardworking. Emperor Yao Xing was highly impressed by him. The emperor felt that the extraordinary brilliance of Kumarajiva must be transmitted to future generations. He assigned ten girls to live with him. Kumarajiva adapted himself to the circumstances and complied with the wishes of the emperor. During his preaching, he warned his listeners to take only the lotus that grew out of the mud and to leave the mud alone. The sons and grandsons of

Kumarajiva failed to live up to the high hopes of this eugenic experiment.

The language of Kucha was Tocharian B which shows a close affinity with European languages like Latin. The Chinese ethnonym *Po* 'white' indicates their affinity to Europeans. Kumarajiva was European and Indian by circumstance of birth. His Chinese version of the *Lotus Sutra* thus represents the cultural strands of Sanskrit, Tocharian and Chinese that symbolise the three major mindscapes of his times: Indian, European and Chinese. A great Japanese poet of the eleventh century Saigyo (1118-90) writes about the Lotus Sutra translated by Kumarajiva into Chinese:

> *Natsu kusa no* Even the white dew
> *Hitoba ni sugaru* Clinging to every blade
> *Shiratsuya mo* Of summer grass
> *Hana no ue ni wa* Does not accumulate
> *Tamarazarikeri* On this flower

The word 'flower' means the flower of the *Lotus Sutra* and dew is the metaphor for conditioned things that come to be, to pass away.

From the ghost of the Gobi desert the author comes to the Yulin caves by the side of the Yulin river. These caves are unique in being contextualised in the hills and dales of the site. They were dug several metres deep, which keeps them exceptionally cool while the surrounds are scorching hot. The Chinese character *shi* for a monastery meant a government office when Buddhism was introduced into Han China. The early translators of Buddhist sutras into Chinese were Parthians, Yueh-chih, Sogdians and Indians. An Hsuan who translated the *Ugradatta-paripriccha* was a Parthian of Eastern Iran, a Buddhist layman, and a commander of the Chinese cavalry. The horses for Chinese army came from Sogdiana and adjacent regions, and thus Buddhism and defence were interlinked. The saying is *dharmo rakshati rakshitah* or dharma and defence are interdependent. It is no wonder that the Yulin caves with the subterranean complex were an extension of the concept of trenches in warfare. The Chinese commanderies could keep a watch for any nomadic intrusion, while they were not visible to the aggressors. Remote from mainland home, the soldiers found it hard to spend lives away from friends and families, and only Buddhist monks could find in these deserted stretches, the void of the self, the echoing of samsara and nirvana, an embodiment of Buddhist teaching. Hence, the monks and monastic establishments. The Chinese poet Wang Wei (701-81) pined as his friend was leaving for the Gobi:

> In Wei township morning rain has wetted the fine dust,
> Your lodging is shaded by fresh new willows.
> I urge you, Lord, to down another cup of wine,
> Going West of Yang barrier, there will be no more friends.

Another T'ang poet Wang Zhihuan (born 695):

> Why should a foreign flute play 'Willow Lament'?
> No spring breeze can reach Jade Gate Barrier.

The Yulin caves have willow trees, the feel of spring breeze in its subterranean depth, and they are rich in the beauty of murals and icons. They reflect the new iconography of the Water Moon Avalokitesvara, and the mandalas of Tantric Buddhism under the influence of Xixia, after the prince of Shazhou had made submission to them. Cave 25 of Yulin has the most splendid representation of the Descent of Maitreya, that supersedes all its eighty-seven illustrations of the golden Tang period at Dunhuang. The *Sutra of Maitreya's Descent* (*Mile xiasheng jing*) was translated from Sanskrit into Chinese by a Yuezhi monk Dharmaraksa in AD 266 at Dunhuang. Maitreya was to descend in remote days to come as a Saviour, an open-ended symbol of a glorious future of peace and plenty, in the euphoria of happy rhythms of life. Maitreya is a metamorphosis of Mithra, the royal god of the Iranians. Mithraism took root among the Romans, and religious life was like enlistment and service under a divine commander or *militia Mithrae*. The Yulin caves are the imposing edifice of the convergence of monastic enlistment and of the protection of the empire by Maitreya, an incarnation of the unconquerable *Sol Invictus Mithra*. Yulin caves are the vigorous and positive, transitive and transcendent sanctuary of Dharma.

The author has a long chapter on Dunhuang, the jewel of the Spiritual Route of Sutras (rather than the Silk Route), that is honeycombed with 496 caves, listening to the pause of time. From the Blazing (*Dun*) Beacon (*huang*) of the Han commanderies it became the illumination of the inner vision. The outstanding colossus of Maitreya in cave 96 constructed in AD 695 is its wonder. Its dedicatory inscription *Mogaoku ji* 'Record of the Mogao Caves' describes how this thirty-two metre high dry lacquer image was made in the reign of Empress Wu. It gives the name of the caves as Mogao. It made a vivid impression in the minds of Lajos Loczy and his companions who reached Dunhuang in 1878 and have left its engraving when it was in a frayed condition. They inspired Sir Aurel Stein to investigate its forlorn wonders in the heart of the Gobi. The author cites the opinion of Chinese scholars on this historic discovery who denigrate it as deceit, treachery, and shameless trickery. Had Stein and Pelliot not researched them they would not have gained international recognition as prime historic treasures. As an academic, I admire their labours of opening up China's heritage of culture and aesthetics in its profound and wonderful murals, sculptures and sutras. They revealed the *sunyata* and *rupam* of these caves as syllogisms of the soul and mind in the luminiscence of wisdom. This cave complex was commenced by an Indian monk named Lo Tshun in AD 366. He dreamt of a cloud with a Thousand Buddhas floating in the sky. The Thousand Buddhas are the core concept in the Avatamsaka tradition with the centrality of the colossal image (*abhyucca-deva*) of Rocana Buddha. He may have been inspired by the colossi of North West India culminating in the Bamiyan Buddhas. The name Mogaoku means 'Cave of Unequalled Height' which is an epithet of the Divine Mount Sumeru. Lo Tshun decided to excavate the caves in the escarpment of Dunhuang in the Avatamsaka tradition whose colossus and Thousand Buddhas were in keeping with its association with impirium. Dunhuang had been established as a garrison commandery in 111 BC by Emperor Wu of the Han dynasty to guard the route to the West. The spiritual and artistic initiative of the Indian monk made Dunhuang outshine the other Central Asian commanderies. It became a centre for the translation of Sanskrit Sutras into Chinese by Parthian, Yueh-chih and other monk scholars who came alongwith their kinsmen trading in the steeds of Ferghana renowned for their strategic necessity. These merchants, monks, and envoys from the distant kingdoms of

Central Asia were recognised as people from afar barbarian wastelands who were deemed to be bearers of tribute as a token of submission in the Confucian world-view. The Central Asian people with their profound study of transcendental philosophy and Buddhist Sutras knew that they inherited a perfection of the Corpus of the Word, which was beyond the comprehension of the Chinese literati. They started to translate the Sanskrit sutras into Chinese so that they realise the radiance of their virtue and learning. As early as the year 2 BC we find a Yueh-chih prince instructing a member of the Imperial Academy in Buddhist sutras. The Sinocentrism of Confucian polity deepened in awareness: 'and there is a rain of precious flowers that robs the very cloud of colours... When we hear the teachings the Mighty Intellect, the seventh heaven is reached'.

The flying goddesses in the murals of Dunhuang are the jade beauties of Serindia. The Chinese were fascinated by them, by their music and their dance while they carried the fragrance of Buddhism to China. The goddesses emerge from the Pool of Seven Jewels in the Pure Land of Sukhavati. They scatter blossoms from the sky to make the world fragrant. With no raiment above the waist, with their bosoms exposed, they were in contradiction to the Confucian order with its meticulous dressing. They bid the onlooker to accompany them into worlds of luminous beauty. Even Chairman Mao appreciated their joyous tenderness, and they were painted all over China during his period.

After the An Lushan rebellion (755-63) the imperial forces lacked the strength to maintain the western possessions. The Tibetans took the capital Chang-an (modern Xian) in 763 and controlled Dunhuang from 781 to 847. Dunhuang thus remained untouched by the persecution of Buddhism in China between 842 and 845. Monk Hong Bian worked closely with Zhang Yichao to expel the Tibetans. An imperial tablet records that Hong Bian could wear purple in commemoration of the return of Dunhuang to Chinese control. On his death around 862, a chapel was dedicated in his honour. It is cave 17 which later on became the Library Cave to preserve the Sutras when Khotan fell to the Islamic onslaught of Kashgar around AD 1000. The risk of Muslims pursuing Buddhist monks of Khotan who were seeking refuge in Dunhuang raised the apprehension of a threat to Dunhuang itself. Cave 17 as the holy symbol of Hong Bian who had saved Dunhuang was chosen to conserve the Sutras for posterity, in the face of impending danger of Islam which had engulfed all the Buddhist kingdoms of Serindia.

The author illustrates a wooden block of a Sanskrit hymn to a Buddha flanked by two Bodhisattvas. The most ancient xylographic plate for printing Sanskrit comes from the Library Cave of Dunhuang. It is a mantra for defence dated 980, to pre-empt the Islamic threat that loomed large on the horizon. It is a dharani to Mahapratisara, one of the Five Goddesses of Protection or Panca-raksa.

The author continues her journey to Urumqi, the City of Lights, where the famed mummies from Loulan are preserved. The face of the lady from Qaurighul looks so peaceful and hauntingly beautiful that she has captured the imagination of the Turkic people who have nicknamed her Beauty of Loulan. She is of Europoid ethnicity with blue eyes and light brown hair. Her wheat basket and winnowing tray, woollen clothing and Caucasian features demonstrate her Western origins. Loulan has yielded Kharoshthi tablets in Prakrit and these texts call it *Kroraina* which has become Loulan in the restrictive phonology of Chinese. The parallelism of Tokharian languages and the textile links tie these Central Asian mummies to European ethnicity.

The next major site visited by the author is Gaochang or Khocho which was inhabited by Tokharian farmers and traders in AD 108. Its control seesawed between the Xiongnu and the Chinese for 400 years (206 BC-AD 220). A Maitreya temple was built in 469. In the sixth century the Buddhist dynasty Qu was ruling with Gaochang as the capital. The famous Chinese pilgrim Xuanzang was welcomed by King Qu Wentai. His son surrendered to the Chinese in 640. The act of making grape wine was introduced to China from Gaochang. In 840 Uigur tribes established their kingdom with Gaochang as the capital, and ruled for centuries until the Mongols swept Central Asia. The Uigurs were forcibly converted to Islam in the fourteenth century. In the Ming period (1368-1644) Gaochang was crucial to the Chinese for its dye for blue and white porcelain. The Uigurs have a history of several hundred years of translating Buddhist scriptures. A few thousand fragments of Uigur texts show their extensive Buddhist literature. For instance, an Uigur text is *Disha-stvustik* or *Disam-svastika* which narrates the story of the two merchants Trapusha and Bhallika. The *Buddhacarita* of Asvaghosa was done in alliterative verse translation in Uigur. A Nilakantha-sutra invokes the protection of Avalokitesvara against all evil. A red sandstone votive stupa from Gaochang of the fifth-sixth century, was excavated from the Khan's palace. The Uigurs used their own script as well as Brahmi script for writing Uigur Turkish. The Turkish written in Brahmi with specially innovated diacritic marks gives precise vowels and is invaluable for the history of Turkish language. The Uigurs were the only people who captioned their murals in Sanskrit. For instance, in the group of six monks in the corridor of temple number 9 of Bezeklik the sixth is *guru acarya ghosa-gotra Jnanasenasya bimbo yam* 'this is the picture of Jnanasena of the ghosa gotra'. Another pranidhi scene in the same temple has the caption:

> *Vasisthasyagamanam srutva sresthi pritiman abhavat*
> *Udyanam mandayitva ca viharam karayamy aham*
> *'On coming to know of the coming of Vasistha,*
> *I the merchant was mighty delighted, had a*
> *monastery constructed adorned with a garden'.*

An interesting find from Astana cemetery is a posy of artificial flowers made from silk gauze from the seventh-eighth century. They are in an exquisite condition. When the kingdom of the Uigurs was vanquished by Chinggis Khan, the Uigur monks were the only well educated class. The empire of Chinggis Khan needed a literate beaucracy and the Uigur bhiksus became secretaries to the emperor. The word *bhiksu* had become *bakshi* in Uigur, and in the new Mongolian context bakshi came to mean a secretary to the state. We have inherited this designation and there are bakshis all over India. Our word *thakur* is from Uigur *tegin*, through the Mongols. Thus Gaochang has left its reminiscences in these words in our language.

The tenth chapter on Kuqa is a readers' delight as the author describes the hidden splendour of the caves, swathed in luminous halos. She watches with emotion the laborious paintings of the monks to whom the Enlightened One had whispered: 'You are the brush of the Buddha...' The 363 caves at Kizil and others at Kumtura come alive in the moving diction of the author in their subtle brushwork, devotion and skill, in the astonishing freedom the artists to express individual features, such as the beating wings of a bird or the beard of a brahmin. The religious culture of Kuqa was a major source of inspiration for the Chinese monk-literati whence they obtained Sanskrit texts like the *Bhiksuni-pratimoksa* or the discipline of nuns. The archeological discovery of Serindia at the end of the nineteenth century began in 1890 when the British major general, H. Bower, found a birch-bark manuscript in Kuqa where he had gone in search of a murderer. Alongwith Khotan, Kuqa had a rich tradition of Sanskrit learning. Kuqa equally enriched the dance and music of China. Sujiva of the royal house of Kuqa was a lute player and he came to China in the bridal train of a Turkish queen in AD 568. He introduced the scale of seven notes which were studied by the Duke of Pei, Cheng I, who headed a committee appointed by the emperor in AD 567 to study musical problems. The theory and vocabulary of Sujiva shows that Kuqean music was derived from that of India, as pointed out by Prof Sylvain Levi. The Tocharians of Kuqa who spoke an ancient Indo-European language were absorbed by the Uigurs and eventually converted to Islam by the Chagatai Khanate.

The author is in Kashgar with its marvelous monuments of the Idgah Mosque, Apakhoja Tomb and its bustling bazaars recalling those of India. She traces its history from the second century when it was invaded by the Kushans. The Turks of Kashgar embraced Islam in 960 en masse in all their 200,000 yurts, the first and the largest ever conversion in Central Asia. The author refers to its forerunner, the ancient kingdom of Shule with a number of stupas, some dating back to the first century. Shule (or Sogdiana) is mentioned in Sanskrit literature as Sulika. Kumarajiva stayed for a year in Kashgar with his mother to study the Vedas, astronomy, and mathematics.

The author regales the readers with the details and travails of the journey to see some surviving stupas in the sands to track the Light that emanated from the stupa of her birthplace Kushinagara. They are draughts of the Ideal from Form's flagon. The Rawak stupa is a reminder of times when Buddhist monasteries had orchards and grew grains, the monks developed architecture, sculpture and painting, studied philosophy and translated Sanskrit sutras. Buddhism gave rise to a rosary of oasis towns strung around this great desert. Jacques Gies and Monique Cohen call 'Serinde, terre du Bouddha' which it once was with its lavishly decorated convents, grottos and stupas.

The author wends her way into Tibet with its overflowing metaphysical filigree of scrolls and statues to carry eternal depths to the eyes of the faithful. In the Tibet of today, we see shadows of evanescence and envision the rags we pick and stitch as the insubstantiality of samsara. The author takes us to see the throbs and surges of the spirituality of Tibet in the fragments of enchantment.

Her penultimate chapter is on Avalokitesvara, the visive symbol of the omnipresence of compassion, to rescue the world from its restless and trembling in the fleeting breeze of transience. A Tibetan hymn on the virtues of Avalokita seeks:

The rays of Your knowledge open the lotus
of the mind.
Your rays of morality cool those scorched by
defilements.
From Your cloud-mass of Love, the downpour
of Compassion
Soaks Faith's fields and ripens the leaves of Bodhi.

Bodhisattva at Kumtura Caves, Kuqa

The Korean annals *Samguk-yusa* record a hymn sung by a country woman named Huimyong who lived at the time of the Silla King Kyongdok (r 742-65). Huimyong's child was blinded at the age of five. She took the child to a temple and sang the following to the Thousand-eyed Avalokitesvara, painted on its north wall:

I fall on my knees and implore You
Thousand-eyed Bodhisattva
You have so many eyes,
Can You not spare two for my child?
Your compassion is so great.

And with this song, her child's sight was restored.

The author is imbued with the profound culture of the Buddha and has tried to see it in the charm and grandeur of China's architecture, statuary and nature in its immensity. I shall leave the reader to roam around with the author and can only repeat Andre Gide: 'toutes choses sont dites deja'.

I have been a pilgrim with this fascinating book across several thousand years and immense spaces in their poetics of Buddha's Way of Values and Beauty. This book is a ferry boat and you, dear reader, its passenger in a pilgrimage to the yonder shore. The words flow smooth as water, Supernal in their message, they are the heyday of the youth and poesy of Buddhism. The book is an anguish of loss and a passion of quest, to sow precious seeds of wisdom:

Dwelling in tranquility,
Seeing the Dharma,
returning to the Source
Without hatred or violence,
Joy and peace overflow.

Lokesh Chandra
2009

The splendid Amitabha, wearing a monastic robe and holding an alms bowl sits in his Western Paradise preaching the Dhamma to his devotees. In his compassionate grace the Amitabha offers devotees a place in his Sukhavati or Paradise. The colossal painted statue has been carved out of the rock at the Baodingshan grottoes in Dazu county of Chongqing in Sichuan province of China.

Introduction

In tracing the story of the Silk Road I have before me a vast amount of literature by eminent travellers, historians, archaeologists, geographers, linguists both Indian and foreign who dealt with the exciting but arduous subject. This travelogue, in the shadow of the Buddha, has been aided and enriched by the accounts of all those who have traversed the Silk Road before me and chiefly by those who have researched, translated, and published them.

A Safari on the Silk Road

I am uncertain when Buddha first walked into my life. Perhaps in my childhood when I ran barefoot across the green fields to play at the giant mound of bricks called the Ramabhar stupa, a little distance from my house in Kushinagar. Or perhaps when I saw a mysterious Chinese monk living on a peepal tree that had taken roots in the loose bricks of the stupa. May be when I saw the Dying Buddha in a temple on the banks of the Hiranyawati river or when one night the golden Buddha on my bookshelf entered my dreams. In the dark of the night, I looked into his serene eyes in search of light, in happy times I whispered my joys to him and when there was no one else to talk to, I shared my secrets with him. He always seemed to be there....but I never did imagine that the Buddha would one day permeate so much of my being that I would trudge along rivers, mountains and deserts of the Silk Road to search for him.

The Silk Road had its own beginnings, its own story[1] to tell—'a story of trade and commerce, of plunder and conquest, of peace and religion, of art and history; of life itself.' It was the conduit between the East and the West, the oldest and greatest international route that traced its beginnings to the first step of nomads and traders that sunk into the wild, boundless steppelands and deserts to mark the birth of a historic path that paved way for the later Silk Road and thus sowed the seeds of the present globalisation. It stretched long, gathering tributaries on its way to connect the continents of Asia and Europe. From the China Sea to the Mediterranean, it journeyed through the dreadful deserts of the Gobi and the Taklamakan, climbed the snowy ranges of the Pamir, Hindukush and the Karakoram, meandering through innumerable oases, beautiful river valleys, forests, pasturelands and high passes of Central Asia, Afghanistan, India, Iraq, Syria, Turkey, and finally reached Rome.

We learn that the Great Route stretched thousands of kilometres from the ancient capital of Chang-an (present Xian) in the province of Shaanxi of China and crossed the Gobi desert to the oasis of Dunhuang. Here it bifurcated into the northern route (which passed through Hami, Turfan, Korla, Kuqa, Kashgar) and the southern route which passed through Miran, Keriya, Khotan, Yarkand and met the northern route at Kashgar. From Kashgar the route split again with one branch running down the Alai Valley to Termez and Balkh, another running through the Ferghana Valley and Karakum to Merv and a third running north of the Aral and the Caspian to the Black sea. Running across Central and West Asia the routes reached the ports on the eastern Mediterranean from where ships carried the cargoes to Rome.

For sources see Reference

LAND AND SEA ROUTES CONNECTING ASIA AND EUROPE

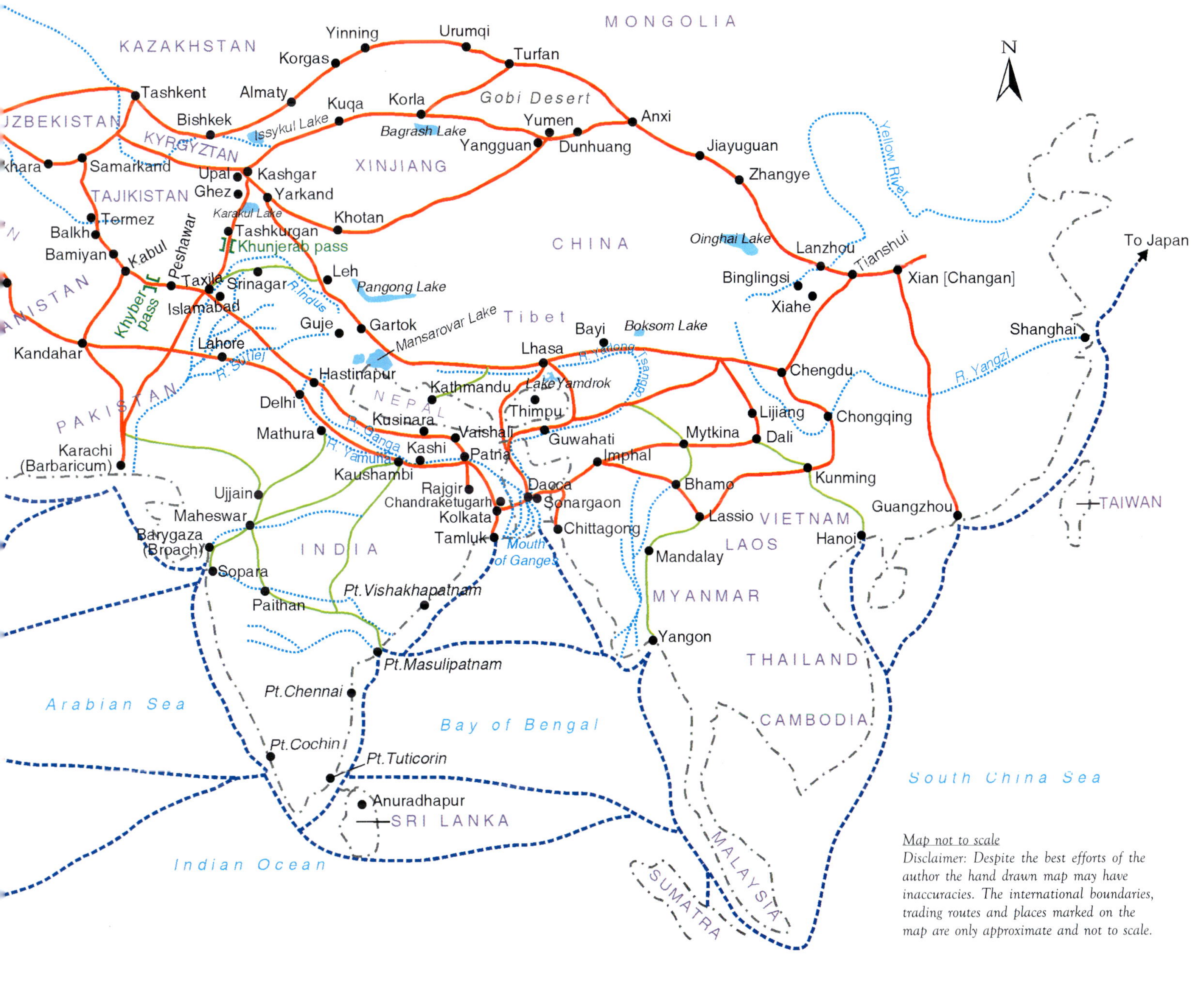

Map not to scale

Disclaimer: Despite the best efforts of the author the hand drawn map may have inaccuracies. The international boundaries, trading routes and places marked on the map are only approximate and not to scale.

Southern Silk Road through India

We learn from various sources[2] that a loop of this important Asia-Europe route called the Southern Silk Road, arose in the southern provinces of China running through Burma (now Myanmar), India and via the Uttarapath or the Northern Highroad to Taxila onwards to Central Asia and Europe. It is believed that over two thousand years ago this Southern Silk Road linked the Yunnan province of China to the North-eastern provinces of India.

India was the hub of this Southern Silk Route because of its links not only with East and South-East Asia but also due to its close ties with Tibet, the Pamir regions, Central and West Asia. Apart from these external links India had well established internal routes that criss-crossed its entire its length and breadth. India could also provide important sea routes on its eastern and western coasts, at the Bay of Bengal and at the mouth of the Indus.

Interesting historical records traced by Sobhan Rehman of the Dhaka University (*Rediscovering the Southern Silk Route*) suggest that Emperor Ashoka (r. 268-32 BC) of India travelled (presumably by this southern Silk Road) to Talifu then the capital of Yunnan where he married a Chinese princess named Chien-meng kui. 'Ashoka returned to India but his descendants from this marriage are reported to have ruled Yunnan upto AD 902'. Even during the times of the great Venetian traveller Marco Polo (AD thirteenth century) Yunnan was in direct contact with India:

'In this province (Yunnan) also are bred large and excellent horses which are taken to India for sale', says Marco.

(Henry Yule, Henri Cordier, *The Book of Ser* Marco *Polo* Vol. II, Chap. XLIX p.76)

This southern route dropped from the main route at Xian and ran southwards towards Chengdu (in Sichuan)

and passing through Kunming, Dali and Baoshan (in Yunnan) ran westwards through Burma and entered the North-East regions of India at two points. One route ran into Assam and another into Manipur.

According to the *Gazetteer of Bengal and North-east India* the proximity of India and China on India's north-eastern borders takes us back to the pre-historic days when the region drew its inhabitants from the Mongolian race in western China from where they migrated to the frontiers of India, Burma, Siam etc. Many migrants took the Brahmaputra river route and travelled along its banks to Assam and thence further to Bengal.[3] Since ages river-borne trade of commodities like Assamese silk, gold washed from the river, musk, agar, pepper had been travelling by boats through Bengal to all parts of the country and abroad. Apart from the river route there were also overland trade routes through the Himalyan hill tracks leading from India to the neighbouring regions of Tibet, China and Burma. Thus we have the famous Muga silk of Assam reaching the Szechuan province of China.

According to B.G.Verghese (*India's North East Resurgent*; p.368) two routes, being part of the Southern Silk Route, were described going to 'Purvadesa or Brahmadesa'. The southern most route passed through Ruili into Myanmar and crossing the Chin hills and Chindwin river reached Manipur in North East India. The northern route passed through Mytkina, Hukwan Valley and the Paktai and Naga Hills into Assam. Upinder Singh (p.290) also mentions the Bengal-Myanmar route as being important.

About fifty kilometers from the Lamaling temple in Nyingchi is the majestic confluence of the Niyang river with the mighty Yarlung Tsangpo or the Brahmaputra river in southern Tibet. The river flows west to east for about 2000 kilometres before taking a grand U-turn to enter India.

The Kunming to Bay of Bengal

The Kunming–Calcutta (now Kolkata) road is said to follow the path of the ancient Southern route through Myanmar and Pragjyotisha (present Assam) to Chandraketugarh (thirty-five kilometres north-east of present Kolkata). Existing upto recent times the head of this 1700 kilometres long Southern Silk Road lay at Kunming in the Yunnan province of South-west China leading through Myanmar to Ledo in the Indian province of Assam. Called the Ledo-Burma Road (also named the

The Karakorum Highway runs from Renmin Xi Lu in Kashgar and leads south for over 2000 kilometres over the Khunjerab Pass into Pakistan tracing the ancient route to Taxila. For thousands of years traders and pilgrims travelled on this mountainous route (a branch of the Silk Route) connecting China, Pakistan, India, Afghanistan and Tajikistan.

Stilwell Road (after General Joseph Warren Stilwell) it passed through Lekhapani, Jairampur, Nampong and Pangsau pass on the India-Burma border, winding up the passes of Patkai Range and running upto Myitkyina and Bhamo and onwards to Kunming.[4]

Another overland route from Kunming via Ruili, Mandalay, Imphal passed through the towns of Moreh and Tamu on the Indo-Myanmar border along the present National Highway-39. It could run upto Sonargaon (in Narayanganj district of Bangladesh, twenty-seven kilometres south-east from present day Dacca in Bangladesh) to join the eastern arm of the Uttarapath (later the Grand Trunk Road) or take the route to Chittagong, the traditional port on the Bay of Bengal.

Interestingly, the Southern Silk Road has been identified as a 'possible route for the Asian Highway', under the Asian Land Transport and Infrastructure Development (ALTID) project. The highway project, initiated in 1959, by U. Nyun, executive secretary of the Economic Commission for Asia and Far East was 'designed to provide uninterrupted travel from Asia to Europe'.[5]

It is believed that this great Asian Highway linking China and Europe through India was in reality a combination of the Southern Silk Road and the Mauryan Royal Road (also called the Uttarapath or the Northern High Road.) Historical records placed by Romila Thapar (*Early India* pp-177, 183) suggest that the territorial foundations of Chandragupta Maurya's empire (321-185 BC) stretched from the Indus to the Ganges plain and that as early as the fourth century BC a 'royal highway' linked Taxila to Patliputra terminating at the mouth of the Ganges. During the reign of Sher Shah Suri (r. 1540-1545) the ancient highway was developed into the famous Grand Trunk Road. Starting from Sonargaon (now in Bangladesh's Narayanganj district) it traversed through

Kolkata, Allahabad, Delhi, Amritsar, Lahore, Peshawar and crossing the Khyber Pass terminated in Kabul.

Zhang Qian –'Father of Silk Road'

We read in Zhang Yiping's *Story of the Silk Road* (Trans. Jia Zongyi, p.19-27) and in Jonathan Tucker's *The Silk Road-Art and History* (p.26) about Zhang Qian, the famous royal emissary of the Chinese court and an outstanding diplomat who sowed the the seeds of the great inter-continental highway and is called the father of the silk road. His life sized image, seated on horseback stands majestically at the Yangguan Pass deep inside the Gobi Desert. He holds aloft the royal standard of yak tails in his right hand while holding the reins of his horse is racing through the desert towards the western regions, his cloak billowing in the fierce desert wind and a more fierce determination on his face.

It is said that in 138 BC under the leadership of Zang Qian intelligence operations were first sent by the imperial court of China to areas west of the country to search for the Yuezhi tribe and forge a strategic alliance with them for subduing the maurading tribes of Mongolia, called the Xiongnu or the Huns. He and his mission took gold and silk with them and visited Loulan, Lopnor, Quici, Kashgar, Khotan, Wusun and other places of Xinjiang and Central Asia. His deputies also visited Iran and India.

It was Zhang who first informed about unknown states to the west of China and of a larger breed of horse that lived their and its suitability for the Han cavalry.

In 115 BC the emperor is said to have once more sent a convoy of 300 men headed by Zhang Qian to the western regions to gather support for a war against the Huns. After a year or so the countries which Zhang visited sent their envoys to the imperial court of Changan.

A fragment of an exquisitely woven ancient textile probably of a super fine attire found by Aurel Stein on the Silk Road oasis site during his explorations in the early twentieth century.

FACING PAGE:
The royal emissary Zhang Qian, called the 'Father of the Silk Road' racing his horse through the western regions of the Gobi. The magnificent statue stands proudly at the Jiayugguan Pass near Dunhuang in China.

Thus offical relations were established between the western countries and the Chinese imperial court at Changan. Messengers were also sent by the imperial Chinese court to Parthia, (Persia), Kizil (Kuqa), Hindu (India) and other countries.

First Silk Yarn from China

The Silk Road owed its name to the gossamer fabric obtained from the silkworm cocoons. The Chinese first spun the gauzy yarn into fabric almost 5000 years ago.[6] Only the best of weavers could extract the flimsy thread and weave it into the superb fabric. We get a glimpse of silk weaving in Xinru Liu's *Silk and Religion* (p.17). The looms were not sophisticated, but the weaver used variations of the warp and the weft to create magical patterns of auspicious birds, animals, plants and sacred symbols in brocade, twill, damask and polychrome. The beautiful fabric not only draped the bodies of emperors and people of high social status but tribal kings living in yurts, the gods residing in temples and also the dead in burial rites.[7] The nomadic chiefs are said to have plundered the caravans on the trade routes for silk. While their own robes were made of the finest brocade, their numerous wives and favourite cocubines wore sat in dresses, slept on the soft silken bedrolls and wrapped themselves in lustrous quilts. We have first hand accounts of the nomadic chiefs' lifestyle in the travel records of the Chinese monk Xuanzang (AD 603-64), Venetian traveller Marco Polo (AD 1254-1324), Spanish envoy Ruy Gonzalez de Clavijo (d. AD 1412) and in Susan Whitfield's *Life Along the Silk Road*.

When Xuanzang visited the court of Yeh-hu Khan, the nomadic king of the Western Turks he was impressed by the use of embroidered silk in his camp and on the body of the Khan and his officials (Hwui Li's *The Life of*

Hieun-Tsiang p.42). In the camps of other nomadic chiefs, Caidu Khan and Kublai Khan, Marco Polo was tongue-tied at the grand display of brocades, silks and gems. There were Chinese cloaks of blue silk. The throne room was like a museum of silk and gems. Kublai himself wore a gown of 'gold watered silk'.[8]

In Justin Marozzi's *Tamerlane* we read about Ruy Gonzalez de Clavijo, Spanish ambassador who travelled six thousand miles from Cadiz in Spain at the behest of the king to Samarkand. Clavijo met Tamerlane in AD 1404 in his Bagi Dilkusha and described the 'blinding opulence' he saw in the nomad's favourite park.[9] It was a city of paradise with tents of silk and the sleeping chamber inside the palace had 'silk mattress embroidered in gold thread'. The walls were covered with silk hangings ornamented with emerald, pearls and other precious stones.

The merchant, Nainavandak (in Susan Whitfield's *Life Along the Silk Road*) travelling from Samarkand to Chang'an in AD seventh century saw the summer camp of Turghiz Kaghan on the northern borders of the Issykul lake amidst rich pasturelands.[10] His white felt yurt was adorned with 'rich silks and brocades' and dazzling 'gold and silver ornaments covering its walls and ceiling'. His officials

A fragment of an embroidered banner depicting the Thousand Buddhas dating to the sixth-seventh century, from Dunhuang. The banner embroidered in silk thread used the famous Kashmiri chain stitch. The ragged border exhibits the donors.

wore embroidered silk robes and the Kaghan himself was wearing a 'long green robe of the finest silk'.

In monasteries and temples, gods were adorned in the finest of silks and offerings were made of silk banners, says Xinru Liu (*Silk and Religion* p.13). We come across description of the images of Buddha clad in silk robes or gold woven silks donated by the pilgrims. In the convents the images were covered with silken fabric. The silk banners were painted with the Paradise of the Buddha, Amitabha, Avalokitesvara, Bhaisajyaguru etc. Sutras were written on silk and worn as charms for curing ailments. Numerous such silk banners from Dunhuang lie in the National Museum of Delhi and other museums across the world.

As early as the second century BC a special non-mulberry silk was also being produced in the villages of Assam in India and traded through branches of the Southern Silk Road passing into China. It was called unbleached or Muga silk, considered to be the most popular and fashionable silk in China. Besides, brocade weaving, especially with gold and silver, had been an age-old tradition in India. Brocade from Benaras in deep vegetable colours and intricate designs was most popular because it was considered the finest. In poet Asvaghosa's *Buddhacharita* (Sanskrit, AD

A uniquely designed piece of ancient textile found by Aurel Stein on the Silk Road oasis site during his explorations in the early twentieth century. The small fragment of the exquisitely woven fabric was once brilliantly coloured.

second century) we find that the silk robe worn by the Buddha had the motif of golden geese embroidered on it,[11] (probably woven in city of Kashi also called Benaras).

However, culture of silkworm, extraction of the silk yarn and weaving of fabric remained a secret for centuries, perhaps the most zealously guarded secret in history. There are countless stories about how silk reached the West where the people were still wearing coarse clothes made of wool and flax.[12] Some say a Chinese princess seeking a marriage alliance with the king of Khotan smuggled out the silkworm stock under her hat and some seeds of the mulberry tree when she set out to marry the king.[13] The soldiers on the border checked everything except the princess herself. Others owe gratitude to Persian merchants and Indian monks who arrived in the court of Emperor Justinian[14] with silkworm stocks hidden in their hollow bamboo staves. Whatever the story, the gleam of the silk fabric did have the Western world gaping in awe and admiration. It became the most coveted commodity and people were ready to trade gold, silver, corals, precious stones, horses, furs... just about anything for a bale of silk. Xinru Liu mentions (*Silk and Religion*) that although silk was a bulky commodity, it continued to be the best medium of exchange. People used silks to make payments as it was more acceptable than coins. The emperors also issued edicts to punish those who refused to accept silk as payment. Silk was an essential part of government revenue.[15] Even during the time of Kublai Khan although paper money had been introduced the economy was backed by reserves of silk.[16]

A complicated, diagonally patterned silk weave in brilliant colour design, created by the genius of the artist, depicted on the garment of a deity (probably Buddha, standing on the lotus).

Silk became the buzzword but the road through which the precious fabric reached the Western world was as yet anonymous; it had no name. It had to wait until late eighteenth century for German geographer Ferdinand von Richthofen to christen it the Silk Road,[17] the name that defined the romance of silk on the international highway.

Silk Route by Sea[18]

We learn from *The Nearchus* and *The Periplus of the Erythrean Sea* (source: William Vincent, 1998; p.384) about the importance of sea routes between Europe, East Africa and India through navigation in the Red Sea, Gulf of Persia and the Indian Ocean; about the routes taken by the travellers and the commodities that were imported and exported from the important port cities viz. Barbaricum, Barygaza, Sopara and other places further south along the Indian coastline.

We have the accounts of commerce carried on from the Red Sea and the Coast of Africa to the East Indies, the exchange of produce between Europe and India by channels and also about the Arabians as the first the navigators of the Indian Ocean and the first carriers of Indian produce to the West.

According to Upinder Singh (*A History of Ancient and Early Medieval India*; p.407) The port cities on the coastline of India emerged as a significant factor in the India-Mediterranean maritime trade in the late or early second century and the demand for Chinese silk in the Mediterranean region was a major stimuli to trans-regional and trans-continental trade during the second century BCE to third century CE (p.408).

It is believed that in order to quench the insatiable thirst for silk, merchants brought cartloads of Chinese silk to the Western world and adventurous traders set out by sea to the East in search of silk. Some drifted with the favourable winds, their cargo vessels swiftly crossing over to the Indian Ocean. Here they anchored at Indian ports of Barbaricum, Barygaza, Cochin, Calicut to buy the Chinese silk and Indian sandalwood, cotton, pepper and aromatic spices. Others went right up to the Chinese port at Zaytun (Guanzhou). According to Joseph Needham (*Science and Civilisation in China*) the existence of 'middlemen... along the overland route' encouraged the tapping of the sea route at 'intermediate stages'. He mentions routes through which Chinese silk came to the Indian ports: over the passes of the Hindukush and through the Khyber pass to Taxila and then down the Indus; over the Tibetan plateau through Ladakh or Sikkim or other Himalayan passes to Palimbothara or Patna on the Ganges where it met foreign ships at its mouth; He also points to the connection between Yunnan province of China and Burma (now Myanmar) which served to bring silk to the ports at the Bay of Bengal.[19]

A painted clay bowl on display at the Banpo Neoloithic Museum near Xian.

We learn that as early as second century BC Chinese ships were already sailing along the South China coast as far as Annam.[20] The invention of the stern-post rudder in the mid-Han dynasty (AD 923) is believed to have helped in maritime trade with South and Southeast Asia. From the times of the Song dynasty (AD 960-1126) the use of magnetic navigation compass helped the Chinese junks to sail to Malaya, India, Persian Gulf and later also to East Africa.[21]

It is said that by the late eighth century the sea route as an alternative to the land route was becoming popular. Following the direct military confrontation between Arabs and Tang China at the Battle of Talas in AD 751, the trade between the two was mostly by sea. The sea route was considered to be easier and safer.[22]

From *The Life of Hieun Tsiang* (by Shaman Hwui Li, Trans Samuel Beal) we learn that the sea route between China and India in the Tang (AD 618-907) dynasty was by way of Java, Sumatra, Strait of Malacca, coast of Burma and Arakan to Tamralipti or by way of Ceylon and many Chinese monks were travelling by sea route to India.[23] Among these we read about I-tsing, who in the year AD 671 boarded the ship at Canton and arrived at Tamralipti where he stayed at the famous Varaha temple for three years; Hieun-Ta, a priest of Kung-chow who travelled in a Persian ship. He arrived at Sribhoj, Malaya and then in a royal ship towards eastern India; Ming-yuen, a 'doctor of law' travelled in a ship of Cochin-China and arrived at Kalinga and thence left for Ceylon; I-long (a priest of Yih-chau) boarded a merchant ship and arrived at Langkia and thence to Ceylon.

According to T.W. Rhys David (*Buddhist India*) Indian merchants are believed to have traded from the ports on the south-west coast of India with Babylon from very early times (as early as the seventh century BC.[24] They made use of the strong monsoon winds. From the Jataka tales we learn that traders went from Videha to Gandhara, from Magadh to Sovira (Surat) from Bharukaccha (Broach) around the coast to Burma, from Benaras down the river to its mouth and thence on to Burma. Trading journeys to Babylon and China is also mentioned.[25]

Ibn Batuta (AD 1304-69), a Moroccan, took the sea route from Cambay and journeying along the western coast of India passed through the of Bay of Bengal to China. From his travel accounts *Travels in Asia and Africa 1325-1354* (H.A.R.Gibbs) we get a glimpse of the cities he crossed on way from Tangier in Morocco to the Mongol capital of Khanbalik in China through Delhi.[26] At Aden, the port of Yemen, Batuta mentions that boats from Indian ports of Cambay, Quilon, Calicut and other Malabar ports arrive. At Dohar he informs that horses are exported to India and rice is imported from India. Crossing

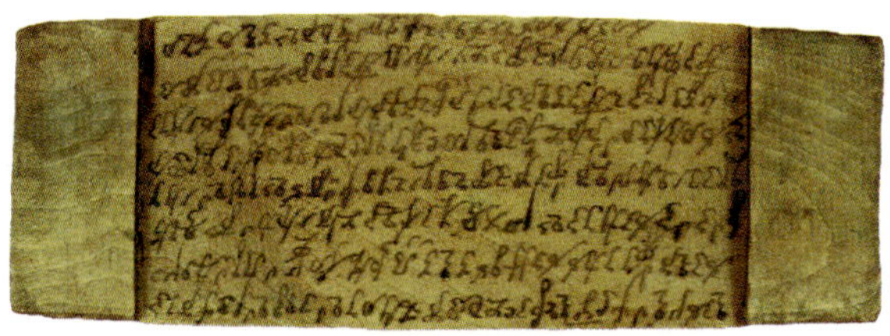

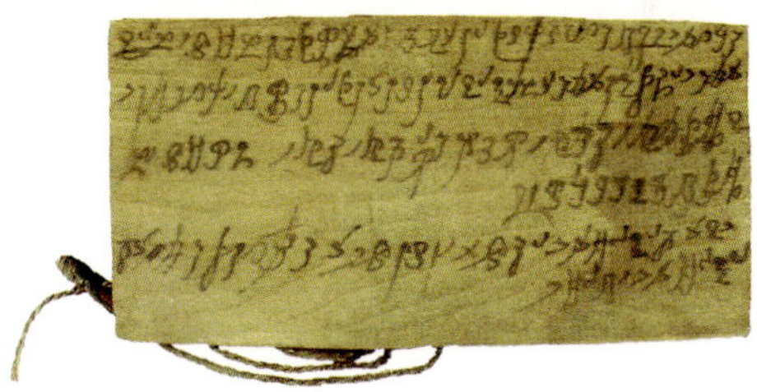

FACING PAGE:
A rectangular wooden under tablet with a covering bears an inscription in Kharosthi in black ink belonging to the third-fourth century. The tablets were tied together with fibrous string and then sealed with clay. Such tablets were used as documents or letters in business transactions.

BELOW:
A herd of wild double-humped camels grazing on thorns and shrubs in the desert around Kuqa.

Panjshir, Parwaan, Gazna he reaches Kabul and thence to the great Indus river in Sind from where Delhi is only fifteen days march. Through Aligarh, Ujjain, Daulatabad, he reaches the port city of Cambay where he boards a ship to sail around the western coast of India to Goa, Onore, Hili, Calicut. At Calicut, thirteen Chinese ships are waiting to leave for China. He sails to Maldives, Ceylon, Bengal, Sumatra, Tawalisi on his way to China.

Zheng He in Cochin

During the early years of the Ming (AD 1368-1644) the Chinese emperors are said to have launched a number of maritime expeditions. Among these were the several voyages led by Admiral Zheng He (1371-1434) to Southeast Asia and India, and as far as Arabia

and the east coast of Africa.[27] In AD 1405 the expedition of Zheng is known (Tucker, *The Silk Road-Art & History* p.366) to have consisted of 27,000 men and a fleet of over 60 gigantic ships, as well as a massive amount of cargo. The 'treasure ships' halted at the coastal cities of Cochin and Calicut on the West coast of India on their way to the Persian Gulf. The Chinese fishing nets still in use in many villages in Kerala are said to have been introduced by Chinese people coming to the Cochin region. Other Chinese influences observed at Cochin are the dragon boats at the beaches similar to the ones found in China and the hosting of the dragon boat festivals.

Over the years, the trading routes became synonymous with silk, but silk was not the only commodity traded along the route - even spices, jade, tea, salt and horses had their ardent takers. And some branch roads[28] borrowed their names from the commodities they carried. Thus we learn of the Spice Road that ran from India to China and Central Asia, the Jade Road that ran from Khotan rivers (the Urungkash and the Karakash) eastwards to inland China; the Tea Road from Yachao westwards to Lhasa and the Salt Road from the lakes of Changtang area of northern Tibet to Xinjiang and Gansu provinces of China and to the Nepalese border. Likewise there were the Musk and the Horse roads. It is also learnt that from Lhasa to South Asia and Central Asia there were not one but three Tea-Horse trade routes. One was from Lhasa to Yadong, another from Lhasa to Nepal, and a third through Xigaze and Ladakh and Kashmir to Afghanistan (*China's Tibet*, Vol.16. No.4, 2005).

Indian Doctors and 'Tantriks' in China

Beside silk merchants, there were many other people travelling along the great trade route. Prominent among these were Indian 'vaidyas' or physicians. We learn of such 'clever physicians who by opening the brain and extracting worms' could cure blindness.[29] According to Needham (*Science and Civilisation in China*; Vol I, p.204) a 'Buddhist sutra ...has the son of emperor Asoka being cured of blindness by Bactrian physicians at Gandhara'. There were a host of medicine men, herb gatherers, magicians and also 'tantriks' who practiced 'tantra'.[30] They were famous for their potent aphrodisiacs, magical formulae, secret incantations and charms and were known to achieve the impossible. They caused quite a rage in the royal courts of China interested in *rasayana* (alchemy) and 'tantra vidya'. Indian alchemy was renowned for its magical potions and elixirs not only for curing ailments but supposedly also obtaining immortality. Alberuni who visited India in AD 1030 wrote about the horrors of *rasayana* or Indian alchemy in his book on India (*Alberuni's India*, trans. Edward Sachau)

It is believed that from very early times India was famous for its potent aphrodisiacs. These formed part of gifts exchanged between the Mauryas and the Seleucids and the Hellenistic states further west as early as the fourth century BC. (Romila Thapar *Early India* p.177).

In *Marco Polo's Asia* (Leonardo Olschki pp.415-24) we read that the court of the Chinese emperor Kublai Khan was surrounded by a host of astrologers and physicians and many of whom were from India. Marco Polo who stayed at Kublai's court for several years is said to have been struck by the 'legendary longevity attained by Brahmans' (of India) who according to him 'are the people that live the longest in the world'. According to Marco, the yogis of India 'lived to be a hundred and fifty even 200 years old by using an elixir which they made of sulphur and mercury….' (Leonardo Olschki, *Marco Polo's Asia*, pp.415-24).

Indian dancers, much sought after by the royal courts, also journeyed on the trade routes. Many 'lithe' Tamil women 'contortionists' from India were found dancing at the court of Kublai Khan by Marco Polo (journey AD 1271-95). We read of Indian girls clad only in loin cloth and a narrow strip over their breasts dancing erotically at a party thrown in honour of the Polos' at Shangtu. Indian conjurers also travelled to entertain the emperors.[31] According

Sakyamuni Buddha at the Baodingshan grottoes in Dazu county of Chongqoing in Sichuan province of China. Carved out of stone, the deity looks magnificent. The face is round with soft features and dreamy eyes.

to the travel records of the Moroccon traveller Ibn Batuta (journey AD 1325-54), a hundred Hindu dancing and singing girls and brocade (probably from Benaras) were among the things that had been sent to the Chinese royal court by the Sultan of Delhi in AD 1342.[32]

The tallest outdoor Bronze Buddha seated on a lotus flower smiles and blesses all from a hill top above the Po Lin monastery at Lantau island in Hong Kong.

A Hundred Flowers Bloomed[33]

For several centuries the road reverberated with the 'sound of the bugle, the clash of the swords' and was blinded by the shining armour of conquerors like Alexander (356-23 BC), Atilla (AD 406-53), Genghis (AD 1162-1227) and Tamerlane (AD 1336-1405). It also witnessed the propagation of Buddha's Dhamma by *dharmadutas* and *mahamatras* (messengers and preachers) of Mauryan emperor Asoka (269-32 BC) and carried the message of the prophets viz.

Zoroastra, Jesus Christ, Mani, Niestorius and Prophet Mohammad. Many religions walked this path, many empires flourished, many a flower bloomed and many an idea grew along the way.

The contact between the East and the West catalysed the spread and coexistence of various religions on the Silk Road. Of these, Buddhism was the earliest to make its presence felt. About the first century AD it had travelled from north-west India to several parts of Central Asia and from there to China.[34] The new religion slowly spread eastwards through the oases towns on the fringes of the Taklamakan desert, with the merchants, missionaries and pilgrims carrying along the words of the Buddha. Faith took various forms, and acquired innumerable hues.

However, Buddha was not the only one worshipped on the Silk Road. By the AD fifth century the Nestorian sect of Christianity, which was outlawed in Europe, was traversing the trade routes of Asia. Syrian monks brought the faith along the Silk Road into China and the first Nestorian church was consecrated in Changan (Xian) around AD 635 during the rule of Emperor Taizong (AD 626-49). The famous stele called the 'Nestorian Stone' of AD 781 stands in the museum of Xian.[35] Manicheism, started by Mani, a Persian (AD 216-77) was also popular on the trade routes. After his persecution and death in AD 276 his followers spread eastwards through Central Asia and India and eventually reaching China in the seventh century.[36] In AD 236 the Sassanian Dynasty in Persia adopted Zoroastrianism as the state religion. As Persia and China were allies and trade partners on the Silk Road, the religion spread eastwards and its presence in China was recorded in the history of Tang dynasty in AD sixth century.[37] The first Muslims are said to have arrived in Guangzhou by AD seventh century. Facing persecution in Mecca in AD 616, over a hundred Muslims fled to Abyssinia for asylum and from there travelled to Guanzhou by sea where they began to preach Islam in the south-eastern coastal areas.[38]

My Adventure on the Silk Road

My own tryst with the Silk Road began much after the sound of the horses' hooves and the swirl of the desert sand had been forgotten and the glory had all but faded into oblivion. Through growing up and the tortuous and blissful twists and turns of life, the golden Buddha stayed with me. I continued to look into his serene eyes for answers; I continued to whisper my secrets unto him. But I never imagined that I would one day trudge through the Silk Road. I did not know it would have an unusual beginning in an unusual place—almost thirteen years ago in the tiny island of Lantao, Hong Kong.

It was the summer of 1995. The magnificent Victoria harbour was walking distance from my hotel in Tsim Sha Tsui that sat smug at the tip of Kowloon peninsula. Taking the Canton road I reached the Star ferry terminal where black clouds were gathering over the harbour and the Chinese 'plum rain' of June was expected any moment. Half a dozen ferries were already unloading workers, shoppers, traders and tourists from the outlying islands.

A strong wind blew over the China Sea as our ferry sailed on to the Mui Wo pier at Silver Mine Bay, that borrows its name from the silver mines that once dotted the fringes. I could feel the silken sand beneath my bare feet, I built sand castles, stared at sun peeping from behind the clouds, let the breeze from the palm fronds caress my skin and when afternoon came I dug my fork into the scrumptious seafood platter. A waiting bus drove passengers to the longest beach, the Cheung Sha on the Lantau. Red flags had been stuck at certain danger zones where crocodiles lay in hiding.

Far away from the busy metropolis, Lantau, the island of Buddha remained tranquil as no motor vehicles were allowed beyond a point. Here at the Po Lin monastery, a thirty-four-metre bronze Buddha lorded over a hilltop. I climbed up a hundred steps to the precious lotus amidst which the Buddha sat in *abhay mudra*, his hand raised in blessing. I was mesmerised as Buddha looked down from his lotus seat and smiled; he looked so much like the golden Buddha that had almost become a part of me. That was not the only Buddha I would see that day; in the museum at the foothills I stumbled upon paintings and graphics about giant Buddhas living along the Silk Road. That moment I knew I would some day walk the Silk Road.

Later at the large dining hall of the monastery where I was invited to a special vegetarian lunch, I met an old Thai monk who had just returned from Japan and was headed to Xian through Hangzhou, Shanghai and Chengdu to follow the famed Silk Road up to Dunhuang. His stories fascinated me and steeled my resolve to make the journey on my own.

Back in Delhi, I poured over books by historians, travellers and archaeologists all of whom had woven romance into the Silk Road. The more I read, the more curious I grew. I wanted to explore the monuments of the glorious past that India and China had shared. I wanted to feel the hot sand of the Gobi and the Taklamakan under my feet, the touch of the silk carpets and the jade of Khotan. I longed for the melons of Hami and the grapes of Turfan. I wanted to breathe in the chill of the mighty Karakoram and the Pamirs. I did not care for the black storms and the infamous demons of the desertland that had killed so many caravans; nor the evil bandits who ambushed and plundered.

My marathon across China began sooner than later. My first encounter with the giant Buddhas (after Lantao island) was at the Maijishan grottoes near Tianshui, often called the eastern terminus of the Silk Road. The highway is said to approximate the ancient Chinese route starting from the city of Changan (Xian), heading up the Gansu corridor and reaching Dunhuang on the edge of the Taklamakan. Several other Buddhas were ensconced in beautiful caves and temples across the Gansu province and in the oasis towns. At Binglingsi, near Lanzhao, the tall Buddha sat in a cave at the foot of which flowed a stream; at Dafosi the huge Nirvana Buddha lay peacefully in eternal sleep just as the Reclining Buddha of Kushinagar (India); the most magnificent Maitreya Buddha sat in the double-storey temple at the Yulin grottoes of Anxi; at Dunhuang a nine-storey temple had been built inside the mountains to house the Maitreya; at Leshan near Chengdu, the Buddha sat between two huge rocks overlooking the torrential confluence of three rivers, which met just below his feet.

It is believed that the construction of these caves or grottoes began in China during the Han dynasty with the introduction of Buddhism. By the first century BC the most precious commodity travelling from India to China was Buddhism. The religion travelled from north-west India to many parts of Central Asia and from there to China. When the early monks cut caves in the mountains they chose the site with an eye to the landscape and their own

The author inside the Taklamakan desert near Khotan. Preparing for a hearty meal amidst an ocean of sand before the long march to the Rawak stupa. This was the desert of 'no return' which ancient travellers dreaded most.

need for food and shelter. Water came from the river that usually ran at the foothills or from a stream trickling down from a melting glacier. Dense foliage concealed the grottoes from wild animals. The site's proximity to the main caravan route enabled access to the travellers and ensured its upkeep in the form of rich offerings to the deity. Alms for the begging monks also came by easily. Sculpted and painted images of Buddha and bodhisattvas were installed as central figures in these caves just as in Ajanta (India). The walls were decorated with paintings depicting the life of Buddha, the Jatakas and themes from the everyday life of the people.

With each mile that I trudged I saw more of Buddha; the more I saw him the more I wanted to see him. Often I stood incredulous at the vignettes of faith; I could envisage pilgrims dipping their brush into emulsion to paint their favourite Buddha or diligently chipping off mountains to give Buddha another home. But if there were the devout, there were the plunderers, the ones who hacked away Buddha images from their heavenly paradise, exchanged a few pieces of silver for thousands of rare manuscripts....There were the explorers who literally gouged out the frescoes from their walls with axes and knives....

During many moments on the Silk Road, I often shed a tear at such sacrilege; I often mourned the desecration of the Buddha monuments and statues, I often wondered what the Silk Road would have looked like if it had not fallen to the vagaries of Nature and Hopkirk's devils.[39] I often wondered at the whys...but before I accosted the whys on the sidewalk, I had begun my romance with the Silk Road.

Men driven by fear go to many a refuge,
to mountains, and to forests, to sacred trees, and shrines.
That, verily, is not a safe refuge, that is not the best refuge.
After having got to that refuge a man is not delivered from all pains.

But he who takes refuge in the Buddha, the Law, and the Order,
he perceives, in his clear wisdom, the four noble truths.

(The Dhammapada, C XIV, Buddhavaggo; 188, 189, 190;
Trans. S Radhakrishnan; Oxford University Press, 1950, Madras; p191)

The Famen temple where the holy 'sarira' of Buddha is buried. The octagonal pagoda known as the 'True Pagoda' houses the finger bones of Sakyamuni Buddha.

1

My Journey Begins from Xian

There was a pleasant nip in the air as I left Delhi and boarded an early morning flight MU 564 (China Eastern Airlines) to Shanghai and a transfer to Xian. From the window of the aircraft I could see the fluffy clouds play with the golden rays of the rising sun. My heart was pounding with excitement—it was my maiden journey along the Silk Road. I was no merchant carrying bolts of silk, nor gems, nor spices. Neither was I looking for that magical herb that would grant me eternal youth. I was only an adventurer seeking the aura of Lord Buddha on every inch of the great highroad; and searching the ancient roots that bound the two giants of Asia—India and China.

A few hours later, the HU 7846 (China Hainan Airlines) descended on the city of Xian dropping among its many passengers, an Indian. I was greeted with loud cheers by the representative of my tour agency. While I gladly scanned the gleaming yellow coach parked outside the airport lounge that waited to receive us, the natty representative's eyes were glued on my purse tied securely around my waist. Before I hopped into the coach I had to sacrifice a thick wad of dollars for the first leg of my journey up to Dunhuang.

I felt a jab in the side! But in the land of Buddha such 'mortal' thoughts I threw to the wind. With a song on my lips and a spring in my step I hopped into the coach and sank into the cushioned seats as it sped towards Huangcheng Hotel that lay smug in the heart of the city. By the time I checked in and arrived at the dining hall, the waiters were clearing the tables, the sauces were being stacked back on the shelves and the breadbasket was being carried back to the pantry. Breakfast time was over; I snatched a hurried meal of rice porridge and sautéed cabbage and mushrooms. I knew I had a hectic day ahead and so was happy for that simple refreshing bite.

The yellow coach that brought me from the airport was still parked outside and it would drive me through the western gate to first pray to the great Buddha of Famen monastery. I was sticking to the ancient Chinese tradition of seeking His blessings before starting my journey along the Silk Road. In the olden days, caravans comprising Bactrian camels loaded with merchandise and accompanied by groups of merchants and monks left for the Silk Road from this gate. After a tearful farewell to their family and friends at the city gate they trudged westwards for two days before making their first stop at the Great Famensi to worship the *sarira* (body relics) of Buddha and beseech the lord for their safe journey and return.

Taking the grand six-lane Baoji expressway my guide Xingxiaochun and I drove for 120 kilometres to reach Famen. The East–West highway pierces through the fertile plains that hem Xian. Winter wheat had already been sown and the dainty emerald green spikelets were swaying in the frosty November breeze. Suddenly I heard a rumble and saw a black shadow that seemed to throw a veil over the sunshine. Thick clouds were rolling over the landscape and it was getting quite dark. Very soon there was a drizzle and I could see tiny raindrops hurrying down the windowpane. That moment they did not seem absolutely innocuous; the little drops of rain had me worried about bad light. I knew they would spoil all photo-ops.

The towering pillar of the Crowned Buddha is visible from the expressway and is the light that guides the devotees to the temple. We left the road and turned towards the pillar driving into a shopping arcade where the driver parked the coach. On this pillar of grey marble sat

four Buddhas facing the four directions. The image in *dhyan mudra* (meditating posture) holds the lotus flower. The *triratna* – the three jewels of the Buddha, the Dhamma and the Sangha, hang in a jewelled crown over his head. We walked through a blue gate with golden eaves into the temple precincts right into the heart of the Famen.

Buddha's *Sarira* at Famen

Thankfully, Famen was dry; I had left the dark clouds behind on the expressway. But it was not sunny either; the sun was still hiding behind layers of mist. The vast temple area looked hazy, gloomy and grey. Set against the sky, the temple looked ethereal; I tried to take a wide angle shot, but the haze blurred the lens. I fiddled with the camera, said a prayer and hoped for just a moment of sunshine, but it was not to be. A few more attempts to capture the temple failed, I conceded defeat and ran up the steps that led to a sidewalk ambling alongside the temple into the front courtyard. The concrete pathway was laced with beautiful flowers and the voices of women selling lotus and incense sticks added a hint of clamour.

As I shifted my gaze from the geraniums and the poppies, I noticed the thirteen-storied red octagonal pagoda that seemed determined to scrape the sky. Known as True Pagoda, it is said to have housed the finger bones of the Sakyamuni Buddha. It is also believed that over the years, the Pagoda has tilted—perhaps with age, or a structure burdened with the history of 2,500 years. Surrounded by thousands of monks and tourists, the pagoda brings to life the stories associated with the Mahaparinirvana of Buddha and devout Buddhist emperors of China who worshipped the relics of the Great Master.

The precincts seemed laden with piety. Hundreds of monks in maroon and grey robes were swarming, their whispers imparting an odd drone. Dozens of tourist buses were parked in another courtyard from which streams of pilgrims were emerging. Most of them indulged in the ritual of being photographed in front of the pagoda. Inside the monastery

FACING PAGE:
The thirteen-storied red octagonal pagoda at Famen scrapes the sky. It brings to life stories associated with the Mahaparinirvana *of the Buddha and the devout emperors of China who worshipped the relics.*

there were incense burners where pilgrims had gathered to offer prayers. Countless fragrances mingled with the serene air – the unique concoction providing a surreal touch to the place.

It is said that after Buddha's *sarira* was brought to Famen it was placed in the basement of an underground structure built specially to house it. Later a bigger pagoda was built over the holy remains. The crypt was enlarged; an adjacent palace with several courtyards and a Buddha temple was constructed in AD 147. However, the relics, the crypt and the palace lay hidden from the outside world until the archaeologists put the shovel to the ground and revealed the presence of the holy remains.

The plaques and boards at the site have you believe that the royalty worshipped the relics in private, allowing public access to the holy site only once in ten years. The kings and their kin were convinced that worshipping the relics would bring good fortune and protect their country from foreign invasion and evil spirits. The Tang emperor Taizong let the public have a look at the *sarira.* There were altogether eight Chinese emperors who had the *sarira* brought to the royal palace in Changan and Luoyang for worshipping.

In 1981, half of the pagoda collapsed and the rest just seemed to have slid down. During the renovation in 1987 the Buddha's fingerbones and other relics made of precious stones were discovered. The bone relics were found placed in a tiny stupa of pure gold encased within eight gold and silver caskets in order of size. The other relics were similarly housed in stupas and caskets. Many royal treasures and jewellery were also found here. Presently, this is the biggest Buddhist underground palace so far discovered.

From the pagoda, a path led through dense foliage of willows and poplars to the courtyard of Grand Palace of Buddha. Here the air was thick with scented smoke as hundreds of devotees were burning joss sticks in the massive incense holder. Long, thick decorative candles were being lit. I had gone there empty-handed, but a monk graciously offered me a bunch of candles. When I rummaged my purse to pay, he smiled generously. He would not take money from me. I was touched; I bowed in gratitude and headed towards Buddha.

Inside the massive hall sat the central image of the enlightened Buddha in *dhyan mudra*, his eyes half closed in meditation and a curious smile on his lips. The hall reverberated with the loud chanting of monks who were holding lamps and circumambulating. There were far too many devotees, and very little space with all of them jostling for a look at the deity. Many were prostrate on the ground, mumbling their prayers, almost unaware of the world around them. A few monks quickly drew a tight rope at the hall's entry to bar the devotees from rushing inside or touching the deity. I got trapped in the crowd, with not even enough elbow room to stand still for a moment and take a photograph of the Buddha. Every time I tried to get the frame right, I would be edged by someone in hurry for his tryst with Him. With every passing moment, the crowd around me seemed to be swelling further, but ultimately I did manage. Suddenly someone tapped my shoulder. I looked back and saw a monk gesticulating fervently at me to shut the camera. I did as he said and walking out of the temple took the road that ran into the museum, which housed precious relics discovered during the renovation.

Emperor Asoka's temple

History boards at the site inform us that the relics were brought here during the reign of Asoka, a Mauryan emperor who is believed to have enshrined the Buddha's relics at the Famen temple. It was therefore called the Asokan Temple. Scholars have debated whether Asoka actually ever set foot in China. While historians continue to debate that issue, records traced by Rehman Sobhan of the Dhaka University (in *Re-discovering the Southern Silk Route*) point to Asoka's trip to Yunnan province of China where he reportedly married a Chinese princess.[1] However, they do agree that the emperor's *dharmadutas* and *mahamatras* (religious messengers and preachers) spread the religion of Dhamma not only in India but across the borders: 'among the Yavanas, Kambojas and Gandharas, the Rashtrikas and Paitryanikas and other people dwelling about the western borders of my (Asoka) dominion', as the major rock edict of Asoka No. V, the *Manshera Text* written in Kharoshti script and translated by D.C. Sircar in *Inscriptions of Asoka* reads.[2]

Historical material on Emperor Asoka (by Lama Taranath, Radhakumud Mookerji, Bhadant Sawangi Medhankar, D.C. Ahir) have us believe that Asoka's *Dhamma-Vijaya* campaign spread beyond the boundaries of his own empire; to the furthest corners of the world in far off countries of West Asia and Europe:

> '...Dharma-vijaya... has been won by His Sacred Majesty both here (in his dominion) and among all his frontier peoples even to the extent of six hundred yojanas where (are) the Yona king, Antiochos by name, and beyond that Antiochos, the four kings named Ptolemy, Antigonos, Magas and Alexander....'
>
> (Excerpt taken from Edict of Asoka XIII, Shahbazgarhi.)

The above authors (quoting the *Mahavamsa*) also give a list of Asoka's missionaries who were sent to Kashmir, Gandhara, Yavana or the Greek country, Burma, Himalayan provinces, Sri Lanka among others.

However, Buddhism did not gain prominence soon after the death of Buddha. The ardent trek of the followers is believed to have begun after the Third Buddhist Council at Asokarama at Patliputra which was held under the chairmanship of Mogaliputta Tissa exactly 260 years after Buddha's *mahaparinirvana* (Great Decease).[3] The *dharmadutas* are learnt to have gone as far as Khotan as Asoka is believed to have 'conquered the northern Himalayas, the snowy ranges beyond Liyul, the entire land of Jambudvipa... and fifty small islands.'[4] Although there are no historical records of the visit of *dharmadutas* to Xian, the possibility cannot be ruled out, considering the fact that India and China had bustling trade relations. Also because Khotan, where Asoka's messengers are believed to have visited, lay on the trade route to Xian.

History does talk about how Emperor Asoka unearthed and divided the relics of the great Buddha. It is said that he did so by excavating the relics from seven stupas; the only one to remain untouched was the stupa at Ramagrama (on the banks of the Jharahi river in Nawalparasi district of Nepal which was guarded fanatically by a dragon.[5] According to legend, Asoka divided the remains of Buddha into 84,000 parts that were enshrined in various stupas across the world. If one were to count them, it would probably run into thousands. China alone has nineteen stupas that house portions of Buddha's *sarira*. Asoka decreed daily worship at each stupa with thousands of lamps, incense and garlands.

Asoka's search of the relics took him to far-flung areas. And there lay a precious one that King Ajatsatru of Magadh had received. The relics lay buried in Rajgriha (modern Rajgir), that almost abutted Patliputra, the modern city of Patna. We learn of the interesting event in *Taranath's History of Buddhism*. As the story goes[6] Asoka started digging but his search was disrupted by a burning iron wheel that seemed to rotate at the speed of light. Despite his attempts Asoka could dig no further; he could not stop the rotating wheel. He was almost at the end of his tether when an old woman's advice came handy. She exhorted the emperor to turn the flow of a river that cut through the belly of a hill (possibly the hot sulphur springs of Rajgriha). The emperor did exactly that. Surprisingly, not only was the fire extinguished but even the wheel stopped rotating. On digging further Asoka found a copper plate with an inscription 'Here lies the relics of the Tathagata'. The relics were preserved in the innermost of the seven gem-studded chests placed one within another. Asoka took some of the relics and left the rest in the chest hidden as before. However, he did not want anyone else to access the relics and to prevent this he re-diverted the stream to its usual route. Once again the wheel started burning and moving at an unimaginable speed. Asoka knew nobody else could now reach the relics.

It is said that most pilgrims walking the Silk Road carried bales of silk and velvet pouches spilling with gold and silver. However, they were not ready to barter all for a night in the inn. The pilgrims would also trade it with the relics of the Buddha; they scoured temples looking for a willing seller who would part with a relic for a yard of silk. The basic motive was to carry these relics to their emperors and gain favours and rewards.

In the seventh century the rulers of Kapisa happily parted with the 'small parietal bone' (presumably of Buddha) in exchange for 4000 bolts of silk[7] (Xinru Liu in *Silk and Religion*; p.47). Another pilgrim, Wu'kung, is said to have carried Buddha's tooth. In return, Wu'kung and other pilgrims who bought relics were granted official position and honours.[8]

When Chinese pilgrim Xuanzang set out on his journey that would make him famous, he not only packed essentials in his valise, he also carried huge quantities of silk and gold which he later offered at a number of temples. While worshipping the parietal bone of Buddha at the Nagarahara and other stupas on his route, Xuanzang is said to have donated gold coins and silk.[9] When it was time to return to China, in his bag the great monk packed relics and images of Buddha alongwith Buddhist scriptures.[10] Perhaps the great pilgrim managed to buy a number of relics from the monasteries in India.

In Memory of Xuanzang

When I began my journey, I thought of Xuanzang, I thought of the man who seemed to have spent an entire lifetime travelling, chronicling stories about neighbourhoods and people whose tales nobody else was telling. The pilgrim achieved fame through his travels, which remained well nigh unmatched. The day after my trip to Famen when I was headed to the Wild Goose Pagoda, a virtual treasure trove of relics, I was reminded of Xuanzang again. Wild Goose Pagoda is the city's most famous landmark that was built by Emperor Taizong (AD 626-49) to house the relics and scriptures brought by Xuanzang from India. There is a plaza in the pagoda premises and in a corner stands Xuanzang - carved out of stone. Next to him is a huge stone on which an inscription narrates the story of his travels to India.

Much before I noticed the spires of the pagoda standing arrogantly against a blue sky I was fascinated by the colours of the sky. That day the blue sky was spangled with innumerable hues - fancy kites with tails like snakes swirling in the gentle breeze. Locals told me that kite flying was

FACING PAGE:
Xuanzang stands proudly in the plaza of the Wild Goose Pagoda built by the Chinese emperor Taizong for housing the scriptures brought by the great monk from India.

one of the favourite pastimes of the Chinese and if the speckled sky was any indication, I believed every word of that.

I looked at Xuanzang, saluted his courage, walked across the plaza and passed through the south gate to the bell tower which was swarming with people—tourists taking photographs and devotees lighting lamps. Every morning the sun rises with the clank of the bells and glides down the pagoda in the evening amidst the beating of drums. The ancient pagoda lies in front, rising from the precincts of the Hall of Buddha where nuns in brown robes were guiding the pilgrims and indulging in crowd control like old-hand cops. I looked at the Buddha, closed my eyes and fell at His feet, thanking him for making this visit possible; for holding my hand and bringing me to the place where the great monk spent several years translating Buddhist scriptures and writing the *Si Yu Ki*, the most valuable records of his travel to India. The temple was decorated with the scenes from the life of Buddha. On the left wall was depicted the Nativity scene of Queen Maya dreaming about the white elephant entering her womb at her palace in Kapilvastu, followed by the birth of the baby Buddha at Lumbini, the penance and Enlightenment at Bodh Gaya and 'turning of the wheel of law' at Sarnath. The last painting depicted the Reclining Buddha at Kusinagar in eternal sleep between two *saal* trees and surrounded by a multitude of disciples mourning the Great Decease.

I crossed into another courtyard where a huge hall was devoted to the great monk himself. It displayed his writings and translations bound in thick covers sitting securely behind glass. The walls were not stark either, even they recounted the story of the monk's travels and life—with motifs depicting his endless search for scriptures and the monk hunched over a notebook penning his greatest work, the *Si Yu Ki*.

It was in AD 629 during the reign of Emperor Li Shimin (Taizong) that the monk went on a pilgrimage to India in search of the Buddhist scriptures. In India he acquired a profound knowledge of Sanskrit. When he arrived back in Changan after sixteen years through Kashgar and Khotan he is said to have carried so many images, scriptures and relics

A painting at the Chengdu Daci temple depicts the return of the great monk Xuanzang with huge loads of Buddhist scriptures. He is seen here sitting in a howdah *on elephant back.*

that he had to hire twenty horses to carry them! The booty comprised 150 particles of *sarira* of the Buddha, his images carved in gold, silver and sandalwood[11], Mahayana scriptures and works of monks belonging to other schools.

There is an interesting anecdote about Xuanzang's return from India.[12] As the story goes, Xuanzang's fame preceded him and as he neared Xian, the news about his impending arrival spread like wild fire. Hundreds of people left their daily chores to join the crowd that was milling around the entire town. The streets were so full of people that the monk could not walk a step. He was completely stranded in the crowd that was present to have a look at him. When evening came he could neither inch towards the town nor could he wriggle past into a neighbouring inn. The monk actually spent the night by the canal! When the sun rose out of the clouds in the morning, the crowd took him in a huge procession to the Hongfu or the monastery of Great Happiness. Here he devoted himself to translating texts that he had acquired during his travels in India and retranslating older one that he felt were inadequate.[13] By the year AD 648 he had completed fifty-eight books, including the *Si-yu-Ki*. The emperor composed an introduction to his works which was later inscribed on a stone tablet.

Kashmiri Scholars Settled in Xian

It was in Xian that renowned Indian scholars found patrons in the royal courts. Buddhist scholars from Kashmir and Taxila (now in Pakistan), the great centers of learning, were widely acclaimed for their knowledge of Sanskrit and Chinese. They were invited by the royal Chinese court to settle in Xian and translate Buddhist texts into Chinese.[14] According to historian and sinologist P.C. Bagchi,[15] Kashmir took the lead in transmitting Buddhist traditions directly to China. The number of scholars who went to China from Kashmir, the most flourishing centre of Buddhist learning, was larger than that of those from other parts of India. Kashmir also attracted scholars from outside, mentions Bagchi.

Kumarjiva, an erudite scholar of Buddhism studying in Kashmir, was invited by the emperor in AD 401. He was appointed *purohit* (priest) of the Caotang temple in Xian where he delivered lectures on Buddhist doctrine and translated Buddhist scriptures with the assistance of three thousand Chinese disciples.[16] Of Kumarjiva, it is said that he was completely at home in both Chinese and various languages of India and Central Asia. He is said to have not only produced elegant translations but also coined much of the Buddhist terminology.[17] Among his translations the 'most valued and revered' is the 'Lotus of the True Law' or *Sadharmapundarika*.[18] which embodies the ultimate teachings of Buddhism, namely 'all beings—whether good or evil, male or female, high or low—will ultimatetly achieve enlightenment if they put their faith in the Buddha'.[19] On his demise he was buried at the Caotang temple and an octagonal pagoda was built in his memory.[20] There is a well in the backyard of the Kumarjiva temple from which every morning a magical mist is believed to appear.

Other Kashmiri scholars who went to Xian were Vimalaksa, Dharmamitra, Buddhyasa, Budhabhadra, Sanghabhuti, Gautama Sanghadeva and Punyarata. Here they set about translating Buddhist scriptures.[21] Another great Indian monk and a devout Buddhist who made Xian his home was Amoghavajra—he translated 278 volumes of Buddhist scriptures into Chinese. Amoghavajra was in charge of the temple of great Xingshan.[22] The temple that lies three kilometres from the city is said to be one of the oldest, its history dating back to almost a thousand years. The temple is also regarded as the fountainhead of Vajrayana (mystic Buddhism).

The mystic form of Buddhism is said to have been taken to China by Vajrabodhi and extensively preached by his disciple Amoghavajra. According to P.C. Bagchi 'it was generally known as Tantrayana but included various forms of mysticism known as Vajrayana, Kalchakrayana, Sahajayana'. The practice introduced many new Buddhist gods and goddesses and 'involved some form of yoga, use of mystic gestures and formulae'.[23] Amoghavajra was in China from AD 724 to 731 and again from AD 746 to 774 working incessantly for the propagation of mystic Buddhism.[24] Kala Acharya's *Buddhanusmrti* tells us that magical Buddhism is based on *tantra* involving spells and formulae, repetition of mystical syllables, yoga postures and meditation. *Om mani padme hum* is the famous mantra of Vajrayana.[25]

According to Edward Conze[26] (*Buddhism–Its Essence and Development*), 'Tantra is not a new creation, but the result of absorption of primitive beliefs by the literary tradition, and their blending with Buddhist philosophy'.

View From the City Wall

Having thanked the Buddha and marvelled at all that the great monk had brought with him from his travels, we drove around the magnificent gold-topped Bell Tower in the heart of Xian. This was the busiest roundabout flanked by one of the biggest malls in the city—the Xian Tayuan shopping mall. On the plaza outside the mall, men and women were trading in small items, trying to eke a living out of whatever they could spread on the make-shift kiosks. In a corner a shoeshine boy sat next to a stack of polish arranged neatly on the stand; one could see the tans and the blacks and the neutrals. Not too faraway sat an old woman with wrinkled hands, her money-making tools comprising a sharp needle and an assortment of threads and buttons. The impromptu seamstress was beckoning people to get their torn clothes mended or have a missing button sewn. Red buttons were not all the red I saw in the plaza that day; there were succulent red plums huddled in a wicker basket which the fruitseller was serving in bowls made of mulberry leaves. Surprisingly, there were no beggars, nobody intruded, nobody interrupted, nobody asked an unwarranted question.

In the hoary past, when not all wrists were laden with watches nor all walls nailed with a clock, it was the gleaming bell that doubled up as a timekeeper. The bell would clang at the hour, a sound that would be heard miles away. It was around the regular clanging of the bell that people living inside the city walls wove their everyday chores, they had no other way of knowing time. Today, the bell hangs silently, like a forgotten remnant of a glorious past. The double-storied tower that was constructed in AD 1384 sits on a rostrum of blue bricks, its roof the colour of emerald and contoured with eaves. Huge rows of orange and red flowers laced the tower resembling the axis of a huge merry-go-round, around which revolved speeding limousines and city buses.

Driving a little further into the market area my guide Xingxiaochun and I left the vehicle at a parking lot and walked to the ancient twelve-metre high city wall within the confines of which once lay an entire city replete with paved streets, bustling markets and gilded shrines. And among the two million inhabitants from various lands also lived Indians.[27] The wall was originally said to have been made of mud beaten with lime, rice husk and natural glue that was famed to have more strength

The magnificent tower of the thousand-year-old City Wall standing in the central urban area of Xian. The Wall once enclosed the ancient capital city spread out in a radius of thirty-five kilometres with four gate towers and arrow towers for defence.

than modern-day cement. Once the walls were dressed with a layer of mud they were embellished with stones. The wall had withstood the vagaries of nature and the intrigue of people; even 1400 years later it looked sturdy!

The western gateway of the wall meandered through a long alley adorned with colourful satin flags and red chandeliers that looked like inflated balloons. Walking along we reached the watch tower where a long flight of steps took us atop the wall to an eleven meter wide street. I took a walk on the top street to get a bird's eye view of the city below. It was so quiet and peaceful at the top, and in sharp contrast the city below seemed to be in a hurry what with cars hurtling in the maddening traffic and people striding fast to their destinations. Not too far away I saw that a train had stopped mid-track. The gardens that lined the streets were being watered from the deep blue channel and in the adjacent park, children were gamboling in ponds. I looked to my right and saw tall, shiny glass skyscrapers that reflected the burnished orange of the setting sun, while on my left I saw the banal brown of the rubble; several flyways criss-crossed the skyline but none matched the grandeur of this ancient flyway. An electric vehicle was parked nearby for those unable to walk or just wishing to take a ride. In the eras gone by, these streets resonated with the gallop of the horses that sauntered alongwith the wooden carriages. Even today ramps for horses lead to this ancient expressway running like an elevated metro.

Xingxiaochun tells me that once upon a time sharp shooters were perched at vantage points on the street to keep an eye on the movement of people, specially intruders and strangers. In case of an attack they rained flaming arrows from their perch. The surrounding moat provided further security; several gates and watch towers have found room along the wall.

Elixir of Immortality from India

In the Chinese capital, faith and the relics were not the only things the emperors were obsessed with. They were deeply passionate about Indian alchemy and *tantra vidya* involving mystic practices. They sought the elixir of life, which would ensure an unending youth and magic rituals that would awaken *shakti* or the divine force. They lived in incredible luxury and knew money could buy them anything–except eternal youth. They dreaded wrinkled skin and a weakened body–they wanted to enjoy life's pleasures forever. To escape the inevitable, they sent emissaries to India to fetch magic potions prepared by mendicants and *vaidyas* (doctors) that could not only cure ailments but could also ensure immortality. India was a country well known for its experts on alchemy who could prepare certain compounds which could restore the health of those who were ill and could bring back the vigour of youth. Al Beruni who visited India in the eleventh century described *rasayana* (alchemy) as the 'Hindu sciences which prey'.[28] They also sent for Indian *tantriks* who were armed with enigmatic incantations, secret formulae, prepared charms and practiced some strange and mysterious kind of magic.

Not surprisingly, along the Silk Road trudged not only traders with bolts of silk, but also Indian physicians carrying strange concoctions with them and mystics who were armed with secret formulas and practices.

I was reminded of the story of the legendary Wang hsuan-Tshe (Needham: *Science and Civilisation in China*).[29] He had captured an Indian prince accompanied by an Indian scholar who seemed to have the immortality secret up his sleeves. He claimed he could make people live for two hundred years! Emperor Tai Zong was impressed and invited the scholar to live in his palace. According to the scholar, there was, in India, 'a substance called Pan-chha-cho water produced from minerals in the mountains, which could dissolve herbs, wood, metal and iron'. Taking his word, the emperor exhorted the scholar to prepare such drugs.

P.C. Bagchi[30] also mentions that a Chinese officer Wang Hiuan-tso was sent by the Chinese emperor to India for the third time in AD 657 to take back home an Indian *tantrik* who professed that he was acquainted with the means of securing long life.

He was not the only one, though. In AD 664 Chinese pilgrim Hsuan Chhao received an imperial order to return to India to search for famous physicians and to collect medicinal plants.[31] According to *Si Yu Ki*, the monks who came on Buddhist pilgrimage to India were also keen to buy Indian medicines of various kinds. We read of Hieun-Chiu (same as Hsuan Chhao) who in the year AD 664 came to India and 'proceeding to South India, purposed to return to Tangut, taking with him various sorts of medicine'.[32] Bagchi also reports about Hiuan-chao going to South India to collect different kinds of rare medicines for the Chinese emperor.[33]

Even during Genghis Khan's rule there was great fascination for such alchemy. The Great Mongol was interested in employing the magic powers of the Taoist monk Ch'ang Ch'un to gain immortality.[34] The aged Chinese scholar arrived at the camp of Genghis Khan then camping in Khwarazm after travelling a distance of five thousand kilometres. When the Khan questioned whether he actually possessed the secret potion, the monk said that there were various ways of prolonging life but no such medicine existed.

However, this obsession with immortality was not without its follies, its casualties. The first emperor Shi Huangdi died in 210 BC probably as a result of consuming the elixir of life to attain immortality.[35] This was because 'most alchemical concoctions were highly poisonous and had ...claimed lives of many victims, including a fair number of emperors'.[36]

An interesting incident or misadventure is revealed in Leonardo Olschki's *Marco Polo's Asia*. When Polo, who was on way to Venice from China, halted at the court of King Arghun of Persia while bringing his intended bride princess Cocachin from China, he learnt that the king Arghun had died. 'Rumours were then circulating that the king Arghun had been a victim of a potion of sulphur and mercury administered to him by some Indian, "bacsi" as an elixir to assure him a long life'.[37]

Before death quashed his search for eternity, the emperor had sent thousands of young boys and girls to fairy islands where immortals were supposed to live and where herbs of immortality grew.[38] The story goes that the three thousand girls and boys sent by the emperor under the leadership of Xu Fu never returned. Then the scholars Hou and Lu were sent to hunt for the magic herbs of immortality. The two ran away after their mission failed. The emperor in great frustration and rage ordered over a thousand scholars to be buried alive.[39]

But the emperors' quest for immortality did not end there. Perhaps they knew that death was inevitable, but even in death their quest for eternity would not cease. Some even got jade burial suits for themselves. These were no ordinary suits; jade, which is believed to preserve the body and prevent decay, was sewn with gold thread to encase bodies before burial. One such green jade burial suit lies at the Beijing Museum. The emperors also spared no efforts in building extravagant tombs where they would live in great luxury in their after life.

Heavenly Paradise After Death

Evening had settled in when I set off to see the mausoleum of Emperor Shi Huangdi (259–10 BC) located in Lintong county, thirty-five kilometres east of Xian at the foot of Mt. Lishan. History is replete with Emperor Shi Huangdi's cruelty, but his love for mortal pleasures–beautiful women in his harem, shiny cannon in his armoury, caparisoned horses in his stable–would one day feature his mausoleum in the UNESCO World Heritage List–the only royal tomb in the world to have this honour. Even 2300 years after his death, every evening as the sun sets, a battalion of soldiers in ancient headgear of long felt caps topped with white feathers and protective armour come marching to the beats of bronze drums. As if to salute the emperor, they display their prowess in martial dance.

Mausoleum of Chinese emperor Qin Shihuangdi whose quest for eternity never ceased. More than seven lakh convicts built the royal mausoleum over thirty-eight years at the foot of Mt. Lishan in Xian. It now features on the UNESCO World Heritage Site.

The emperor's royal chariot of gold and silver ready to take him on a tour of his 'wonderland' that he built inside the mausoleum.

A blackboard at the plaza narrated the history of the emperor and facts about the mausoleum in gilt. An audio-video programme in the campus transported the visitors to third century BC when the emperor conscripted more than seven lakh convicts to build his mausoleum immediately after he ascended the throne. It took thirty-eight years to finish the monument made of earth and wood in the shape of a tunnel.

Inside a huge hall a beautiful model of the mausoleum is on display and visitors like me were provided audio aids to have an idea what the mausoleum looked like. The emperor built an opulent world so that he could live in luxury even after death had knocked at his door. He had imagined what heaven would look like and created a replica inside the mausoleum. Built of brilliant gems, the sun and the moon would smile on him and the nights would be starry. His nobles would sit around him and his concubines would provide him pleasure. Rivers and lakes of mercury were constructed to symbolise the earth and eternal lamps were lit with grease. The coffin chamber which was estimated to be about thirty metres deep was bored through three springs. The tomb was also protected with cross-bows, which could catapult automatically if anyone

tried to plunder the tomb. His army of terracotta would defend him and his chariots built of gold and silver would take him on a tour of the 'wonderland'.[40]

It is said that the emperor chose this site for his tomb because of the beautiful landscape of the Li mountains said to be rich in gold and jade, and the Weishui river. But this 'heaven' was not without its tales of gore and brutality. To keep his harem intact and indulge in pleasures even in after-life, childless maids and concubines were killed so that they could follow the emperor to the other world. The workers who slogged endless hours to build the mausoleum were also killed and buried so that they could not divulge the secret of the tomb's architecture and décor.[41]

The emperor's fascination for eternity not only led to bloodshed and death of innocents, it also resulted in environmental disasters. I was informed that so much mercury was used to recreate lakes and rivers that an area stretching over 12,000 square metres around the grave mound has shown high levels of mercury contamination.

There are about 1000 steps cut into the hill that take visitors to the top of the mausoleum. While I was raring to go my guide backed out. I made my way alone to the top. The way led through orchards and flower gardens and dense pine forests. On the wayside benches were laid to enable the visitors to catch their breath. Vendors were selling ice creams and cold drinks, coffee and snacks. My climb to the top took about half an hour. But it was worth every second. The view from the top of the mausoleum was absolutely spectacular! The blue sky descended to meet the emerald hills. On the horizon the huge golden fireball was slowly turning into orange. I sat on a bench to watch the beautiful sunset on the royal grave. The birds were chirping loudly as they settled in their nests in the forests below the hill. Those who lived far away on other hills were making the last dash to their homes before it got dark. As the sky faded into pink and then purple the birds started chirping at the last visitors. Suddenly there was silence. The guards at the mausoleum came checking on the hilltop for lingering tourists like me. It took barely ten minutes to retrace my steps to the waiting vehicle below.

The emperor's terracotta warriors discovered in pits near the mausoleum seem to be always in action readiness. The paint on their face and the design on their uniform have barely faded.

The courtiers and nobles who once gave company to the emperor in his mausoleum now stand guard in front of the Xian museum.

But my tryst with the emperor was not yet over. The following day a CNG cart took me to the pits where his terracotta warriors and horses and golden chariots were standing in battle formation to fight a war. It is said that in March 1974 villagers discovered the pit while sinking a well. After several years of continuous excavation by archaeologists the museum of Emperor Qin Shihuang's terracotta warriors in military robes and horses was officially opened at the site of Pit.no.1 in October 1979. There are altogether three pits on display called Pit 1, 2 and 3; they showcase horses, chariots and the entire army of the dead emperor.

Thousands of real weapons were unearthed from the pits including swords, axes, crossbows, arrows and arrow heads. Some weapons had still not lost their sheen as they were chrome-plated. Beautifully ornamented bronze chariots harnessed by horses and shaded by umbrellas were unearthed. An army general with a sword hanging from his waist was riding it. One of the chariots carried a sitting room which had windows on four sides. It was decorated with gold and silver ornaments. This two thousand-year old army is now one of the eight wonders of the world.

Xian is littered with lavish palaces built inside tombs by reigning kings; even after death they did not want to leave anything to the descendants or courtiers. Apart from the mausoleum of Shi Huangdi, one can see about thirty mausoleums including those of the emperors of the Han and the Tang dynasties. Some of them were large cone-shaped tombs of earth resembling the Egyptian pyramid.

Drive to Banpo Village

Driving back from the terracotta warriors to my hotel I passed by the Huaqing Hot springs, the celebrated romantic retreat of emperors at the foot of Mt. Lishan. It was famed for both its picturesque setting and the romantic love story of Tang Emperor Xuanzong (AD 685-762) and his concubine Lady Yang Guifei. The story goes[42] that the emperor became infatuated with the beautiful consort. He built a palace over the hot spring and each year would take Lady Yang to the retreat so that he could gaze on her gorgeous body while she bathed in her 'Lily Pool'. While the emperor dallied with her, one of the generals, An Lushan, acquired control of the whole north-eastern frontier forcing the emperor to flee to Sichuan. The troops revolted on the way and forced the emperor to have his lady love executed.[43] Presently, the hot spring has been turned into a museum opened to visitors.

I made a last stop at the village of Banpo, five kilometres from the eastern outskirts of the city. Inside the forest of poplars and willows a naked maiden clad scantily in animal skin stands with a water pot beside a fountain. She symbolised the people of the Banpo village – their culture, dress, habits and mores. The inhabitants used a primitive script evident in etchings on pottery and rock drawings.

Paintings on the rock surface take their cues from hunting and ploughing; birds, animals, trees, spade and hoe were drawn in black. In another drawing, two persons were depicted, one of whom had a crown on his head and holding a string. The rock diagrams did not appear as mere canvases to give vent to creative instincts, they seemed more like a language that the Neolithic village dwellers used to communicate with one another. Behind the forest were the dwellings, round domes resembling igloos, topped with thatched roofs that looked like granaries still found in the villages of India. I climbed the wall to take some photos as entry inside the domed structures is prohibited. Strange as it may sound paper was being made in the Banpo village four thousand years ago. One can still see traces of a large pottery kiln. Evidence of a Neolithic settlement was reported with the discovery of burial jars, kilns and hunting tools dating over four thousand years.

Discovered in 1953, the Chinese Academy of Sciences took to large-scale excavation, the find comprising 45 houses, two stables, six kilns, 200 storage caves, 250 burial places in pottery burial jars, 10,000 pieces of tools and utensils and cores of fruits, bones of animals and rotten millet. The Banpo Museum was built in 1958 to display the antiquities, including photographs of the archaeological site, stone axes, knives, spades, wooden digging sticks and hoes. I saw utensils with animal designs and geometric patterns and a bowl with a pattern of fish and a human face. The stone grinder on display is exactly like the ones still used in Indian villages.

According to archaeologists, a matriarchal system existed at Banpo. The inhabitants led a rather primitive life; their women engaged in pottery making, weaving, raising domestic animals and farming while men hunted, fished and fought. A huge cave inside the village served as the paper-making unit. It is not certain as to what paper was used for, as the drawings were done mainly on rocks. In the excavated graveyard, adults were found buried with their faces up and limbs straight and some with faces down and limbs bent and burial articles placed along with them. Children were buried in jars with a hole in the lid for passage of air. Next to them were kept stone bracelets and shell ornaments.

As I stepped out of Banpo, I thought of the era gone by, of an age so different from the one we live in; of Lady Yang whose beauty was the cause of her suffering, and of the emperor's grief on losing his love; my mind wandered to the maids and concubines who were killed to pander to the whims of an obsessed king, the workers who lost their lives because with their tiny hands they could turn coarse mud into a breathtaking artifact; the blacksmiths who sat through whirls of smoke to make axes and spades; the terracotta soldiers that were moulded to defend an imagined invader....

But my reverie was broken by a hollering guide. It was time to step out of Banpo, another day, another destination, another Buddha awaited me.

FACING PAGE:
Paintings engraved on the rock walls of the Banpo Neolithic village, Xian take their cue from hunting and ploughing. Primitive figures drawn in black wear a crown and hold a string from which probably hang hunted birds.

After leaving Xian, travellers who were headed westwards first came to the Majishan hills to seek the blessings of the Maitreya for a successful journey to the Western Regions. The journey was perilous and the travellers feared beasts, serpents and marauders who killed and plundered.

(2)

To the Pavilion of Buddha at Majishan

Leaving Xian the Silk Road headed west along the Wei River valley towards the Majishan caves, the first important halt on the border of the Shaanxi and Gansu provinces. The site is believed to have been an active Buddhist centre from AD fifth to thirteenth century.[1] The thousand kilometre long corridor of the Gansu province, also called the Hexi Corridor linked China with Central Asia through the province of Xinjiang (earlier called East Turkestan). It was also the conduit to India and Southeast Asia through the province of Sichuan and Tibet. About one thousand kilometres of the Silk Road passed through this corridor –westwards to Central Asia and southwards to India; just as the modern Asia-Europe Railways that connects China with Europe. Located on the upper reaches of the Yellow River and Yangtze River, Gansu is believed to be the confluence of Indian and Chinese art and culture that flowered at the grottoes of Majishan, Binglingsi and Dunhuang.

To reach Majishan I took train K-119 to Tianshui, from where the site was south-east at a distance of fifty kilometres. I reached the crowded station a little early. I looked at the watch and saw it was close to 11 pm. I was feeling a bit drowsy and wanted to stretch out on a bench and snooze. But the train was a few miles away and I waited in the lounge.

寺
来看六朝山
行经千折水

FACING PAGE:
The Majishan hill rises dramatically like a huge pagoda from the earth, surrounded by hills covered with silvery pine and a great variety of wild fruits and plants. The caves are carved on the Majishan hillside like a bee-hive and lie hundreds above from the ground. They can be reached by steel ladders that have replaced the ancient wooden ones. The Pavilion of Seven Buddhas cut deftly into the rock face and the high standing Maitreya Buddha can be seen from afar.

Minutes ticked away, with no sign of the train. Thirty minutes in the waiting room seemed to stretch till eternity. No, the train was not late, perhaps, for a change, I was impatient. I looked around, the waiting room had comfortable chairs; there was a small shop that stocked snacks and some Chinese silk carpets and paintings. I had hardly begun looking at paintings when a gregarious bunch of young men entered. They pulled chairs from all over to form a group of eight and began playing cards. They did not seem to be in a hurry, nor seemed impatient. They whiled away their time, for, until ten minutes before the arrival of train no passengers are allowed onto the platform.

When the train's arrival was blared from hidden PA systems, I fell into a queue with other waiting passengers to march out. A lady conductor checked our tickets and then led us all to the platform for boarding. It was all so meticulous—there was no clamouring, no pushing, no porters lugging baggage, no hawkers selling eatables; the platform was scrupulously clean and shining. Everyone awaited their turn; the passengers stood on the place marked for their bogie number and boarded without a whisper. I could not find my compartment and the lady conductor helped me most graciously.

After an exhausting day in Xian, particularly the tiring climb to the hilltop of the emperor's mausoleum I found some comfort here. I took a few deep breaths of the jasmine fragrance sprayed in the coupe and sank into the cushioned berth covered in an exquisitely embroidered sheet. The touch of a soft pillow under my head felt heavenly. The person on the opposite berth was fidgeting with a magazine. From behind half closed eyes I saw him pouring some hot tea from the flask on the side table. I was unaware how long that person sat drinking tea and reading his magazine nor how much time it took to reach my destination. All I knew is that when I alighted at Tianshui station early morning, my guide, Lijing, was waiting for me. We headed toward the Sunshine Hotel, a cosy place with a beautiful vista of the pine-hills and apple and peach orchards by the side of a gurgling stream. My room had a lovely view and I stood by the window soaking in the vignettes. I freshened up and headed to the dining hall for a hot meal of vegetable fried rice, noodles, mushroom soup and salad. By nine in the morning I was on my way to the Majishan grotto corridor, barely an hour's distance from Tianshui.

As we drove past streams, grasslands, orchards and dense forests I began soaking in the sheer beauty of the place. Silvery streams trickled from pine covered cliffs to form lakes at the foot of the mountains where wild pheasants, ducks and long necked cranes descended for their meals. The natural water bodies nourished the lush grasslands and forests of oak and poplars. Numerous fruits like gooseberries, cherries and loquats were growing abundantly in the wild. On the tree trunks grew mushrooms and wild fungus. I signalled to Lijing to halt for a few moments so that I could shoot a video film of a beautiful green lake blooming with lotuses by the side of the road.

From a distance I saw the Majishan hill rising dramatically like a huge pagoda from the earth. Surrounded by hills covered with silvery pine and a great variety of wild fruits and plants, the hill was home to thousands of parrots, blue pheasants and eagles that flew overhead and chattered incessantly. As I climbed up, I saw baby parrots peeping from crevices on the hill side. I was informed that once upon a time, wild animals like leopards and reptiles roamed here freely. The golden monkey and the musk deer had made the Majishan hills their home. The monks must have chosen this spot for its natural beauty and seclusion. It was a kind of cliff monastery where monks lived, studied and preached.

A huge fifty-eight-metre high Maitreya, believed to be the Future Buddha waiting to be born in Tusita heaven, had been carved majestically on the hill face. The Maitreya was flanked by two standing bodhisattvas believed to be Padmapani and Manjusri. The Buddha blesses all those who seek him.

It is said that after leaving Xian, travellers who were headed westwards through Gansu first came to Majishan where they halted and prayed to the Maitreya for a successful journey. The road was perilous, there were mauling beasts, poisonous serpents and marauders on the way who killed

FACING PAGE:
The huge fifty-eight metre high Maitreya, believed to be the Future Buddha blesses all those who seek him. The Maitreya is flanked by two standing bodhisattvas believed to be Padmapani and Manjusri.

and plundered. I saw that hundreds of caves were carved on the cliff like a dense beehive, which narrated the history of a bygone era when monks lived and studied here. According to records exhibited at the site, two well-known Buddhist priests Xuangao and Tankong lived and preached a group of three hundred monks. Between AD fifth and thirteenth century, the site was a flourishing Buddhist centre. However, the caves were not carved at one go, they gradually took shape over different dynasties and centuries. Despite earthquakes and destruction over the years, 194 grottoes, thousands of stone and clay sculptures and over 1000 square metres of mural painting are still intact. Renovation of the caves is said to have been done as late as the early twentieth century.

The caves lie hundreds of feet above the ground and can be reached by recently built steel ladders that have replaced the ancient wooden ones. The narrow winding staircase can scare the faint-hearted; many give up after climbing a few rungs. The sheer height makes one breathless, light headed and dizzy. I took one trembling look at the caves perched hundreds of feet above the ground and another at the wirey steel ladder clasping the cliff sides. My courage gave way. Even before I took the first step on the steel my legs began shaking and refused to move. I had already been pushed aside by other tourists who were in a hurry to go up. I saw a bunch of overweight English tourists peering down from the top caves. Miraculously, I regained my resolve to climb right to the top. Holding the side of the ladder I forced a trembling leg on the first step, second and then... up, up and up, without looking down or sideways. Many tourists had deserted under the pretext of taking a walk in the surrounding forests and a peep at the Ruiying temple in the foothills.

On reaching the cave galleries I was spellbound and forgot that I was on a mountain cliff. It was like walking inside a huge palace where lived the graceful Buddha and bodhisattvas, where dark apsaras danced and where the divine horses draw the deities' chariots. Strange birds which were half human, rode the rolling waves of black clouds. With

FACING PAGE:
The painted images of Buddha and bodhisattvas have chubby cheeks and long face and are wrapped in an elaborate halo from which light seems to radiate. In some images, the halo seems to burst into flames.

splendid mural work and thousands of stone and clay figures, the caves looked more like an art gallery.

The caves have been dug out on the vertical cliff of the mountains. I learnt from my guide that fire wood was stacked close to the mountain and workers stood on wooden planks to excavate the caves, carve images and paint murals. The painters were said to have employed the same technique as in Ajanta to prepare the walls for painting murals. After the caves had been dug, the inner surface was smoothened with a thick layer of mud and wood dust. Occasionally horse hair or husk was mixed with yak dung and mud to smoothen the rock surface. This was followed by a thin layer of finely powdered gypsum that was washed with pigments to obtain a uniform background. This became the soft surface over which images of Buddha and Bodhisattvas were drawn and painted. The craftsmen used special techniques to prepare the basic mixture of clay and other ingredients so that the statues appear as fresh and firm as fired pottery.

At several points wiry streams have caused seepage in the caves. Several murals have been destroyed due to high moisture in the air but the clay sculptures are pretty well preserved. Most of the smaller caves with murals and images have been sealed with wire meshing making photography impossible.

If one sees the images, their drapes and adornments, the Indian influence is very

evident. Surprisingly, in some caves Buddha bore a striking resemblance to the Hindu god Lord Shiva—eyes bloodshot, dreamy and intoxicated; multi-coloured rays dancing around the body, hair held high in a top bun or the *jata* of Shiva and a blissful mien of detachment from the mundane world. The jewellery that adorned the bodhisattvas had an Indian feel about them. Apsaras and devas wore anklets on their feet and thick bangles on their hands. Some of them were semi-clad like the images in Ajanta caves, their chests bare, their unstitched clothing falling just above the knees. Some of the apsaras were tall and dark.

Around the colossal Maitreya were eight, long cave galleries or corridors known as 'Gallery of Oriental Sculptures'. Among these, the 'Hall of Scattering Flowers' and 'Pavillion of Seven Buddhas' occupied by the bejewelled Buddha and flanked by bodhisattavas are the hallmark of Majishan grotto art. The former, the most gorgeous was cut and adorned in the sixth century by the famous general Li-Yun-Xin with an inscription composed by littérateur Yu-Xin. Eight pillars support the cave and divide it into seven niches, with beautiful mural work depicting celestial beings playing musical instruments. Apsaras can be seen

ABOVE AND FACING PAGE TOP:
In some caves the Buddha resembles the Hindu God Shiva. There is a deep protuberance on the forehead that was once coloured in vermillion. The mark on the forehead appears to have been sculpted like the third eye of Shiva.

showering flowers from heaven. There were beautiful statues of Buddha and dozens of sculptures and painted reliefs of bodhisattvas and disciples. The clay images had a stone core. Approximately 250 square meters of murals are still preserved on the ceiling.

The images of the Buddha and the Bodhisattvas have chubby cheeks and a longish face; with a deep protuberance on the forehead that once was coloured in vermillion. Many images had motifs painted on the body and face. The clothes fell heavily from the shoulders in neat pleats and their necklaces and armlets were exquisite. Interestingly, I noted that the images had Mongoloid features but their clothes and jewellery were Indian. Their thick curls were rolled up in high buns; the Buddha had ringlets and an *ushnisha* or a bun on top of the head.

There is beautiful mural work on the walls and ceilings of the caves depicting rare birds and animals. The ceiling of Cave 5 depicts a 'heavenly horse' galloping away.

I climbed higher and passed through long cave galleries. My head was reeling as I looked down several hundred feet below; perched up there, all I could see was the top of the forest cover over high mountain peaks and black crows floating in the air. Crossing Caves 31 to 38 and going through Caves 10 and 13, I reached cave 9. It was a huge cave located under a cliff cut in the sixth century. It had a long shed with seven niches and is called the Pavilion of Seven Buddhas. Each niche had a Buddha image flanked by two bodhisattvas and two disciples. An interesting and rare painting of *Kalavinka*, a bird with a human head and long wings can be seen on the ceiling of niche 4.

The images of Buddha in the seven niches sat in different postures and the halo around their head was differently designed. One halo showed bright rays, orange, green and yellow emanating from the Buddha's head and encircled like snakes around the head of Lord Shiva. In another niche the halo around Buddha's body showed deep orange flames emanating from his body and reminded one of the miracle of Sravasti when the Buddha's body burst into flames. In each niche, the robes of the Bodhisattvas and disciples were in similar colours, but draped differently. In some niches, there were gilded umbrellas embedded in the roof just over the Buddha's head.

The double-storey 'Thousand Buddha Corridor' is about 32 metres long and houses 258 clay Buddha figures, built around a core of stone. It resembled the Teen Taal Buddhist cave at Ellora in India. The famous heavenly horses galloped on the ceiling of Cave 5. There were sculptures of Buddhist deities and a beautiful illustration of Buddha's Paradise on the main wall. A masterful illustration of the Nirvana Buddha decorates Cave 135. Another 'Ten Thousand Buddha' chamber (Cave 133) decorating the western cliff had Buddhist deities carved into the walls and flying apsaras on the ceiling. Inside stands the Amitabha Buddha.

Three other giant Buddhas adorned the eastern and the western cliffs of the Majishan mountains. It was said that repeated earthquakes over the years caused the Majishan mountains to split into two halves —the eastern and the western cliffs. Access to both cliffs was provided

An interesting wall painting at the Majishan caves depicting horse riders following a horse driven chariot. The riders are holding banners and seem to be part of a royal entourage.

ABOVE: A mountain stream has been trapped into the rocks below to form a beautiful lake at Xianrenya, surrounded by towering cliffs and dense forests. The lake appears dark green as scarcely any light reaches through.

TOP: At a short distance from the Majishan lie the beautiful grottoes gallery "the Xianrenya, which in essence is said to be a symbol of harmony and religious co-existence. A wall painting shows warrior kings.

by a narrow bridge of steel that carried tourists from one cliff to another. A sixteen metre high Buddha flanked by bodhisattva Manjusri stands in Cave 13 cut in the sixth century. The local guide informed me that the sculpture was of clay but the core was made of stone. Another huge Buddha flanked by bodhisattvas stands in Cave 98 on the western cliff. An interesting image of bodhisattva Vajrapani holding a sceptre can be seen in Cave 191.

Xianrenya Caves

Another beautiful grottoes gallery, the Xianrenya Caves, was waiting for me.

A short drive through lows hills and forests of pine took me to the Xianrenya mountains. Our vehicle was stopped about two kilometres from the caves and an electric car transported me along a gushing stream up the hill to the Xianrenya gardens. Here a mountain spring has been trapped into the rocks below to form a huge lake. Shrouded by towering cliffs and covered by dense forests on all sides, the lake appeared dark green as scarcely any sunlight gets through. But thousands of yellow and pink lotuses blooming in the lake send out a strange luminosity and stand out in the darkness like sentinels of lights. Giant cliffs crowned by pines, silvery streams, scattering and dancing in the air before getting lost in the dark lake, the radiance of the lotus all lend a divine ambience to the place. Small wooden pavilions with dragon eaves popping out of the rocks invite visitors to enjoy the scenic beauty.

The electric car stopped near a refreshment stall where two women attendants sat knitting sweaters. The journey hereafter to the Xianrenya cliffs was by foot. Many tourists preferred to sit by the side of the lake warming themselves over bowls of steaming soup and soaking in the beauty of the place, but I decided to head off to the caves with my guide. I climbed hundreds of steps cut into the grey and black rocks and negotiated several cliffs to reach the Xianrenya caves. Like the Majishan mountains, the Xianrenya hills are carpeted with dense forests and inhabited by beautiful birds and wild animals (I thankfully did not come across any). All creatures big and small were thoroughly enjoying the wilderness just as I was. Huge juicy beehives, full of sweet honey hung like black bags from the rocks. The steep climb to the caves was invigorating. There were wooden benches on the way for travellers to rest awhile and catch their breath.

Religious Co-existence

It is said that the immense beauty, isolation and rich resources of the hills also called the 'Immortals' Cliff' attracted scholars and priests who lived and studied here. I do not know why the hills were so named. Perhaps the scholars were alchemists in pursuit of the herbs of immortality; perhaps magic herbs actually grew here. But one thing is certain that before the Buddhist monks swarmed the area it was already inhabited by Confucian thinkers and Taoist priests. As a proof of this, some caves on the cliffs displayed a unique confluence of Confucian, Taoist and Buddhist deities. It is believed[2] that while the Buddha and his disciples were preaching in India, his near contemporaries in China like the great philosopher Confucius (551-479 BCE), Mencius (372-289 BCE) and Taoist philosopher Laozi (369-286 BCE) were helping to establish early Chinese ways of thinking. After Buddhism arrived in China around the beginning of the Christian era, the basic Confucian and Taoist traditions are believed to have remained largely intact. But by the end of the fifth century Buddhism had swept across China and emperors lavishly patronised the Buddhist church.[3]

The co-existence of the three traditions could be observed at the Xianrenya caves—said to be the confluence of Confucius, Buddha and Laozi. The wall paintings depicted scenes from everyday life and religious themes. The first cave called the 'Three Officials' was cut in the Ming Dynasty (AD fourteenth century). Carved under a hanging cliff the cave hall had statues of the Nature deities—heaven, earth and water. I saw the 'Three Masters' in Cave 2 cut in the Qing Dynasty (AD seventeenth

The massive black marble stone slab standing near Cave 4 at Xianrenya in Tianshui displays royal instructions from the emperor of the Ming Dynasty to the local officials and a record of all temples standing on the mountains.

century) also carved out of a mountain cliff. There were images of Confucius, Buddha and Laozi (founder of Taoism) and decorative murals on the side walls.

The Lamaism Hall (Cave 3) was in the natural shape of a mountain cliff and had the images of the Tibetan Buddha (Lamaism is a special form of Buddhism acquired from Tibet). Another hall, Cave 4 was the main Bodhisattva Hall cut during the fourteenth century. The central image here was that of the 'Guardian king' made of iron. A little further I came across a large black slab of stone in which royal instructions had been inscribed. The orders of the emperor of the Ming dynasty to the local officials and a record of all the temples existing at the Xianrenya mountains begin with a letter which was an exact replica of the Sanskrit 'Aum'.

We began our long walk to the south cliff of the mountains to reach the 'Ten Thousand Buddha' niches where the image of Guayin Buddha, (or the bodhisattva Avalokitesvara also called the 'Goddess of Mercy' shown to be female in appearance), sat in the center of the cliff. The Guayin Buddha is widely worshipped and is believed to bless barren women and keep away misery.

A neighbouring hill, which is closed to the public, has thousands of caves which seem like small holes from afar. Long ago monks had made the hill their home. Now only birds and bees could be seen darting in and out. I was very eager to take a look but there was no easy access.

We retraced our steps to the foot of the mountains and joined several other tourists sitting in a pavilion under the shade of peach and apple trees. A big tray of goodies was spread out on the table before them and two women attendants, their nimble fingers playing on the knitting needles, were coaxing all to try the fish soup prepared at the nearby restaurant. I was amazed at the whole lot of attention tourists were drawing to themselves. There was some rice porridge and sweet buns on my tray and I lapped it up quickly. The corridor surrounding the lotus lake was by now crowded with tourists who had assembled for a quick snack before embarking on the steep climb to the Immortals' Cliff.

The sun was going down and I had one more destination on my itinerary—the Fu Xi temple. I bade goodbye to the lovely lake and hopped into the electric car to reach the parking lot. There I climbed into the waiting vehicle and was driven through the hilly landscape bathed in the radiance of the setting sun. An orange glow settled over the sky, the fluffy clouds sailed over the hill peaks taking on a violet hue. The verdant vegetation was slowly turning dark. There was a loud chirping of the birds as they fluttered over tree tops, vying for space in the foliage and settled down in their nests.

Shrine of Fu Xi

Passing through the huge City Square I reached the shrine of Fu Xi, the great ancestor of the Chinese who was believed to have been born here. He was said to have been the first to use ropes to make nets for hunting and fishing He sat in the main hall of the temple as the reigning deity. The ancestor was dressed like a Neanderthal; his skirt made of leaves, leaf necklace snaking around his neck. In his hand he weilded a disc called the 'eight diagram' representing the eight directions and eight elements in nature—the sky, earth, water, fire, wind, thunder, mountains and the river. The core of the disc is believed to represent the cosmic energies Yin and Yang. The active Yang and the passive Yin cooperate as male and female energies. It is said that Fu Xi had a strong observation of nature. He discovered that everything in the world is the result of a combination of the negative and positive energies.

On the walls there was a huge mural depicting primitive scenes of hunting and ploughing. Men and women clad in short skirts made of animal skin with naked torsos were dancing and making merry while hunting birds with bows and arrows. One primitive woman was feeding her baby while others were busy with household chores. In the courtyard under the shade of ancient trees lay a huge incense pot. We lit candles and paid homage to Fu Xi.

A Trip to the Market

In the evening I headed towards the market to have some roasted sweet potatoes. The seller had a mobile oven in which he had stacked a heap of them. I relished a bowl tossed with salt and lemon juice. Along a narrow lane, I found women selling trinkets, embroidered items and toiletries. A shop in a bylane sold paintings of Bodhisattvas and enamelled woodwork. I was keen to buy one, but they were priced exhorbitantly high!

A woman cyclist who rode into a pedestrian lane found her bicycle chained by female cops. In another winding lane, I chanced upon a hawker selling sweet popcorn laced with sugar and absolutely delicious. As I emerged from this small market onto another back lane, I found women selling vegetables and lotus flowers. As I walked in the dusty lanes, I was reminded of the Indian daily markets. Women were hollering at me to buy their goods. All I wanted to buy was a lotus, I asked the price of one, but a generous woman packed an entire bunch for one yuan.

Here skyscrapers stood in contrast to small markets. Although traffic was heavy there was very little pollution because the preferred mode of transport is the bicycle. By evening the place was swarming with people. There was music at the square; people were sitting on benches enjoying a pleasant breeze. Life is hectic by the day and peaceful in the evening. I returned to my hotel late at night after taking several rounds of the market wondering at the similarity of everyday life in India and China —the flavour of roasted tubers, the corn cobs, the lotus sellers outside the temple gate, the deafening din in the vegetable market and in the mural of the Fu Xi temple depicting a simple village life, a scene that looks straight out of an Indian village.

I am not sure what awaited me at Zhangye, but I was ready to go anywhere for the Buddha. Anywhere...!

A twenty-seven metre high Maitreya Buddha sits in deep meditation in a huge cave cut vertically along the mountain cliff at Binglingsi, near Lanzhou. The Buddha appears to be sitting on a throne and has some resemblance with the Leshan Buddha near Chengdu.

(3)

Along the Yellow River at Lanzhou

In a Speedboat to Binglingsi

From Tianshui I headed towards Lanzhou—the capital of Gansu province. It was an important strategic town on the ancient Silk Road connecting China with the Western regions, and is now a key link on the modern Asia–Europe Railways. It is the crossing point on the Yellow River which flows through the city from the east to the west and owes its historical significance due to its geographical position.

I found myself at the Tianshui railway rest room waiting for the T-568 train to Lanzhou. While I was pre-occupied in my thoughts, I knew the train must be hastening past verdant fields of the Hexi Corridor. I was shaken out of my reverie by the loud hailer that announced its arrival. I squinted at the large, round white clock, which showed 10 pm. Yes, the train was not a minute later than scheduled. My guide Lijing who was still with me would leave only after I had boarded the train. In the neon lights of the platform I looked for my compartment and spotted it a few steps away.With bags in tow I jumped in. Clean, thick comforters were neatly folded and placed on the soft seat. In one corner I noticed an embroidered dark blue butterfly. A shiny flask full of hot water for morning tea stood in another corner of the berth. I could feel the warmth around me, thanks to central heating. The compartment looked well-appointed; I was happy I could sleep well through the night. Very soon all travellers were snuggled in their berths, wrapped in the blue comforters. I must have been half-way through a dream when I woke to the thud of a closing door. The woman in-charge of the compartment was locking the toilet door so that people would not use it at the station. Throughout the night the noise of the closing door kept waking me up. It was a routine task – the lady would lock it as soon as the train halted and would unlock it as soon as the train chugged out of the station. But that was not her only duty; she kept the toilet sparkling clean by scrubbing it with a special duster.

One can see hundreds of nooks cut into the rocks at Binglingsi. In one nook there are three pagodas having spires like the Hindu temples.

During the night, I must have run through a hundred dreams, I no longer remember them; all I recall is that I slept very well. Lanzhou was not too far away and the attendant woke us up just before the train chugged into the station. At Lanzhou station, there was a sea of nameless travellers, all that looked familiar was my own name, scribbled on a placard. It was my guide Cengxing who would later take me to a small hotel—only for a short halt. I freshened up, had some breakfast and left for the Liugioxia dam at the foot of the Binglingsi caves. It is situated in Dasigou valley of Mount Jishi, about thirty-five kilometres southwest of Yongjing town. In 1961 Binglingsi was tagged a National Heritage site and I was curious to see it.

We drove along the Yellow River. Well, I always thought colour names for rivers were mere euphemisms. A Dead Sea could not be dead, a Red Sea could not be red and a Yellow River certainly could not have been yellow. But how muddled was my geography—the Yellow River actually looked yellow! We headed to the pier of the dam where several speedboats were anchored. The speedboat that cut through the water of the dam with vengeance took me to the foot of the mountains where steps had been carved out of rocks. The carelessly hewn staircase made for a narrow path flanked by two hills that took pilgrims to the cave.

There are innumerable legends about the caves, the most plausible of which was the story that began in AD 420 when the first rock was cut for the cave. However, the cave was not built in a day; legend has it that hundreds of workers cut rock for more than a thousand years to give the cave its present-day shape. When the dam was being built several caves at the base of the mountains were submerged. Thousands of cultural relics including pottery, thangkas and gold and silver images of Buddha were removed either to the upper caves or preserved in the museum. A beautiful life-size Reclining Buddha and rare Buddhist scriptures were moved to a temple on the opposite cliff.

A three-feet wide wooden bridge on stilts was built along the mountain to take the visitors from one cave to another. The caves exist in several tiers and reaching the top is quite an arduous task. However, fixed wooden ladders leaning against the cliff take the visitors to the top caves. I saw hundreds of nooks cut into the rocks, some holding small carvings of the Buddha and his disciples, others adorned with pagodas having

The Reclining Buddha inside an ancient temple at Binglingsi. The image had been salvaged from a submerged cave at the foot of the mountains when the Liugioxia dam was being built on the Yellow River.

The Buddha sitting in abhaymudra *smiles at his devotees. Huge* kundals *hang from his ear lobes. Colourful rays emanate from his body while disciples hold fans or* chavar *over his head.*

spires like the Hindu temples. Some caves were deeply set into the mountains and held large images of the Buddha and bodhisattvas. The cave walls were not barren either, they were replete with murals, stretching more than 1,000 square metres.

Buddha like Shiva

Against the charcoal grey of the caves, the bodhisattvas looked absolutely splendid, their bangles, armlets, necklaces and earrings gleamed even in fading light. The Buddha wore large *kundals* or earrings, while some bodhisattvas even had the trident, which is synonymous with the Hindu god Shiva and is a common accoutrement of Indian sages and saints. Some of them held *kamandals* like Indian sadhus.

A wide angle view of the Maitreya Buddha cave and other multi-storied caves on his right. A three-foot wide wooden bridge on stilts has been built along the mountains to take the visitors from one cave to another.

Looking at the bodhisattvas and the Buddha it was difficult to believe that they are made of stone, one cannot but marvel at the dexterity of the sculptors. Even in the sculpted images the expression on the faces is soft. The clothes appear transparent and the folds of the garment are visible. One can decipher the serenity in the eyes, the veins that run through the slender hands, the folds of the fabric that fall carelessly on naked torsos, the curls that cover the forehead mischievously...! The sight is all the more marvellous because there were no machines with which stone could be carved in a jiffy; there was no emulsion that could add a colour in a moment.

The halo around the Buddha was painted in various designs. In alternating bands of black and green, rays emanated from the head while some had a corrugated surface from which flames seemed to flicker. From the roof of the arched caves hung flowers, crowns and chandeliers over the central image of the Buddha. The dominant colour used was malachite green and red which had turned black over the years. In the Avalokitesvara cave the head dress and skirt of the deity was gold rimmed and the red paint was still visible.

A twenty-seven metre high Maitreya Buddha sat in deep meditation in a huge cave cut vertically along the cliff. I found a place to fix my camera on the opposite cliff. I waited for the sun to rise over the mountains so that some light fell on the image and I could capture the Buddha in the slanting rays.

Along the Hilly Stream in an Open Jeep

A small bridge over a hilly stream led me to the mountains on the other side. The stream meanders through a narrow alley for five kilometres before reaching the dam. Here we found an ancient Tibetan temple where the Reclining Buddha salvaged from a submerged cave had been placed. Near the cave, several monks had their homes. I lit incense sticks and offered prayers to the Buddha and climbed down the mountains into the alley. Here, by the side of the stream Cengxing hired an open jeep and we drove upstream to reach the Lama temple. The valley had hairpin bends and we parked the jeep on a broad open landing inside the mountains. Buddhist banners along the rocky path fluttered in the breeze. Tiny alcoves seemed to have been carved inside the mountains; it was here that monks found shelter. All along the way I saw monks in brown robes going about their daily chores nonchalantly. Some caves were perched on the hill top and it was in one of these high caves that the head lama, until recently, lived. I noticed a silk flag and freshly-painted floral motifs on the wall. Having come so far I wanted to meet the lama; but my wish was met with absolute silence. The lama had passed away a few days ago; the cave had been deserted as the new lama was living within the temple precincts.

A flight of steps led me to an ancient stupa near the Lama temple. Here lamas were preparing lunch and butter tea. One lama picked insects from a plateful of brown rice that would be cooked alongwith lentils and beans as porridge. Inside the temple Guru Padmasabhava was seated on a throne. The sanctum sanctorum was dark and a huge lock was staring at us. I urged the lama to open the door but he refused–he could not disturb the sleeping deities! Not too far away was another mountain cave where more statues of Maitreya Buddha and Padasambhava occupy gilded thrones. However, there was not an air of antiquity around them; the statues looked rather new.

The open jeep brought me back through the mountain alley to the giant Maitreya. I walked to the pier to hop into the jetty that would take us to the other side of the dam from where I would head towards Xiahe.

The ferry took me across the dam and I alighted at the Liugioxia gorge. Here the streets were lined with fishermen; I saw nets everywhere. A group of women were proudly sitting next to a pile of freshly caught fish, snails, water snakes and tortoises. I was waiting for the driver, but he was nowhere to be seen. Suddenly I spotted him sitting on a bench, enjoying a lunch of rice and snails that had been cooked on a small woodfire. A heap of tiny fish was being smoked in the dying embers and I too sat down for a quick lunch.

ABOVE: A Lama temple near the Binglingsi caves. An image of Guru Padmasambhava sits on a throne inside the temple.
BELOW: The path to the lama temple is through a narrow alley cut through the mountains by a rapid stream. All along the pebbled path one can see numerous alcoves cut into the mountain sides, many of them inhabited by monks.

Lama Dance at Labrang Monastery

Instead of going back to Lanzhou we took the road along the Xiahe river (a tributary of the Yellow River) which flows at the foot of the Dragon mountains. Unlike other mountains that seemed to wear a sheath of brown or black, the Dragon mountains look green, covered as they were with long grass and trees.

The road was bumpy and the journey was back-breaking, the only distraction—and solace—being the beautiful Tibetan villages and monasteries that were lined all along the route. I reached Xiahe well after nine. All I needed then was a bed on which I could stretch myself and give my back a little rest. Not many moments later I tucked myself to sleep in a small but cozy Xiahe hotel that lay in the neighbourhood of the Labrang Monastery.

The sprawling Labrang Monastery at Xiahe on the banks of the Xiahe river, a tributary of the Yellow River. The 300-year old monastery is a prestigious national monument and has six colleges. At the Kalachakra College students study Sanskrit poetry among other subjects.

I was so tired that I did not even notice that the room overlooked the lone Tibetan market. Fresh after a good night's sleep, I looked at the room, which resembled a doll house—small and beautifully painted with floral designs over the walls and the wooden roof. Perhaps the only aberration from a doll's house was the whirr of the heater that provided the much-needed warmth as the temperature often dipped below zero at night. I looked out and saw hundreds of lamas; the entire town seemed to be teeming with lamas in brown robes and maroon shawls. They were everywhere. That day wherever I went I saw lamas, even at restaurants digging their forks into Chinese and Tibetan food.

It was pure coincidence, for that day in Xiahe was not just any other day; the monastery dance was scheduled for the day. The town was cluttered with foreign pilgrims who had descended on Xiahe to see the dance. I thanked my good fortune and quickly took a vantage position in the open ground at the foot of the mountains. The performers were lamas, wearing yellow hats and maroon robes. There were so many of

The famous Lama dance to mark the passing out ceremony of the students of the Labrang Monastery at Xiahe.

FACING PAGE:
An image of Maitreya Buddha adorns the Golden Temple at the Labrang Monastery.

them that the entire ground seemed to have borrowed the yellows and the maroons from the lamas' robes and hats. As the first sound of the conch shell and the trumpet rent the air, the performers broke into small rhythmic steps that gained momentum slowly. The mellifluous strain of the trumpet was joined by the reverberation of the metal cymbals. I held my breath for the final moments when the music would reach a crescendo and the lamas would twirl speedily. As the music began to fade, the movement of the lamas got slower. The change in rhythm was absolutely fascinating, the steps matching the beat of the cymbals and the breathlessness of the trumpets. Between tapping my foot along with the lamas and getting mesmerised by their agility, I bonded with the lamas. On that ground that day in Xiahe, a friendship flourished.

The lamas so fascinated me that I rushed to a shop selling Tibetan knick-knacks, incense sticks made of the bark of wild trees, Chinese brocade and lama shawls. But I was not interested in these trinkets; I was looking for a lama dress. I finally found one, quickly slipped into it and got a photograph taken. That day in Xiahe, I became—at least for that one brief moment—a lama.

I was amazed how quickly the day had ended and melted into another. The next morning I began the day with a Tibetan breakfast at a neighbouring restaurant. There was no option; the tiny Xiahe Hotel did not offer meals. At the restaurant I was taken by surprise, not by the chicken-noodle soup that came accompanied with puffed buns, but at the large television screen on which played dubbed Hindi dance videos. The music was loud but the monks inside the cabins, digging on their plateful seemed to be enjoying not only every morsel but even the music. Who would have thought that far way in Xiahe I would get a hint of Bollywood! But Bollywood too was in for a little remix here. There were Tibetan clones of the Bollywood popular songs–no, not dubbed in Tibetan, but Tibetan actresses copying each gyration and the flutter of the eyelashes complete with sarees and Indian jewellery. While I sipped on endless glasses of Tibetan tea a monk told me that the remixes were a rage in Xiahe. Going by the din of the tapping feet within the restaurant I believed all about the 'rage'.

The wait outside the Labrang monastery was too long. I was not waiting for salvation, what I was looking for was the English guide who would take all foreign tourists inside the monastery. Lama Jam Young was not English, he just spoke good English. The monastery had been standing there for nearly three hundred years and its moment of glory arrived when in 1982 the State Council of the People's Republic of China listed it among prestigious national monuments that deserved special preservation.

Tantra Colleges in Monastery

The Labrang Monastery, a world resource for Buddhism, was founded in 1709 by Washu Byawang Tsendu, the second highest Lama in the history of the Gelupa (Yellow Hat) Sect. There are six colleges in the monastery, each teaching a different subject. According to the temple brochure the Labrang monastery has two Tantra Colleges that teach meditation on the three deities of Samvara Chakrasamara, Guhyasamaja and Yamataka. The study of Dhilwa Shidak (the four explanations of the Tantric doctrine) is also offered to eager students. In Kalachakra College, students practice meditation on three deities of Kalachakra, Kunruk and Eyon Shang and study Sanskrit poetry, religious dancing, making sand mandalas and chanting prayers.

In the Medical College of the monastery, the three deities mediated upon were Bhaishajyaguru (medicine Buddha), Mintrupa and Hayagriva (horse-necked one). Here the monks studied the ancient basic Tibetan medicine text, the *Gyushi*. Lamas themselves collected medicinal herbs

The Labrang monastery is famous for its beautiful butter sculptures prepared by the monks. These are of animals carved out of yak butter and embellished with vegetable dyes.

and prepared medicines. As we walked inside the College of Medicine I felt heady with the whiff of the herbs stacked in bags. There was not one, two, or a handful, the storehouse had hundreds of herb bags that were spilling with different varieties of herbs. We were first welcomed by the statue of the Medicine Buddha and a photograph of the tenth Panchen Lama before whom a large yak butter lamp burns incessantly. Here lamas studied 'medicine tantra' to keep alive the tradition of Tibetan medicine that is said to have a panacea for several critical ailments. The deities of Havajra College are Havajra, Vajrapani and Naljor Namka. The college offers astrology and Tibetan culture as part of the syllabi that also comprises lessons in composing Tibetan and Sanskrit poetry.

The biggest and most important college in the monastery is the Philosophy College, where the five volumes of the Gelupa Sect are studied. Astronomy, geography, mathematics and compiling the Tibetan calendar and the science of forecasting solar and lunar eclipses are also part of the curriculum.

Inside another hall was a huge statue of Tantrik Buddha who held a vajra. Ancient thangkas covered the walls and important scriptures adorned the shelves of wooden cupboards. There were precious statues of two huge golden Buddhas. We crossed into the great hall of Knowledge Buddha (Thungkapa Buddha) who founded the Yellow sect in the fourteenth century. Old scriptures are still kept inside this hall where the students sit for their examinations. There were beautiful statues of the Green and White Tara and a thousand enlightened Buddhas.

When in Labrang, the Monastery Museum is a must-see. Full of prayer wheels, countless Tibetan cultural relics, rare Buddhist works of art, tens of thousands of Buddhist sutras in Tibetan language, the monastery lives up to its reputation of being a great Buddhism resource. It is also famous for its butter sculptures, the art of which is taught in a huge hall. Several Buddhist sculptures have been carved out of butter and embellished with vegetable dyes.

Winter Dance and DohDar Music

Dance forms an integral part of several religions and Buddhism is no exception. However, most of the dance festivals entail dancing by young monks who wear interesting masks of lion, deer and dog. The Havajra Winter Dance that attracts tourists from across the world is dedicated to the different religions of the world. During the religious festival the grasslands change their colour—they all look white, borrowing that colour from the thousands of tents that are pitched on these special occasions. Not only have the festivals become popular with the peripatetic traveller's calendar, even the passing out of the lamas is celebrated with a lot of dance. As we emerged out of the hall we noticed hundreds of lamas in brown robes who had gathered to watch the passing out which was observed as a Tibetan festival. The young lamas had formed a huge circle and were dancing to the beat of drums and metal clangs.

At the Golden Temple where white and green images of Goddess Tara are seated lamas were pouring yak butter in burning lamps. Inside there was the huge image of Avalokitesvara with a thousand arms. Images of the Maitreya Buddha and eight bodhisattvas were made of gold and copper. About eight hundred students were chanting mantras while the senior lamas were supervising the prayer and teaching session. The lamas were pouring water in large receptacles, burning incense and filling the lamps with butter and prostrating before the Buddha. We climbed up the White pagoda to get a view of the entire Labrang monastery sprawled on the foothills.

Another interesting annual festival was the Festival of Saving of Lives. The Festival is not about gods or humans, it is about animals. On this day, a few animals are chosen and marked. They are the lucky ones; they would never be killed and would be allowed to die a natural death. The Sunning Buddha is another fascinating festival where an ancient thangka of Buddha is placed on the side of a mountain. The following day is marked by religious dance, circumambulation by devotees and offerings of yak butter to the deity.

Winter dance and DohDar music form an integral part of the religious activities at the Labrang monastery and attract tourists from all over the world. Here lamas play the traditional musical instrument and young lamas dance to the beat of drums and metal clangs.

According to monastery records, DohDar, the famous music of Labrang dates back to three hundred years and has, in recent times, elicited a lot of interest from scholars and researchers. Music was brought into Labrang Monastery by the second Jamyang Lama. Originally, music was played by only twenty-one monks from the six colleges of the monastery. The eight-piece music (the principal three pieces are named Lama Dhandin (inventing Lama), Tupchin Jachu (eighty saints), Rinchin Charbip (raining jewels) would not pipe in the monastery everyday—it was the privilege of the Jamyang Lama, the music played only when he was leaving or arriving at the Monastery. The music which was once the preserve of Jamyang Lama is now played only on ceremonial occasions.

Over the years, the instruments, if not the DohDar music, have evolved with each incarnation of the Jamyang Lama. During the reign of the first Jamyang Lama the only instruments used were the dragon-head banjo, the (two-string) guitar, flute and Milong Gudong.

In the biography of Guntang Thanbi Dolmi Lama, it is mentioned that when he came from Lhasa to the Labrang Monastery, some monks from Mongolia along with others from Kalachakra College played DohDar music for him in the Thuptan Palace as an offering. DohDar music was also played during the enthronement of the third Jamyang Lama. The biography of the fourth Jamyang Lama shows that he too helped develop the music. The fifth Jamyang Lama incorporated DohDar music into many traditional Tibetan dramas and sermons.

The music was given a more complete and distinctive sound when the sixth Jamyang Lama added a number of different Tibetan instruments to the mix—the banjo, Tse, Kangling, two-string guitar, Jumang, drum and small cymbal. To help rebuild and develop traditional Tibetan Buddhism music and encourage its development, he also began introducing it to the rest of the world.

Lama Jam Young

Too much happened in these couple of days in Xiahe. There were Buddhas everywhere, there was faith everywhere. And during my days in Xiahe, my guide Lama Jam Young stayed by my side, narrating interesting stories and sharing nuggets of history in his impeccable English. The more he shared, the more he shed his identity as a guide and became my friend. He had gauged my curiosity for detail, and wherever possible he handed me literature about places and monastery. He took me to Excellent Hotel which the monastery has generously built for foreign visitors. It was on the banks of the Xiahe river and had a mountain for a beautiful backdrop. Inside the Hotel I was welcomed by the chief lama who wrapped a white silken scarf around my neck and mumbled prayers for my success and good health. They graciously served boiled mutton and yak milk curd, the meal concluding with a rice and milk pudding that was specially prepared for me. The lamas were being very generous they did not charge me for the meal. They smiled and added that it was their honour. I bowed in gratitude to the host and headed towards the hotel for the night.

I spent two shivering days in Xiahe; the third day I returned to Lanzhou where the mercury had dipped further. On my way back to Lanzhou I did not take the previous route; this route was longer and better and was dotted with many more Tibetan settlements than what I saw earlier.

In the Lingxia Muslim region I saw many mosques and madrassas. I climbed down the coach to visit a green-tiled madrassa in a small town that was in the midst of an orchard and looked very ancient. I was told that students came there to learn Arabic. The imam's tomb was nearby. The present imam and his family lived in the residential quarters behind the mosque.

We passed through the Deben mountains and drove along the banks of the Tao river strewn with blue and green ink stones which are harder than jade. In ancient times, mural artists ground the stone to obtain

FACING PAGE:
The seven-storied octagonal pagoda built in the thirteenth century in honour of a Tibetan lama, stands seventeen metres high. Images of Buddha adorn the eight sides of the pagoda and dragons carved in red bricks peep from each corner.

cobalt blue and emerald green. Soon we reached the Lingtao area. Passing through the Gao mountains I came to a one and a half kilometre long dark tunnel. On the other side of this tunnel was the city of Lanzhou.

On the Yellow River At Lanzhou

It was a long ride and by the time I reached Lanzhou it was already dark. The mighty bridge over the Yellow river was swathed in spectacular lighting. I was unable to see the yellow of the water; it was completely enveloped in fog. The temperature was below zero and I knew the night would bring no succour–there was no chance of the fog vanishing at night. I decided to walk on the Yellow river bridge to get a feel of the pristine mountain air and the bustling city. Interestingly, I saw more bicycles than cars! It was fiercely windy and the mist and fog blew into my face. I took a few more brave steps, but the fog was so dense that it almost burdened my eyelids. I could hardly open my eyes and when wisdom dawned on me not to stay out too long in the chill I turned back for the hotel.

Next morning the sky was overcast and stout raindrops were slipping down the window pane. It was my last day in Lanzhou, the weather was daunting but I could not leave without having a look at the White Pagoda. I put on my jacket and cap and with my guide drove toward the Yellow River bridge.

I was wearing a light jacket, and with every passing step I could feel the chill cutting through my bones. My wad of dollars was precious; I did not want to splurge on a new jacket. I shivered and as if to beat the frosty breeze, I walked bravely over the bridge, crossed the river and reached the beautiful promenade. However, the cold wind seemed to be unsparing; it was far colder at the promenade. I envied those who were pedalling through the promenade gleefully, as if the cold had no relevance in their lives.

From the riverfront steep steps and paved passages led to the pagoda on the mountain peak. From the top of the pagoda I looked at the Yellow river below, its expanse stretching till eternity. There were boats lined up on the banks; the boats were unusual; they were not made of wood, but of goat and yak skin. I spotted four farmers sailing merrily in a goat skin boat to the opposite hills.

Surprisingly, despite the silt, the river flows fast. A ropeway takes tourists to the Peony Pavilion, the highest structure on the hilltop. Built in the 1950s, it was the first modern ropeway funded by the Chinese government. The hills were covered with luxurious pine; the fragrance of wild flowers wafts in the air and the twitter of birds added a musical note to the panorama. As I stood on the mountain top I saw the entire city with hundreds of its high-rises making an appealing skyline. A lone mosque with green domes flanked by white minars looked matchless.

The White Pagoda hills believed to belong to the Qilian mountain range was the most beautiful landscape over Lanzhou. The hills are named after the white pagoda temple that stands on the peak of the hills which I reached after an hour of climbing.

A board at the White Pagoda informed me that it was built in honour of a famous Tibetan lama who died in Lanzhou of disease while on his way to meet Genghis Khan in 1228. It was first built in the Yuan dynasty (AD 1279–1368) during the reign of Zhang Tang and renovated during the Qing dynasty in AD 1715 by Zhao Qi, the local governor of Gansu.

The seven-storied octagonal pagoda stood seventeen metres high. Images of the Buddha adorned the eight sides of the pagoda. Dragons carved in red bricks holding iron bells hanging from their mouth could be seen from each corner of the octagonal structure. In the courtyard there stood a high white marble elephant carrying a drum made of elephant skin on its back. According to legend, the drum was a gift from an Indian monk who visited the White Hills pagoda at the end of the Yuan dynasty.

When a war broke out, the drum was destroyed; the present drum is a replica of the original made during the reign of the Qing dynasty.

In another corner of the courtyard hung a bronze bell weighing about 153 kilos. Counted as one of the gems of the monastery, it was cast in AD 1718 when the Qing dynasty was at the helm. The bell had square geometrical designs etched on it and even hundreds of years later its sound resonated loudly. An exhibition of the antiquities found at the pagoda hills was on display in a hall just above the pagoda. There were beautiful jade statues of the Buddha and paintings of bodhisattvas and apsaras. In a nearby shop, one of the hottest selling items was Longjin tea, every tourist seemed to pick at least one sachet.

Old Man Living in a Crevice

While descending from the mountain I met an old man who had made his home in the curve of the hill. What he called home was actually a tattered hut. Locals told me that once upon a time the old man was in-charge of a nearby temple. However, when the temple was renovated and even having reached the age of retirement, he refused to leave the temple premises. He chose a hole in the mountain abutting the temple and called it his home.

He had seen me walking down the hill; he peeped out of the crevice and beckoned me. I hesitated but did not refuse his invitation and entered his dwelling. Even in the crevice I saw modern equipment—a flaming red heater was providing warmth while the old man munched on monkey nuts. He offered me some nuts and biscuits and got ready to prepare tea for me on the heater. Our communication was a little muddled—he only spoke Chinese while I knew not even a smattering of it, but inside the mountain crevice, we seemed to communicate. Interestingly, he showed me the urns where he stored his daily ration. He gestured as if to say that food and warmth were the most important to him. Of the many tourists, the old man had chosen to invite only me. I was touched by his kindness and I munched on the peanuts and

FACING PAGE:
The White Pagoda hills across the Yellow River at Lanzhou. Belonging to the Qilian mountain range providing a beautiful landscape over the city. The hills have been named after the pagoda temple standing on its peak.

sipped on the tea that he made for me. I warmed myself by the fire. He was frail and hunched over with age. As I walked away I felt his eyes trailing me, and it was as if I was leaving behind a long-lost friend.

I took a stroll on the bank of the Yellow river and stopped to take a look at the colossal Mother Sculpture of a reclining mother playing with her baby on the river bank. She symbolised the Yellow river–the mother that has nurtured the Chinese civilisation for thousands of years. Lanzhou is the only city that has the Yellow River flowing across it, giving it a magnificent landscape, fertile soil, water for irrigation and power generation. It blesses the town with abundant fruits and vegetables, rare sunflowers and Lanzhou pears. The pears are a great thirst quencher and also a sure cure for pulmonary ailments.

I found the river front teeming with schoolchildren who were sitting with their drawing books and painting the Mother sculpture under the sharp eye of their teachers. A little distance away a giant wooden wheel was drawing water from the river and diverting it to a wind mill which,

Mother Sculpture on the banks of the Yellow River. The reclining mother plays with her baby. She symbolises the Yellow River that has nurtured the Chinese civilisation for thousands of years.

The Yellow River runs through Lanzhou. Despite the heavy silt which give it the yellow colour the river flows fast. It blesses the town with abundant fruits and vegetables. Bridges and ropeways have been built over the river to take people across to the opposite hills.

in turn, ran a flour mill and a huge grinder. In ancient times, the Chinese used the water wheel or river energy to run their grinders and flour mills. It is said that such a system, which was invented by Duan Xu in AD 1556, was in use even in the 1950s.

I got a peek into the ancient Chinese culture in the small museum on the riverfront. I saw paintings from the Dunhuang caves and replica of the wooden wheels drawing water from the river for the royal town. The energy of the rotating wooden wheels was used to press oilseeds for extracting oil and for grinding grains to make flour. There were ancient sculptures and paintings of the heavenly horses. It was still very cold outside and I took shelter inside the exhibition hall where a massive heater kept me warm.

Immortal Springs of Lanzhou

From the banks of the Yellow River we drove up to the Spring gardens where a huge gateway of flowers welcomed me. The garden was blooming with flowers of many varieties, the area redolent with their perfume. The park named after its five crystal springs was a place of tranquil beauty with lush gardens, gurgling streams and ancient temples. It was believed that the springs gushed out when an army general, Huo Qubing, searching for water for his thirsty troops whipped up a stone. He had been sent by the Han Emperor Wudi to defend the northern borders under attack from Huns in 120 BC. The springs flow to this day.

I crossed the grand gateway guarded by stone lions and entered a temple. Here stood the lofty statue of the great philosopher Confucius (551-479 BCE) surrounded by beautiful trees and flowers. Looking at his pensive eyes, long grey beard, flowing robes and the gesture of his hands it seemed as if the great thinker was in the midst of expounding some deep philosophical thought. A lane to my left led into another park where a statue of Sun Yat Sun welcomed me. He was a popular and revered political leader predating Mao Tse Tung and Chiang Kai Shek. I turned to my right and climbed a flight of about hundred steps to reach the Spring Garden on the peak of the hill where stood a magnificent Mahayana temple, said to be the biggest Buddhist temple in Lanzhou.

I descended through a different route and counted at least five mountain springs on the way. The highest one was called the sweet dew or the 'Amrit Spring'. Legend has it that anyone who drank water from this spring would gain immortality. A big crowd was pushing and jostling as all visitors wanted to dip their hands and scoop out some water! I moved to another spring called 'Moziquan' (Spring of Son) and descended

The Magic Spring Garden at Lanzhou. The park has been named after five crystal springs. It is a place of tranquil beauty with lush gardens, gurgling streams and ancient temples.

to the bottom of a dark cave where a shallow glacial spring was flowing quietly. Here visitors were mumbling prayers and throwing coins. Some were trying to fish out pebbles from the bed of the shallow spring in the hope of begetting a son. It was rumoured that those who retrieved the pebbles would be blessed with a son. Another spring that brings good luck is the 'Moon Scooping' spring or the Juyue where the reflection of the moon is seen on the surface of the water in the Autumn festival. I came across two other springs in the garden–the Benefit or the *Hui* spring and the *Meng* or the dangerous spring. The latter was believed to be inhabited by demons and evil spirits.

Crossing the heavy vegetation I reached an ancient Tibetan Mani temple where monks were chanting sutras. Under an old tree was a large incense holder whose antiquity, like that of the temples, goes back several centuries. It was evening and the weather was getting worse. The afternoon sun had made way for twilight and the gentle breeze for a fierce wind. I knew I would not come here again; despite the chill I could not resist the temptation of taking a walk on the glittering Lanzhou bridge.

In the days of yore, so many pilgrims and devouts must have braved the pitiless winds to keep their missionary zeal alive, to keep the flicker of the lamp from being snuffed out... I am sure it was the Buddha alone that gave them the strength to strive against all odds; it was faith that lured them on. I borrowed a little of that faith, stood a few more moments at the glittering bridge and then headed back to the hotel. When I slipped into the warm bed, I was no longer angry with the vicious frostiness; that day faith had taught me forgiveness.

The following day I caught the T-658 train to Zhangye to see the great Reclining Buddha at the ancient Dafosi Monastery.

A carved panel on the exterior wall of the Dafosi Reclining Buddha temple at Zhangye. The panel probably portrays a scene from the Buddha's Paradise. Several such panels portraying scenes from the Buddha's life decorate the walls of the temple.

(4)

To Dafosi at Zhangye

Reclining Buddha at Dafosi

After crossing the Yellow River at Lanzhou the Silk Road travels northwest along the Hexi Corridor to Zhangye (ancient Ganzhou). History records Zhangye as an important silk trading center since ancient times when 'local officials regulated the passage of silk' by issuing certificates signed by the commandant of Zhangye.[1] It was in Zhangye that the Chinese emperor Yangdi of the Sui dynasty held his first audience with the kings and emissaries of the Western regions in AD 609 which was hailed as the 'first international trade fair on the Silk Road'.[2]

Apart from the sky-rocketing Kumarjiva Pagoda, built in the heart of Zhangye in memory of the great Indian monk Kumarjiva, the city's claim to fame is also the Marco Polo street and a huge marble statue of the great Venetian who is recorded to have stayed here for a year[3] probably awaiting an appointment with the great Mongol emperor Kublai Khan. Marco Polo and his father Maffeo Polo who were on their way to Xanadu (Shangdu) in AD 1271 to meet the Chinese emperor carried the holy oil from the lamp from Christ's Sepulchre in Jerusalem.[4]

I was now headed towards Zhangye, my next destination. The train whizzed through the Gansu Corridor and I arrived at the station along with dusk. Liu Chunling, who was travelling with me, guided me to the Zhangye Hotel. Smart choice, I thought. For all tourist sites were scattered around my hotel and for a change I was not huddled in taxis from one site to another. In Zhangye, we could actually walk to all the sites picked from history books and listed on the itinerary.

Ah! But then there was my nemesis. The biting cold that had made me look weather-beaten, rough and red. There was an unbeatable chill in the air. But I was not daunted; I could not afford to waste time in hotel rooms. In the evening I went for a walk to the People's Square, which was brightly lit and resplendent with myriad blooming flowers. There were a hundred others like me, walking lazily without any hurry. From one television screen stared footballers trying to win a game and from another, Premier Hu Jintao looked gleeful after signing a deal. The street near the square was bathed in green light and trees arched over the boulevard and malls and markets buzzed with countless footfalls.

I had picked up facts about Zhangye before stepping into it, but I had perhaps missed the most important one. I figured that out when I saw what looked like a sea of silk flowers. I was told Zhangye was the centre of production and sale of artificial flowers. If one looked from far one would not know they were artificial! I picked some lotuses, cherry blossoms and carnations for my home. I began to feel hungry after all the walking I had done and noticed some crispy savouries being sold. I bought a packet of the salted, straight out of the oven cheeslings and with a cup of coffee I sat at the Square and watched middle-aged men flying kites. The kites spangling the evening sky were of various hues and designs, some in the shapes of clowns, snakes and butterflies. It seemed as if an entire animal kingdom had been let loose in the sky, wagging their tails and fluttering in the air. I was completely mesmerised. As soon as it got dark the kites were rolled back and the sky looked vacant again. I was still hungry and craving for yoghurt. I flitted from one lane to another but could not find any. I was certain some shop had it, but since I could not pronounce its Chinese name, I had to return empty-handed. But in my quest, I did get to see the real Zhangye.

The grand entrance to the magnificent Dafosi temple situated in a lane near the Bell Tower and surrounded by lush trees. The blue gate adorned by dragons provides a splendid view of the Buddha Hall.

FACING PAGE:
The grand seven-storied Pagoda of Kumarjiva stands loftily in the heart of the city. The monument is a reminder of the close religious and cultural ties between India and China and a befitting memorial to the great Indian monk.

Though I roamed from one corner to another, I knew I could not get lost because the hotel, our landmark, was just round the corner. I was amused to see lead curtains in front of restaurants; the owners had no choice, they needed it not just to fend the icy winds, but also because fierce winds tore and blew away fabric curtains.

Suddenly I saw something familiar–the large yellow arch of McDonald's. I stepped in to find myself amidst a chirpy bunch that was seated in the small joint. Within minutes I felt a little uneasy what with all eyes gazing in my direction. They had never seen an Indian before and a few crowded around me to be photographed. I was bathed in the light of the flashing camera bulbs and felt like a celebrity even though for a brief moment. It was foggy and freezing outside but this brush with celebrity-hood warmed the cockles of my heart and I returned to my hotel room happy. I was not in the least sleepy and so stood by the window from where I saw two golden palms lit for the night by which couples were gyrating to the beat of a live band.

Kumarjiva Pagoda

The following morning while walking to the Dafosi Reclining Buddha temple I passed by the grand seven storied Pagoda of Kumarjiva standing loftily in the heart of the city. The monument was a reminder of the close religious and cultural ties between India and China and a befitting memorial to the great Indian monk who was said to have won an 'unparalleled reputation in China as the most efficient interpreter of Buddhism' and for introducing Mahayana Buddhism in China.[5] Kumarjiva, who knew thirty-six different languages including

Sanskrit and Chinese, had a profound knowledge of Buddhism and had the unique honour of having more than three thousand Chinese priests as his disciples.[6]

Kumarjiva's arrival in China in AD 401 is a story in itself. By the time the monk was captured at Kuqa during a political expedition by Chinese forces in AD 383, the fame of his merits and talents had already spread far and wide. He was first brought as a prisoner to Liangzhou (Wuwei). In AD 401 he was invited by the Chinese emperor to Changan (Xian) where he was appointed the emperor's *purohit* (royal priest-counsellor). Here he lived and translated ninety-eight Buddhist Sanskrit texts until his death in AD 413.[7]

Reclining Buddha at Dafosi

Taking a round of the Bell Tower I reached the Great Monastery of Dafosi where I spent most of the afternoon going around the precincts that houses the 34.5 metre long Reclining Buddha, the largest in China. The temple was built in AD 1098 by Xixia Tanguts (a tribal group) who had invaded the area around AD 1038 and are said to have established an independent state.[8]

The magnificent Dafosi temple inside which lies the Reclining Buddha. The temple itself is said to have been built in AD 1098 by a Tangut (a tribal group) queen.

The 900-year old – 34.5 metre long Reclining Buddha inside the great hall of the Dafosi temple at Zhangye. The idol representing the Nirvana scene at Kushinagara (India) is said to have been placed along with two other idols by a Tangut.

From the notes in *The Book of Ser Marco Polo*, we learn that the monastery of the 'Lying Buddha' was built in AD 1103 by a Tangut queen who placed there three idols representing Buddha in the reclining posture, representing the Nirvana scene. They have since been found in the ground on this very spot.[9]

The temple was magnificent, surrounded by lush trees on a lane near the Bell Tower and a row of shops by the boulevard. The unique red orifice at the temple gate offered a splendid view of the Buddha Hall from the street. A side opening led the visitor to another gate over which sat huge blue dragons. A paved path led to the 900-year-old Reclining Buddha in a grand hall which was marked by huge wooden carved doors.

Inside, the Great Master lay on a lotus pedestal on his right side, sleeping blissfully, eyes half closed, one arm folded under the head. There was a swastika on his chest and his robes were neatly pleated in deep folds over his body. His disciples stood near his head mourning the Great Decease (Nirvana). I was reminded of Kushinagara in India where the Great Master breathed his last between two *sala* trees by the side of the Hiranyawati river.

I circumambulated the huge Buddha. At the back was a dark alley lit only by red bulbs. Nothing was visible. I could barely trace the outlines of golden Buddha images that reflected light and were lined in a row in the back room. Other Buddhist deities flanked the main image.

Several monks were reciting prayers and kept a strict vigil over the visitors. I sat on the steps of the Dafosi before the huge Nirvana Buddha. It was an incredible sight; I had not seen anything like this before, not in Kushinagara, not in Mingsha mountains, not even in the Binglingsi caves or at the Dazu grottoes. Marco Polo during his stay at Zhangye had seen the great Buddha at the Dafosi temple:

'The people are idolators, Saracens and Christians and the latter have three very fine churches in the city, while the Idolators have many ministers and abbey after their fashion. In these they have enormous number of idols, both small and great, certain of the latter being a good ten paces in stature; some of them being of wood, others of clay and others yet of stone. They are all highly polished and then covered with gold. The great idols of which I speak lie at length. And round about them there are other figures of considerable size, as if adoring and paying homage before them'.

(*The Book of Ser Marco Polo*; Vol. I, Chapter XLIV–Of the City of Campichu/City of Kanchau; pp. 219-20. Henry Yule, Henri Cordier)

At the back of the temple were several ancient halls surrounded by dense trees. One of these was the exhibition hall displaying rare relics unearthed in Zhangye, some of which were nearly 4,000 years old dating back from the Neolithic Age to the Qing dynasty covering the history, politics, economy, art, and culture of the region.

A flight of steps led to another hall where were displayed various styles of brick carving–there were wood carvings, decorations, stone

FACING PAGE:
At the back of the Dafosi is the Earth Pagoda touching the sky from the base of a double-storied ancient temple. The pagoda is made of clay and has beautiful ornamental and geometrical design on its surface.

and brick inscriptions, sculptures and drawings. Painting and calligraphy works were displayed in another hall with beautiful landscapes, figures, scrolls, imperial edicts and stone seals of the Ming and Qing dynasty.

It is said (John Man, *Kublai Khan* that the five-year old ex-Song emperor Zhao Xian, grandson of empress dowager who had formally surrendered to Kublai Khan in AD 1276 was sent away to become a monk in the Dafosi temple.[10] The ex-Song emperor who had been locked away from the outside world so that he may never pose a danger to the Mongol rulers of China committed suicide in the temple in AD 1323 at the age of fifty-three.[11]

Legend (in the same book) has it[12] that long after the surrender of the Song royals to Kublai, the Mongol had a dream that a dragon shot up from a particular spot in the palace. Next day the young Song prince Zhao Xian came to see Kublai and happened to stand at the same spot from where the dragon had appeared before him. This unnerved Kublai and alerted him of a possible coup by the prince. Zhao was then packed off to the monastery with the royal orders to adopt priesthood.

In early AD 1252 Sorkaktani, the Christian queen of Tolui, the daughter-in-law of Genghis Khan and mother of Kublai died at the age of seventy and was buried in Zhangye at the Dafosi, which was then a garrison town on the Silk Road. Some believe that Kublai was 'actually born in the Dafosi temple' or that Sorkaktani was pregnant with Kublai when she first arrived at Zhangye.[13]

Not too far away is the Palace of Buddhist Scriptures that stacks rare Buddhist sutras written in gold. According to temple records, in AD 1411 the Chinese Ming emperor donated about 600 volumes of imperial Buddhist scriptures, a collection of the Ming dynasty. This was printed by using the official printing plates of the Ming dynasty. In the same year the governor of Gansu and Shanxi provinces ordered scholars to copy 800 volumes of the *maha prajna paramita sutra* in gold. These were known as the golden Buddhist scriptures of Zhangye. Along with the gold scriptures are the ones copied in Chinese ink.

At the back of the Dafosi is the Earth pagoda touching the sky from the base of a double-storied ancient temple. This pagoda has ornamental and geometrical designs on its surface and is made of clay. As the name denotes, the earth pagoda is one of the five such pagodas built in Zhangye during the Ming dynasty. It was originally called the Pagoda of Buddha and consists of a body in the shape of an inverted bell. A row of arched niches and designs embellish the pagoda. The conical top has a jewelled crown.

As the sun set over the pagoda the pilgrims started leaving the temple. I returned to Buddha's feet to bid farewell. Looking at the Dying Buddha I was overwhelmed with emotion. I was transported to my roots in Kushinagara where once upon a time the real Buddha actually lay dying under the *sala* forest on a full moon night of *Vaisakh* in 543 BC. His last words were: Decay is inherent in all composite things. Work out your own salvation with diligence.

Cold Evening in a Coffee Shop

I loathed the idea of returning to the hotel room. But staying out in the biting cold would have been foolhardy. It was frosty and I was not sufficiently warm. I spent the cold evening in the coffee shop of the hotel nibbling away at melon seeds. I peeked into an antique shop in the hotel arcade and learnt of the cultural evening at the hotel where entry was by invitation only. I had no choice but to while away time in the coffee shop and talking to the owner. I could hear the wind whistling outside, desperately trying to breeze past the curtains. Through the chinks in the curtain I could see the golden palms burning brightly and heard the band playing. Suddenly the music was drowned by a loud chant from the Dafosi. Perhaps a cry from the last mourners still sitting at the feet of Buddha. Perhaps they were wailing, beating at their chests, tearing away their clothes at the demise of the Great Master whose last words ring in my ears: 'You should live with yourself as an island, with yourself as refuge, with no one else as refuge; with the doctrine as an island, with the doctrine as a refuge'.

I closed my eyes, said a prayer and hailed the Holy One.

The gigantic Great Wall snaking through the Gobi desert at Jiayuguan. It was built in the Ming Dynasty and was the western starting point of the Great Wall through which the old Silk Road passed. Beyond the wall is the Gobi desert and to its south lies the Qilian mountains. The wall served as a defence against the marauding Mongols. The Ming general Feng Sheng in AD 1372 built an impressive fort along the Wall to guard a strategic pass between two mountain ranges.

(5)

To the Great Wall at Jiayuguan

Zhangye onwards I shunned the train and decided to travel by road. I left early morning in a taxi on National Highway A312 north-west to Jiayuguan, about 200 kilometres from Zhangye.

National Highway A-312 is one of the longest and prestigious highways of China running for over 4000 kms from Shanghai through Louyang, Xian, Lanzhaou, Anxi, Hami, Turfan, Urumqi to Yinning cutting across several provinces of China from east to west and north before it touches the border of Kazakhastan near Korgas.

I was amazed at how well maintained the Zhangye-Jiayuguan stretch was; there was never a pothole and vehicles seemed to fly on the six-lane highway. The early morning drive through the north-west part of the Hexi Corridor passed through some beautiful desert landscape interspersed with grain planting regions. Snow capped mountain peaks were visible from a distance. The farmers rose with the sun, heading to their fields along the Taolai river and along numerous snow-melting streams running from the Qilian mountains to pick up a fresh crop of carrots and sweet potatoes. Some of the farmers were enterprising; they had spurned the hand ploughs and taken to using hand tractors which made ploughing easier and faster. We drove past apple orchards where large golden apples were burdening the boughs. In a parsimon orchard women had spread a cloth under the tree that was being shaken.

Dried Berries at Lingza

The Lingza county was primarily a corn-growing region and the local markets were spilling with green corns. My guide Liu Chunling and I stopped at a berry farm to buy dried berries; they were sweet and delicious. The area around Zhangye was like a fruit belt, as far as one's eyes could see there were only orchards–apples pears, berries and parsimon. The entire land was laden with the aroma of ripe fruits.

I stopped at Goutai, a small town, for lunch. Here the owner, a lady, prepared hot food for me. Inside her restaurant, fish, prawns and snails were floating in large tubs full of river water. For lunch, she picked large prawns from the tub, steamed them, tossed them in vinegar and voila! lunch is ready. But my plate had more than just prawns, there was rice, noodles, some congee and mixed vegetable and shredded chicken. I had clearly overeaten and felt sleepy. There were no beds in sight and I took a short snooze on the chair itself.

On the way to Jiayuguan I passed through jungles of tamarisk. Villagers had built small reservoirs for collecting snow water flowing from the mountains. I was still in the Hexi corridor. I saw more farms and orchards. Onion growing belts were interspersed with crops, sweet potatoes, carrots and berry tomatoes. Farmers were getting their fields ready for the winter crop, women wearing trousers were shepherding the cattle while others sat knitting in the sun. The first hint of a desert was evident the moment we approached Jaiyuguan. From far I saw hamigua (water melon) climbers. The yellow loess soil had made way for the porous sand mixed with earth.

As I reached Jiayuguan I saw the gigantic Great Wall snaking through the desert. At about 9 pm I reached the Great Wall Hotel which abuts the Great Wall. I had travelled through the Hexi corridor and my bones were creaking after a long haul. Soon after a light dinner, I dozed off.

Sunrise at Jiayuguan. The snow-capped Qilian mountains become aflame as the first rays of the morning sun bathes them in a golden hue.

Sunrise over Jiayuguan

I wanted to stay snug in bed, but even before the sun rose I was reminded of my guide, Liu Chunling's praise for the sunrise. 'You should not miss it,' he had exhorted. Thankfully, I did not have to step too far; for that stunning view of the rising sun all I had to do was go to the hotel terrace. The alarm rang at 5 am sharp and I ran up the stairs and requested the staff to open the locked terrace. At 5.30 I took my seat on a beautifully carved pavilion with long upturned eaves. The great event was heralded by the loud chirping of the birds and the flight of a flock of white swans right over my head. They too were waiting to chase the first rays. The snow-capped Qilian mountains blushed. The grey sky was glowing in a lustre of faint purple and suddenly turned orange and pink. Finally, the huge orange ball started emerging from behind the snow and went up in the sky. The mountains became golden. With the first rays of the morning sun the snowy mountain changed its colour. It was indeed a mesmerising sight.

Steel City

Back in my room I flipped through historical information about Jiayuguan. It was the first town on the Chinese side of the Great Wall; it was a frontier post since the Han dynasty when the Great Wall reached as far as the Yumen pass in the Gobi desert (Jade Gate). The Pass sat on the juncture of the Mazong mountains to the north and the Qilian on the south. It was a hunting ground, a grassland, a pass and a fortress. The wall was built in the Ming dynasty and was the western starting point of the Great Wall through which the old Silk Road passed. It was known as the majestic pass under the heaven. Beyond the pass was the Gobi desert and to the south the Qilian mountains. The wall served as a defence against the marauding Mongols who puntered on horseback. The magnificent Qilian mountains was covered with snow throughout the year. The grassland on the foothills was dotted with wild flowers and gurgling streams.

Since iron-ore was found in the desert of Jiayuguan it is also called the steel city. After it was discovered here in 1958, Jiayuguan has really shone as one of the biggest iron and steel complexes of the world and the wealth gave rise to a dazzling city and an industrial town with its own airport, rail links, big hotels and wondrous landscape.

Spending a Day at Jiayuguan Fort

The impressive old fort was five kilometres outside the town and stood in a dramatic spot guarding a pass between two mountain ranges. During the Ming dynasty it was the westernmost point of the Great Wall. The fort was built in 1372 with 33-ft high walls and a circumference of 770 yards.

It is said that in 1372 the Ming dynasty General Feng Sheng defeated the last of the Mongol armies of the Yuan dynasty that had ruled China since 1279 and built a fortress at Jiayuguan guarding the entrance to the Hexi corridor in Gansu province. This part of the Great Wall was made of bricks and was more durable than the earthen walls of the earlier dynasties.

I bought my entry ticket at the fort plaza and walked through a garden that laced the fort area. A metalled road shaded by poplars and willows ran by the side of a wide artificial lake to the main entry point.

The Jiayuguan Fort represents a unique defensive structure. During wars, guards could stay hidden in enclosed structures and rain arrows at the invaders. Usually, the enemy was repulsed by the onslaught of arrows from atop the high walls. But even if they managed to breach the front gate they would be confronted with another huge heavy gate and would be trapped in a rectangular space with arrows and spears being shot on them from the four high walls. It was like a fort within a fort with trap points inside. Over the wall inside there were arrangements of shooting arrows on stuffed Hun warriors fastened to earth below with the help of bamboos. Visitors could shoot three arrows on them for a small price of one yuan.

The folding doors of apartments inside the fort are decorated with paintings of warriors and royal personages wearing exquisite robes and accessories. A warrior clutching a sword in one hand and something like a flying whip in the other appears on the folding of an apartment door inside the Jiayuguan fort.

FACING PAGE:
An array of exquisite paintings of royal personages, tales from life in the desert and beautiful flower arrangements adorn the huge folding doors of a royal chamber inside the Jiayuguan fort.

There were other forms of entertainment here. Royal ensembles of princes and princess, of kings and queens were displayed on large hangers. For a small fee tourists could get themselves photographed in the attire. Many foreigners dressed up like the Chinese royals were in the queue. The folding doors of the apartments that dotted the fort were decked with paintings of royal personages and warriors and served as a good backdrop.

I climbed the Great Wall and saw the vast expanse of the land to the west and mountain ranges on the north and south through which it criss-crossed. This wall was not as high as the Great Wall near Beijing but lengthwise it covered a vast expanse.

It is said that the territories to the west of Jiayuguan was a place of banishment to the Chinese. Only those who were exiled, courageous monks and Silk Road travellers and invading and defending armies could enter it. The fourth century Drum Tower lies in the heart of the city and points the way to the western land.

Portrait of a royal personage inside another chamber of the Jiayuguan fort. The royal ensemble worn by the royalty like the one above is actually on display in the corridors of the fort.

Xuanzang

It was at this frontier outpost of Jiayuguan that the Chinese pilgrim, Xuanzang waited for a month. Here his companions deserted him, his horse died and spies had informed the local governor that the monk was leaving for the western regions. Undeterred, he bought a new horse. It was also here that he met a Central Asian named Bandha who offered to conduct him past the Jade Gate and the five watch towers in the desert. Later, at this post Xuanzang exchanged his newly bought horse with a lean and thin red one belonging to an old foreigner who is said to have made the to and fro journey to the west at least thirty times.[1]

I bade goodbye to the great pilgrim who left on his red steed to the western regions and returned to the Great Wall Hotel to prepare for the next day's journey to the Yulin river to explore the caves of the bodhisattvas and apsaras.

It was at this frontier post of Jiayuguan that the great monk Xuanzang waited for a month. Here he exchanged his horse for a lean and thin red steed belonging to a foreigner and left for the Western Regions on his way to India. A painting from the Chengdu Daci temple.

Yulin grottoes, also called the Valley of Ten Thousand Buddhas are located on the cliffs of the Yulin River valley of the Nanshan mountains of Anxi on National Highway 313.

(6)

To Yulin Grottoes at Anxi

Grottoes by the Side of the Yulin River

It was the dawn of another day and I took another highway. This time, National Highway 313 was taking me westwards to Anxi, about 270 kms from Jiayuguan, while NH 312 (coming from Xian) sped away north-westwards through Hami to Urumqi. Anxi was not just another town, it had its own geographical importance; it was at Anxi that the Silk Road split into the northern and southern route; the former going to the western regions along the foot of the Tienshan mountains up to Kashgar while the latter going along the foot of the Kunlun range through Khotan to meet the former at Kashgar.

On way the luxuriant fields seemed to reluctantly give way to the desert. The ghost of the Gobi was gradually emerging before me; the rich fertile soil of the foothills was disappearing as I travelled northwest from Jiayuguan. Numerous streams were rising from the snowy Qilian and gushing into the grasslands at its foot.

It was very cold and I was shivering but my guide Liu Chunling consoled me saying that the weather was still not at its worst; in December the temperature often dipped to minus nine degrees! People stayed indoors and fed on dried vegetables, stored poultry products and frozen meat. The temperature hadn't fallen much but I saw farmers getting ready for the chilly days and nights—they were stocking fodder with haystacks and firewood heaped on the high boundary walls of their houses. The fields were empty and poplar trees were thinning out. Flocks of sheep with long hair herded by women dressed in trousers, short coats and boots were desperately looking for fodder in the dry fields.

In the severe winter months when everything is buried under deep snow, even the trees are not happy; they are threatened by frost and often wilt if the water in their pit freezes. The farmers prevent this by wrapping the trunks in cloth and covering them with plastic. Everywhere the field had been submerged in water so that in spring the soil would be still soft for ploughing. Otherwise it would be difficult to break the earth with a plough.

I reached Anxi, took a round of the main road crossing and turned southwest to drive another seventy-five kilometres to reach the Yulin caves in the valley of the Nanshan mountains. Standing on the western

The Yulin River runs at the foot of the caves and is lined with thick yellow poplars. On both sides of the river the soft rocks have been cut into rows of caves.

Caves cut deep inside the rocks have a front open space where sits a small pagoda. Such spaces in front of caves are said to have been used by monks to hold meetings.

end of the Hexi corridor Anxi is linked with Dunhuang, being its prefecture in the Western Han dynasty.

Yulin grottoes, also called the Valley of the Ten Thousand Buddha, are located on the cliffs of Yulin River valley. The grottoes were possibly dug up in Sui (AD 589-618) or early Tang (AD 618- 907) dynasty and thrived up to the Yuan (AD 1279-1368) dynasty.[1] The roof of the caves was almost at ground level; an inexperienced driver could never notice where the rocky pathway to the grottoes cuts away from the main road. The car stopped in the desert and I walked a few yards before reaching the stone steps descending several feet below to the swift flowing Yulin river.

The river ran at the foot of the caves and was lined with thick yellow poplars. On both sides the soft rocks had been cut into caves, arranged in several tiers and decorated with painted statues and murals. On the eastern side of the valley there were about thirty-two caves while on the western side there were about eleven.

It was freezing in the windy valley as the temperature dipped below zero. But the sun was shining brightly upon us. I came upon a huge stupa standing at the base of a cliff as if welcoming the visitors and reminding them of the glory of yesteryears.

The monks of the Yulin calculated every possible risk to the deities that would be housed in the caves, the splendid art work on the walls and the danger to their own lives from nature's fury and wild animals that lived in the river valley. To protect the caves, narrow entry passages had been cut into the rocks which spread out deep into the mountains. Well protected from sun, rain, snow and storm and guarded against moisture from the air, the grottoes were like an air conditioned structure. Even the sand which filled them over the ages, was like a protective layer. Such a structure had protected the Yulin wall paintings from erosion from sandstorms for hundreds of years and the colours were still fresh on the walls. Of the forty-three caves only ten are open for public viewing.

Picture of Paradise

Special caves had special entry fee. One such cave was No.25. where a unique style of line diagram depicts the everyday life of the people. While a woman swept the floor with a broom, others were ploughing the field and winnowing and threshing grains. It was a lively village scene in brilliant colours that appeared three-dimensional. The strokes of the artist's brush were delicate yet imposing and conveying movement.

The murals of *Maitreyasutra* and *Manjusrisutra* were painted in rich hues and were evident of the artist's skill in breathing life into the deities. The picture of paradise in the *Maitreyasutra* depicted the bodhisattva Maitreya in *abhayamudra* (hand raised in blessing) and surrounded by numerous bodhisattvas. While the Buddha appeared unornamented, the latter wore elaborate headgears and jewellery. Bodhisattva Manjusri was seated on a bejewelled white lion and was accompanied by a brightly painted disciple who appeared to be a royal personage with long robes, gem-studded crown and heavy necklaces. A dark young boy was taming the lion. A beautiful chandelier with bells on its edges hung over the head of Manjusri.

The ferocity of the roaring lion was brought out by clever strokes of the brush. His mouth was wide open and his fierce tongue hung out. Manjusri's procession on the back of a lion and followed by other bodhisattvas who were beautifully adorned with jewels and brocades seemed to be actually moving. The attendants who held the royal *chhatra*, a huge jewelled crown over the head of Manjusri had bells hanging from its edges. The bells seemed to be swaying with the movement of the

Depiction of a village scene on the walls of the Yulin grottoes. A farmer ploughs his field while another sows seed. In the right corner a man who appears to be a monk is seen delivering a discourse.

FACING PAGE:
The painting on the wall of Cave 25 depicts Bodhisattva Manjusri seated on a lion. This famous painting of the Manjusrisutra *has a three-dimesional effect.*

procession and one could almost hear them ringing.

On another wall there were human figures dressed in cloaks, feasting and celebrating. Another scene depicted men and women in the process of ploughing, harvesting and sweeping, while a monk recited sutras.

The depiction of bodhisattva Manjusri sitting on a lion was repeated in Cave 12. Manjusri resembled the Hindu goddess Durga who also rode a lion and was a symbol of power. The walls displayed an array of bodhisattvas seated in paradise or the 'sukhavati'. Musicians were playing the *pipa*, while the apsaras adorning the ceiling were flying and dancing happily. From the ceiling the Thousand Buddhas were peering down. Buddha's chief disciples Kasyap and Anand also adorned the cave wall as did bodhisattva Bhaisajyaguru or the medicine Buddha, the healer of all mankind. Sun su Miya, the famous doctor of the Tang dynasty, is depicted as holding a conference with his students. Built in the tenth century the cave was beautiful with statues of heavenly guardians. On the back wall the king was worshipping the bodhisattvas while donors adorned the gallery.

A Buddha statue in Cave 14 was destroyed by the local people or taken away by the Taoists it is believed. Another image of Buddha sat in *dhyan mudra* (posture of meditation) under a low roof decorated with the lotus and a beautiful Bodhi tree in the backdrop. The tree, however, appeared like a pineapple tree. The cave was guarded by *Lokpala* or the heavenly guardian. On a wall of the cave bodhisattva Samantabhadra rode a white elephant with six tusks. The elephant reminded me of the 'six-rayed' elephant seen by Gautam Buddha's mother Queen Maya in her dream while she slept in the Hamsawati palace of Kapilvastu.

The bodhisattva is a favourite theme at Yulin. A precious, intricately carved ivory elephant, said to be from India,[2] was recovered from the grottoes by a monk. It was transferred to the National Museum of Chinese History at Beijing. On the back of the elephant sat bodhisattva Samantabhadra holding a relic pagoda. The skillfully carved elephant opened on hinges into two halves and portrayed Jataka tales of the previous life of Buddha. According to Jonathan Tucker,[3] it may have been carried to China by one of the several monks who travelled to India during the Tang dynasty to seek Buddhist scriptures.

Nomads With Tiger Skin

The warriors in Cave 15 appear like nomads wearing tiger skin with a tail. The cave is said to have been built in the ninth century by the Tibetans. The heavenly guardians look angry while the apsaras have pleasant faces. One guardian deity was holding a fox in one hand and a *vajra* or the thunderbolt in the other. The fox was spitting pearls, the metaphor, according to the local guide being that even devils become righteous upon the touch of virtuous Bodhisattvas. Inside, there were murals of bodhisattvas Kasyap, Anand and Manjusri and other disciples surrounding the central painting of the preaching Buddha. Beautiful apsaras played the lute. The Guanyin Buddha depicted on a wall as a female goddess had large breasts. Perhaps the concept of the half male and half female god has been borrowed from the Hindu concept of 'ardhnarishvar' another name for Lord Shiva. Guanyin is also the Avalokitesvara or the 'goddess of mercy' and is female in appearance.[4]

One mural depicted an interesting fight between bodhisattva Sariputra and a demon in Cave 16. Both were seated on high pavilions. While Sariputra appeared calm and poised, the demon had a furious look. The painting is said to depict a fight between the Han and the Mongolians. Or perhaps, and more appropriately, it represented the struggle within every human–between his Buddhist spirit or virtuous values and the demonic destructive desires. The cave was built in the tenth century in the late Tang and the early Sung. There are donors Tao Cao and his wife, an Uighur princess in the corridor and thousand Buddhas on the roof of the cave.

A 24.7-metre high giant Maitreya sits in Cave 6 built in the Tang dynasty. The artists are said to have worked from the top to the bottom of the cave. On the wall were the Mongolian people who contributed in building the great Buddha. The wheel of life painted in Cave 19 depicted

Temple of the Great Buddha in Cave 6 of the Yulin grottoes. Inside the cave sits a 24.7 metre high Maitreya.

the eight dragons inside the human body. The eleven-headed Guayin Buddha can be seen in Cave 23 built during the Tang dynasty.

Anxi Museum

We drove back to Anxi as I wanted to visit the museum. Beautiful pottery found in the burial tombs on the trade route between Anxi and Dunhuang was on display. A large grinder found near the Yulin caves is said to have been used by monks who once lived here. There were ancient Chinese documents on bamboo strips and other relics also from the Yulin caves, like clay Buddha statues, painted pottery, bronze statues, bronze ware and gold and silver ornaments. The latter were probably offered to the deities living inside the cave temples by merchants and travellers.

On display were a large number of Neolithic Age implements and painted earthenware excavated from Anxi county. Some other relics including ceramic figurines of a lady and soldier were found in a tomb alongwith a ceramic Bactrian camel. There were tricoloured horses from the Tang dynasty tombs and other tombs built in the graves of the Gobi dating from the Wei and the Qin periods. These graves had chamber rooms from where objects like mural bricks were unearthed.

By evening I finally reached my small rest house in Anxi to spend the night. After the long tiresome journey from Jiayuguan Great Wall to the Yulin grottoes I had no energy to venture out either to the market or the city square. A simple dinner comprising a bowl of green vegetables and meat soup and some steamed white buns was all that I could manage for dinner.

In my sleep I found myself in a dark cave on the tallest cliff of the Yulin. To my horror the ladder leading to the cave had disappeared. The brown robed monks had left me alone. I called out for help but my voice was stifled. Just then a ray of light from the Maitreya temple dispelled the darkness. I woke up feeling fresh and I soon left for Dunhuang, my next destination.

Several pagodas lie at the entrance along the path leading inside the great art gallery of the Magao grottoes at Dunhuang. The World Heritage Site is described as a 'brilliant star in the history of Chinese civilization'. The first grottoes at Magao are believed to have been dug in the fourth century AD.

(7)

Highway 313 to Dunhuang

The Silk Road came with its own surprises, its own wonders, its own paradoxes, its own idiosyncrasies. And I was ready to soak in whatever it had to offer to me.

From Anxi, National Highway A-312 runs north-west towards Hami, a town famous for its sweet and juicy melons. I had to travel west to Dunhuang, about 200 kms away. So I took State Highway A-313. There was a chill in the air and the sun was just beginning to rise. The barren desert was bathed in a hue of orange and purple. Only a painter's brush could capture the divine sunrise in Gobi. I passed through the coal mountains and salt areas interspersed with rich iron and copper regions.

The world was flitting by but I needed to breathe in the Gobi air. As if on a whim, I stopped midway to take a stroll. Everywhere my eyes wandered, the earth appeared black and rocky; there was not even a hint of sand. Forget trees, there were no shrubs either. The only other colour I saw was a thick crust of salt that covered some portions of the terrain. I scraped the brittle surface and tasted the white. Well, it was no different from tablesalt that I kept neatly in a porcelain pot on my dining table. As I caught my breath on an odd rock, the strong wind played with my hair. I smiled. But the wind was not benign; it carried spiky rough rock particles that blew cruelly on my face.

There was no sign of human life; the only vestige of human habitation was the empty green soda bottle that lay carelessly where workers must have put up tents during road construction. The four-lane road that ran through the most difficult terrain in the world glistened like the skin of a snake. It stretched for hundreds of miles before converging like a triangle far away on the horizon.

A Gurgling Stream

Liu Chunling, my guide, directed me to the Dunhuang Hotel by the side of a gurgling mountain stream that perpetually sings paeans to the Mingshaw mountains and the exquisiteness of the Moonlake. The snow that capped the mountains melted in summer forming hundreds of streams that murmured past hamlets and hills quenching the thirst of the people and irrigating parched fields. A river front laced with weeping willows ran along the stream and I saw dozens of men and women walking along its banks going about their daily chores with amazing calm. The window of my room opened onto the children's park where little kids in pigtails and pinafores were occupied in typical childhood pranks.

Sitting in the hotel lobby I glanced at the shopping center. The walls of the entire hall were covered with paintings of apsaras and bodhisattvas on silk, paper and canvas. There was a beautiful collection of calendars abounding in apsaras, lokpalas and bodhisattvas. I walked towards a shop and saw beautiful jade jewellery. There were dainty pieces in distinct colours and were selling briskly. I selected a delicate string of shining yellow jade, but it was too expensive. I held it in my hands for a few moments and then quietly placed it back on the velvet tray. A painting of lovely red cherry blossoms caught my eye. Next to it sat figurines in carved wood, painted Buddha on flattened slate and stone sculptures. Svelte and large-eyed apsaras were everywhere; they were in various dancing poses and seemed to be the favourite motif of artistes on the Silk Road. I wanted to take an apsara home and I picked an exquisite one painted on tussar silk.

Teeming With Foreigners

It is said that as early as the first century BC, Dunhuang, owing to its position in the western part of the Hexi Corridor, was the 'hub of international trade' and exposed to foreign influence being the 'gateway' to the Western regions. According to Zhang Yiping (*Story of the Silk Road*), Dunhuang was the first to receive Indian influence and became one of China's early Buddhism centres. By the time of the Tang Dynasty (AD 618-67) there sprang up 'sixteen grand Buddhist temples with more than 900 monks.'[1]

I found Dunhuang a squat little place, its skyline not too cluttered with high-rises or hotels. I was surprised to see so many foreigners; many of them walking or cycling on the boulevard. Early morning Dunhuang was covered with dense fog, even the pansies and daisies in the nearby garden looked grey. People were sitting on stone benches embellished with pink roses entangled on the white lattice.

I spotted a small market by the side of the stream that was not too far from the hotel. Every morning fresh vegetables and fruits were brought here on donkey carts. In the evening I went for a walk and found freshly picked oranges and red apples. The entire market was spilling with fresh produce. I saw a crowd gathered in one corner; I got curious and wriggled my way in. There was a man baking sweet potatoes over a slow fire in a portable mud oven that was cut out of a large drum. The scent of the baking potatoes was heady and I bought a bowl and sat with it on the steps of a large building. It was delicious and while I dug a little twig that served as a fruit fork, I was told that baked sweet potatoes were the most popular snack in China. The young man was also roasting corn and rice flakes in a pressure cooker. I was amused at how quickly boiled and roasted groundnuts were flying off his makeshift oven.

A stone's throw away from the hotel was a curio shop selling wine cups made of jade. They were delicate and transparent and available in dark green and pearl white. There were Plaster of Paris images of decorated Buddha and Bodhisattvas that were stacked next to jade

FACING PAGE:
The magnificent nine-storied Buddha temple at the Magao grottoes of Dunhuang houses the 35.5 metre high image of Maitreya Buddha. The image has been cut into the rocks. The Maitreya is draped in an orange robe with an elaborate blue border.

BELOW: *The guardian deity Vaisravana painted on the cover of the* Prajnaparamita Hridaya Sutra *was retrieved by Aurel Stein probably from the Library Cave of the Magao grottoes. It is now a prized antiquity at the National Museum, Delhi.*

jewellery. However, Dunhuang is most famous for its silk flowers; everyone picks a flower as a souvenir.

Mogao Grottoes – the Great Art Gallery

Early next morning I was headed to the World Heritage Site of UNESCO—the great art gallery of the Mogao grottoes Described as a 'brilliant star in the history of Chinese civilization', it is believed to be at par with Ajanta and Ellora in India. Hewn along a 1,600 metre long corridor along the eastern hills of the Mingshan mountains, the grottoes are located twenty-five kilometres southeast of Dunhuang on the banks of the Dangquan River.

It was a forty-minute drive through the desert past the sand hills of the Gobi. Clasped tightly to my heart was a copy of Duan Wenjie's book on Dunhuang Art (*Dunhuang Art Through the Eyes of Duan Wenije*). Since I was only a lay traveller I intended to go entirely by the account given by Wenjie, the eminent director of the Dunhuang Academy, a copy of whose work I managed to bring along from Delhi. Wenjie and his predecessor Chang Shuhong are said to have 'lived in the caves of Dunhuang as custodians, art historians and painters'. But at the grottoes office near the gate not only my bag but also my camera and my guide book on Dunhuang were taken away and put in a locker. A special guide of the Dunhuang Institute was there to escort me and other visitors to the caves.

It is said that for centuries, the grottoes lived in the womb of the earth anonymously; nobody had heard of them, nobody had seen them. Its glory would have had to wait for a swooning monk who walked this path in AD 366. According to legend,[2] one fine day while monk Lo-tsun was passing through the Gobi desert, he fainted and had a vision of 'a Thousand Buddha appearing to him in a cloud of glory'. The pious monk did not dismiss the vision as an ordinary dream; he actually mustered the help of people to dig so that he could find the Buddha who had appeared in his vision. With great trepidation the shovel was put to earth and the first cave was dug in AD 366. The digging continued for about a thousand years, much after the monk had left his mortal body. But Lo-tsun did not slip into oblivion; he is still remembered as the first cave builder of Magao. The caves were dug but they were not left barren – the caves on the cliffs of Mingshan mountains were adorned with magnificent wall paintings and sculptures. In all, nearly 492 caves were dug of which only ten are currently open for public viewing.

A dancing apsara *or* deva *adorns the ceiling of a cave. The flying celestial beauties found on the walls and ceilings of most caves are wrapped in diaphanous clothing and long fluttering ribbons. They seem to be in the act of scattering flowers on the central image of the Buddha.*

Illustration of Buddhist Sutras on Cave walls

As I walked into the dim caves a mystical world of 'Buddhist paradise' unfolded before my eyes. I was wonderstruck at the luminous three-dimensional figures of the Buddha and bodhisattvas, apsaras and devas. They seemed to light up the caves with their radiance. Their gold and silver ornaments studded with gems, their shimmering robes with beautifully designed borders and heavenly crowns, the near naked apsaras wrapped only in ribbons and fluttering like butterflies, singing and dancing in obeisance to the Buddha. All presented a perfect picture of joy and beauty.

In cave after cave the breathtaking beauty of the Buddha and bodhisattvas cast a spell on me. I gasped in amazement at the gorgeous designs and the splendour of the jewelled crowns, the armlets, the bangles and necklaces worn by the bodhisattvas. Bathed in the fragrance of flowers falling from heaven, and soft music played by the lute wielding devas, the caves appeared mysterious.

Says Tan Chung, (introduction to *Dunhuang Art Through The Eyes of Duan Wenjei*) the cave art was meant to 'wean people's mind away from unreality of the material world where ego, greed and false pride dominated'.[3]

Using ordinary raw materials, the artists had created images that seemed to walk straight out of life. The painted images were arranged symmetrically with the Buddha in the center, Anand to the Buddha's right and the old and wrinkled Kasyapa to his left. The attendants were not seated—they were either standing or kneeling. The guardian deities called the Lokpala were placed at the entrance of the caves. Painted images of the Buddha and bodhisattvas occupying the niches of the cave walls or standing in the centre of the caves were stucco; they were modeled in clay over a central core of wood and straw.

However, the most beautiful were the apsaras – the flying celestial beauties playing the lute, dancing and offering flowers to the Buddha. The apsaras were semi-naked or wearing transparent clothing; they were holding or playing various musical instruments and the devas wearing ornamented crowns danced in joy. These celestial figures are the treasures of Dunhuang art and imparted a distinct beauty to the caves.

In the hands of the ancient artists the walls of the Mogao caves became a vast canvas for the illustration of Buddhist Sutras. Chief among these were the portrayal of the '*Sukhavativyuha Sutra*' highlighting the heavenly bliss of the Buddha's domain, the '*Maitreya Sutra*' depicting the re-incarnation of Maitreya in Tusita Heaven and the '*Saddharma pundarika*' or the *Lotus Sutra*. The richest illustrations were those from the *Lotus Sutra* and many caves were therefore termed as the Lotus Sutra caves picturising whole chapters of the *Lotus*. However, my own search for the Sutra illustrations viz.of the 'phantom city' and the 'treasure tower' that hung in mid-air proved futile as these caves were locked.

The mystical city of treasures said to be an illustration of Chapter seven of the *Lotus* on the walls of Cave 217 had been conjured up by the 'Master' to revive hope among an exhausted people in their search for the Ultimate truth. There was also the 'great treasure tower' that had emerged from below the earth and was suspended in mid-air. Seated on the tower was the Buddha worshipped by innumerable bodhisattvas and benevolent deities illustrating Chapter eleven of the Lotus Sutra in Cave 23.

Fortunately for me, the above rare illustrations of the Lotus and many others based on Buddhist parables from Caves 23, 33, 61, 98,159, 217 of Dunhuang which I could not see on the walls of the Mogao were on display at a rare exhibition organised in Delhi by the Bharat Soka Gakkai, Indian affiliate of the Soka Gakkai International (founding president

Dr Daisaku Ikeda) to highlight the 'Relevance of the Lotus Sutra in contemporary society'.

On display were twelve rare manuscripts, sixty-three photographic panels depicting the relics, documents, manuscripts and facsimile editions of the Lotus Sutra in Sanskrit, Chinese, Xixia (Tangut), Sogdian, Khotan, Saka, Tibetan, Korean, Odi Uighur and Romanised texts. The exhibits came from Cambridge University Library, Columbia University Press, the Lushun Museum Collection from China, the Royal Asiatic Society of Great Britain and Ireland and the National Archives of Nepal.

Though not all caves were open to the public, I learnt that the murals of Magao caves covered an incredible 45,000 sq metres. They illustrated stories from Buddha's life, the traditional life of ancient Chinese, scenes from 'Jataka' propagating Buddha's good deeds in his previous birth and also stories from the 'Hetuprataya' or the miracles of the Buddha.

Cave that caused a furore

I began my walk from Cave 17. This was the mysterious cave where a hundred years ago was written a 'tale of deceit' and 'shameless trickery' in the light of a flickering candle. A tale of two men who stealthily carried away rare manuscripts from this cave; an act that caused a huge furore in the historical and archaeological world. I remembered the doings of the two men as the guide from the Dunhuang Research Academy started his commentary in impeccable English. It was said that in the early twentieth century Aurel Stein, a Hungarian from British India and French Sinologist Paul Pelliot tricked the Taoist priest, Wang Yuanlu, into giving away thousands of rare manuscripts for a measly fifty grams of silver![4] At another place I read that the transaction cost only 130 pounds. The story reeked of 'treachery' and as I headed towards the cave I wondered at the greed of us humans.

But I was wrong to think of priest Wang Yuanlu as a man of greed. As I later found out, that one of the chief reasons behind Wang's action in selling the manuscripts to Stein and Pelliot was his utter disappointment with the government's failure to protect the Sutra cave. Priest Wang also needed money for building a three-storyed structure and a bridge and also for clearing the sand that buried the caves.[5]

The most famous item to have fallen into the hands of Stein was the Diamond Sutra printed in the year AD 868 – the earliest printed book, currently on display at the British Museum.[6]

The passage to Cave 17 was through Cave 16. There was a common entrance to both the caves; at the entrance we were greeted by an ancient bell that hung on a wooden frame and a drum that might have served for worshipping of the deities or, as the guide informs, keeping time in the monastery. It was struck at dusk to call the monks for prayer. As I entered the cave's large opening I noticed the steps that led into Cave 17. The right wall of the doorway was sealed and it was here that over ten thousand Buddhist scriptures, documents, sculptures were found. It was here that the two explorers Aurel Stein and Pelliot sat night after night rummaging through the manuscripts and escaping with the best.

A statue of monk Hongbian occupied the cave. Said to be the high priest of the temple of Buddha, it was Hongbian who built the Sutra Library cave in the Tang dynasty around AD 851. He had preserved thousand of sutras, manuscripts and silk paintings in the sealed cave. The mysterious cave was discovered by priest Wang in the year 1900. As soon as the discovery came to light foreign scholars from Britain, France, America, Russia and Japan swooped on the cave and carried away a lot of precious scriptures, murals and silk banners. Several of these carried by Stein to India make for some of the finest collections of the National Museum at Delhi.

The image of a woman painted inside Cave 17, holding a towel in one hand and a stick in another seemed to be in attendance on the monk who was sitting under a Bodhi tree. On one branch of the tree hung a bag which could possibly have belonged to the lady who might have travelled a long distance to meet the monk. According to my guide she was an *upasika* who had converted to the Buddhist faith and was attending on the monk Hongbian. Her hair was tied in two top buns and she wore the robe of a nun, tied at the waist and hanging loose thereafter in hundreds of folds.

Bejewelled Bodhisattvas in Indian Apparel

According to Zhang Yipping (*Story of the Silk Road*) it was a fashion for women in Dunhuang during the Three Kingdom (222 BC-AD 80) to wear Indian styled costumes. This was because the region was deeply influenced by Indian culture.[7] The outer wall of Cave 17 shows five bejewelled bodhisattvas, their torsos decked with jewels and the lower body covered in a diaphanous cloth that resembled the Indian dhoti that was also draped carelessly over the bare shoulders. Their crowns were studded with gems, multi-stringed pearl necklaces snaked around their neck and a halo added to their aura. In their broad hands they were holding flowers for the main deity in Cave 16. On the left wall of Cave 16 there was a giant Kuber or a guardian deity Vajra reclining leisurely and looking furiously at a mongoose. The deity is shown pressing the neck of the animal who drops jewels from his mouth. The roof of the cave that belonged to the Tang dynasty was ornamented with square patterns in gold. Designed bricks provided strength to the base of the cave while wooden tablets were loaded with scriptures.

Cave 328, a well-kept small cave, belonged to the early Tang dynasty (AD 618-704). Here the Nagaraja pays homage to the Buddha. Whether he is the same Nagaraja who blew forth poisonous smoke and flames on the Buddha or the ones protecting the Buddhist stupa at Ramagrama, or guarding the Buddha's pool at Sarnath, the serpent king had none of his ferocity and was worshipping the Buddha. It is said[8] that once Buddha went to the hermitage of a Brahmana called Uruvela Kassapa. Here he was lodged in a room where a 'savage Naga' or the serpent king lived near the sacred fire of the Brahmana. On seeing the Buddha the serpent became angry and sent forth a cloud of smoke. The Buddha excercising his magical powers too sent forth a cloud of smoke. The serpent then blew flames and the Buddha conquered the flames and

The Magao grottoes are embellished with beautiful painted images of the Buddha and bodhisattvas. In Cave 45 the seated Buddha in abhaymudra *blesses his disciples. The two most favoured disciples Anand and Kasyapa are seen standing on the Buddha's right and left respectively.*

subdued the serpent throwing him in his alms' bowl.

At the entrance of the cave stood three bodhisattvas painted in a combination of green and brown. The bodhisattvas on either side led to the front room where guardian deities, said to be Vajras, were standing with thunderbolts. In the centre was the Buddha seated cross-legged on a pedestal and surrounded by his disciples. In the front of the central deity there was a void—the seat was empty, the image was missing. One can imagine the missing image sitting in front of the Buddha and seeking his blessings. The other images were wearing gold-trimmed apparel in red, black and green.

My guide told me that originally there were four bodhisattvas on each side of Buddha but one was stolen, presumably by the American explorer Langdon Warner of Harvard's Fogg Art Museum who is said to have entered the cave in 1923 much after Stein and Pelliot. Warner did not come empty-handed, he is said to have carried a chemical with which he could peel the paintings off the walls. However, his wile did not work due to the extremely cold weather of Dunhuang. But he did manage to remove paintings and some clay sculptures.[9]

Inside the cave what caught my eye was the magnificent clothing of the Buddha and bodhisattvas. While two images were fully clad in what looked like a cloak, the others were semi-clad; below the waist they were covered with unstitched cloth that loosely draped their torso like a sash or an Indian dhoti. Buddha's disciple Anand was standing on the Buddha's right, while Kasyapa looking grave with his eyes closed and knitted eyebrows had his hands folded in obeisance. Two half-clad bodhisattvas sat on small tables with one leg hanging and another folded; another bodhisattva sat on a lotus seat below listening to the sermons of the Buddha.

The main hall of the cave depicted the Buddhist paradise or the 'Sukhavati'. The preaching bodhisattvas were bedecked in beautiful jewels–armlets adorned their broad arms and huge necklaces with colossal pendants covered their chest. They wore large *kangan* or bangles on their hands; their hair tied in a top bun and the upper lip had traces of moustache. On the roof were painted several crowned bodhisattvas and princes who offered obeisance to the central deity. The edge of the roof had a flowery motif in green and brown which matched the colours on the wall and statues.

Tiger Devours Prince Sattva

Cave 428 that belonged to the Zhao dynasty (AD 557-81) was layered in bright blue that was acquired from lapis lazuli. It is said that a thousand monks pored over their palettes for unending hours to replicate a paradise inside the dark cave. The painted paradise had a beautiful garden full of flowers and trees set against the backdrop of dark mountains. In this paradise animals roamed freely, monkeys frolicked on the trees and heavenly horses carried warriors safely across the western regions. The Jataka tale of prince Sattva also came alive on the wall. A tiger was feeding on the body of the prince who sacrificed himself so that the animal would not go hungry. The story of prince Sattva[10] is that one day the prince went to the forest where he saw a hungry tigress about to eat her own cubs. In order to save the cubs the prince offered his own life. He went close to the tigress and stretched his body before her. Since the hungry tigress was too weak to kill her prey, prince Sattva himself pierced his neck with a sharp stick and offered himself to the tigress who feasted on his flesh. His grief stricken family later collected his remains in a casket and built a stupa over it. Another scene portrayed the stupa of bodhisattva Sattva being worshipped by disciples.

There is another story of prince Sudana portrayed on the walls of the cave. Sudana, a generous prince gifted away the precious white elephant belonging to the king. Since the elephant was the main defender of the country, the king became furious and exiled the prince. Sudana drove away on a chariot with his wife and sons. On the way he gave

FACING PAGE:
A bejewelled bodhisattva sits on a low stool listening to the sermon of the Buddha. He is bedecked in beautiful jewels including armlets and necklaces. Below the waist he is wrapped in unstitched cloth draped like the Indian dhoti.

away his horse to a Brahmana and himself pulled the carriage. This too he gave away in alms. Suddenly in the wilderness he came across a wonderful city where lived the celestial beings. Here Sudana and his family lived for sometime. Then came a brahmana who begged him to give away his sons as slaves for his wife. The prince forced his two unwilling sons to go with the brahmana who took them to the market to sell them. Finally they were bought by the king's men and brought to the palace. Later, on learning about the prince the king sent his men to bring Sudana back.[11] As is wont in cave paintings, there were apsaras too—beautiful women dressed scantily and striking different dance poses. Two of them—wrapped in thin ribbon-like sashes with a round vermilion mark on their forehead—were playing the musical lute and the Chinese harp. On the lower half of the wall were four preaching bodhisattvas wearing beautiful crowns.

Cave 259 belonged to the Wei dynasty (AD 386-543) and is famous for a rare image of the smiling Buddha called the Monalisa. This image lent the cave its more popular name of the Cave of the Smiling Buddha, who was flanked by bodhisattvas wearing *dhotis.*

A lively hunting scene in Cave 247. A man riding a horse is seen taking a fearless ' back shot' at a tiger who is chasing him from behind. Another is in hot pursuit of three wild gazelles and is in the act of drawing the bow.

Hunting in the Forest

Not too far way was Cave 249 that belonged to the Western Wei dynasty (AD 456-540). It depicted a lively hunting scene where two men riding horses were hunting in the forest. One of them took a typical nomadic 'back shot', so famous of the Hun talent in archery, at a tiger who was fiercely chasing him. Another was in pursuit of three wild gazelles and was drawing the bow. The fierce movements of the tiger and the gazelles were depicted with the flourish of an artist's brush.

A host of Hindu gods added a subtle touch to the roof and to the influence of Hinduism on Buddhist art. There was Indra, the god of wind, and gods of light, rain and sun. An evil *asura* with four eyes and long ears held the sun and the moon. Two ferocious demons on either side stood in ankle-deep water near mount Sumeru. On his left was the

god of wind and on his right the gods of thunder and lightning. Flying celestial beings and animals surrounded him. Another scene depicted a sow and her piglets scouring the forest in search of food. On the walls were numerous bodhisattvas and preaching Buddhas. Dating back to the Sui dynasty (AD 581–618), Cave 427 had heavenly guardians killing demons and flying apsaras playing the lute. On the side walls were painted images of the donor king and his wife. There was an interesting array of the images of past, present and future Buddhas flanked by bodhisattvas. Their clothes had phoenix motifs in dominant red and green colours obtained from vermillion and malachite.

Giant Buddhas

So many more Buddhas I would see that day, each so different from the other. Of all the tallest were two Buddhas at the Mogao grottoes: the Maitreya Buddha in Cave 96 and the Meditating Buddha in Cave 130.

Passing through the entrance of Cave 96 where a huge drum and a bell were kept I reached the colossal central hall. Here a magnificent 35.5 metre high Maitreya Buddha welcomed me. The priest told me that the image had been cut into the rocks – no straw or wood was used to make the resplendent Buddha who wears an orange robe with an elaborate blue border. Dragons painted intricately looked magical.

The twenty-six-metre meditating Buddha in Cave 130 had also been cut into the rock then modelled and smoothened in clay and finally painted. The unique halo round Buddha's head had a floral design in a combination of green, white and black. The body was unornamented. A protuberance marked with vermillion sat on the centre of his forehead, his eyes half-closed in a state of bliss. But he was not alone, a large, flying apsara adorned the roof.

My guide told me that work on the two huge Buddhas started from the top and continued to the bottom of the cave. In the beginning, windows were carved on the face of the mountain through which craftsmen could excavate for the caves. Before hammers and chisel struck the rock to carve the Buddha, parallel ladders were placed to make the chore of sculpting easy. Accurate measurements were taken by the artistes to attain perfect proportions; careful research was done before the correct mudra or posture was imparted to the deities and the folds of the robe set with amazing precision.

The priest took me to the original windows which were the first to be carved, much before the deities found a place inside. Originally, the artistes used the drilled spot to excavate and later turned them into windows. However, the windows now had another task, they served another purpose—providing the much-needed light that was essential for the preservation of the cave and the art therein.

The Nirvana Scene in Cave 158 depicted the fifteen-metre long Nirvana Buddha surrounded by mourning disciples. Buddha slept in the bliss of total emancipation, his eyes half closed in the joy of salvation. His right hand was under his head, resting serenely on a beautiful pillow decked with painted flowers, the Buddha breathed his last peacefully while his disciples from various kingdoms wailed in grief. Many of the disciples were at his feet in distress, some were even mutilating and hurting themselves in anguish. One disciple was piercing a dagger in his chest while another sliced off his ears. They were all bawling, not just common disciples but even kings, their head still covered in jewelled crowns. Like elsewhere, even here the apsaras were present; they were floating in the clouds, playing divine music and offering a garland of pears to the dying Buddha. On the ceiling, there were a thousand other Buddhas. On a wall sat Avalokitesvara amidst paintings of the paradise of Amitabha Buddha. Interestingly, the cave belonging to AD 705-80 had rare black stone tablets that chronicled the family history of the Tang dynasty.

Whistling Mountains and the Moonlake

On my way to the grottoes I came across Mingshan or the whistling sand mountains and decided to visit them the following day. The

The whistling sand dunes around the Moonlake in the Gobi. The Moonlake in the shape of a half moon is said to have been a huge lake fed by snow mountains but over the years has turned into a small pond.

mountains, five kilometres south of Dunhuang, formed a corridor of sand mountains about twenty kilometres wide and stretched forty kilometres east to west. The word Mingshan comes from Ming (sound) and Shan (mountain). The ridge of the high sand mountains resembled a huge dragon and their edges are said to be razor sharp. With that sharp edge, they cut the flow of fierce desert winds and made a whistling sound. If one slides swiftly from the top to the bottom, a whistling sound is created, hence the name Whistling Mountains. Visitors can reach the peak by using the rope ladder that hangs from the top of the dunes. Once at the top, they leave the rope ladder and slide down the hill at great speed. For the less adventurous, there are caparisoned camels that take the tourists for a ride.

Several electric cars were parked inside the area of the Whistling Mountains. As soon the visitors enter the Mingshan they are driven to the Moonlake situated at the base of the mountains. It is a perpetual spring with clear cool waters in the shape of a half moon that embraces an ancient pagoda. The Moonlake is said to have been a huge lake fed by the snow mountains but over the years has turned into a small pond near the pagoda.

Inside the pagoda, a museum housed antiquities that were salvaged when the original pagoda was destroyed during Mao Tse Tung's Cultural

Inside the Moonlake pagoda in the Gobi, the museum houses antiquities that were salvaged when the original pagoda was destroyed. Its priceless antiquities include a huge Reclining Buddha sculpted out of a single piece of stone.

At the Dunhuang museum lies the oldest and the most precious printing plate of a Buddhist sutra in Sanskrit illustrated with the image of the Buddha and other deities.

Revolution. A replica that was constructed later also houses a Reclining Buddha and other sculptures.

Sanskrit Scriptures at Dunhuang Museum

Next on my itinerary was a desert safari but before that I wanted to see the artifacts in the Dunhuang Museum, especially the written scriptures unearthed in the Library Cave No.17, also called the Buddhist Sutra Cave. The scriptures displayed in Han and Tibetan languages were exquisite and often referred to as a priceless treasure. The oldest and the most precious artifact was the printing plate of a Buddhist sutra in Sanskrit illustrated with the image of Buddha and other deities.

Bricks decorated with flower motifs and geometrical designs, which once embellished the tombs of the Tang dynasty, were also housed in the Museum. Of the innumerable bricks, the most valuable was the one unearthed at the Sanwei mountains. It had a galloping unicorn with its head raised and the tail flying in the air. There was also a miniature five storied stone pagoda with Buddhist deities on each of its four facets.

Buddha Caves in the Gobi

That night I dreamt of the unicorn; in my blurred dream I saw him racing with the clouds, hastening past the dragons and resting on snow-capped mountains for a gasp of breath. But there was no rendezvous with the unicorn planned for the following day; instead we were to head to the Western Thousand Buddha caves. We drove thirty-five kilometres from Dunhuang on the road that snaked through the Gobi. Initially, the grey and brown of the desert looked interesting, but it soon got monotonous. For miles, all that stretched was the desert. I did not see a human figure; there was no sign of life. It was so rocky that nothing grew there. The unending stretch was fallow; there were no trees, not even a weed to add that green for respite.

After an hour of driving and what must have been a hundred miles of the Gobi desert, the driver skewed to the left and screeched to a halt. The guide led me through a jagged path that descended twenty feet below and ended in a large iron gate. The landscape was different; we seemed to have left the desert way behind. I looked beyond the gate and saw a verdant patch replete with lush green elm, willows and poplars. Through the thick foliage and stout boulders, the Danghe river murmured by. On the left were mountains that had been cut into caves, their roofs almost at ground level.

I knocked the gate and waited patiently. Minutes ticked by but there was not even a whisper of a footstep. I knocked again. The silence remained unbroken. Holding the coarse rod of the iron gate I waited for someone to appear in the desolate desert. My wait seemed futile. The silence was deafening but my grit would not melt so easily. I knew I would not go without looking at the caves. In desperation, I hollered. In the expanse and silence, my voice reverberated. I waited. I was clinging to hope; maybe someone would hear my loud call. The silence was not broken yet. I was about to turn, when I saw what looked like an apparition. The person turned out to be a monk who lived in the quarters below. He was walking up a path that was flanked by elm trees. As he neared the gate, I told him I had travelled a long distance; I had come from India. The word India worked magic, the monk who looked reluctant till a few moments ago suddenly changed his mien–he unlocked the gate and led me to the caves.

The cave was absolutely deserted; we were the only visitors. That day we lorded over the isolated site that looked picturesque with the elm and poplar trees providing the green and yellow for the divine canvas. But entry was not free; we bought tickets and the guide took me through the series of caves that were hewn on the cliff. The monks who came here first chose to settle by a river for convenience, as I walked around the caves I could hear the gurgle of the river.

The Western Thousand Buddha caves situated along the Gobi road to Yumen pass. The isolated site looks picturesque with a thicket of elm and poplar trees and River Danghe rushing by.

In all there were sixteen caves of which five were built during the Wei and Jin dynasties and the rest during the Tang dynasty. However, only six caves are open for public viewing.

A Hidden Maze of Rooms Inside the Rocks

Even though the caves were poised in a forsaken place, they were not unadorned. There were murals on the wall and images of the preaching Buddha inside. That was not all, though; even the cave turned into the office had its walls covered with paintings. We were led to a peculiar cave which had three extensions, a kind of maze excavated deep inside the mountains. The narrow entry led into a vast cave with two extended caves on the right. The preaching Buddha was sitting in the deepest extension of the cave. Interestingly, the cave had only one opening for all the three extensions. The caves, allotted number 3 and 4, belonged to the Tang dynasty with a history dating back to 1,300 years.

It is said that the special cave structure was needed to obviate threats from the elements and keep wild animals at bay. The monks constructed caves with a narrow entry or corridor which spread out inside the rocks like a network of interconnected rooms. Such a cave structure was also seen at Yulin where a common, narrow corridor opened into a double cave or a multi-cave. The narrow entry prevented sand, strong winds, snow and rain from corroding the cave and the paintings on the walls. Such deep inter-connected rooms inside the rocks provided safe dwelling to the monks. The river was close by and the high cliff provided safety from wild animals.

The common theme of the paintings on the cave walls appeared to be the 'Thousand Buddha' and probably the site got its name from this. However many images inside the caves were found damaged. The earliest cave cut in the Northern Wei (AD 439-535) dynasty was Cave 5. There were two images of the Buddha–a damaged idol lay in the niche of a central pillar while the other intact image occupied another corner. The Thousand Buddhas and bodhisattvas were painted on the walls. There

Even though the caves lie in a forsaken place inside the Gobi, they are adorned with beautiful murals and images of the Buddha. Here the sitting Buddha is giving a sermon to his devotees who stand with folded hands. 'Thousand Buddhas' surround the central image.

were apsaras and devas dancing amid blooming lotuses. The large cave led to a dark ante-room which might have been the home of the monks, a secure home far away from intruders and wild animals.

The back wall of Cave 6 belonging to the Northern Zhao dynasty (AD 557-81) was decorated with a Nirvana Buddha. There was a central pillar having a broken Buddha image in the niche. The ceiling was decorated with beautiful flowers and flying apsaras. There were Thousand Buddhas painted on the wall.

ABOVE: *A watchtower at the Yangguan pass. Large sections of the ruined pass are buried in the desert and only a beacon tower remains on a reddish sandstone hill. A complete township of yurts has been set up as an entertainment centre in the Gobi.*

BELOW: *Famous eighth century Chinese poet Wang Wei bids farewell to his friends at the Yangguan pass leading to the Western Regions of the Gobi.*

An image of the Buddha with mutilated arms lay in Cave 7 belonging to the Western Wei dynasty (AD 535-57). However, the large cave was extremely well kept. There were clay statues of bodhisattvas but some images on the left were defaced. The back wall was painted with a typical Nirvana scene of the dying Buddha surrounded by weeping disciples.

We were next headed to Cave 9 which belonged to the Northern Zhao dynasty (AD 557-81). A gallery painted with the images of donors led one inside the cave which was full of rare images of Buddha in black stone and bronze which seemed like recent additions; certainly there was no air of antiquity about them.

Fortress in the Gobi

By the time I was done with the caves, I realised that I was quite tired. But, as they say, the pilgrim's path is never easy; mine certainly was not. While my knees cried for rest and my camera battery gasped without a recharge, I had no choice but to hop back into the coach that would take me deep inside the Gobi. I was jaded but the sight of the snow mountains and a sleeping bodhisattva formed by the huge precipice of the rocks pepped me up. After driving for about a hundred kilometres we hit a T-junction from where one road runs for about 1700 kilometres through the oasis towns of the southern Silk Road crossing over into Tibet. But that was not where we were headed. We took the road that went straight and arrived at the South Lake city village. In the village we came across a huge reservoir for drawing water from the streams running down the mountains. However, what took me by surprise was a recreation centre in the middle of the Gobi for the tourists who would like to spend the night there. From the South Lake village we could see the massive gates of the Yangguan fortress walls. Not too far away flowed the South Lake river on the right that lent its name to the cluster that sat on the left. The last thing I expected there was a raisin factory! I could see grapes hanging from the beams of the adobe houses. They were being sun dried before being sent to the raisin factory for packaging.

At the Yangguan fortress I was given a rousing welcome by Wang Wei, the famous poet of the eighth century whose stone statue stood at the Pass. The poet, his right hand sweeping to the west and holding a cup of wine in his left, was reciting his famous *Farewell Song*:

'No dust is raised on pathways wet with morning rain;
The willows by the tavern look so fresh and green;
I would ask you to drink a cup of wine again;
West of the Sunny Pass no more friends will be seen'.[12]

(Yuanchong, Xu; *300 Gems of Chinese Classical Poetry*, 2004, Peking University Press, China. p.189)

This was the site of the ancient Yangguan Pass which along with the Jade Gate pass (or the Yumen pass) comprising a series of beacon towers and walls once marked the western border of the Chinese Empire. They were said to be built by Emperor Wudi during the Western Han period when he opened the western frontier region of the Yellow river. The two passes were military strongholds and protected China from invasion from the west and formed the gateway to Central Asia.

In modern times a fortress has been built at the site of the Yangguan Pass. Large sections of the ruined Pass are buried in the desert sands and only a beacon tower remains on a reddish sandstone hill. I went behind the huge fortress onto the Film City where a complete township of yurts (felt tents) had been set up. Locals told that me this had been the locale of several famous Chinese films. Crossing the Film City I came to a paved pathway from where I could see the beacon tower. A group of labourers were engaged in laying a concrete road here, for plans are afoot to develop the barren region into an attractive tourist spot.

Museum of Silk Road

I returned to the front courtyard of the fortress to shake hands with the royal emissary Zhang Qian also called the Father of the Silk Road. He was sitting on a horse holding the royal standard of the emperor and was leaving for the Western Regions. Well, he was a statue. On either

The Han Dynasty (206 BC-AD 9) Great Wall zig-zagging its way through the Gobi. The wall appears soft and ready to crumble with the slightest touch but is hard as a rock. Alternating layers of mud and hay have been tightly packed into the wall.

side of the statue were two halls of a museum displaying antiquities found on the Silk Road.

Hall-1 showed the interesting route of the Zhang's mission (138 BC) to the Western Region—starting from Xian to Afghanistan. There was a picture of Zang's mausoleum at GuXia, Shaanxi along with an interesting painting of General Huo Qubing recapturing the Hexi corridor near the Yellow River. There were Gan Yanshou and Chen Yang on their expeditions to the west. There was pottery, coins, beads and figurines belonging to the Han dynasty. A passport for horse, armour pieces and stone mortar and pestle recovered at the Yangguan pass were among the interesting antiquities.

Another hall displayed clay pagodas from Magao grottoes and statues of Buddha and bodhisattvas belonging to the Song and the Qing dynasties. I saw monk Xuanzang returning from India with Sutras. The legend of the 'heavenly horse,' also called the 'treasure horse' found near Wuwa lake near Dunhuang, was kept alive on bricks. A beautiful horse chariot belonging to the Han dynasty was parked in a corner of the hall.

Great Wall inside the Desert

We left the Yangguan fortress and taking the road towards Dunhuang drove for a distance of sixty kilometres until we reached a T-junction where another road coming from deep inside the Gobi meets. We turned left and drove for about seventy kilometres and entered a rocky pathway that ran between desert shrubs for about two kilometres and arrived at the Great Wall zig-zagging its way through the desert. The Wall built during the Han dynasty was made of thick layers of loess alternating with layers of hay and tamarisk. It stretched from the Jade Pass up to the Taklamakan desert.

It was a hot afternoon, I felt singed with the sharp sun; I looked for shade but there was none. The Wall which appeared to be soft and ready to crumble with the slightest touch was actually as hard as rock.

The layers of mud and hay had been tightly packed. Because of the dry weather and heat the wall had been preserved.

A Donkey Ride at Jade Pass

Our jeep now traversed in the roadless desert for about two kilometres before reaching the Yumen or the Jade Pass, named so because the finest jade produced in Khotan had to travel through the gate before it reached the Central Plains of China. It is said that the brilliant rays emanating from the jade guided the caravans through the desert.

Said to have been established in the Western Han dynasty, the pass resembled a rectangular structure with thick walls, pierced by a high-arched gateway through which the ancient caravans passed in order to take the northern branch of the Silk Road through Hami, Turfan and Korla or entered Dunhuang on their return journey. When caravans came to this pass they first took shelter in the small houses nearby and tied their animals to stone pillars. The traders cooked their meals, filled their supply of water from the nearby Shule river, paid their taxes and continued their onward journey.

While I was taking photographs of the Jade Pass a woman with a blind donkey approached me for a ride. Not many dare to ride a blind donkey, but I was eager to look around and quickly accepted the old woman's ride offer and perched myself on the donkey's back. I was not the only one, though. There were several other tourists taking a donkey ride. The base of the Pass appeared to rest on a huge mound of the earth and far away near the Shule river I could see a row of quarters that were once occupied by officials and soldiers of the Han dynasty who guarded the Pass. The Shule river was hardly a river, there was no water and it resembled a wiry stream.

A Hot Meal of Rice in the Gobi

Taking the desert road we left the Pass behind and drove for a few kilometres and reached a community centre which also housed a handicrafts museum. Even before I headed to the museum, I could smell some food being cooked. There was a large kitchen where food was being prepared for the truck drivers who had broken their long journey through the desert.

Inside the museum there were beautiful paintings of apsaras and bodhisattvas and delicate jade jewellery brought from Khotan. The paintings of the Buddhist deities had been copied from the Dunhuang caves and reproduced on thin silk and handmade paper. Lovely bronze images of Buddha were also on display.

On returning from the museum I found a hot meal of rice, noodles and fried vegetables laid on a table by the side of a rabbit enclosure. Here dozens of stout brown rabbits were playing with hens. Must have been pets, I thought. I was wrong; they would soon be killed, dressed and thrown in a boiling cauldron to be turned into a soup or stew or skewered and hung over fire for a sumptuous roast. As I looked into the gentle eyes of the rabbits, I loathed the idea of killing them for the palate. I looked at my simple vegetarian meal, and ate it uncomplainingly.

At the hotel I wanted to retire for the night, but sleep would have to wait as I rummaged through the book store at the hotel and found a copy of the collected poems of Wang Wei, the poet who held a cup of wine at the Yangguan Pass and beckoned his friends to drink and get drunk. As the full moon rose I heard his whisper in the song of birds, his words meandering through the hills that dissolved into the horizon.

I switched off the light and tried to sleep; I had to catch an early morning flight to Urumqi from where I would embark on the second leg of my journey along the Silk Route.

This is not a hill station but an oasis inside the Gobi Desert along the National Highway A 312 on way from Urumqi to Turfan. In the backdrop are the lovely ice-capped peaks of the 'Holy Mountains' or the Tienshan.

8

To the Grape Valley at Turfan

Instead of going to Turfan directly on the second leg of my journey along the northern Silk Road I took flight CZ 9110 to Urumqi on the north-western branch of the Silk Road (A 312) that passes through Yinning into Kazakhstan.

It was evening when I landed in the exciting tourist city. Habibullah, my Uighur guide, had been waiting for me at the airport. He waved to me as I struggled with my luggage. He was to accompany me throughout my journey from Urumqi to Kuqa.

It was a long drive from the airport; thankfully, the road was excellent. A gentle breeze blew into my face and soothed my jaded limbs. The moonlit night greeted me in the desert land of western China. Soon we had reached Hoi Tak, the first star hotel in Xinjiang province. After a quick meal I went to bed as I had an early start the next morning.

Such was the beauty of Urumqi that it was called Dihua (City of Lights). It is a precious piece of earth in the expanse of the Gobi Desert. Situated at the foot of the Red Hills, Dihua (later renamed Urumqi) became the capital of the western region of China which was declared a province in 1884 and named Xinjiang or the new territories.

Loulan Beauty – the Mother of Uighur

But what actually stirred in me the desire to see the town was yet another beauty—the famous Loulan Beauty. She was called the Mother of Uighur, as the Uighur stock is believed to have descended from her. I had seen an artist's impression of the beauty in Jonathan Tucker's book on the Silk Road. She had a flowing reddish mane crowning her beautiful brown face with deep-set hazel eyes and a chiselled nose.

Before going to the Museum of Corpses to see the beauty my guide Habib took me to an exhibition of jade handicrafts and musical instruments where exquisite jade work and a variety of musical instruments were on display. Yellow, green and white jade from the Khotan rivers had been chiselled into sculptures. There were intricately carved figurines playing a variety of instruments. From the exhibition we headed straight to the Museum of the Xinjiang Autonomous Region which displayed frescoes and ancient corpses.

Finally, we were face to face with the Loulan Beauty. Called the Tienbahe Female Corpse, it is believed to be nearly 4000 years old. This Mother of Uighur corpse was unearthed near the Tienbahe river at the north end of Lopnor in 1980. She had been found buried in simple clothes of wool and fur at the ancient settlement of Qawrighul (Gumugao), seventy kilometres from Loulan in Xinjiang.

Scholars would have you believe that the Mother of Uighur was 157 cms tall and breathed her last at the age of forty-five. A scientific test concluded that she was of European origin with deep eyes, dark brown complexion, high nose and thick brown lips. Sinuous curls fell on her face and her hair parting was neat and still visible. There was a feather in her cap and she seemed well protected with shoes and gloves. Found alongwith her in the grave was a winnowing tray, a comb and a basket containing wheat. She was not alone, though; she was preserved in a glass case in an air-conditioned room with other corpses.

Another female corpse of European origin was found at Karduwa in Kumul (Hami) on the northern Silk Road. The young girl must have been twenty, from about 1200 BC; her remains were excavated in 1978.

A corpse of an infant from an ancient tomb on the Kongque river in Loulan is said to be nearly 3,800 years old. Aged four-five years, the infant's body has been wrapped up in woollen textile that was held together by sixteen wooden pins.

Another baby corpse called the Qiemo Baby is about eight to ten months of age and is nearly 3,000 years old. Found in a tomb in Zhahongluk, Qiemo, in 1985, the baby lies on a small carpet with its eyes covered with stone and a milk feeding vessel kept close by.

The most interesting corpses are that of a couple, a thirty-two-year-old male and a ninety-year-old female belonging to the Tang Dynasty put together in one chamber. It is believed that the husband, a patient of tuberculosis died at age thirty-two and the wife lived on till the age of ninety. But they were buried together. Another couple with Mongoloid and European racial characters was excavated from Zhahangluk, Quiemo.

There was ancient pottery from Yarkhote (ancient Jiaohe city in Turfan) and an arrow bow pot also from Jiaohe; some items from Gaochang (ancient kingdom in Turfan) and fabric from Jiaohe. A beautiful painted tomb guard of clay with a man's head and an animal's body, from Astana cemetery dates back to the first century BC. Another tomb guard had a lion's head, also from the Astana cemetery dating back to the seventh century.

The corpses were fascinating and I wanted to take photographs. However, photography inside the museum was strictly prohibited, and all my pleadings with the staff fell on deaf ears.

For lunch, we stopped at a wayside Uighur restaurant. The place was crowded and young Uighur waitresses in skirts scampered from one table to another holding large tea kettles. At the reception a young lady sat making entries. In front of her were big jars of raisins and walnuts which the customers could have for free. Habib made a quick round of the kitchen to check whether it was clean. Actually, he wanted to confirm that the food was not cooked in pig lard. We settled for pilaf, the restaurant's specialty. The pilaf was scrumptious; it was full of soft meat, raisins and nuts.

A Day at the busy Bazargaha

The following day was indeed glorious. The sun peeped shyly over the Red Hills and cast a smouldering reddish glow over the horizon. Soon the entire landscape was lit up by a million sparkling diamonds. We were amazed to see morning walkers walking backwards. Habib informed me that walking backwards not only benefitted the body, it also sharpened the mind!

At the People's Square young and old alike were doing aerobics to the accompaniment of music, others were flying kites that were sailing in the morning breeze. The square was crowded with hawkers who were peddling their wares on tricycles and rickshaws. In the evening the square took on varied hues with coloured beams of light playing upon huge bill boards. Flower pots and hanging baskets lent a charming beauty to the Square.

The streets of the Erdaoqiao Bazargaha market were lined with small shops selling a variety of handicrafts and woollen carpets. Traders brought their goods in donkeycarts on which they stood, beckoning people in their loud voices.

As evening fell the city took on a dazzle. A colourful nightlife emerged out of nowhere. Roadside eateries played some loud foot-tapping music; it was time to dance and join the crooner Abdullah in a karaoke bar. Large bunches of lamps hung from ornate posts. Restaurants sprinkled water on the pavements, put out low chairs and tables and switched on neon lights to welcome customers. A chef set out his huge tandoor oven on the pavement outside. Next to him on a high table were spread out heaps of minced lamb meat and an array of spices. He fired the oven with a hand fan till the embers turned red. A thick column of smoke emerged as kebabs were rolled over skewers set on charcoal pits and served hot with chilli chutney.

The street food market does brisk business. After 9 pm people crowd around eateries selling hot *naan*, cakes, hand-made noodles and kebabs. Local fruits like the hamigua, pomegranate and the luscious grape were plentiful. Perhaps, in the entire Xinjiang region, food was cheapest here. In this fruit belt one can have peaches, melons, grapes and other nuts, both fresh and dried. The famous Hentegri Shopping Arcade in the heart of the city is the place to be.

Food market at the Grand Mosque was out of bounds for women. So it was everywhere. I pleaded with the imam to let me in. He relented, but only a little; he only allowed me up to the outer courtyard into which opened the main gate. After taking photos of the green-domed mosque I ventured in a side lane looking for some good Uighur music.

I instead found a food market. Small restaurants provided Uighur food and shops were selling meat and chicken. The Muslims after offering *namaz* bought their daily requirements and had a quick meal here. I walked a little further and found shops selling musical instruments, CDs and video and audio cassettes.

To my utter surprise I found audio cassettes of Hindi playback singers like Mohammad Rafi, Kishore Kumar and Asha Bhonsle. Dubbed CDs of Indian movies seemed very popular as I was to find later while moving along the desert oasis towns. I asked for Uighur music CDs and on the recommendation of Habibullah, I picked up a few of Abdullah, a famous Uighur singer and Arken.

As I stepped out I saw vendors squatting on pavements with their baskets of fresh green figs. They were laid out delicately on leaves over small slabs of ice. I could not resist the temptation and approached a vendor. He quickly sliced the figs into two pink halves and sprinkled some salt and pepper. They were juicy and delicious and melted in my mouth.

I wanted to taste the famed Urumqi desserts and walked into a coffee parlour. I found ice creams in various flavours and ordered some peach cream. It looked pretty—rose-coloured fresh peaches crushed into layers of smooth ice cream. Perhaps the owner realised I was delighted and served an extra helping. He said it was his welcome gift to Indian tourists!

It was noon, the fierce sun was right overhead as we embarked on a three-hour journey through the Black Gobi to Turfan, the enchanting oasis of grapes and sweet wine.

Through the Black Gobi to Turfan

In the land of Buddha I would have only imagined serenity and peace. There certainly could be no room for fear or warnings. Or, so I thought. But a few days into the Silk Road and there came a warning–for my journey through the Gobi to Turfan. There came the warning of dry heat, the fierce wind, the storm and the blinding glare of the sun. And the devils that appeared in the form of illusions and apparitions tricking the travellers and driving them to their death. Stocking on water, colas and fruits–and the warning that could even daunt the intrepid traveller –I took Highway A 312 south east of Urumqi.

I fretted about the five-hour journey, but was nonetheless raring to set foot in the Gobi. Thousands before me had undertaken this journey in caravans, on foot, camels, horses, stocking nothing except a little faith in themselves and their god. I had read several horrifying tales of

The glistening four-lane Highway A 312 to Turfan runs through the Gobi Desert like a black flying snake. Although the sun beats down harshly the drive in a speeding eight-seater is like a dream. Nothing grows in the black rocky soil of the Gobi except thick crusts of white salt.

the desert; many of these travellers and their animals succumbed to thirst and hunger or were killed by bandits who ambushed and looted them.

There was plenty of water in the boot of the car, but it was hot inside and to beat the heat the driver turned on the air-conditioner. To break the silence and monotony, Arken and Abdullah were ready to blare out songs from the car stereo. There were enough accoutrements in the vehicle to keep me company, to drive away the desert ghosts that had struck so many travellers before and to dispel the depressing feeling of barrenness that had engulfed so many in the black Gobi.

Before we hit the road, Habib looked towards the sky and muttered a prayer. The engine of the car revved and soon we had inched into Gobi. To my utter surprise there was hardly any sand in this desert. Only dark, rocky soil. No trees in the vast expanse. Only a few dried shrubs and barren mountains far away. Suddenly on our left appeared snowy white caps of the Tienshan mountains, shining against the azure sky like crowns of massive diamonds, more blinding than the sun. The four-lane road slithered like a snake through the desert. Smooth and black rising above the ground by a few feet. There was another road running parallel to the one we were on for the return traffic. On both sides hung power lines on wooden poles providing electricity to the oasis towns all along the desert.

The weather was sweltering and we had to cover 200 kms of the Gobi. Despite the burning sun, I enjoyed every moment of it. Arken was singing a peppy song. I could not decipher the lyrics but it was enchanting. I was soon tapping my feet to the beat.

The journey that I dreaded was so exhilarating. The lovely ice-capped peaks of the Tinshan mountains, the rich blue sky, the floating clouds, the snaking road and the speeding eight-seater seemed like a dream. More beauty was awaiting us. An hour later I noticed thousands of windmills lining the desert on both sides of the road through a distance of ten kilometres. Like everywhere, wind energy here too is cheap. Habib told me that all villages and towns were powered by these windmills, a fact that was corroborated when I visited some of the remotest places in the desert. There was a halting point for tourists and we stopped to take some photographs.

Down the road we reached a detour which led to a small pastureland and a forest of poplar beside a salt lake, two kilometres away. The driver was reluctant about driving up to the lake, so we walked to taste the salt. The lake's upper crust, especially the fringes, was thick and white. Several centimeters of pure white salt floated on the surface of the lake on the periphery. A Korean oyster-shaped machine was whirring to extract salt. I dipped my fingers in the icy waters, broke the crusted salt and placed a bit on my tongue, which tasted just like table salt. Never before had I tasted salt straight out from a lake and I was ecstatic.

A salt factory along a lake inside the Gobi. It is in the shape and colour of a massive pearl. The surface of the lake is white and crusty with salt deposits.

Around the lake there was a carrot crop that looked like green lace. We plucked a few baby carrots, washed them in the salty water and munched away. Beyond the field there was grassland dotted with grazing sheep and goats and the shepherds who were keeping a watchful eye on them. As if like a blessing, a dense growth of poplar had sprung up near the lake providing shade in a green valley. The landscape looked divine with the snow-covered Tienshan enveloped in a perpetual mist as the lake's backdrop—the view was as heavenly as it could get.

After soaking in the beauty of the valley and the lake, Habib and I walked back to the car and resumed our journey. This time, instead of taking the main road to Turfan the driver drove into the gate of the Korean salt factory. It was a one-way road and a U-turn was prohibited. We wasted half an hour trying to get back to the highway. The driver looked flustered; and confessed he could not find a way out of the maze. To my surprise he added that Urumqi—Turfan was his beat; an everyday route, surely he would know all exits and bends like the back of his hand. I could see drops of sweat on his forehead—it suddenly dawned on me that perhaps it was not bad geography, but anger. Perhaps he was angry that I spent too much time at the lake. Until we took that break near the lake, he was driving smoothly; suddenly there were uncalled for bumps and jerks. But I preferred to remain silent; a word from me would have fuelled his anger. We were at his mercy and there was not much we could do about his tantrum. Thankfully, Habib came to my rescue—he saw a paved pathway that went under a bridge and merged into the main road. I heaved a sigh of relief. At long last we were out of the labyrinth.

About fifty kilometres short of Turfan we came across Daheyan station on our right. We drove ahead for an hour and turned right leaving the desert highway that ran up to Korla, the next big oasis on the Silk Road. It was close to three pm when the car screeched to a halt in the patio of Turfan Oasis Hotel. My room was small and had no beds! What made up for the bed were two mattresses on raised platforms decorated with carpets and cushions. Trust me, it looked very comfortable. I noticed the carpets that swathed the wall. The window opened onto a lovely grape garden, the pink and purple bunches resplendent in borrowed light. In one secluded corner was a courtyard reserved for the evening opera for guests who had arrived for the Grape Festival.

The Grape Festival of Turfan

It was by sheer chance that I happened to be in Turfan at the time of the Grape Festival. It was the thirteenth year of the festival, but there was much more to celebrate as it was the 2100th anniversary of China Silk Road and the celebratory theme was 'A passage to the mysterious and joyous Turpan'.

The festival is held every year between 26 August-5 September at the City Square to promote trade and tourism. The history of grape cultivation in Turfan goes back two thousand years and the grapes of Turfan are perhaps the most coveted in the Xinjiang province. So are the raisins and wine that Turfan is so renowned for. Almost ninety percent of the grapes are marketed; raisins, wine and canned grape juice fetch a good price nationally and internationally.

For the festival, we drove to the grape valley which was teeming with tourists. Lying at the base of the western end of the Flaming Mountains the grape valley is eight kilometres long and 500-2000 metres wide. Springs flow along the valley and water the vineyards. Almost every house seemed to be a vineyard as grapes were everywhere, providing an interesting backdrop to the men and women sitting in their verandahs and going about their daily chores. The creepers served another purpose; they provided a cool touch to the Turfan summer which otherwise singes at forty-eight degrees.

At the grape gorge where the mountain stream gushes out of a huge hole into a large pond, traditionally dressed Uighur men and women danced and entertained the tourists. There was a grape park and a museum of folk customs. Here tourists are offered grapes and a brief introduction to the traditional folk culture. Just behind the gorge was the beautiful Tienshan or the Heavenly Mountain. One can climb up the mountains and get an overview of the grape valley. Thousands of raisins and dryfruit sellers lined the length of the valley. There were endless varieties of grapes in as many shades of green, purple, pink and red hanging in bunches from the trellis that covered the entire valley. The best and the sweetest are the seedless grapes, however, they were not for sale; visitors can have as much as they want without paying a penny. Such generosity takes me by surprise. All you had to do is raise your hand and pluck a bunch. But no one touches the grapes; they hang wantonly on the wooden trellis.

What was on sale were top-grade raisins and dryfruits. Pushy sellers thrust a handful of the raisins at the visitors for free tasting. They were available in a variety of colours–light yellow to brown, coffee and green. They were offset by dried apricots, peaches, raw walnuts and almonds that added to the fascinating palette. I looked at the porcelain skin of the gorgeous Uighur women; maybe it was the sweet grapes and melons that lent the incredible sheen to their skin.

Where there are so many grapes, can wine be far behind? Predictably, the valley produces great wine and is often referred to as the sweetest place on earth. There were countless restaurants under the grape trellis and visitors were lunching on grapes and Uighur cuisine. The waitresses

Almost every house in Turfan seems to be a vineyard as grapes grow everywhere. The thick creepers provide a cool touch to the excessive Turfan heat. The luscious grapes are the most coveted in the Xinjiang province.

had a pair of scissors hanging from their waists. After lunch they would snip off bunches of ripe grape from the trellis and offer them to the customers as souvenirs. This is the bounty of Turfan.

While Habib preferred to walk around I sat down for lunch at a restaurant under the shade of, what else, grapes. I was offered a large bowl of yellow grapes. A carpet had been laid under the creepers for those wanting to take a nap. The dense creepers provided shade and prevented the hot rays of the sun to peep past the canopy. Hundreds of huge grape bunches were hanging over my head. The lunch was being cooked on charcoal fire. I was tired after walking several kilometres in the grape valley. Gorging on too many grape bunches had made me feel sleepy. I shifted the low table kept in the centre of the high divan to one side and put up my feet to relax, but the sweetness of the fruit acted like a sedative and I soon fell into a deep slumber. Only when food was on the table did I wake up. The meal was lavish; there was sheesh kebab, mixed mutton vegetables, naan and pilaf. Habib who had been loitering in the grape valley arrived just in the nick of time to join me for lunch. The large spread concluded with slices of deep red Hamigua or melon from Hami that was served on a large platter as dessert. The owner of the orchard gave me two kilos of green and purple grapes as a parting gift.

I returned to my hotel laden with a variety of raisins and grapes, a shawl woven from real lamb wool and a wall-hanging of a camel caravan trudging along the Silk Road. Little did I realise that I had added at least six extra kilos to my baggage.

To Gaochang on a Donkey Cart

It is said that Turfan was the home of the Cheshi people who lived here during 770-221 BC.[1] Situated at the crossroads of China and the Western Regions (now the Chinese province of Xinjiang) Turfan was a conduit to India and was therefore counted as one of the most important political, economic and cultural centers on the Silk Road. It was the place where

Buddhism and Hinduism flourished along with other major religions of the world including Taoism, Manicheism, Nestorianism and Islam. As evidence of this, papers written in seventeen ancient languages have been discovered in Turfan.[2] Of the several ancient historical sites and cultural relics buried underground, five have survived and are now under the aegis of state protection.

Turfan got me curious, I wanted to know more about it and I set aside the next day for just that. I requested Habib to take me to ancient sites that were deep in the desert. From the map, I picked the ancient kingdom of Gaochang which sat fifty kilometres south-east of Turfan inside the barren deserts of the Gobi at the foot of the Flaming Mountains. Built as a garrison town called Gaochang Bi for the Western Han dynasty[3] in the first century BC, it was once a sanctuary of world religious culture and Buddhist pilgrim Xuanzang is said to have visited Gaochang on his way to India.

However, there was a glitch; the place was inaccessible by car. All I had as a means of travel was a donkey cart. Habib was certain that I would be aghast at the thought of a donkey ride, but to me it sounded very exciting and I prepared to leave for Gaochang hurriedly. By the time I arrived outside the ancient city it was noon. The sun was directly overhead and I knew that we had an extremely hot day ahead of us. Dozens of donkey carts were parked in an enclosure by the side of the road winding through the desert. But surprisingly there were so many foreign tourists that we feared we would have to wait very long for our turn for a cart. We spotted an empty cart decorated with red upholstery, a red carpet covered the wooden seats and a red tarp hung over an arched roof. Even the donkey who was reined into the cart wore a garment with red floral chintz. A dozen American tourists had surrounded the cartman Irfan and were haggling for a good rate. I hopped into one without asking any questions. Habib followed me into the side seat. Irfan was so happy to see an Indian; he asked nothing either, he let out a yell and hit the donkey with a long stick. The animal started off with a big jump and off we went waving to the other tourists

Donkey carts are a popular carriage in Gaochang near Turfan.

who were dumbfounded at Irfan's behaviour. The animal first broke into a trot and then started running furiously behind other donkeys. Though it was a donkey ride, it was so jumpy, it felt like a roller-coaster.

This was my first donkey cart ride ever, and I was thoroughly enjoying it. At least six carts followed us; they were desperately trying to overtake us, but our donkey kept up the speed and ran faster to the yells of his master Irfan. Imagine participating in an impromptu donkey race on the sands of an ancient desert town! Irfan soon broke into a song, now and then whipping the donkey to go faster. The mud tracks were deeply grooved and the wheels of the cart were following the grooves like a rail on its tracks. As they ran faster, the bells of the donkeys clanged louder, making the entire race all the more dramatic.

Our donkey seemed to be on a winning spree; on the four-kilometre stretch it did not stop even for a breath. On reaching Gaochang we were welcomed with the brays of a dozen donkeys and the hollering of the cart-owners who were beckoning people for the return journey. There were dozens of camels standing next to the donkeys; it was the camels that would take tourists around the meandering lanes of the ancient city. However, I preferred to walk.

The paved roads were flanked by innumerable rock structures with brick base and ancient caves with ruined door and window openings. After walking for a kilometre inside the city we came to the gate of the imperial palace. Right in front of us was the massive pagoda of the royal temple that had niches arranged in rows. Once upon a time these niches were not vacant; they were decorated with murals and held statues of Buddhist deities. It is believed that they were either stolen by foreign explorers or destroyed by the onslaught of Islam. The central pillar was said to have held a giant statue of Buddha. The walls of the temples were built of large bricks cemented by rocky mud. Outside the courtyard there were several rooms that once housed monks. An inscription[4] found at Gaochang recorded the flourishing state of Buddhism during the reign of King Qu. This was confirmed by the discovery of a wooden statue of Buddha, stone pillars having Buddhas in the niches, a silk painting of Bodhisattva called Guayin Buddha, clay sculptures and carved stone images of Buddha in different postures.

Xuanzang's Visit to Gaochang

History is replete with evidence of Xuanzang's visit to the kingdom of Gaochang on his way to India. In his travelogue[5] the pilgrim writes that when he entered the city of Gaochang, the king along with his attendants bearing lit torches, came to meet him and pay their respects. The great monk was conducted to a monastery where he was guarded by eunuchs. Here senior monks Tun and Kwo-tong-wang persuaded Xuanzang to remain in the monastery and not take the onward journey to India. But the monk was keen on his India visit; he refused the request of the king and other monks. After a ten-day stay at Gaochang, he sought the king's permission to continue his journey to India.

EXTREME LEFT: The king and queen of Gaochang bidding farewell to the great monk Xuanzang on his departure for India. A painting from the Chengdu Daci temple.
BELOW: Inside the Gaochang ancient city camels wait to take tourists on a trip around the ruins.

EXTREME RIGHT: A massive Buddha temple at Gaochang. The high wall once carried a huge image of Buddha. Even now the niches where Buddha idols were placed are visible in the sides of the wall.

However, the king refused permission. Assuming that he would be detained, Xuanzang gave up food and water for three days. On the fourth day the king relented. Before leaving for India he presided over a religious conference at Gaochang which was attended by 300 people. Everyday the king himself conducted Xuanzang to the pulpit walking with a brazier of incense before him.

Adjacent to the temple was a large mosque built in the tenth century AD when Islam was adopted by the city's rulers. It was a curious round flat structure with a low roof and arched niches in the wall. I took a look inside the mosque which, far from being a grand structure, was built of mud and rocks.

It was an eventful day at Gaochang. However, when we reached the cart parking lot, we could not find Irfan. But there were a dozen others shouting for passengers. Their donkeys too were craning their necks and braying loudly. The sun was setting and the Flaming Mountains

hanging over the landscape of Gaochang were awash in the burnished orange of the setting sun. We hired a cart and galloped to the main road where our vehicle was parked.

Along the Flaming Mountains to Bezeklik

The Flaming Mountains seemed to be emitting orange flames from their purple peaks. We drove towards it on our way to the Bezeklik caves. At the foothills hundreds of camels were waiting patiently to take visitors for a ride into the burning mountains. As we went closer we found that the mountain slopes were deeply corrugated; it looked as if high logs of wood had been piled and a huge pyre lit. Actually it was the heat and the colour of the sandy mountain alongwith its corrugated slopes which gave the impression of rising flames. It was an optical illusion. The ten-kilometre wide mountains running for about a hundred kilometres from east to west-east of Turfan city were blazing at eighty degrees, heating the sandy rocks and causing the air flowing over it to look like flames.

We continued to drive along the mountains and parked our vehicle in the foothills. Walking along a shopping arcade we descended several steps down the hill side to approach the caves which were completely hidden from view as their domed roofs merged with the mountains. They appeared like small roundels embedded in the rocks. A long row of caves to our left were closed while a few on our right were open for public viewing.

Several hundred feet below the caves ran a stream surrounded by lush green dense poplars. The monks who cut the caves must have chosen this site with great care; all along the barren mountains this was the only stretch with dense foliage. It kept the monks safe from predating animals and curious intruders. However, not all was easy for the monks; they had to descend several hundred feet before they could reach the river. Even in the early twentieth century when Albert von le Coq visited Bezeklik he saw the 'horse-shoe gorge full of wolves howling at the moon'.

Bezeklik caves cut into the cliffs of the Flaming Mountains near Turfan. The domed roofs of the caves appear like roundels embedded in the rocks. There is a curved pathway running along the cave gallery. Standing at one point in the middle of the gallery a visitor can view the entire group of caves.

These were man-eaters who feasted on their dead friend, killed when the wolves were fired upon. Earlier the pack had eaten away a twelve-year-old child, writes Coq.[6]

We walked along a narrow curved pathway leading inside the caves which had been built in a semicircle. A series of dome-shaped roofs protruded from the surface of the mountains. Standing at one

spot one could see the entire series of caves; some of the caves had paved verandahs and stairs leading to other caves on a higher level.

The caves were manned and the visitors were watched carefully. No cameras were permitted inside and the guide provided information about the cave's interiors which was sated with faded paintings. The caves were in a shambles, badly destroyed by explorers like von le Coq. The paintings had been cut away alongwith several inches of the wall and large craters were left behind. The faces of the deities were also scratched away; it appeared as if mud had been rubbed on them. The callousness of the marauders was evident in the gaping holes; at places the holes were all that remained of the glorious past.

All visitors to Bezeklik were aghast at the cruelty of those who came here under the guise of exploration and destroyed the heritage of the Buddhist world. Without the images of Buddha and the decorative wall paintings it was difficult to imagine how beautiful the caves might have looked originally. The dilapidated walls and empty niches were the only remains of the once beautiful grottoes that weaved the story of splendour and magnificence of an artist's skills. Most caves were long and cylindrical and approached by an arched doorway. A special technique of brick laying for constructing a dome was said to have been used in the grottoes.

There were about eighty-three caves, forty of which have murals that portrayed stories from Buddha's life and teachings. The Thousand Buddha and the Nirvana scenes adorned several caves. However, the 'Dying Buddha' statues had been snatched away from their platforms at the back walls of most caves. We know only from the mourners painted on the wall that the lost image was that of the Reclining Buddha.

Since photography was strictly prohibited my attention was immediately drawn to two life size portraits of Buddha put on display by the authorities outside Cave 37. That meant that without violating any rules I could take shots of the cave's exterior alongwith the portraits. The posse of cops guarding the caves had no objection to this and I merrily clicked the beautiful Buddha preaching to his disciples. I cursed the German and Russian explorers who had axed the rare paintings

Copy of three life-sized portraits of the Preaching Buddha *put on display in front of Cave 37. These paintings and several others had been gouged out from the cave walls of Bezeklik and taken away by explorers in the early twentieth century.*

FACING PAGE:

Copy of a portrait of the Preaching Buddha *on display outside Cave 37. The Buddha is unadorned. His feet are clad in rope sandals and set on lotuses. Royal attendants surround him listening to his sermon.*

from the walls of the caves. But back in India when I chanced upon P. Banerji's *New Light on Central Asian Art And Iconography* I was shocked to learn that a part of the same painting from Bezeklik was lying in the National Museum at Delhi. It was probably cut away and brought to India by Stein during his third expedition of 1913-1916. But the painting was not on display at the National Museum, Delhi and, I am sure, had been locked up in some wooden box. What a pity! The Buddha was unadorned. He was wearing the Indian 'dhoti' which covered his left shoulder. His feet were clad in rope like sandals and set on lotuses which seem to be growing in a stream. One hand was raised in 'Abhay mudra' while the other touched his clothing. Attendant figures numbering six to eight surround the Buddha. Some of the attendants were bearded and wore crown over their top knots. One attendant had his hair plaited and also wore a crown. They appeared to be kings of different regions as they were all adorned in precious jewels and were in the act of worshipping the Buddha and offering him eatables on trays.

Banerji, (*New Light on Central Asian Art and Iconography*)[7] noting the important aspects of the painting viz 'Buddha's journey in a raft like boat and the great honour shown to him by his devotees' finds similarity with the Buddha's journey during the last days of his life from Rajgir to Vaisali where he had to cross the river. On the way he found the river Ganga in floods but he, alongwith his monks, crossed the river miraculously. A mention of this miracle of Buddha crossing the river without a boat by the force of his magic, we find in Asvaghosh's *Buddhacharita* (Trans E.H.Johnston: Canto xxii no.8-14)

It is said that once the inhabitants of Vaisali were dying of plague. They invited the Buddha who was then staying at the Bambo Grove (perhaps the *Latthivana*) monastery at Rajgir, to come to Vaisali and cure their affliction. When the Buddha reached the other bank of the river the Lichchavi nobility came to receive him and greeted him with gifts, flowers and food. As the Buddha set foot on the soil of Vaisali there were heavy rains which washed away the disease. Buddha preached the 'Ratna Sutra' and eighty-four thousand people embraced the faith.[8]

Of the other caves that were open for public viewing, Cave No. 17 belonged to the Tang period. It was a rectangular cave with an arched roof. There were remnants of seven damaged statues of Buddha and three painted images of Amitabha, Avalokitesvara and Bodhisattva.

In the center of Cave 20 was a central room with a painting of Avalokitesvara. On both sides stood donors–king and queen of Gaochang; Jataka stories from Buddha's previous life adorned the walls.

Cave 27 was bereft of all images. Statues and paintings had been cut away, and there was mud on face of the Thousand Buddha on the roof and walls. The photographic copies of the wall paintings that were taken away by von le Coq to Berlin were, however, kept in front of Cave 31, 32, 33.

Cave 31 belonged to the eleventh century and had the Thousand Buddhas painted on the roof, painting of Nirvana Sutra on the front wall and a platform which once held the image of the Reclining Buddha, now cut away. Only the *Sala* tree on the walls proved that the image was that of the Reclining Buddha. There were damaged images of Bodhisattvas and eight paintings of Nagas on the right. A prince mourned on the left wall. Between them was fire that depicted the Mahaparinirvana and the Holy cremation. There was also an interesting mural depicting the war among eight kings for the holy *sarira* of Buddha. There were also scenes from the Jataka about *Sarvadaan* in which Buddha

A painting from Bezeklik depicts king and royal personages with folded hands listening to the sermons of the Buddha. According to another version they are mourning the 'Great Decease' or the Mahaparinirvana *of the Buddha.*

donated himself and went to Heaven. A board informed that the back part of the eastern wall was stolen by Stein in 1914.

In Peter Hopkirk's *Foreign Devils On The Silk Road* we read about Albert von le Coq and Theodor Bartus, the two Germans explorers,[9] who cruelly cut away the clay walls of the caves to obtain the great murals of Bezeklik. They were said to have used a sharp knife, pick axe, hammer, chisel and foxtail saw. It is said that after removing sand from the northern caves they discovered paintings that were well preserved.

Many murals are now believed to be in the collection of the Museum für Indische Kunst (Museum of Indian Art), Staatliche Museen at Berlin, Germany.

According to another version Von le Coq and Bartus were the discoverers and conservers of the paintings. They discovered and explored the caves around 1905. It took half a century until the Chinese government started to protect the place by declaring it a cultural spot under state protection. In order to prevent further destruction, some caves are now protected by glass walls.

Camel Ride into the Flaming Mountains

While returning from the caves, we stopped near a small restaurant providing snacks and cold drinks. Here camels were available for a ride into the Flaming Mountains. I got onto the back of a huge, double-humped camel. Before I could hold onto the reins the camel took off on grassy foothills leaving the master far behind. As I shouted for the master the camel happily raced along the mountainside with a tearful me on its back. The bronze bells tied around her neck were ringing furiously. From the sound of the bells the master could trace the camel's whereabouts. In no time he hurried along, twisted her ears playfully and informed me that his animal had a special bonding with female tourists. I saw hundreds of camels running along the mountains with tourists on their backs. Countless bells were creating an enchanting sound; they all seemed to be in a joyous mood. Soon all of them would retire for the evening as the sun was setting and the orange mountains were turning a deep purple.

Visit to Jiaohe Ancient City

The next day we travelled west of Turfan to the Yarnaz Valley where lay the ancient city of Jiaohe with a history dating back 2300 years. Its peculiar location on a 300-metre wide and 30-metre high islet set between two rivers precluded the need for a city wall. The steep cliffs on all sides acted as natural defence. The former capital of Cheshi kingdom is said to be the largest, oldest and best-preserved earthen city in the world.

We stopped at a stream running around the site. The vehicles could go no further. After crossing a small bridge on foot we were at the massive gate of the city where a huge board displayed the name 'Yarhu Khadim ke Shahre'. A paved road running from north to south through the city gate went up a steep incline towards the inner precincts and passed through a dense foliage of poplars. I suddenly came upon a huge cave cut out of rocks and supported on a base of red baked bricks and mud. I walked inside the cave and found that the structure was arched and there was sufficient space inside for a living room. The guide told me that in the ancient times this was the tax collector's office. Actually this cave, like several others, served as administrative offices.

On either side of the brick paved road were innumerable cave-like openings in the rocks supported by baked bricks. The caves were interconnected and were said to have served as a base for garrison troops and houses of officials. The road turned to the left and led to a magnificent eighty-eight feet high watch tower used for round-the-clock vigil against invaders. There were side rooms that once served as chambers for guards. The road snaked further past the tower to the royal temple. The ruins of the temple were in the form of four huge pillars in the center of which was a cone-like pagoda. It is believed that there was a huge statue of Buddha on top of the pagoda that could be reached by a flight of stairs.

A pagoda inside the ancient Jiaohe city in the Yarnaz Valley. The ruins are in the form of four huge pillars in the centre of which is a cone like pagoda. A huge statue of Buddha once adorned the top of the pagoda that could be reached by a flight of stairs.

Remains of stucco images of Buddha in the niches of a square stupa inside the Great Monastery of Jiaohe. Here the Buddha once sat cross-legged preaching and smiling down upon those who sought him. The ruined foundations of the square stupa have visible signs of hinges which once held a huge statue of the Buddha.

The road went further north towards the Great Monastery. Two huge mounds indicated that the gates must have been massive structures. Inside the gates stretched the vast expanse of a courtyard with an ancient well from which monks once drew water. Stairs led to the inner precincts of the Buddhist temple, the largest of its kind in the kingdom. It once had a huge Buddha statue on top of the square pagoda. The ruined foundations of some Buddha statues sitting cross-legged in preaching posture can still be seen in the niches of the square pagoda. There were traces of wall paintings in the niches. A look around the great monastery revealed living rooms of monks built of mud and large bricks, toilets with drains and an ancient well for the residents. A multitude of pagodas bunched together like a forest lay to the east. The highest of these could be ascended by a flight of stairs and commanded a bird's-eye view of the entire ancient city. It is believed that the relics of the Buddha lie beneath this pagoda.

A Cup of Sweet Water

Emerging from the ancient city we drove towards the Karez Paradise located in the Yal village in the western suburb of the city lying close to the Jiaohe city. There was a huge crowd at the underground spring. A large wooden wheel was drawing water from a stream and irrigating a grape corridor. Here several Uighur beauties clad in yellow and blue skirts with grape motifs were dancing and singing.

The path to the karez went across the stream and zigzaged under the cool and refreshing shade of a huge grape trellis. It sloped into an underground tunnel. We went down the karez several metres deep. A clear mountain stream coming straight from the Tienshan Mountains gushed into the tunnel. This was laboriously dug a thousand years ago by the local inhabitants in their bid to quench their thirst and channelise the mountain streams to irrigate their land.

After walking for several yards in the dark tunnel I came to a place where several metres above my head was an opening in the roof from where sunlight was streaming in. Actually this was the place where a well was dug to excavate mud from the karez tunnel. From this opening a bucket could be lowered to draw water from the stream flowing through the tunnel. In Turfan every household digs a well about twenty-metres deep to reach the karez (water channel) bringing cool fresh mineral water from the mountains. In the heat and fierce sandstorms of Turfan this underground water system prevents contamination and evaporation. This wondrous irrigation project is as famous as the Great Wall and the Canal System of China.

In order to understand the working of a karez I visited the nearby Karez Museum which displayed a model of karez and explained how it was dug and how mountain streams were tapped into the channels to irrigate fields and provide drinking water to the inhabitants. It is said that the karez system provides Turfan oasis with 220 million square cusecs of water every year and is therefore called 'the spring of life'.

I returned to the source of the stream at the foot of the Tienshan Mountain where Habib was waiting for me. A massive hole had been dug into the mountain walls to lead the stream into the karez channel. Here a huge crowd was waiting to taste the water. A glass sheet covered the channel to let people walk over it and actually see how the stream ran for hundreds of kilometres into fields and houses. A girl handed me a cup of mountain water for a yuan. It was sweet, clear and cold.

On returning to the exit point, there was a kiosk selling Turfan grape wine. I tasted some out of *Scent of a Woman* bottle, which was indeed very nice.

Corpses in Turfan Museum

After a great day at the grape valley and a tour of the ancient cities I wanted to see those who lay calmly in their after life—the ancient corpses found along the Silk Road. A study of these corpses has provided an important insight into the history and culture of the trade routes and the kind of people who trudged them. The bodies were preserved in air-conditioned chambers of the Turfan Museum, one of the largest in Xinjiang. It was several stories high and displayed antiquities from different parts of the province. At the entry there was a massive fossil of a dinosaur and other extinct mammals found in Xinjiang.

The corpses belonging to the fifth and the sixth century AD lie in the museum section dealing with Astana cemetery. I dreaded the whiff of putrid odour from the dead; I puckered my nose, but could smell nothing foul. The air inside seemed as pristine outside; I breathed easy thereafter. The air-conditioners worked non-stop to maintain a certain temperature to prevent the corpses from decaying. Surprisingly, the dead were in good shape; only the skin had wrinkled and dried up and clung to the bone. One young woman had a decorative comb in her bouffant. She must have spent hours in front of the mirror to arrange her hair in a chignon and stuck the comb to prevent any sinuous curls from falling on her forehead and marring her beauty. A

Buddhist monk in a brown robe lay with his begging bowl beside his body. He probably lived in one of the cave temples and begged for alms along the Silk Road. Perhaps, the bowl was his only belonging and he was buried alongwith it. Some coffins have couples buried together. One couple belonged to the Tang Dynasty dated AD 640, another Uigher couple dates back to AD 502-640 and a Mongolian couple dated to AD 502-640. The oldest corpse was that of a man hailing from the ancient city of Jiaohe and belonging to the first century BC.

The corpses and their fabric appeared fresh and well preserved, surprising because they must have weathered centuries of the desert's dry climate. There was pottery from Yarkhoto (Jiaohe) and Gaochang and tomb guards from the Astana cemetery.

We landed at the burial chambers of the Astana cemetery to check three graves opened for public viewing. The cemetery occupying an area of ten square kilometres was called an underground museum as plenty of historical relics had been found here. Since 1959 more than 400 graves have been excavated and studied. A number of human bodies were unearthed from the chambers and are now displayed in the Turfan Museum. The cemetery located in the north of Gaochang is said to have been the common graveyard for ancient inhabitants in the period from Western Jin dynasty to Tang dynasty (AD 200-800). Several nobles and royalty of Gaochang were buried here.

I entered the long, sloping rock-hewn staircase that went several metres below the ground into an underground passage leading into an earthen burial chamber. It was like a deep basement of a mud house with its four walls tapering like a cone a little above the ground. It was very cool due to natural air conditioning. Instead of a coffin there was a

FACING PAGE:
Steps lead inside the underground burial chamber at Astana cemetery near Turfan. Nobles and royalty of Gaochang city are said to have been buried here.

BELOW LEFT AND CENTRE: *Paintings retrieved by explorer Aurel Stein from burial chambers at Astana. It is believed to be of Fuxi and Nuwa.*
Another painting depicting two women in a garden.
BELOW RIGHT: *A brightly painted tomb guard. The fierce animal stood outside the grave to drive away evil spirits and prevent theft of valuables kept inside the burial chambers.*

bier made of bamboo. The dead were laid here wrapped in exquisite silk for their eternal sleep. Along with the body was buried the record of the person and numerous articles for his use in afterlife. Sometimes more than one person was placed inside the chamber. Tomb guards stood outside the grave to drive away evil spirits and prevent theft of valuables kept inside. Paintings, some of which exist to this day, adorned the walls.

Some of the chambers are believed to be royal tombs in which members of the ruling family were buried. According to the Turfan Museum records (*Turfan Museum* p.56) in Tomb 383 was buried Peng Jian, wife of Juqu Mengxun, king of the Northern Liang dynasty. In Tomb 177 was buried the Juqu Fengdai, prefect of the Gaochang prefecture.

When Aureal Stein went down into the burial chambers in 1914, he found biographical data of the dead inscribed in Chinese on special funereal bricks. He also found large quantities of beautiful silk in which the corpses were wrapped.[10]

The Amazing Royal Lady of Emin

Habib guided me to Emin Tower. I found a huge crowd at the thirty-seven-metre high tower. Tourists were racing up a long flight of spiral

stairs to reach the top from where they could view the entire city of Turfan. Also called the Sugong Tower, it was built by Suleman in 1776 in the memory of Emin Khoja, the prefectural king of Turfan. The pillar with a huge base tapers gradually to the top like a cone. Its surface was decorated with grey sun-dried bricks replete with geometrical patterns, water waves and flowers.

The dead lady was the most amazing antiquity lying in a small section of the museum near the tower. This thousand-year old mummy of a young Uighur woman was found inside the tomb of Imam Kazim, the famous ninth century missionary from Saudi Arabia. I asked Habib what a young woman was doing inside the tomb of the religious Imam? He said that she was probably forcibly put inside the coffin and buried along with the Imam. She may have been his consort and when the Imam died she must have been compelled to die and buried alongside. This was not an exception; in ancient times when an important person died his consorts and parlour maids were all buried in order to provide comforts in after life.

The young lady was strikingly beautiful; she was dressed in a regal maroon gown, embroidered shoes adorned her tiny feet. She had high cheek bones, a cream-and-peaches complexion and lovely tresses. Her mouth was wide open and her well-set teeth were visible. There was a touch of royalty around her, but it would be ridiculous to assume that she could have died so young or on her own accord. She must have been strangled, for her tongue was slightly protruding between her teeth. She lay in a glass case by the side of a large coffin. I looked at her and felt a little lump in my throat. I did not know her name; I had no idea what her life was before being forced to die. But I did feel sad for her. She would have grown into an exquisite woman for whom many a prince would have pined.

Murals and fabrics found in Lop area and woollen carpets of Turfan were also on display. Another section had pottery found near Karakash and from the tombs near Khotan, Sanpula, Bugei and Suwatkum. Shelves were stacked with Uighur writing equipment including a pen made of

At the grand Tower of Emin in Turfan. Also called the Sugong Tower, it was built by Suleman in AD 1776 in the memory of Emin Khoja, the prefectural king of Turfan. The towering cone like pillar is decorated with sun-dried bricks.

special wood and a wooden roof support found in Niya Kingdom.

There were bronze spoons and spades from Niya, arrows from Karakash, pots and fabrics from Sanpula cemetery. Ancient moulds and face masks found in Guma and displayed at the museum revealed that artistes used special moulds for making different parts of the body of Buddha; there were separate moulds for the ears, hands, torso of Buddha. The parts were created individually and then joined to form a symmetrical image. Not just body parts, there were moulds for ornaments that were used to embellish the image of bodhisattvas.

Back at the hotel I had an early dinner and booked my seat at the open-air theatre under a grape trellis. Here a group of musicians played lively folk music of the grape growers. Beautiful Uighur dancers in long skirts sang melodiously; they sang of the grapes that have ripened and the lovers who have not returned. The lovers arrived after much pining and joined the dancers. In a sweeping motion their hands extend to the grape trellis above, they pluck bunches of grapes and lovingly feed the young girls. The crowd, tipsy after several rounds of drinks, gleefully clapped and jumped onto the stage to join the whirling dancers. Humming the grape lovers' song I retired to my room. But before I hit the bed I had to pack several kilos of raisins and bottles of wine that I had bought in Turfan. The next day I had to leave the city of grapes. I did not want to. But I knew I had to.

The Highway A-314 loops along the northern fringes of the Taklamakan desert to reach the Korla oasis. The Iron Gate (above) is situated along the foot of the Tienshan mountains. A road actually goes under this gate and until recently caravans are reported to have taken the road east to Turfan and west to Kuqa.

(9)

To Korla on Desert Express

South-west of Turfan, the highway A314 (a branch of the NH A312) loops along the northern fringes of the Taklamakan desert to Korla oasis, which was my next destination on the Silk Road. But Habib was not too confident of the road and we therefore headed to the Turfan station in the evening to catch the N 944 train to Korla.

I was excited to travel to the place that I had read so much about. We had to drive fifty kilometres from the city to get to the station. After driving about forty-three kilometres on the Urumqi highway we turned right and took a narrow road that led to the railway station at Dahiyan. To avoid the fierce desert winds we arrived early and made ourselves comfortable in the waiting room which, with its huge lobby and swank toilets, looked more like a hotel. The walls were covered with silk carpets depicting pictorial motifs of the famous musicians from Kuqa playing instruments and royal hunting scenes. In a corner of the hall was a well-stocked bar with Turfan grape wine, Maotai vodka and dry fruits. At another counter silk garments and embroidered linen were on sale. Since I had arrived early I needed to while away hours; I spent some lovely moments admiring the splendid carpets which were unrolled one by one by a female railway staff. Her diligence surprised me, she knew I still had a long way to go along the Silk Road and could not have lugged the carpets, but she still showed me everything as if I was the first buyer. The train arrived at 11.30 pm and foreign passengers for Korla and onwards were led down to the platform and guided to their compartments. There was no panic, shouting or jostling. I spent the night comfortably in a soft seat.

Actually my destination was Karashahr (called Yanki), south-west of Turfan, which was the ancient kingdom of Agni or Okini. Unfortunately, the midnight express train did not halt here. Instead, it hurtled further south-west for about a hundred kilometres to the petrochemical city of Korla early next morning.

It was very windy outside the Silver Star Hotel. After checking in I sat on the porch waiting for the taxi to return after refuelling. I planned to take the road straightaway to Yanki, (Karashahr) about sixty kilometres north-east from Korla.

The Iron Gate Pass through which the ancient trade route ran. The pass lies at the entrance to the Kongqu River that flows alongside. The gate and the double storied structure adjacent to it are a memorial to the original Iron gate Pass.

Xuanzang's Agni

The place was called Agni in Sanskrit; in his memoirs Xuanzang calls it Okini.[1] It is said that after leaving the kingdom of Gaochang the monk passed through the oasis town of Toksun and arrived at Agni in AD 630. In his travelogues he describes Okini as a place surrounded by hills where numerous streams that mingle were channelised to irrigate the fields. The soil was rich for red millet, winter wheat, scented dates, grapes, pear, and plum. About the people, the monk writes that they went about in shorn locks and without head dress.

He found ten or more sangharams with 2000 priests of the little vehicle of the school of Sarvastivadas. 'The doctrine of the Sutras and the requirements of the Vinay are in agreement with those of India'[2] and 'the books from which they study are the same'. The written character (the script), according to the monk was, with a few differences like that of India.

Another great explorer and traveler of British India, Sir Francis Younghusband (1863-1942) passed through 'Korlia' in 1887 on his interesting overland journey from Manchuria via Beijing to India through

Chinese Turkestan (now Xinjiang).

He described Korla as a pretty town along the river bank covered with trees and cultivated fields more than in any other town he had passed.[3] Maize, rice and wheat were the main crops of this well cultivated and prosperous town. There was a small Chinese town, about four hundred yards square with mud walls about thirty-five feet high and a mile south was the Turk town, but its walls were in ruins.

Bad Road

Surprisingly, Habib had never heard the name Karashahr or Yanki. Having read in *Si-Yu-Ki* that the place was near Lake Bagrash I decided to leave for the great lake, now called Lake Boston.

On the way to the lake I crossed the Korla river and the Iron Gate on a detour. The road was rutted but the landscape was so beautiful that I ignored the bumps. The lakes had been formed by the mountain streams and were full of pink and purple lotuses. Wild water fowls swam happily, dipping their beaks for a mouthful of shrimps. Small wild birds flew over the surface or sat on the flowers looking for insects.

The road soon ran through village Tashidian, a picture of immense beauty. The fields were covered with blooming sunflowers, which were not meant for vases, they were pressed for edible oil. In another village I saw tonnes of red juicy tomatoes hanging in green houses that lined the streets. Very soon they would be plucked and turned into ketchup and juice in a nearby tomato factory. We then hit Hoshit, an oasis town on river Hoshit; its 'industrial town' tag evident in the massive ongoing construction work.

Near the lake the fields were aflame with heaps of red chillies laid out on the sand to dry under the harsh sun. Together they looked like a red carpet spread under the heaven's blue canopy. I got off the car to shoot the massive hill of chillies lying against a backdrop of the poplar forests at the foot of the snowy Tienshan. Women labourers were unloading the chillies from trucks and spreading them out on the sand while others had settled for a quick lunch under the scanty shade of a date palm tree.

Lake Bagrash, the Hawaii of Xinjiang

As we turned right from the main road towards Lake Bagrash I noticed the unending fields laden with watermelons (hamigua and seagua). I reached Jinshatan Beach Resort on the lake where hundreds of holidayers had arrived. While many were circling the lake on speedboats, others were sunbathing on the golden sand. Once inside the premises of the holiday resort, we drove along a narrow road running parallel to a stream that crossed a tomato farm and joined the lake.

The massive fresh water lake rises upwards to meet the sky. Blue merges with blue while a thick grey mist envelops the snowy mountains. The lake with its beautiful resorts was called the Hawaii of Xinjiang. Bagrash or Boston, the largest lake in Xinjiang, is fed by the Kaidu river and forms the source of Kongqu or the Peacock river. Situated in Buohu county, it is the largest inland fresh water lake in China with an elevation of 1000 metres, covering a total area of about 1000 square kms. Surrounded by small lakes, this lake looks colossal like a sea.

The kingdom of Yanki was, even in ancient times, famous for a variety of fish, fresh water mussels, shrimps and oysters and even today adds to the allure of a great seafood platter for the tourists.

Heaps of red chillies left out on the hot sand to dry up in the deserts of Korla.

In a Speedboat

While Habib rested in a shop on the beach, I walked up to the jetty, put on a life jacket and hopped into a waiting speedboat along with three other tourists from Singapore. The boat whirred loudly, leapt into the air, and landed with a thud on the surface of the lake. We were drenched in a jet of icy water but took several rounds of the lake exploring the flora and other aquatic life. Fish farms had also been cultivated on the periphery.

Tourists enjoy a boat ride on the massive fresh water Lake Bagrash. The lake with its beautiful resorts is called the 'Hawaii of Xinjiang'. It is the largest lake in Xinjiang fed by the Kaidu river and forms the source of the Kongqu or the Peacock River.

I took my seat under an umbrella on the sand and ordered some grilled fish from the nearby restaurant. The menu was large, it was difficult to pick from the water mussels, oysters, carp, shrimps... I ordered Bohu fish, the delicacy of Boston. A group from Hangzhow (near Shanghai) was engrossed in a game of cards on the sand and invited me to join them. They spoke English and told me about the beautiful West Lake in Hangzhow. They were amazed to know that I had stayed on the West Lake and taken a ferry ride by moonlight only a few years ago.

It was evening when I arrived back in Korla. I stopped at the Xinhua bookshop and asked for an English translation of classical Chinese poetry. It was expensive but I was ready to shell out the precious yuans as the anthology included my favourite poets Li Bei and Wang Wei, among twenty others.

Iron Gate Pass

Early next morning we drove twenty-seven kilometres north from the city to reach the Iron Gate pass through which the ancient trade route ran. A steep ravine, the pass lies at the entrance to the Kongqu river that flows along the road. The massive gate with green eaves was built on the road that goes through the mountains. The gate and the double-storey structure adjacent to it are a memorial to the original Iron Gate pass.

The travellers on the northern branch of the Silk Road coming from the Gansu corridor and traversing through Hami and Turfan had to pass the Iron Gate in order to go westwards to Kuqa and Kashgar on their onward journey to India in the south or to take a westerly route from Kashgar to cross into Tajik territory. They halted at the Iron Gate and paid tax on the caravan goods.

The mountains at the pass looked silvery grey and I wondered if the silver mountains described by the Xuanzang in the kingdom of Agni were the ones that I was seeing. Once upon a time silver was dug from these mountains. I climbed up the ravines to get a feel of the high mountains. On the top I found the tombs of two lovers, Thyre and

Zohra. I learnt about their tragic love story: Zohra, the daughter of a rich tax collector at the Iron Gate, fell in love with Thyre, the son of a poor farmer. But not many were happy about the mismatch; the lovers knew that their love would never reach fruition and killed themselves.

The Iron Gate was a symbol of struggle that the early travellers on the Silk Road had to undergo. The biggest danger was the brigands who plundered and killed travellers. There was a dearth of potable water and the travellers were scared of this stretch of land running at the foot of the mountains. Many a caravan had negotiated this rough stretch with great suffering but managed to tread on.

A road actually goes under this gate and caravans, till recently are reported to have taken the road to Turfan in the East and Kuqa in the west along the foot of the Tienshan mountains. The pass is at a strategic spot at the entrance to the Tarim basin. The mountain is steep; a river flows along the pass and falls from great height into the plains below. By the side of the river tourists huts had been erected for visitors who might want to spend the day here.

The evening at Korla was leisurely. I arrived at the beautiful Korla river front where luxury boats were waiting for tourists. Many couples were sitting on the steps that descend into the river. A beautiful double-storey yellow boat shaped like a dragon was ready to leave for a night cruise.

The river front was a nice place to spend the evening. There was music and dance. A young man was gyrating to the beat of a Chinese song. A crowd had collected under the grape trellis to watch him perform. Encouraged by the spectators he climbed onto the rostrum set up for the evening gala show on the river front.

The boulevard runs for about two kilometres along the river bank. As the sun set there was loud music and more crowds. A cool breeze from the river heightened the pleasure of an evening walk along the boulevard. I sat along the steps listening to music and soaked in the flavours of Korla.

The small oasis of Korla was like a village—an insignificant place until oil was struck here. Surprisingly, it does not find mention even in Xuanzang's travelogue despite the fact that the Iron Gate pass was located near the village. It was Karashahr (Yanki) near Lake Boston that was an important site on the Silk Road. With the discovery of rich oil fields the place became an important town next only to Urumqi. In the 1960s it was established as the capital of the Bayingolin Mongolian Autonomous covering one-fourth of the entire territory of Xinjiang. Today, the city is dotted with numerous skyscrapers, beautiful river fronts and parks. Considered one of the richest cities in China, it is connected to all parts of Xinjiang by good roads, telecommunication and civil aviation network. It sits on a huge reserve of oil and with the opening of the Tarim oil field Korla has become one of the richest petrochemical centres of China.

You can see drilling going on, but fortunately modernisation has not blemished the beautiful landscape. Lying at the base of the Kurutag mountains the oasis with its numerous streams and fertile soil is considered to be the fruit and vegetable belt of the desert, with scented soft pears being the most sought after. From early summer to late autumn there is a regular supply of hamigua, seagua, pomegranate, peaches, walnut and apricots.

Amidst the glistening skyscrapers, newly-surfaced roads and the polished boulevards, one can find paths leading into the mountains and caravans of camel laden with watermelons and pears gently trudging along the side walks. On the fringes of the city are natural lakes full of white and pink lotus and wild water fowls. A scene of beauty straight out of a postcard.

A view of the Kizil site at Kuqa where visitors from all over the world flock to see the exquisite wall paintings still preserved inside the Buddhist caves cut into sides of the Mingutag hills along the Mozart River. The grottoes are believed to have been dug in the third century and are among the earliest caves in China.

(10)

Kuqa—the City of Kumarjiva

I left Korla early the next morning after bidding farewell to Thyre and Zohra who lay in their graves on the top of mountains. As I began my journey to Kuqa 300 kilometres on Highway A 314, a splendid scenery unfolded before my eyes. Different from the drive through the Gobi, we were now travelling through the Taklamakan desert, the land of death from where travellers seldom returned. But that was long, long ago. The terrain was no longer arduous, there was a four-lane road running through the desert.

I was passing through the fruit belt between Korla and Kuqa and could see yellowish-green pears and red pomegranates hanging from small shrubby trees. To my right the snow peaks of the Tienshan melted into streams that appeared like twisted ribbons that were sucked in by the orchards and thirsty maize fields of the numerous villages lining the foothills.

Desert Rain

I was in for more surprise; rain suddenly lashed the desert. First, large drops came shooting down on the windscreen and later there was a downpour. The torrents followed us into Kuqa. Habib told me that it seldom rained in the desert and we were very lucky. The temperature suddenly plummeted from forty degrees to a cool twenty-five.

On the way we passed through Yengisar where women sat on both sides of the road with heaps of hamigua, seagua and apricots, picked from orchards in the nearby oasis villages. There was fruit everywhere; it was the perfect time to come to Xinjiang. At village Buguar the roadside was stacked with vegetables growing near a stream. But in the pouring rain, there were no takers for the high mounds of brinjals, lettuce, cabbage, yellow carrots and tomatoes. Suddenly, we felt hungry. We had not eaten anything since morning. We looked for a dry place to sit for a short lunch but all roadside restaurants were soaked with rain.

We soon came across a bridge on a huge stream that we later found out was the Subashi river. The scenery was breathtakingly beautiful. The snowy peaks of the Tienshan seemed to have descended on the road and numerous streams gushed out like rivers of milk. Thick green forests of poplar grew on both sides. Just below the pearly ranges there was a line of purple and orange hills which added to the beauty of this emerald river valley.

Lunching in the Subashi Valley

We decided to have lunch here. Looking around Habib found a small village eatery and settled down in its outer courtyard from where we had a full view of the mountains and the river valley. The hostess welcomed us with steaming jasmine tea. Soon a large plateful of hamiguas arrived, followed by several courses of spiced brinjals, noodles, *naan* with mutton gravy and sweet buns.

By the side of the courtyard a rubber pipe carried a mountain stream to the footsteps of the eatery. Cool, refreshing and sweet, the water gushed forth as if some pump had been working on the mountains. Nearby was a large cattle shed where a dozen cows and donkeys had been locked up. Outside the cattle enclosure soup was being prepared for the cattle. Leftovers from the restaurant were being boiled in a large aluminum pot on a kerosene stove. It looked and smelled awful but was considered good food for milch cattle. Adjacent to the shed was a toilet where wooden planks had been set on a deep trench that had not been cleaned for months. I peeped inside but could not bear the sight or the stench. I remembered the story of an American who had fallen into a similar trench when the wooden plank broke and had to be rescued!

Habib told me that Kuqa was just about thirty minutes away. At many villages heaps of coal had been deposited by the side of the road. These had been mined on the other side of the mountains and kept there for quick delivery to purchasers.

We travelled non-stop to our hotel where there were no porters to pull out our heavy suitcases. We dragged them out and carried them over the double landing to my room. Immediately after, I regretted having bought several bottles of wine and five kilos of raisins in Turfan.

Kumarjiva–the Brilliant Monk

I learnt that Kuqa had quite a history not only because of its position on the Silk Road and being the capital of the ancient kingdom of Quici but also that it was the home of the towering monk Kumarjiva (AD 343-413). He is said to have played an important role in the expansion of Buddhism in Central Asia and China. His virtues were such that the kings fought over him. According to Saroj Kumar Chaudhuri (*Lives of Early Buddhist Monks*) not only was he brilliant but also 'handsome as a god'– a deadly combination. Chinese emperor Fu Chien of the Tsin dynasty in AD 383 sent a large force to attack Kuqa giving orders to his general Lu Kuang to 'bring Kumarjiva as quickly as possible'. Lu Kuang defeated Kuqa, killed the king and captured Kumarjva and brought him to China where the monk was appointed 'guru of the nation'.[1]

Chaudhuri says (*Lives of Early Buddhist Monks*) that kings, monks and the laity were in so much awe of his brilliance and knowledge that 'nobody dared to sit above him'.[2] 'Whenever he delivered some religious discourse, kings kneeled down beside his seat so that he could step on their knees to take his seat'.[3]

Kumarjiva who was recognised as an encyclopaedia of Indian learning including knowledge of the Vedas and 'heretical shastras' (Charles Eliot in *Hinduism and Buddhism*)[4] was also well versed in astronomy and mathematics. In addition he had the miraculous power of divination and whatever he said proved to be correct.[5]

Writing about the parentage of the great monk, B.N. Puri (*Buddhism in Central Asia*), tells us that Kumarjiva's father Kumarayana joined the Buddhist order and left his home in search of enlightenment. Crossing the harsh terrain of the Pamirs he arrived in Kuqa where he was appointed the royal priest. He married Jiva, the sister of the king of Kuqa; their son was christened Kumarjiva. After Kumarjiva completed his studies on Buddhist literature and philosophy under Bandhudatta at Kashmir he returned to Kuqa with his mother after visiting various centres of Buddhist learning in Central Asia.[6]

We find mention about Kuqa in Sir Charles Eliot's *Hinduism and Buddhism*. During the Western Tsin dyasty (AD 265-317) it was described as 'a seat of Buddhism'. It was 'enclosed by a triple wall and contained a thousand stupas and Buddhist temples...'[7]

Wu-K'ung who visited Kuqa in AD 788 mentioned an Abbot who spoke with equal fluency the language of the country, Chinese and Sanskrit.[8]

Xuanzang Accepts Grape Juice

It was here that the great Chinese monk was given a rousing reception by the king and the Kuqean priests who had brought grape juice for him.[9] It is said that in the seventh century when Xuanzang passed through the Taklamakan desert to Kuqa the king accompanied by his ministers and a celebrated priest Mokshagupta came to meet him. Several thousand priests gathered at the eastern gate of the city to welcome him. Here they had erected a pavilion inside which they placed a statue of Buddha.

Xuanzang worshipped the Buddha and stayed in Kuqa for about two months as he had to wait for the snow to melt in the mountain passes.

He mentioned in his records that the soil was suitable for rice and corn. It produced grapes, pomegranates, numerous species of plums, pears, peaches and almonds. Minerals like gold, copper, iron and lead and tin were also found here.

He further mentioned (S. Beal; *The Life of Xuanzang* by *Shaman Hwui Li*) that the style of writing was Indian and the Kuqeans excelled in playing music especially the lute and pipe. They wore garments of embroidered silk and cut their hair and wore a flowing covering. There were a hundred convents with five thousand and more disciples, belonging to the Little Vehicle of the school of Sarvastivadas.

Wild Camels on Way to Kizil Caves

The following day I got up early to leave for the world-famous Kizil cave temples called the bright pearl on the Silk Road. The Kizil caves were among the four groups of grottoes lying within the territory of Kuqa which go by the name of Quici grottoes. They were among the earliest cave temples in China whose digging started in the third century. Currently, they are 236 in all of which 135 caves are in a good condition. However, very few are open to the public.

Taking Highway A 217 we drove for about eighty kilometres to reach the famous grottoes in the county of Baichung. On the way we came across a high beacon tower and large herds of double-humped camels grazing on the low bushes in the desert. Habib told me that the animal was a precious gem for the desert-dwellers as it could go without food and water for weeks. If there was no green fodder it could survive on thorns, dry wood as no other animal could. It also knew how to draw water from beneath the seemingly dry and prickly bushes of the desert. And that lovely hump on the camels back not only provided excellent meat but when sliced and dipped in hot tea it gave delicious butter.

We stopped the car and got down to see the ancient tower and mingle with the shy creatures. I wanted to feel the soft, silken hair on their long neck which Habib said could be woven into carpets. Before we could get

near them the camels lifted their head from the bushes and stared at us for a while in amazement. But they were not amused; very soon they started running towards us; scared, we ran for our lives and hopped into the car.

We left the highway and turned right towards the township of Kizil.

On entering the cave area we were greeted by a huge black statue of the celebrated Indian monk Kumarajiva. He wore a monk's chivar and sat on an inverted lotus. His head was shaved and in great modesty he lowered it in a shy gesture. The statue was set up in front of the Kizil caves in 1994.

High up on the mountain cliffs of the Mingutag the Kizil grottoes are reached only by wooden ladders. The caves present a 'heavenly world' of the Buddha, bodhisattvas and apsaras and devas depicted in the murals. The famous music of Kuqa still reverberates inside the caves.

RIGHT: Herds of wild double-humped camels graze on low shrubs in the Taklamakan Desert. along the National Highway A-217. In the absence of food and water in the desert these wild animals can survive even on thorns and dry wood.

BELOW: A colossal statue in black marble of the celebrated Indian monk Kumarjiva (AD 343-413) greets visitors at the entrance of the Kizil caves at Kuqa. Apart from its strategic position on the Silk Road Kuqa was also famous as the hometown of this brilliant monk. He was recognised as an encyclopaedia of Indian learning.

To the left of the statue were the Mingutag hills the sides of which had been cut into barrel-shaped caves with vaulted roofs. The monks and merchants chose the site with great care—river Mozart flowed nearby and the mountains were made of soft rocks so that they could be easily cut. The cliff provided safety from wild animals. From the roundabout of the Kumarjiva statue I moved towards the caves. But near the wide stairs at the entry gate I had to deposit the cameras as photography was strictly prohibited. I waited outside cave number one for the local guide to arrive with keys as the caves were locked.

Unique Style of Kuqa Art

Perched high on the hill side, the caves were reached by steps cut into the rocks or by ladders. Most caves consisted of an outer room or the front room and an inner room called the main room. Most of the outer rooms were roofless and looked like open verandahs, though the inner rooms were still intact. They had a central column with a niche where once sat the preaching or the meditating Buddha. Two narrow passages on either side of this central pillar called the circumambulatory passages, led to an inner chamber where a huge platform against the back wall once held the Nirvana Buddha. There were sculptures of Buddha and other deities in several other niches of the walls.

It seemed that the life in these ancient caves had not dimmed over the centuries. One became a part of the heavenly world of the Buddha, bodhisattvas, apsaras, devas, benevolent kings and also of the animal world depicted across the mud walls. Blue, brown and green rock colours had been used profusely, though red had turned black over the ages. In many caves mud had been splashed on the bodies of deities to disfigure them. The murals drawn from the Jataka stories, Buddhist sutras and folktales prevailing in India form a popular motif on the walls and the arched roof. Most of the pictorial representation had been done inside rhombic checks which imparted novelty to the paintings inside the Kizil caves. The stories, full of pious legends and worldly wisdom were believed to be helpful in propagating the Dhamma to the vast audience who came to the grottoes.

The beautifully painted cave walls portrayed a picture of a blissful paradise. There were drawings of human figures, Buddhist deities and apsaras in sensuous apparel, some naked, some half-clad against a backdrop of gardens full of flowering trees. Here the deer roamed and the birds sang. Apsaras danced in gay abandon, female figures with exposed breasts sat listening to the sermons of bodhisattvas, while blissful lovers played the lute or the *pipa* in an intimate posture.

There were about a hundred Jataka stories painted inside rhombic checks. It is said that Kuqean art had absorbed influences from Persia, China and India. This was because in the middle of the seventh century AD a large number of Persians fled Persia and sought sanctuary in Kuqa as the Sasanian empire had collapsed. At about the same time the town was brought under Chinese control and became the headquarters for the entire Tarim basin.[10]

Mount Sumeru

I entered Cave 1 that had two chambers, a main chamber in front and a back chamber connected with the main through two narrow passages on either side of central pillar. In the niche of the pillar once sat an image of the Buddha supported by plinths resting in the numerous holes in wall. The pillar which supported the cave was corrugated and designed as the Mount Sumeru, the heavenly abode of the gods. Describing Mount Sumeru, Xuanzang said that 'its stands up in the middle of the great sea firmly fixed on a circle of gold around which the sun and the moon revolve and where the gods live'.[11]

The dominant theme of this cave portrayed the Buddha in the '*Dharmachakrapravartana mudra*', or 'Turning the Wheel of Law'. On the side walls were painted three groups of bodhisattvas being preached

Nude art is said to have been prevalent in Kuqa when the caves were cut. Wall painting in a cave showing half-clad devotees listening to the Sermon. A female devotee standing in the middle is wearing diaphanous fabric.

by the Buddha. The human figures had high noses, large eyes and a top knot on the head. There were flying apsaras on the arched ceiling dancing in joy on hearing the sermons. As He taught the 'end of suffering and Nirvana; the truth of suffering and Dukkha; the cause of suffering and the Noble Path' a soothing light seemed to have illuminated the heavenly realm above. The gods of the Sun, Moon, Fire and Wind, depicted on the roof of the cave rejoiced. It appeared as if Brahma himself was rejoicing on seeing the Buddha heeding to his request to preach the Law. According to Buddhist legend, five weeks following his awakening Buddha remained seated under the Bodhi tree and other trees in the vicinity in great ecstasy. Even as he rejoiced, he debated whether or not he should teach others what he had attained. This conflict was resolved when Brahma appeared before Buddha and requested him to preach the Law.[12]

There were rows of sitting Buddhas apparently pointing to the 'Miracle of Sravasti'. The Buddha is said to have performed this miracle before an audience consisting of the king of Kosala in response to a challenge from non-believers. Levitating on a thousand petalled lotus he caused fire and water to leap out of his body and multiplied his person a million times in air.[13]

The four main rock colours used were red, black, blue and green. The walls of the cave had high niches in which once stood sixteen donors and sixteen swordsmen. The back chamber had a raised platform on which once lay the Nirvana Buddha. On the wall above the platform were painted several kings and royal personages who were mourning the Great Decease. Semi-clad deities wearing crowns were showering flowers on Buddha. To complete the scene of the *Parinirvana* of Buddha a *Salavana* had also been painted in the Nirvana Hall.

Flying apsaras on the ceiling of a cave dancing and singing joyously and showering petals on the main image of Buddha below. The apsaras are bare-breasted and are clad in the Indian dhoti.

Dormitory for Monks

I followed the guide to Cave 10 where the main door led through a very narrow corridor to a dark room which was once a dormitory for the monks. A raised platform on the right side of the room was meant to be a bed for at least four monks. Opposite the bed was a large hole in the lower part of the left wall said to be the fireplace. It was from this dormitory that Korean researcher Han le Ran conducted his research on the Kizil caves and the murals. His students also assisted him in his work and researched, recorded and excavated seventy-five caves and copied the paintings. Such a dormitory structure was repeated in Cave 18.

While some caves are closed to the public, many lie crushed and fallen. Many new caves are also being discovered under the debris of fallen structures, including Cave 15 in 1994. It was in the form of a single room and here was a modern Buddha statue presented and placed in the cave by a Japanese monk.

Jataka Tales

It is said that the Kizil caves are 'a sea of Jataka stories'. This is true of Cave 17 which has interesting wall paintings depicting the birth stories of Buddha in his previous incarnation. Animals bring life to this cave as most Jatakas are fables about animals who have either noble human traits or are as evil as humans. One can see monkeys frolicking on trees, a bear caught in a snow-storm, a hunter chasing a game on horseback. Deer listening to sermons in a park having all kinds of flowering trees bringing to mind the Deer Park at Sarnath. There is also a wicked crocodile being speared to death by a fish feeder and his wife. The story from Vikannaka Jataka (no.233) tells us about the fish-eating crocodile who was ordered to be killed by the bodhisattva king of Benaras.

A beautiful elephant in another rhombus reminds one of the royal elephant Chhadanta.[14] The story goes that the bodhisattva was born as a six-tusked elephant and lived in the Himalyas with his two wives, Mahasubhadda and Chullasubhadda. The latter was jealous of Mahasubhada who was the favourite of Chhadanta. In her next birth Cullasubhada sent a hunter to cut off the beautiful tusks of Chhadanta.

In another rhombus sits the emaciated meditating Buddha being offered sweet *kheer* by Sujata. It is believed that prince Siddharth in order to attain Enlightenment and become a Buddha applied himself to self-mortification and severe austerities. His body was reduced to a skeleton. His arms and legs resembled dried twigs and his spinal cord looked like a string of beads and his belly touched his spinal column. After six long years he realised the futility of self-mortification and decided to give up austerities. At that time Sujata had came to a banyan grove to make the offerings of milk and rice. Seeing a holy man under the tree she gave the offerings to him.[15]

Another scene showing a royal personage riding away on a horse is said to be a depiction of prince Siddharth leaving his palace at Kapilvastu on the back of his favourite horse, Kantaka.

The cave had a front room, a main room and a back room. The central pillar inside the main room had a niche which once held the devotional image of the Buddha. On the right wall was the painting of Buddha preaching his disciples.

There were other stories of the 'Sarvadaan', depicting a king who gave away everything in alms. He was like prince Vesantara[16] who was known for his generosity and charity. He even gave away the supernatural elephant gifted with the power of bringing rain to the kingdom. For doing this the prince was exiled. Another pious and generous king was Sibi, the king who tore out his eyes and gave them to a Brahmana.

At another place sits the Greek king Milind or Menander[17] from Bactria who ruled over North-west India from around 155 BC-130 BC. The scene seems to have been picked up from the '*Milinda Panha*' (Questions of King Milinda) where the king is debating with the Buddhist monk, Nagsen.

It is said that Nagsena[18] was a disciple of Ven. Dhammarakshita and had mastered the Buddhist doctrines. Once he journeyed to Sagal (Sialkot) the capital of Milind, in the company of 80,000 monks and was staying at the Sankheya monastery. When the king learnt of the arrival of the famous monk he arranged a debate with him in order to

It is said that the Kuqa caves are a 'sea of Jataka stories' inside rhombic checks. This is the unique style of Kuqa art. The above painting portrays the Mahakapi Jataka.

test his knowledge of Buddhist theories regarding 'soullessness', the 'nature of man and his survival after death...'[19] Another rhombus depicts the story of brothers who killed the dragon and saved their country. There is the story of a woodcutter who requited kindness with cruelty.

On the front wall sits the Maitreya Buddha preaching in Tusita heaven. He is surrounded by numerous bodhisattvas listening to his sermon. The roof carries the entire cosmic order of the Buddha. In the backroom was the Nirvana scene. Here was a high platform on which once lay the Reclining Buddha. The image seems to have been cut away. On the wall, among other mourners crying and mourning the 'Great Deacease' is the portrayal of the 'Mahasravaka' Kasyapa, the great disciple of Buddha. His face distorted and eyes in deep sorrow. It is said[20] that at the cremation ground in Kusinara when the great Master's body was placed on the 'sweet-scented' pyre, a lighted lamp was applied thrice but the pyre did not catch fire. This was believed to be due to the power of Kasyapa's wish to see the holy remains of the Buddha as he was still travelling on the road to Kusinara. The moment he reached the cremation ground and paid his obeisance to the deceased Buddha that the pyre immediately caught fire.

There is a vivid portrayal of the dissensions in the Buddhist Order led by Devadutta who wanted the Buddha to give up the leadership of the Buddhist Sangha to him. He even conspired to kill Buddha.

The back wall of the pillar carried the story of the king and the mad elephant depicting Devadutta who let loose a mad elephant at Buddha. It is said that at Rajgir there was an elephant named Nalagiri which was fierce and killed humans. Devadutta went to his stable and told the elephant keeper to let loose the animal when Buddha passed by. On seeing the mad elephant Buddha was not perturbed. He caused 'his love to pervade Nalagiri who put down his trunk and stood still before Buddha'. The animal then lifted the dust from the feet the of Buddha and sprinkled it over its head.[21]

Similarly Cave 32 has the unique painting depicting the struggle between the Devadutta and Buddha. It showed Devadutta hurling a huge stone at Buddha. It was outside one of the caves at the Griddhakutta in Rajgir that a large rock was hurled by Devadutta to kill Buddha. Buddha had a narrow escape but was injured. He was taken down the hill to the Mardakkukshi where the royal physician Jivak nursed him.[22]

The Celestial Musicians

We also learn that Kuqa was specially famous for its music. Native artists from Kuqa sang and danced at the Imperial Court.[23] In Susan Whitfield's *Life Along the Silk Road*[24] we come across the courtesan Larishka who belonged to Kuqa and had been trained as an entertainer. The story set in AD ninth century tells us how from childhood Larishka attended classes in music, singing and dancing. She specialised in the Kuqean lute, a four-stringed instrument.

Writes Whitfield[25] that Kuqean music was famed along the Silk Road, from Samarkand to Changan. Kuqean singers could also sing in Sanskrit and many musical dramas had their origin in India. The title of some songs 'South India' and 'Watching the Moon in Brahman Land' indicated their Indian origin.

The pictorial representation of dance and music for which Kuqa was so famous found ample space on the walls of Kizil. The beautiful, lively and scantily attired apsaras were depicted in various dance postures. They symbolised the beautiful women of Kuqa who were gifted musicians and dancers and were patronised by the kings and aristocrats. Even the common people and monks had great love for music and they sang hymns in the praise of Buddha and other deities.

The famous Cave 38 is called the Musicians cave. Here a dark half-clad devata was playing a musical instrument something like the *veena* and a beautiful, white skinned female apsara who was bare breasted and bejewelled played the lute. To me they seemed to come straight from the *Canda Kinnara Jataka*[26] where '*Canda kinaras*' or moon fairies lived in the mountain caves and played by the silvery stream. They anointed themselves with perfumes, ate the pollen of flowers, clothed themselves

Kuqa was famous for its music. Native artistes from Kuqa sang and danced at imperial courts. The singers could sing in Sanskrit and many musical dramas had their origin in India. The famous Cave 38 is called the Musicians Cave. Here a dark half-clad devata *is playing the* veena *and a beautiful white-skinned* apsara *is playing the lute.*

in flower petals and made a swing of plant creepers. They played sweet music on a bamboo flute, singing and dancing by the side of the stream. Just the kind of setting that the hills and streams of Kizil could have offered.

It also reminded me of the dark Krishna and his beloved Radha playing the flute in a blissful state–a scene right out of the twelfth century Indian poet Jayadeva's *Geetgovinda*. The dark devata and his consort were lost in the blissful moment like Jayadeva's Krishna and Radha in their love for each other. But the central deity in the cave was the Buddha himself and the celestial musicians were playing divine music in obeisance to him.

The musician couple was depicted in various dancing postures. The bare upper half of their body was covered with heavy jewellery. From their ornate head dress they appeared to be royal courtesans or heavenly musicians. They wore beautiful gem-studded crowns. Hanging from their ears were large rings or 'kundals' and droplets of coloured gems clasped their necklace. Golden chains adorned their forehead and bangles played on their wrists. The doe-eyed male played the Pipa while the female musician blew into a bamboo flute. They also danced and sang joyously. As a soft breeze blew from the whispering wind god above, the wild birds danced in a moonlit sky and joined the celestial couple with their chirpings. Sadly, many apsaras had their lovely faces splashed with mud and disfigured.

An interesting story of the Mahakapi Jataka[27] was represented on the walls of the main room. A monkey formed a bridge over a river by stretching his body and several monkeys were seen climbing over him to cross the river. The noble monkey is believed to be a bodhisattva born as chief of the monkey tribe. This tribe lived on the sweet fruits of a mango tree by the side of the river Ganga in the Himalayan region. When the king learnt about the sweet fruits he surrounded the tree with his soldiers. The chief monkey, in order to save his tribe, formed a bridge over the river by tying a bamboo shoot to his waist and stretching his body to the other end of the tree. All escape but Devadutta, rival of

Buddha who was also born a monkey crushed him under his weight by jumping over his body. The king took pity on the chief monkey and brought him down. Before his death the monkey delivered a discourse to the king.

Huge Buddha Cave

Cave 47, at 16.5 meters high, is the largest cave temple in Kizil. It once had a huge image of standing Buddha like the Bamiyan Buddha but is said to have been built earlier than the Bamiyan. One can only guess the size of the huge Buddha image from the remaining holes in the walls which once held it. The hall is colossal. The roof of the hall has a window with a ten-metre long Reclining Buddha inside. The wall is adorned with a Naga couple, flying apsaras, a meditating Buddha and a unique painting of Mokshavajra.

Cave 48 has a central pillar and a painting of Mogallana, a favourite disciple of Buddha. Bejewelled flying devatas with halos round their head have been depicted on the vaulted ceiling. Draped in exquisite dress with the upper half of their bodies unclad and floating in the air, they are making offerings to Buddha. The apsaras with exquisite wings are bare breasted and full-figured. They are all in the act of making offerings to the central image of Buddha which has been cut away and stolen from the central pillar.

Nude Art at Kizil

Many wall paintings at Kizil provide evidence of nude art prevalent in Kuqa in the third century AD. There are female figures in diaphanous fabric listening to the sermons of Buddha and bodhisattvas, naked apsaras floating in ether worshipping devas. Even the male figures were half naked. According to critics, the recurrent appearance of the nude female images in Kuqa murals was to convince believers that only through total detachment from the mundane life and lust could they achieve enlightenment and attain salvation.

Two different origins of the art have been traced by Feng Fei, historian and art critic. According to one school the Quici nude art had its origin in India, while some trace its origins to Greece. A third school of thought traced the art to the Quici people themselves.

According to Feng Fei, nude art was already prevalent in China when the Kuqa caves were cut. This was proved by the discovery of nude terracotta figurines, nude hunting scenes engraved on sacrificial urns, nude stone sculptures on tombs and rocks in various provinces of China.[28] Some murals portrayed secular activities like cultivation of crop, playing of musical instrument and dancing for which Kuqa was famous all over the Silk Road.

Sadly, the caves of Kuqa have suffered massive damage and Buddha statues have been pilfered from almost all the caves. The sculptures have been carried away by foreign explorers who came to Kizil under the guise of researchers.

Many foreigners hung their heads in shame as guides from Kizil Research Institute recounted how cruelly Buddhist images had been cut away and stolen. Angry tourists wanted to know what China was doing to get back its stolen wealth. A simple question that should set the Chinese government thinking.

Visit to Subashi Ancient City

The Subashi site was located twenty-three kilometres north-east of Kuqa county and large ruins of Buddhist temples could be seen on both sides of the Kuqa river. The site on the western bank had several stupas. The biggest and most important stood on a high base and steps led to the upper part. Numerous grottoes had been preserved at the site. I climbed the steps of the huge temple which led from the back in a winding fashion and opened into a small open courtyard of the main temple. Two arched openings led inside the temple where Buddha images once adorned the niches. Where the steps began there were several small rooms called meditation grottoes where monks once lived.

On the eastern bank too there were stupas, grottoes and temples.

Explorers have found a large number of ancient coins from the Han and Tang dynasties and documents in Chinese and Qiuzi languages and Buddhist relics.

The Subashi ruins were identified as the Zhaohuli of Xuanzang. They are the largest group of ruins in the eastern region with a hundred temples.

During his stay at Kuqa Xuanzang visited the Zhaohuli convents.[29] He mentioned Si-Yu-Ki that there were two convents close together on the slope of a mountain, but separated by a stream of water both named Chau-huli. Here he saw a statue of Buddha, richly adorned and carved skillfully. In the hall of the eastern convent, called the Buddha pavilion, there was a yellowish-white jade stone, shaped like a sea-shell and on its surface was traced an eight inches long foot of Buddha which emitted a 'bright and sparkling light'.

He mentions two huge images of Buddha, about ninety feet high adorned the western gate of the chief city. In front of the statues the quinquennial assembly was held where priests assembled from all over the country. The king and all his people, from the higest to the lowest, abstained from public business and observed a religious fast, and listened to sacred teachings of law.

The images of Buddha in all the convents, he says, were decorated with precious substances and covered with silken stuff. On festive occasions these were carried in processions. Another convent called Oshelini, situated across a river had a precious temple having a beautifully carved image of Buddha.

French Sinologist Paul Pelliot during his 1907 visit found many coins in the area, about fifteen clay and wooden funeral urns which can be seen in the Musee Guimet, Paris. A particularly beautiful urn found here was said to be covered with cherub-like figures dancing and playing musical instruments. The Otani mission had earlier discovered a similar

A Buddhist temple at the ancient city of Subashi. The site is located twenty-three kilometres north-east of Kuqa on both sides of the Kuqa river.

ABOVE: *Steps lead to the Subashi temple from the back in a winding fashion and open into the small courtyard of the main hall.*
BELOW: *Two arched openings lead inside the Buddha Hall of the Subashi temple where once Buddha images had been installed in the niches. The hall is now empty.*

casket covered with cherubic figures on the lid and a complete orchestra of Kuqean musicians now kept in the Tokyo Museum.[30]

High Entry Fee for Kumtura

Kumtura grottoes comprising 112 caves and 4000 square metres of wall paintings are located 20 kms west of Kuqa on the east bank of the Weigan river. They are considered to be the second largest grotto temples of Xinjiang.

The site is difficult to reach and therefore seldom visited. Tourists wishing to see the site have to take special permit from Urumqi office of the Institute of Archaeology. Unaware of this in Urumqi, I was now in Kizil and preparing to go to Kumtura.

I approached the director's office at Kizil and was informed that the permit fees would be five hundred dollars and for photographing the caves, an additional thousand dollars per cave. I knew that indirectly the permission had been refused. I quietly backed off after purchasing a dozen slides from the Kizil Institute on sale at the book stall near the director's office.

I found out from my guide that an ancient trail along the Muzart river led to the site of Kumtura and researchers were required to walk a considerable distance on foot. However, what deterred me was the prohibitive fee.

But I thought of the Buddha–of the man who attained Enlightenment and showed the world the Middle Path. I thought of all that ails the world, I thought only if there was a little Buddha in all of us, it would have been such a beautiful world to live in.

The beautiful Lake Karakul at an elevation of more than three thousand metres lies between the two famous ice-capped and several metres thick glacial peaks of Mt. Mustagha Ata and Mt. Kongur. The lake is surrounded by high mountains and rich pasturelands.

11

Kashgar—A Heady Mix of Old and New

The Desert Express N 947 chugged along the Taklamakan. Not far away, the snowy Tienshan glistened in the first rays of the sun. Huge glaciers metamorphosed into myriad streams, some gurgling towards the south slope feeding small forests and orchards, others burgeoning into rivers that nourished the oasis cities along the Silk Road, formed lakes, or bravely murmured along the dry desert before losing their identity—and existence—in the thirsting sand.

The Chinese-speaking Uighur guide Habib had left me a day earlier and now I was on my own, without a guide and with no reserved ticket. I was told the Sunday Bazaar was one of the best ways to see the real Kashgar. But to partake in the bustling bazaar I had to cut short my trip to Kuqa and take the evening train. As I stepped in, the folly of not having a reservation hit me. The bogies were spilling with people, there was no elbow room. But I could not afford to miss the train, so I edged, nudged, jostled and jumped into the general compartment. Forget a seat; there was no room to even stand. All I mustered with great difficulty was a little space near the toilet to stand, with my huge pile of luggage jutting out of the open door. Kenji, a Japanese friend who had joined me at Korla, was appalled at my pathetic situation. He took pity, accosted the lady conductor and passed on my request for a sleeping berth. She smiled beatifically. I had my fingers crossed and was hoping she would wave a magic wand and procure some seats for me. And voila! She did. My prayer was answered, I was allotted a berth in the next compartment. I saw my watch. It was 6 am. The sun was waking out of the clouds, the dawn was breaking. But my body clock was disoriented, at wake-up time I dozed off. I must have slept like a log, nine hours whizzed past and I was completely oblivious of the morning that had melted into afternoon and was beginning to look like evening. I slept for nine hours only to find myself at Kashgar where the railway tracks end after traversing the desert.

At the station, Hasan Usman was waiting for me. As I stepped out carrying my luggage but feeling fresh after the long sleep, little Uighur boys pulled at my clothes. They wanted the used train tickets! I later learnt that old tickets could be resold!

A Heady Mix of Old and New

Kashgar, a verdant desert oasis, is China's western-most city and separates the vast Taklamakan deserts of the Xinjiang from the glacial peaks of the Pamir and the Karakoram. It is a heady mix of the old and the new; it juxtaposes the Minority City with its mud wall, no sewerage and the raucous animal market with the novelty of the Central Asian Grand Bazaar. Both the old and the new vie for attention. Hasan takes me to both.

The oasis is believed to be the ancient Shu-le kingdom.[1] The heartland of the Uighurs, it is said to be the soul of the Silk Road that has droned with trade for over two thousand years. Standing at the eastern foot of the Pamirs at the junction of the northern and the southern Silk Road, it was an ancient trading center where highways coming from Persia, Central Asia, China, and India met. From Kashgar tracks ran west crossing the Pamirs and Central Asia to Persia and further west through Turkey to the eastern shores of the Mediterranean. Another road ran

Idgah Mosque, built in AD 1442 is the largest mosque of Xinjiang. It has a massive plaza in front that leads to the giant yellow gates. Inside a cobbled path lined with huge trees and flowering shrubs opens into gardens full of flowers amid which stand ancient structures.

Magnificent adornments inside the prayer hall. The richly carpeted verandahs provide sitting place for thousands of men and women who visit the mosque everyday. Huge chandeliers hang from painted ceilings, the doors are richly decorated, and the beautiful arches give the mosque the look of a palace.

south crossing the Karakoram to enter northern India. Caravans from China going to the west and south were loaded with silk, pottery, fur etc. while those coming from the west carried wool, precious stones. Those coming from India packed aromatic spices. It was through these routes that foreign religions spread in China: Christianity and Islam from the west and Buddhism from the south.

It is said that the travellers coming from Central Asia and heading for China would stop at Kashgar on descending from the Pamirs. They would exchange their yaks and mules for camels in preparation for their difficult journey through the Taklamakan desert. Likewise, the west-bound travellers reached Kashgar exhausted after a journey through the Gobi and the Taklamakan deserts. Here they found relief and rest before exchanging their beasts in preparation for the ascent of the mountain of the high Pamirs. In his memoirs Xuanzang mentions that when he visited Kashgar on his way to India there were several hundreds of *sangharams* with some ten thousand followers; they studied the 'little vehicle' or Hinayana, and belonged to the 'Sarvastivada School'. There were many who could chant the 'three pitakas and the Vibhasha'. 'They paint their bodies around their eyelids. For their writing they take their model from India', he wrote.[2]

According to historical records Kashgar[3] (also called Kashi) was invaded by the Kushanas from the Gandhara kingdom around AD 107 and their control over the vast empire spanning Kashgar, most of the Karakoram, the Hindukush and northern India led to the introduction of Buddhism in Central Asia and China through the existing trade routes. Buddhism remained the religion of the kingdom of Kashi up to the tenth century after which it was replaced by Islam during the Qarakhan kingdom (ninth to the twelfth century AD).

The Scene of Great Rivalry

In modern times Kashgar also served as the arena of the 'Great Game' between Russia and Britain for 'political ascendancy in Central Asia'.

We learn about the exciting story of the great rivalry in Peter Hopkirk's classic *The Great Game*.[4] The two super-powers suspected each other of eyeing the new Chinese province of Xinjiang set up by the Qing Dynasty in 1884 and gaining strategic control of the Pamir region where the three great empires–Russia, China, British India, and Afghanistan met. That was not all that they vied for, there was neighbouring Tibet too.

The two rivals had set up their consulates in Kashgar which sat strategically at the foot of the Pamirs from where mountain roads and passes led into Russian Central Asia, India and Tibet. The Russian consulate, Seeman opened in 1880 with Consul Nikolai Petrovsky. Earlier too the Russians had been permitted to open their consulates in Yili and Tarbagatai by the Chinese court.[5] The British Consul George McCartney arrived only around 1890 at Kashgar where he was allotted the 'Chinese Garden' or the 'Chinibagh' that later became the British consulate. McCartney stayed on for twenty-six years as the British consul. Renowned explorers such as Francis Younghusband, Aurel Stein, Albert von le Coq are said to have called at the Chinibagh on their way to the Taklamakan desert for digging expeditions.

It is said that Seeman and Chinibagh consulates were actually 'listening posts'[6] for their respective countries for gathering information and playing the 'Great Game' for the strategic control of the region. While explorers looked for mountain routes and passes through the Pamirs and dug up the ancient sites in the Chinese Turkestan for antiquities, the consuls general kept an eye on each others activities for political alliance and military manoeuvres. Both consulates were closed down in 1949 to be later turned into hotels for tourists.

A peep into *The Great Game* (by Peter Hopkirk) reveals the grand visions of the Russian Tsar in the nineteenth century viz. 'of opening up to Russia the whole of the Far East, with its vast resources and markets...'[7] before these fell prey to the expanding British empire.

By 1885 Russia had already taken the entire area of Central Asia between the Caspian Sea and the Pamirs reaching upto the borders of Afghanistan and set about laying a huge network of railways. By 1888 the Trans-Caspian railway reached Samarkand and by 1905 the Orenburg-Tashkent line was completed. The great Trans-Siberian railway ran for 4,500 miles across Russia from Moscow in the west to Vladivostok and Port Arthur in the east.[8]

However, the Viceroy of British India, Lord Curzon was (in the words of Hopkirk) 'confident that with firm action the Russian steamroller could be halted...'[9]

At the Chinibagh

It was into this consulate that I checked in the following day. At the Chinibagh Hotel, the famous old British consulate, a dancing Uighur couple carved out of white stone welcomed me at the gate. I had read about this hotel in Diana Shipton's book, *The Antique Land,* but where I stood looked very different from what I had seen and read in the book. I was foxed at the discrepancy. I was too tired to find answers to all that was intriguing me, but after a short nap I decided to look for the real Chinibagh. I did not have to go too far. I found it at the back of the new Chinibagh building—the stone-paved verandah, the English furniture and the ancient portrait of a lady inside the lobby.

It was such a delight. The front garden had beautiful trees, some of them believed to be planted by McCartney's wife, Catherine, when the consulate first opened as a mud house. An old-looking tree which was probably planted by Diana Shipton was laden with large red pomegranates. A flight of steps took me to a fabulous verandah that resembled a long corridor flanked by Roman columns. Inside, white diaphanous curtains billowed in the cool breeze wafting through the open window on the back walls of the front room, now turned into a lobby. The consulate had been turned into a dining hall for the hotel guests, the rooms refurbished and the floor carpeted. A couple sat sipping wine near the front desk that also served as a bar.

I could smell the old fragrance of the Chinibagh that seemed like a postcard from the past. I thought of the days of the yore when this place

The animal market at Kashgar is a sea of human and animal heads. Hundreds of trucks bring sheep, goat, cows, horses and donkeys from the neighbouring villages. The entire market, held on the banks of the Tuman river, is enveloped in swirls of dust as animals are dragged away by their new buyers.

must have been bustling with tall, fair men in trousers and short haired women in gowns, the rustle of the silk and the smell of fragrance. They must have waltzed through the night, their guns must have boomed to break the silence of an eerie night but they must have also spent restless days in the mud house, so far away from home, caught in a culture that was so alien.

At the Animal Market

Since I arrived at Kashgar on Sunday, a day earlier than scheduled hence, instead of checking into Chinibagh I had to spend a day at the Taximan Barony, a well-appointed four-star hotel. After settling down in my room I left for the cattle market which remained open only on Sunday. A little beyond the bed of the Tuman river, all I saw was a sea of human heads and all I heard was the buzz of gruff animals. From trucks sheep, goat, cows, horses and donkeys were offloaded and found buyers within no time. Here I waded through an endless stream of animals and people. The market was enveloped in swirls of dust and money was changing hands briskly. While buyers gloated over bargains and dragged away their new purchases, the sellers settled down to a hearty meal of hot sheesh kebabs roasted on burning charcoal.

In the market I must have grazed past hundreds of donkeys and their owners, I had never seen so many donkeys gathered in one place. The scream of the buyers and sellers was drowned in the incessant braying of the donkeys. But in this region everyone loves the donkey; it is still the most dependable in the gruelling mountainous and desert terrain. And in the Sunday Bazaar the donkeys are the most coveted. While other animals waited impatiently for a buyer, the donkeys relished their fate with a few calm brays. In one corner I heard neighs and turn, I saw horses, some the colour of honey, others russet, some white as milk. There were buyers, but they were not pouring their money without a test ride, they galloped on the horses around the bazaar for a few minutes before loosening their purse strings.

Amidst the whiff of unwashed and unkempt horses and donkeys, there mingled the scent of food from outside the market where several kiosks were selling quick meals. Traders had come from far-flung destinations and having finalised deals they sat for a bite of the succulent sheesh kebabs that they wash down with ladles full of tea that was being poured in colossal bowls. Not too far from the donkey carts tumbled sacks full of yellow carrots and white radish that were joined by delicious figs and large green pomegranates brought from the countryside.

Those who told me that the best way to get a feel of the place was to go to the bazaar were right. These fascinating scenes never find mention in glossy brochures or thick history books; you need to be there to see them. I am glad I did.

To the Ancient Kingdom of Shule

The following day my guide Hasan, and I took the road north-east of Kashgar to the ancient city of Hanoi. Driving for about twenty-five kilometres we came to a deserted stretch where we left the road and turned towards a dirt track winding deep into the desert. It led to a ruined city which is believed to be the ancient Hanoi built by the Tang Dynasty in the seventh century. A number of Buddhist stupas have been found near this village which probably was the ancient capital of the Kashgar state, also called the kingdom of Shule. According to Jonathan Tucker (*The Silk Road*), the oldest of the stupas found here is the Topa Tim belonging to the first century AD. Another stupa is the Kurghan Tim, shaped like a mound that lies northwest of Kashgar.[10]

But Mauri Tim or the Mor Pagoda, just north of Hanoi village, was perhaps the best preserved in Kashgar. We could see the remains of the city walls and the huge Mor Pagoda. About twelve metres high, it had a square base designed in four layers on which stood the Buddhist stupa, oblong in shape and built of clay. This stupa was worshipped by the people of the ancient Shule kingdom. Adjacent to it was another ruined structure with a similar square base arranged in four layers believed to

A winding dirt track deep inside the desert leads to the Mauri Tim stupa. All around the stupa lie the ruins of an ancient town believed to be the city of Hanoi built by the Tang Dynasty in the seventh century.

be part of a Buddhist temple once decorated with an image of Buddha. The ground was full of broken pieces of pottery and ancient bricks on huge mounds of earth.

The Three Immortal Buddhist caves, also called the Sanxiandong, are held to be the earliest Buddhist remains in Xinjiang. The three caves lie on a steep cliff on the river Qiakmak near the Urumqi-Kashgar Highway 314. Unfortunately, we could not reach the caves as construction was going on in the ravines below. We had to stand on the opposite cliff to see the caves that looked like little windows in the mountains. In fact, the caves which were barely two metres high and one metre wide on the outside are said to have been cut quite deep inside the mountains and adorned with rare paintings of Buddha.

Mao at People's Square

On day two of my Kashgar sojourn, I decided to take a spin around the town center or the City Square where a huge statue of Mao Tse Tung loomed large. Flower beds had been arranged symmetrically to form a huge flower fountain. Large synthetic pomegranates with electric bulbs inside hung from trees. A coloured fountain added to the glory of the central pool. The City Square was a popular dating place for young men and women. I joined the crowd and sat on the sidewalk observing the world going about its errands and a huge Mao smiling and waving at the people who were walking or stretching on sticky mats and children who were gleefully spangling the sky with colourful kites. At the City Square evenings are special; people throng to see the daily entertainment programmes.

From the City Square I proceeded to Idgah Square in the centre of the city that led to the giant yellow gates of the Idgah, the largest mosque of Xinjiang. Built in 1442 the place was noisy, there were dozens of shops in the massive front square where the Uigur people gathered to celebrate their festivals with great fanfare. Originally, it was a nondescript mosque on the outskirts of the town, but over the years it has become the largest and the most famous mosque in the whole of Xinjiang. I walked through a tree-lined path to the inner courtyard where water pots were placed to enable devotees to wash themselves before attending prayers.

Inside the mosque I found a crowd of men and women sitting on carpeted verandahs. With huge chandeliers hanging from painted ceilings, decorated doors and arches, the mosque looked more like a palace. The courtyards were adorned with lush trees and fountains where devotees waited for the muezzin to invoke the gods.

I went around the mosque and ventured into the backlanes that were cluttered with countless antique shops selling jewellery and pottery. Rare pieces of jade, parrots, knives and musical instruments were all available for a price. The Golden Street, a lane famous for its collection of precious gems and ornaments, drew the largest crowd. Traditional Indian *jhumkas* and hair ornaments were on display. Metal chasers sat by the side of the street cutting intricate designs on copper and brass vessels.

Apakhoja Tomb

All along the Silk Road I had seen fascinating vignettes, had heard enthralling tales, but of all that I had heard there was nothing more captivating than the story of Xiang Fei, the Fragrant Concubine.[11] It was in search of this concubine that I head to the seventeenth century Apakhoja tomb located five kilometres north-east of Kashgar. The dome and minarets of the mausoleum were covered with green glazed tiles and there was a huge burial chamber where lay Apakhoja, the grandson of Muslim missionary Mahatum Ajam from Kazakhastan, the patron saint of Kashgar. There were about seventy tombs inside the compound. One of them was believed to be of a descendant of Ajam called Ikparhan. It was she whose story I had heard. She was Xiang Fei, the Fragrant Concubine. According to legend, the Chinese emperor Qian Long was absolutely smitten by the woman who was not only beautiful, but from her body emanated the fragrance of olive flowers, a scent that had the

FACING PAGE:
The tomb of Apakhoja or the green mausoleum of the 'fragrant cocubine' telling not only the story of the patron saint of Kashgar but also of Xiang Fei or Ikparhan, the beautiful descendant of the saint who is said to have caught the fancy of the emperor.

emperor love-struck. She was believed to be gifted to the emperor for his harem and was carried away to Beijing. But her happiness would not last long. It ended tragically because the Queen Mother disliked her and once while the emperor was away Xiang Fei was killed by the palace eunuchs. Her body was carried back to Kashgar in a procession that was said to have taken over three years. According to another version, says Hasan, Xiang Fei was none other than Rongfei, a concubine of Emperor Qian Long, who died a natural death and was buried in the tombs of the Qing Dynasty in Zunhua County, Hebei province.

I do not know whether Xiang Fei actually carried the fragrance of olive flowers but the whiff of the rose flowers in the front of the mausoleum reminded me of her. Corridors of grape trellis adorned the pathway to the mausoleum. Not too far away was the blue-domed tomb of Yusup Haji, a famous Uighur poet (AD 1019-85) belonging to the Karakhan kingdom. I had heard of *Happiness and Wisdom*, a great literary treatise that he had composed in Uighur language in 1069. I kneeled at the tomb of the great poet and paid my respects.

Grand Bazaar of Central Asia

No trip to Kashgar can be complete without a visit to the Kashgar Grand bazaar, said to be the biggest in Central Asia. On a bazaar day villagers and herdsmen from the countryside ride their donkey carts laden with livestock and agricultural produce to be sold here. Even to this day, the Grand Bazaar is primitive in its dealings, nobody shells out jangling coins or crispy notes after a deal; here everything is bartered.

The carpet shops occupied a vantage point, they lined the front rows of the bazaar. I spotted a carpet with a beautiful pattern and got tempted. But the seller was sleeping on his pile; I woke him up and asked him for the best carpet from his lot. He pulled out large wall hangings of woven silk embellished with geometrical pomegranates and popular motifs like a Uighur singer, a camel caravan and a mountainous landscape. But the quoted price was exorbitant–30,000 yuans! I haggled, but he was stubborn. I haggled further, but he shook his head vehemently. I did not give up and tried every trick for a decent discount. But nothing worked, not my charm, not my pleadings. I finally gave up. I noticed more shops spilling with carpets and traditional wall hangings. I looked for tags, they were not any cheaper. Everything was expensive, a carpet for nothing less than 20,000 yuan. I looked in my purse. I would have loved to spread one of those exquisite carpets in my living room, but the price hurt. I had nothing to barter and was greatly disheartened. But I moved on and looked at the women selling Pakistani laces, scarves and dress material, satin and the famous hand-woven multi-coloured striped Atles silk. In another corner I saw bolts of brocade. This time I did not even dare ask the price. It must be expensive, I assumed. Looked like I was the only one with tight purse-strings, for the brocade had many takers.

The bazaar had an amazing array of products. Well, there were snakes too! Dried and coiled hanging from ropes. But there was more. Jars full of snails, scorpions, lizards, and severed heads of wild animals floating in what could be formalin. Coiled snakes are panacea for skin ailments; each animal serving its own medicinal purpose. I am not sure how potent they are, but going by the number of buyers I was certain they worked like magic. However, my stomach churned at their sight and I ran past hurriedly. I bruised against a wooden dowel and ended up next to a Chinese ginseng kiosk. Ginseng is said to be a magical aphrodisiac and

FACING PAGE

TOP: The Kashgar Grand Bazar, the biggest in Central Asia where barter trade still takes place and villagers and herdsmen still ride their donkey-carts laden with goods to be sold here. Kashgaria knives, Pakistani brassware and Shah Rukh Khan posters are the most sought after items.

BELOW: All kinds of medicines including snakes, snails, scorpion venom with aphrodisiacal and healing properties, sea-shells, salts, herbs can be found at the Grand Bazar in Kashgar.

I spied men stealthily shoving packets in their bags. While men were busy picking their weekly dose of ginseng women were quibbling over dark maroon and orange-coloured saffron.

Alongside there were shops selling Kashgaria knives, Pakistani brassware, hosiery, Sichuanese tea, fresh fruits and dried sarda, hami gua and seagua, peaches, and apricots. Apricot seeds were prepared into delicious snacks and a hundred different varieties of raisins were bought for a hundred different reasons. There were bolts of fabric in captivating colours and chintz. Interestingly, most of them came from Pakistan which has an open border with China. Traditional square Uighur hats in sequined satin and Uighur musical instruments resembling the Kuqean flute and the narrow sitar and drums made of snake skin were also on sale.

In the vast market expanse, there was nothing Indian, there was no Indian making quick money. Nobody understands Hindi but there were two words that everyone identified India with - Hindustan and Shahrukh Khan. Not many knew the name of Indian actor Aishwarya Rai, but her face was pasted on the covers of several Uighur and Chinese music albums.

Shopkeepers beckoned me as Pakistani and many women rushed out of their shops to feel my nose ring. When I told them I was from India, Hindustan, they smiled, shook hands and said, *Ya Shahru Han* (Yes, from the country of Shahrukh Khan). Television sets were providing respite to shop owners who were jaded with too much bargaining, to break the monotony they were watching dubbed Indian movies!

Minority City

In the bazaar, I got nostalgic; it looked so much like an Indian bazaar—the same din, the same eternal propensity to haggle, the same aroma of fresh produce, the same warmth, the same commotion. After a round of the Grand Bazaar we headed to the Minority City right in the heart of Kashgar. Built on a hill top, the history of this city goes back to over two thousand years. Archaeologists would have you believe that the first Uighur potters settled here because the soil found in this region was apt for pottery. The city has nearly forty streets with narrow lanes and bylanes where children with red cheeks shouted and played. In this handicrafts center of Kashgar one could see potters hunched over the wheel, their hands stained with wet clay, women stitching Uighur sequined caps, painters working in ancient studios and women pulling out hot *naan* from charcoal ovens.

The inner lanes were cluttered, spilling with busy people and playful children. Sellers with decrepit wheelbarrows were peddling ice lollies while houses had antiques displayed at the front door. I saw an old spinning wheel which must have been used to weave silk and an old cartwheel parked outside a dilapidated house. The Minority City has a system of dry latrines with no flush toilets. I climbed up the top storey of another ramshackle house to have a view of the river and five-star hotels just across the road. I felt like an intruder, but the people were friendly and welcomed me warmly and smilingly into their homes. They even requested me to try their Uighur dress and embroidered cap. I was only too happy to oblige.

On the Karakoram Highway

The next day I rose just before sunrise. At five in the morning, the sky still wore a black sheath. The clock here adheres to Beijing time, which means it was two hours earlier. I got ready and was craving for some tea and breakfast. But at Chinibagh the breakfast was never laid before eight am even if guests had to depart early. I had no option, but to leave on an empty stomach, hoping to get some grub on way, perhaps at the banks of the Karakul lake in the Pamir mountains.

The green Pajero was large enough for all of us—Kenji, my Japanese friend who had also joined me, and I took the back seat while Hasan sat next to the driver. With us were Abdullah and Arken, the two singers whose taped voice had kept me company all over Xinjiang. I liked their guttural voice, I liked the thump of the drum that resonated with their fast-paced music. In between Hasan kept up his commentary on the history of Kashgar and the Karakoram Highway.

The Karakoram Highway (KKH) starts from the Renmin Xi Lu in Kashgar and leads south for over two thousand kilometres over the Khunjerab pass into Pakistan tracing the ancient trade route to Taxila in north-western India (now in Pakistan). In the olden days this route at Taxila met the *Uttarapath* or the northern high road coming from Vaishali (near modern Patna). At Sravasti a branch of the *Uttarapath* turned southwards and became the *Dakshinapath* (the southern high road) travelling to Paithan in South India. In the fifth and seventh centuries Chinese monks Fahien and Xuanzang took this route to India in search of Buddhist scriptures.

I was informed that the KKH is open from May to October. For thousands of years, traders and pilgrims have travelled on this mountainous route branching into China, Pakistan, India, Afghanistan, and Tajikistan, connecting China, South Asia and Central Asia. Pakistan and China jointly cut this Asian high road across the Pamirs and the Karakoram range during the 1960s, formally opening their mutual borders in 1986. It connects Kashgar with Rawalpindi and Islamabad via the Khunjerab pass through Gilgit.

Outside Kashgar city the road was wide but completely rutted. It was being widened and repaired, and construction materials were piled on either side. Occasional rains and heavy mountain streams from the melting glaciers had taken their toll. At several places the KKH had been cemented to prevent breakage but the streams dodged and changed their course breaking new path and rushing head-on all the same. The Pajero ran into the fast flowing streams at several places and was drenched with muddy water.

It took about an hour to reach Upal village. To our right a small road branched off and ran about four kilometres to the tomb of Mahmud Kashgaria, who completed *The Dictionary of Turkic Language* in AD 1075. He died in AD 1105 and lies buried here.

Into the Pamirs

After an hour the road skewed towards the right and climbed into the mountains and the entire landscape changed suddenly. All around I saw massive peaks and the Gez river running below. The river formed a beautiful vision of shimmering waters and coloured rocks. Most settlements as far as Karakul lake were Kirghiz. A smooth black road ran for about 120 kms to the lake flanked by low shrubs of blooming yellow and purple flowers.

The KKH was undergoing a makeover; it would soon become a six-lane road like the one cutting through the belly of the desert. Thousands of bulldozers, material and men populated its stretch. Thankfully, there were no traffic snarls; the traffic was sparse, all I saw was an occasional truck or tourist van passing by. The water from the streams had been channelised over the mountains to the villages. The water was spring clean and potable, but it got muddy near the road. Several rows of power lines ran by the side of the road and climbed up the high mountains. Every village along the KKH had electricity. Only the yurt of nomads did not seem to have power. Perhaps, the nomads did not need electricity, for they never pitched their tents at one place for long.

A few patches of green by the streams were an exception, otherwise the mountains remained stark–brown, green, red and yellow like an impressionistic landscape set against high peaks and glaciers and a deep blue sky. A lot of pale yellow powdery dust settled on our faces and hair and the strong wind caressed me with sand from the mountains. But I was not disturbed; I took it as a blessing from the gorgeous setting. I asked the driver to turn off the air-conditioner, rolled down the windows not wanting to take my eyes off this mountainous feast even for a second. Who knows if would ever see such beauty ever again!

The stark landscape was interspersed with prairies where yak, sheep and mountain goats were grazing quietly, their heads lost in the meadow grass. The yak with its long bushy tail and hairy body seemed ferocious. Surprisingly, there were not too many camels.

The snowy peaks of the Pamir and the Karakul lake. The beautiful lake is sprawled over ten kilometres between Mt. Mustagh Ata and Mt. Kongur. The cool clear and deep sapphire waters of the lake shimmer in the morning sun.

At several places the road had been diverted into dirt tracks or took a long circuitous route around the mountains before merging into the main road which was under repair. Lorries lifted water from the neighbouring streams, sprayed it on the roads to settle the thick cloud of dust. I could hear the hum of the earthmovers, the clunk of the shovels and the shrill conversations of the men and women at work. Construction material had encroached on what could have been a road and they were moved gingerly by women labourers dressed in trousers or long skirts.

We came to the Gez checkpoint. Our passports were checked and we were permitted to travel further. A long queue of trucks and vehicles was awaiting permission.

The Gez river flowed to my right and its banks were gleaming like freshly polished mirror. On reaching the Bolonkul area watered by the Gez I found that the river had become a massive sheet from the melting glaciers. At the foot of the glistening hills lie several kilometres of a river that suddenly seemed to have fattened around its girth. Not too far away was the Kirghiz village of Moji. I saw a pack of sheep herded towards what was probably a green patch.

The newly laid road led to lake Karakul on our left through a large, red, double-arched gate with upturned eaves.

Black yaks graze in the meadows so green
Like emerald set in the crown of hills
And the blue sky descends
In the sapphire lakes
Fed by milky streams
From snowy glaciers

Karakul Lake

The lake was perched at an elevation of more than three thousand metres above sea and sprawled over roughly ten square kilometres between Mt Muztagha Ata and Mt Kongur. Around the lake lived Kirghiz herdsmen with their animals. Near the lake the mountains were high, and the pastures rich and green. Herds of horses and sheep lazed around. The peaks were ice capped and swathed in several metres of thick glaciers. The nomads had set up tents for tourists. For most budget travellers tents were the preferred accommodation as they were cheap. Eating and living with the nomads was a great way to learn about the nomadic culture and save some precious dollars. I saw an Englishman and his friend who had occupied one tent; they came out for a horse ride wearing Kirghiz caps. They had spent the night in the yurt and were in no mood to leave the lake.

The sapphire waters of the lake shimmered in the morning sun. We had made it early to Karakul, even after the long drive my watch showed 9am. The pastureland and the flanks of the mountains were dotted with grey yurts where several foreigners were staying. Little Kirghiz boys pulled up camels and horses to the lake side to offer us a ride. There were several Kirghiz summer villages in the area, the nearest was Subash. Hundreds of yak were enjoying a rich pasture by the lake side while the nomads drew water for drinking and household chores.

There was a restaurant and a make-shift toilet at the lake. Here I opted for a small breakfast of eggs, bread and some jam. A plateful of biscuits was offered with black Uighur tea. I stood on the platform outside the restaurant enjoying a lovely view of the lake and the snow-capped peaks.

A Kirghiz cemetery lay in a neighbouring village. The graves were domed structures made of mud, some with windows cut into the walls. The villagers lived in adobe or stone houses where low walls served as enclosures for their animals. A large herd of camels suddenly appeared from behind a small hillock and ventured onto the road. We stopped our jeep and I pulled out my camera. They were brown, double-humped hairy camels and did an amusing back and forth on the road. They behaved like dimwits and made me smile.

From Karakul lake the newly tarred road ran smoothly for a few kilometres, then joined a pebbled dirt lane that went up and down several slopes, and finally left the main Karakoram highway which was in a state of disrepair. The vehicles were kicking large swirls of dust; the road disappeared into a dusty lane while dozens of bulldozers and clearing machines were rolling on the main KKH which ran parallel and within a few kilometres of the Tajikistan border. South of Karakul the road passed through Kekyor and from there ran across the marshy Tagh Arma basin.

Several Tajik villages dotted the road, I saw hundreds of mud and stone houses and yurts set in the meadows. Few camels were seen on the road, but horses abounded in the pastureland. Quite like the other cities on way, even here the mule was the most-sought after. Every house owned a mule. I loved the paddy swaying in the breeze. But Hasan set me right; he told me the fields were not sated with paddy, it was actually buckwheat. The golden brown ears looked like laden boughs and were ready to be harvested. On our way we saw more Tajik villages where herdsmen led their donkeys, horses and sheep under the watchful eyes of huge dogs. Tajik women dressed in long hats and dresses sat by the side of streams and rivers washing clothes or cleaning utensils.

Tashkurgan

Two hours later we arrived at Tashkurgan. The Tashkurgan autonomous county stretches from Mustagh Ata up to the border with Pakistan. It is home to the Tajiks who at the last count numbered 20,000, according to Hasan. For thousands of years, the Tajiks have made Tashkurgan area in the Pamirs their home. The area is both a gateway to China's western frontier and a key communications center between West and inland China. Even today it is the vital road from Kashgar to Pakistan. Buses to and from Pakistan stop here overnight.

We went past the main road and then turned left. A few yards further the gateway of the Stone Castle, said to be over two thousand years old, welcomed me. Xuanzang visited the stone fortress and mentions it in his travelogue. In Uighur, Tashkurgan means 'stone fortress'.

Unfortunately, on alighting at the stone castle Hasan took ill; his stomach was churning and he started vomiting. Even Kenji started grabbing his stomach and groaning. I was frightened that I would suffer a similar fate because I too had eaten a large breakfast at the lake. Worried about time and the prospects of an aborted visit, I left both Hasan and Kenji behind and trudged off to the edge of the castle. After walking for a

The two-thousand-year-old stone fortress at Tashkurgan finds mention in the memoirs of the great monk Xuanzang. The fortress is now in ruins.

Children wearing traditional Uighur caps play outside their mud house in a Tajik mohalla of Tashkurgan.

kilometre I looked back only to find Kenji hurrying after me, he was unwilling to leave me alone in an alien land. I was touched by his gesture and together we took a dirt road to the right of the fortress. From the edge of a small hillock I took photographs of the crumbling mud structure that once upon a time, was a massive castle.

I got a little adventurous; I jumped the high wall of the Tajik village in Tashkurgan and walked into a narrow alley where small children were playing with a mud cart. They rushed towards me, nudged at the camera, and said something which I obviously could not understand, but I assumed they were requesting us to take their photos. I followed them to the marshy pastures past an open toilet. As is wont in the desert, toilets have no walls; instead they are covered with plastic or cloth on three sides that serve as an improvised wall.

Several streams babbled into the pastures from the mountains. Sheep, horses and donkeys looked plump; they were grazing, looking absolutely content. On mud houses were hoisted television antennae. The village had a school and a mosque. By now we were hungry; we bought some bread and *naan* that we nibbled on our way back to the jeep. We decided not to hurtle back on the road in a hurry; we strolled on the main road of the small town that boasted of only two streets. All else that it could brag of was a small bazaar, a department store and a post office. However, there were plenty of Chinese hotels on the main street which were lined with poplars and a profusion of winter flowers in full bloom. After a while we traced our way back to the main road to join the KKH for our return journey.

Precious Stones in the Mountains

Our return journey began with loud music that was blaring from the stereo. It was 4 pm; it would take about six hours to reach Kashgar without any stops, not even at Karakul lake.

As it got dark, the mercury dipped and we began shivering. We were in the Gez valley which opened into a vast green belt that resembled grass vegetation covering the mountain sides. But a closer look and we realised that the mountains do not borrow the green from the grass, they are themselves the colour of emerald. There were long stretches of light and dark green rocky slopes. Hasan told me about the loads of emerald and jade that was found in this region. At another mountainous bend we came across rocks with green and black streaks. Dark maroon and red mountains and yellow ochre slopes took us by surprise. It looked as if the heavens had poured paint on them. Hasan seemed to know the topography; he told me about all the precious stones that were found here. The river beds were riddled with garnet, aquamarine, topaz, tourmaline and tanzanite and black, white, green, and yellow jade. Suddenly the river valley opened into a vast pasture land with stretches of sand and white pebbles surrounded by wild shrubs and trees. The mountains rose to the meet the sky and the river again cut into the rocks.

I looked at my watch. It was 10 pm. From behind the mountains a large moon rose to loom over our jeep and scattered silver on the winding road. The stark mountains emitted a strange glow and the myriad gleaming streams falling from the peaks murmured in the borrowed lustre.

On my return I found lots of people strolling in front of the hotel enjoying a pleasant breeze and the music wafting from the old Chinibag. We hopped off the Pajero, tired and dripping with dust, hoping to visit again the following year when the grand KKH was completely repaired into a six-lane road.

The city had not slept either. Nattily dressed couples were walking along the promenade. I changed and headed out for dinner at Entezar Ris to Ran where bamboo chairs had been laid out on the pavements sprinkled with rose water. The night was cool and pleasant and a musical band was playing nearby. I sank into a cane chair and enjoyed the evening over chilled juice and sheesh kebab.

Tashkurgan is the last Chinese inhabited town on the border with Pakistan. A special permit is needed to visit this area. The area which stretches from Mt. Mustagh Ata to the borders of Pakistan is the gateway to China's western regions.

The Karakoram Highway begins from Kashgar as an extension of the National Highway A 314 and cuts through the Tashkurgan county. Entering Pakistan through the Khunjerab Pass in the Hunza region it reaches Hawalian and Rawalpindi.

A Day at Village Awat

On the last day of my stay in Kashgar Hasan and I drove thirteen kilometres to Awat village which was his ancestral home. After passing through several poplar forests and grape valleys on unmetalled roads and village tracks by the side of which mountain streams flow, we reached Awat.

A large padlock welcomed us. His mother was in the fields weeding the corn crop. We waited for her; my eyes fell on the main door that was brilliantly carved. The exquisite door seemed like an anomaly in the house made of mud and unbaked bricks. Hasan fidgeted a little but he knew where his mother hid the key to the large padlock. No, it was not stashed away safely in an iron chest. Hasan walked to the back of the dwelling, dug a little earth and... he was disappointed, the key was not there. He was running out of patience; in haste he borrowed the neighbour's horse and galloped to the field. Left waiting behind I walked by a cotton field which was being watered by a mountain stream. In another field, women were busy plucking white fluffy cotton. From behind a bend in the dirt road emerged an old man with a huge pile of fodder on his bent back. He was Hasan's grandfather who lived in another part of the village. On learning about us he sent another young boy to fetch Hasan and his mother. After a long wait Hasan arrived, but not his mother. He broke the lock and we walked in. To our right was a stable where a couple of cows, donkeys and a dozen sheep were munching fodder. A big donkey cart stood in the courtyard.

Inside the mud house carved wooden pillars supported the roof and the verandah was covered with carpets. Even the mud walls of the rooms were carpeted. Soon Hasan brought a wash basin and jug of cold water. He got some corn from his neighbour's farm and roasted them for me. I was a bit tired and stretched on the poster bed for a quick nap. After what seemed like an eternity, Hasan's mother finally arrived and graciously greeted me. Clad in a long skirt, a coat and her head covered in a scarf she looked very young and pretty. She was the fifth wife of Hasan's father; his four previous wives had deserted him soon after marriage. I asked Hasan whether he would emulate his father. He grinned and shook his head vigorously.

In the kitchen, Hasan's mother lit some firewood to prepare traditional Uighur snacks. She cooked scrambled egg with onions and tomatoes which she filled in fresh dough buns flattened with a rolling pin. She poured a cup full of oil in the wok and flipped the flattened buns with a wooden ladle till it sizzled and rose like a balloon. She removed the brown and crispy buns from the pan and wrung them with her hands till thin layers of the dough separated. She set them in a bronze platter, garnished them with lots of green chillies and served us in the inner courtyard of her house. After the delicious meal I bade goodbye to Hasan (who was to appear for an exam the following day) and his mother and left for Chinibagh.

The Chinese Garden or Chinibagh, the famous old British Consulate in Kashgar first opened as a mud house in 1890. After the consulate was shut down, it was turned into the Chinibagh Hotel. The front garden has beautiful pomegranate trees, some of them believed to have been planted by Catherine, wife of Consul General George McCartney who was posted here for twenty-six years.

It was my last evening in Kashgar. Instead of going out for a leisurely walk on the city streets or the Peoples' Square, I escaped to the backyard of the hotel and climbed up the steps of the Old Chinibagh. I was at the front bar but I abstained from sitting alone. Instead, I sat on the paved verandah burying into the past of the picturesque place. A cool breeze from a nearby fountain blew in my face. Many decades ago Catherine and Diana must have sat here listening to lilting music off an old gramophone, ordering their Turki cook to prepare rice pilaf and roasted chicken or planning the next season's flower beds at Chinibagh. Away from their homes, here they must have waited anxiously for their weekly mails to arrive over the mountains from India; they must have also lovingly unpacked baskets of Kashmiri apples and nuts.

It was nearing midnight when the bar closed and couples walked away to their rooms in the New Chinibagh. I took one last look at the pretty little cottage which was once a prosaic consulate. I looked at the pomegranates and purple peonies and knew that I would remember these days for the rest of my life.

The magnificent stupa of Rawak standing loftily in the Taklamakan Desert. It is surrounded by an exquisite landscape of yellow sand dunes designed into waves from the moving sand grains in the fierce desert storm. The author in foreground.

(12)

Inside Taklamakan at Khotan

To Rawak Stupa in Taklamakan

Before I took the road to Khotan I was reminded of Edward, my Chinese friend in Delhi, and his harrowing tales of the NH A315 road through Yarkand to Khotan. Despite my curiosity he had warned me against taking that road. It did not conclude with merely an admonition. There were more spanners in the form of stringent entry procedures and prohibitive fee that put several historical sites like Niya and Lopnor off limits. Danger rarely daunts me but in an alien land I thought it would be prudent to pay heed to wisdom; from my itinerary I dropped NH 315 and decided to fly on the southern route to Khotan or Hotan or Hetian. I was not sure what I would hit on the way, all I knew was that on this route deep in the desert lay the famous Rawak Stupa where, about a century ago, Aurel Stein had carried out excavations. To the mere geographical truth, I added the wile of the explorer who had nearly broken the stupa to dig out antiquities.

My journey began with a domestic flight across the Taklamakan to the foot of the Kunlun mountains. I was now in the remotest part of Xinjiang, sitting on the southern boundary of the Taklamaken desert and very close to Kashmir. The locals were not unfamiliar with Kashmir; they could climb the top of Kunlun and see the lights in Kashmir.

In ancient times a branch of the Silk Road went north from Ladakh and met the southern Silk Road at Yarkand. From here, Kashgar lay to the left and Khotan to the right. Even travellers from Tibet took the route along the Indus, entered Ladakh, and travelled to Kashgar via Yarkand.

At Khotan airport Gorbustan, my guide, was waiting for me. Gorbustan, whose name meant 'flower of the desert', was fluent in English, Uighur and Chinese and efficiently guided me to the Hotan Oasis Hotel, which almost abutted the airport. The sun was shining bright, it was well past noon and we headed straight to the dining hall. There was a large spread—thick and broad noodles sautéed with mutton,

A thousand-year-old Buddha head from Rawak in the Khotan Museum.

grated and boiled pumpkin served with spinach, a mixed vegetable dish of eggplant, green pepper and tomato alongwith stuffed chicken. Full to my gills, I needed a siesta but that was the last thing I would do! I wanted to see the two precious mummies kept in the Khotan Museum and I requested Gorbustan to take me there.

Famous Corpses

I had read about the thousand-year old mummies, one of a man and another of a young pretty girl, both from Imamomusaka. And I walked into the four-storied museum to look at them and their ancient coffins. I also noticed other priceless antiquities like two Buddhas from Rawak and various kinds of pottery from different cemeteries in Xinjiang. The Museum looked sparse but the in-charge informed me that the antiquities found at various sites in Khotan and the ones on display at the Emin Mosque in Turfan would soon be shifted here. I also saw antique brass and copper ware, stone grinders and hundreds of huge earthen pots in the large hall. In one corner stood large, carved wooden coffins in which the mummies had once been interred.

The small room where the two mummies slumbered was eerie in its darkness. Even before I could step past the threshold of the ghostly room, the in-charge was pushing the keys to the large lock. He was reluctant to let me in. I politely requested him to allow entry. He looked at me strangely; despite my pleadings he continued turning the key into the lock. I looked at my purse; I told him I would pay an extra fee for a mere peep. But he seemed unrelenting. I was determined not to leave without looking at the mummies I had heard about so much. I pleaded one more time. This time he gave in, unlocked the hall and walked along to the dank anteroom. It was so dark inside that almost nothing was visible. There were no switches to be turned on and I was not sure what to do next. Suddenly there was a beam of light, I looked around and saw a torch in the man's hands. And then I saw them–the mummies lying on a low cot. They seemed in deep, eternal sleep, lying on their backs.

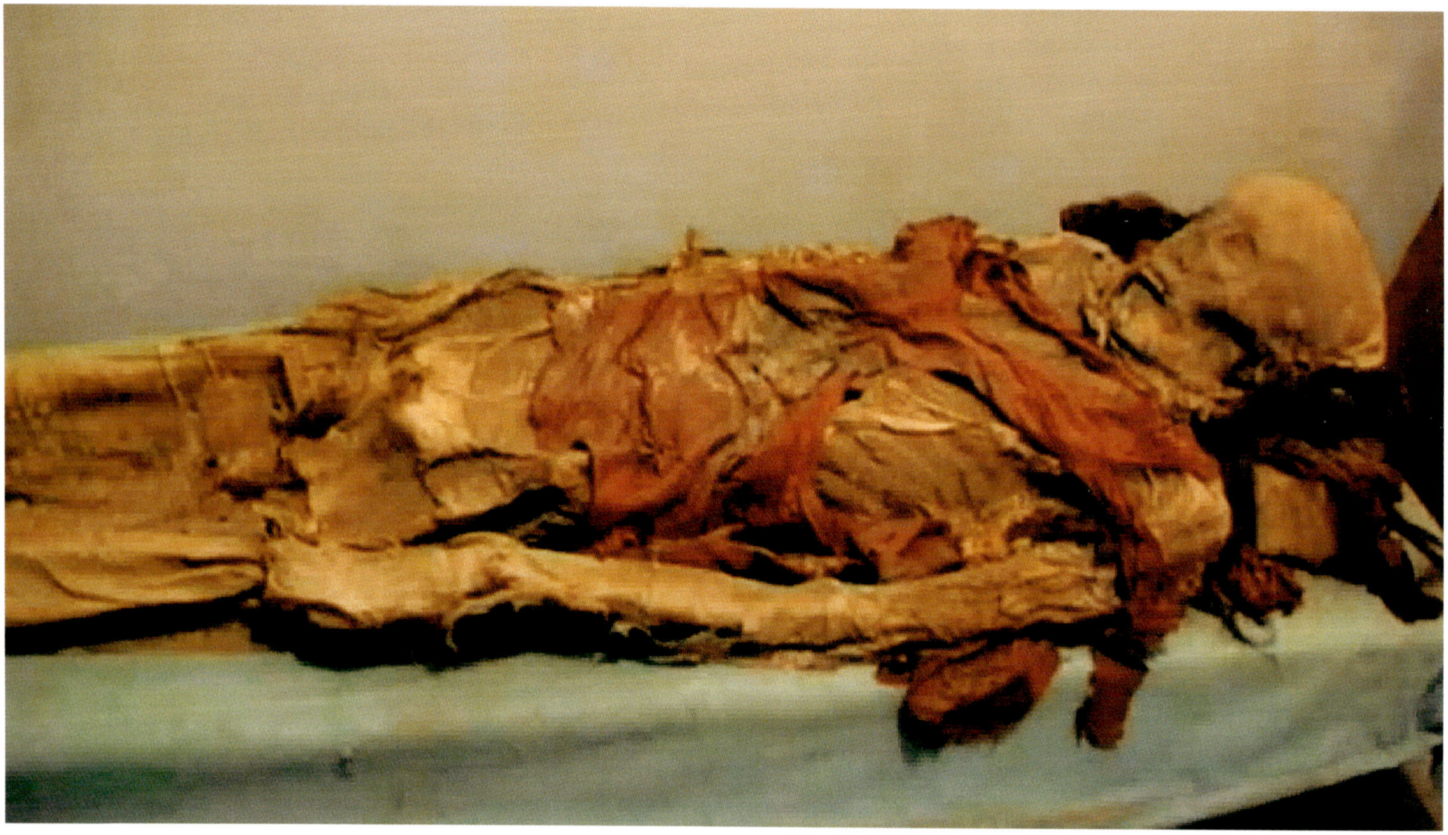

A thousand-year-old mummified body of a man from Imamomusaka lying on a low cot at the Khotan Museum. The mummy is still intact, the skin neither cragged or wrinkled. It lies wrapped in a rust coloured cloth.

The mummies must have been there for centuries; surprisingly, they were still intact, their skin neither cragged nor wrinkled. The skin on their face had not sagged, which must have been so because of the dry air of Xinjiang. Though their bodies were well preserved, their clothes were tattered; they were wrapped in frayed red cloth.

The mummies were not alone in the room; in one corner lay images of the king and queen of Khotan. There was another image of Khotan Buddha sitting on a lotus with eyes half-closed as if in deep meditation. The serenity in Buddha's eyes was in stark contrast to the two ferocious dogs that were chained in one of the rooms—their eyes were bloodshot, their howls intimidating; they were panting loudly and desperately trying to break the shackles that held them caged in the room. They were frail, small and grey in colour—I thought they were foxes. But I was wrong; these dogs were guarding the antiquities, let loose at night to catch intruders and sniff burglars from amidst the crowd. So much security had me thinking; I was wondering if there were more valuable antiquities stashed away from the prying eyes of the visitors, or were the dogs brought in after a recent incident of burglary?

Back at the hotel dinner had already been ordered by Gurbustan—an elaborate seven-course meal and jasmine tea. We were served *Tapanji* mutton that had whole spices cooked in garlic paste, mixed with capsicum and tomato in a light gravy, *Lazros* chicken fry to which capsicum and tomato had been added and sticky rice, and *Permuda* buns, sweet hamigua and fruit yoghurt prepared from yak milk made for dessert. Suddenly there was a lot of commotion, I looked out and saw dozens of luxury buses that had brought scores of Japanese tourists.

Journey into Taklamakan

Conversation at the dinner table turned to the next day's itinerary; we were scheduled to head into the desert to see the Rawak Stupa. But Gorbustan looked vexed; there was no hint of enthusiasm on her round face. I wondered what she was so disturbed about. The weather, she clarified. She was warning me about the gathering sandstorm and the nasty day that lay ahead of me. Gorbustan had me scared for a moment, but I was determined to undertake the journey on foot as camels could not be arranged at short notice. Gorbustan's words were ominous; the sandstorm did not wait for the morning to dawn—that night a fierce sandstorm struck Khotan. It rose in the desert and blew tonnes of sand all over the town. Trees fell as if on cue and electricity poles were uprooted. I could hear its deafening rustle on my window, the angry storm danced violently, loudly knocking and piercing through the crevices in the wooden frame. The funereal sound vanquished my sleep; I stayed up all night, my head cupped between my knees. I knew the next day's plan would have to be aborted but I had not given up hope. I muttered a prayer, asking the gods to give me a calm morning so that I could see the Rawak stupa. Just then there was thunder and lightning and rain fell in torrents. The desert storm had been quelled and a quick calm descended.

I woke up happy, hopped into the four-wheel drive and headed towards the Taklamakan to see the Rawak Stupa, which was not accessible fully by road. I was ready to walk seven kilometres along the sand dunes. I looked at my watch, it was eight in the morning but the shadow of the night was still there, the sun had not yet appeared in the sky. There were no clouds behind which the sun could hide. Does the sun always rise so lazily in the desert? Gorbustan defended the sun; it was not about a lazy sun, blame it on the clock. Khotan was two hours behind Beijing but stuck to Beijing time.

The morning was cold and Gorbustan was stacked for the day, carrying water and fruits in the wicker basket. She was an old hand; she knew we would not find water in the desert. Our vehicle drove past the shade of poplars that stood like sentinels on either side of the road which scampered through immense cornfields. First, the township of Zia fell on our way and then came the village of Imamasun from where the desert began. Soon we hit a grassy and bushy area on the periphery of the Taklamakan. The poplars had made way for statuesque willows that stood next to huts of nomads who had dug feet there temporarily with their camel and sheep. The road skewed right and leapt over a canal. Our jeep was checked thoroughly at the entry point which was manned by the officials of the forest department. Except a few thickets of dry willow trees and grass, the entire stretch looked parched and barren. Soon a sandy lane would lead us into the desert.

The museum officials had accompanied us and we had a permit to enter the desert. The sand had become sodden with the heavy rains that had lashed the desert the previous night and not surprisingly our jeep got stuck in the middle of nowhere. It purred and panted but could not move an inch. I stood by the jeep not knowing what to do. Seconds later, one of the museum officials folded his trousers, knelt by the jeep and started raking sand from under the wheels. From the bonnet I could sniff heat, the engine must have singed. The official poured some water on the heated engine. The engine hissed loudly and then fell quiet. Next, he took the driver's seat, switched on the engine, shuffled the gears and pressed the accelerator. The jeep hopped out of the depression with great alacrity and landed with a thud. We climbed into the vehicle and drove for another kilometre before halting where the road ended.

Hearty Meal on a Sand Dune

We had left the hotel early without breakfast and by now I was quite hungry. A long day lay ahead of us. I looked around for a camel safari but for miles and miles, as far as the eyes could see, there were only high dunes puffing out like hills from endless sand. No human being, no camel. Only the yellow sand adorned with squiggles made by the moving sand grains, their edges sharp like a razor.

We spread a sheet on a huge sand dune and Gorbustan laid a hearty meal. The backdrop was absolutely gorgeous; I felt I belonged to some other land where everything was beautiful. My heart pounded with joy, I felt an explorer–I was reliving the Silk Road experience, I was here to see Buddha, I had flown miles to kneel before the stupas and gaze at the mummies.

I took many photographs as I wanted to capture the exquisite landscape for posterity. And then began that seven-kilometre long stretch on which we would amble along the sand dunes. Walking on the sands of the Taklamakan I thought of the caravans that passed through the desert and recalled exciting stories of travellers and pilgrims and the bandits that sometimes looted them.

It was not reputation, but notoriety, that always preceded Taklamakan. No traveller has ever muttered a word in its praise. Hardened explorers like Aurel Stein and Sven Hedin called it the most dangerous desert in the world. Hedin and his men were chilled to the bone in the fearful desert by the 'cutting south wind' which was vicious enough to kill an entire caravan.[1] During Stein's stay at Dandan-Uiliq 'the night temperature often went down to minus ten degrees while in the day time it never rose to above freezing point. His men suffered from exposure and brackish water'.[2] Hedin's camel transported water through the desert in the form of ice. Men were reluctant to venture into the desert as they feared the 'djinns and demons' that roamed freely. Tortuous thirst gripped the travellers; their feet often sank in soft sand from which they pulled themselves out with great difficulty. Danger waited for them at every bend and the desert was never benign and benevolent.

Thankfully, that day, the weather gods were kind. The previous night's rain had firmed the sand under our feet, the sky was clear; there was no sandstorm to blind us nor fiery winds to scrape us. A cool desert breeze wafted gently. I happily ran about, climbed over the high dunes and shouted in excitement. Never before had I seen anything like this.

Nevertheless, I kept my wits about me. The museum official knew the way well but he preferred to follow the footprints of the camels that had walked before us. The previous night's sandstorm had built new dunes and caused deep crests and impressions of shifting waves on the sand.

Over an hour of walking brought us to a bushy area with lots of dried wood and a dilapidated stupa-like structure. This was the small Rawak. Dried, burnt bushes and fat black barks surrounding it were evidence enough that in the hoary past, the stupas must have been laced by a thicket of dense willows and poplars. I spent some time at the small stupa collecting bits of black and red polished ware with curved lines on them. I even chanced upon a square coin/seal which I diligently handed over to the museum official.

A Gaping Hole in the Rawak

After another hour of walking we chanced upon a patch that had withered plants with leaves as large as that of the Indian corn. We walked on and reached a high dune behind which was the famous Rawak Stupa. Finally, we had reached. But, not really! The Rawak Stupa seemed at an arm's distance but was still a kilometre away. The trek suddenly looked so arduous, but we trudged on. And then, I saw the magnificent Rawak Stupa standing loftily in the desert. The first thing I noticed was a large gaping hole inside the stupa. It looked absolutely anomalous. I knew it was Stein's handiwork. Without any qualms he had drilled a hole in the stupa so that he and his men could enter the holy structure and carry away antiquities.

I looked at the hole again; it was large enough for one person to wriggle through. I climbed the high ramp and reached the opening. I spied upon a narrow path that led into a dark space. I wanted to see what lay therein, but the museum official forbade me to venture inside.

I walked around the high stupa several times, chanting prayers to the great Buddha. Once there was a huge wall around the stupa but all that was left now was a crumbling edifice. My thoughts went back to the second/third century when the nine-metre tall stupa was built; sitting amidst the banal brown of the sand dunes it must have looked magnificent.

In 1929 Huang Wenbi, a Chinese archaeologist found here numerous ceramic fragments, remains of clay Buddha statues and ancient coins that were probably offerings by the devotees. In recent years, the Hetian Cultural Relic Administrative Bureau found a group of statues at Rawak including an elliptical Buddha head whose hair was wavy and tied up in a small bun. The face was round and bulging with large eye sockets and elongated eyebrows. A worshipping female portrait was also found with a partly damaged head, wearing a pleated skirt with a beautiful belt twisted at the waist. The figure held an incense holder in the right hand. There were also interesting murals of door-keeper or Dwarapala facing the entrance.[3]

It is said that Stein camped in the region of the Rawak in 1901 to explore the stupa. He dug into the walls surrounding the courtyard and found that it was adorned with rows of colossal statues in stucco representing Buddha or bodhisattvas with their attending deities and saints. The walls were further decorated with elaborate plaques forming halos above and around the main figures. Added to these were lovely frescoes. There was paint still in the fold of the deities' drapery when Stein discovered them.[4] Stein carried away a considerable number of

A large gaping hole can be seen on the left side of the Rawak Stupa. This opening is said to have been made when explorers drilled a hole to enter it. On close examination one can clearly see a narrow path leading into a dark space. It was from this stupa that British –Hungarian explorer Aurel Stein carried away antiquities.

BELOW LEFT: Men preparing delicious goshikirda *at the Urangkash village market near the Jade river. It is a traditional dish that has minced meat stuffed in wheat dough and roasted in a tandoor.*
BELOW RIGHT: The rounded goshikirda *look like huge roasted buns.*

sculptural pieces to England and the ones he could not carry were buried in sand.

I spent an hour at the stupa resting under a wooden thatched structure and thinking about the monks who lived at Rawak. All around there was only the stark desert. There was no stream, no pond. No water body. How did the monks survive? I learnt from the museum official that in ancient times this was a well irrigated monastic area and a part of the Khotan oasis where at least two crops and some vegetables were cultivated annually. The desert claimed it only after the monks abandoned it. I retraced my steps through the desert to the jeep tired and exhausted and extremely parched.

Goshikirda at Urangkash

On returning from the desert we passed through the Urangkash village near the river. The sleepy village was famous for *goshikirda*, a traditional dish that has minced meat stuffed in wheat dough and roasted in a tandoor. I could sniff the aroma of cooked meat; I was not hungry but

tempted enough. We stopped at the first shop selling the succulent *goshikirda*. There was clamouring all around; the shopkeepers were beckoning people to taste the Khotan specialty. We sat down for lunch and washed down the scrumptious brown *goshikirda* with herbal tea. One bite and whoosh! The spices hit me. It was very spicy, very akin to the Indian kebab. The herbal tea was laden with its share of umpteen spices—cardamom, cinnamon, ginger. The *goshikirda* was cheap, the round, brown balls cost only a yuan and the tea was free. One could pour as much as one wanted out of the large kettle. We were stuffed; this must have been the cheapest lunch on the Silk Road!

Sanpula Cemetery

After a hearty lunch we headed towards Sanpula cemetery, an ancient site in the desert. Located by the side of the river on the northern slope of the Kunlun mountains the cemetery of Sanpula is one of the most important archaeological discoveries in Xinjiang. The cemetery would have remained buried under layers of soil had it not been for a furious flood in 1980 that washed away the top soil, uprooted many tombs and several corpses dressed in fine fabric were found floating on the muddy waters. Or, so say the villagers. When word about the corpses reached those at the helm, they were taken into possession and the cemetery excavated later. However, between the flood and the government's response, a lot of precious ornaments, rich brocade and fine silk that covered and decked the corpses were pilfered by the villagers.

I saw the Khotan river flowing by; it was this river that brought the corpses into the limelight. The flood and that fateful day have not been forgotten but the Khotan river has now settled to doing ordinary chores, like irrigating the fields.

Between 1983 and 1985, sixty-eight tombs and two sacrificial horse pits have been excavated by the Xinjiang Institute of Archaeology and the Autonomous Region Museum. The cultural relics found here include brocade dresses, silk and cotton, felt and leather fabric. These Sanpula

Graves at the Sanpula cemetery, an ancient site in the Taklamakan desert by the side of the Khotan river. The cemetery was discovered after a furious flood when corpses dressed in fine fabrics were washed ashore and found floating by the villagers.

relics have evinced a lot of interest and scholars and researchers across the world are burning their midnight oil to study their design and weave. Scholars would have you believe that since Xinjiang was the confluence of several cultures, the fabric found in Sanpula could be an eclectic pick from West Asia, Central Asia, China, and India dating back to 2000 BC.[5]

Nearly sixty skulls excavated from the cemetery have provided abundant material for anthropological study of the ancient inhabitants of Sanpula, who probably belonged to the Europoid race. Other relics from the tombs include nearly a thousand pieces of ribbons, boots, face

covers, gloves, jackets, pullovers, ornaments, hats etc.

We ventured inside the cemetery where amidst sandy desert lay open graves. Some were rectangular with a mud roof and a tunnel leading inside to the main burial chamber. A narrow pathway cut through the cemetery and led to a large pit where several skulls and bones were lying half embedded in the earth. Some graves had been covered with built structures and appeared like small houses. I wanted to walk into one of the larger graves but the director forbade me; entering the graves is strictly prohibited. Several pathways ran through the cemetery and all around one could see thousands of raised structures which once embodied the corpses.

We sat for dinner with Mohammed Karim, director of Khotan Museum, who regaled us with stories about the strong ties between India and Khotan up to the tenth century. Interestingly, he informed me that until the tenth century AD, Buddha images carved and painted in Khotan, Turfan, Dunhuang and Central China looked very Indian. But things started changing thereafter; now the Buddha images borrow the look of the Chinese.

Karim told me that before Islam made inroads into this region, there were at least ten Buddhist establishments in Khotan which were later destroyed in skirmishes that ensued between the believers of Islam and Buddhism. Temples were destroyed and mosques built on the debris. According to him, Rawak is still considered the best stupa where numerous Buddhist antiquities are still buried under the sand. He talked of the ruins of another Buddhist establishment found in Domoko village where a big headless statue of Buddha was recently unearthed.

For centuries, India and China have been trading partners, with trade commencing between Chinese Turkestan (Xinjiang) and India through Kashmir. The Khotan area was especially close to India and the famous Khotanese rugs, Atles silk and jade carvings were the stuff that Kashmiri markets were made of. However, for political and economic reasons trade with India has been stopped. Now jade, silk and carpets are traded with Pakistan.

On Donkey Cart to the Malikawat Stupa

Deserts around Khotan were littered with the remains of abandoned cities. Yotkan ruins, which was closed for public viewing, is said to be the ancient capital of pre-Islamic kingdom dating from the third to the eighth century.

The Malikawat ruins, thirty-five kilometres south of town at the foot of the Kunlun mountains lay on the banks of the Urungkash or the White Jade river. The Malikawat village still exists on the river bank but the ruins lay scattered four kilometres away. A new airport was coming up near the base of the Kunlun mountains. It took an hour to reach the foot of the Kunlun. The road took a right turn towards the mountains. From a high ground the river looked beautiful and several streams gushed out of the mountains to meet at various points.

On the river bed, machine and trawlers were at work; large-scale mining of the river bed was in progress. The best white jade comes from this river, hence the name White Jade river. Miners take the land near the river on lease and collect jade which goes into the making of jewellery and art objects. Thanks to jade mining and lush orchards, Malikawat is prosperous. Succulent grapes, large pomegranate and precious jade nuggets can be bought from the farmers.

Gurbustan and I stopped near the house of Usman Kasim. But the parked vehicle was not secure and we coughed up ten yuan; that is what Usman charged to keep an eye on our jeep. Many donkey cart owners offered us a ride to the pagoda site. Their fee: twenty yuans. I jumped into the cart of Rossinissa Khan and sat on the wooden seat that was covered with a red carpet. Rossinissa did not need to prod or whip the donkey; perhaps the animal read our mind and knew our destination. Or maybe the ride to the pagoda was his everyday chore; he goes nowhere else; that is his only route. Whatever, he took us quickly to the river bank near the Buddhist site where there was a veritable forest of pagodas lying amidst ruins.

The Jade river quietly flowed by. Once a large Buddhist establishment existed on its bank, but as if on a whim the river changed its course, went further south leaving the site in a vast stretch of sand. It was soon deserted.

I looked around for a bit and then we headed back to Usman Kasim's house. Before we met Usman's family we had to contend with a boisterous bunch of children, their hands full of jade. They wanted to make a quick buck by selling the jade. They pleaded, they begged, they exhorted but I was in no mood to buy. I smiled, shook their hands, and said a 'no'. But this was an adamant bunch; they continued nudging and trailing me. I finally met Usman's family. His daughter-in-law snipped bunches of grapes off the creeper hanging over our head, washed them in a bowl and offered them in a tray. The red grapes were very succulent and delicious.

Usman was a wealthy man, his backyard was full of pomegranate and peach trees. After we had feasted on the red grapes, he pulled out a box of jade that was spilling with stones of various hues. They were rare, looked beautiful but were extremely expensive. I could not afford to splurge. There was so much still to be explored on the Silk Road; I politely refused Usman's offer. He was kind; he understood my predicament and looked stoic about the deal that never materialised. He packed more bunches of grapes for our onward journey. I appreciated his gesture with immense gratitude. But Gorbustan is not so grateful. She said nobody buys grapes here, it is eaten free. On our way back I bought a big hamigua for a yuan to have a nice feast back at the hotel.

I am not the only one in love with Malikawat; the Chinese pilgrim Fahien found Malikawat so pleasant that he stayed here for six months. Well, I could not afford that luxury and headed out.

Indian Monks at Kunlun

About fifty kilometres from the city lies Kakhmarum or the Black Jade river on the banks of which lies a three thousand-year-old cave. It is said that on their return from India, Fahien and Xuanzang stayed in this

The Urungkash or the White Jade river flowing past the Malikawat village in Khotan. The best jade comes from the river and large-scale mining is carried out to collect jade from the river bed.

cave. The double-storied cave was large and cut deep inside the mountains. Near the mouth of the cave was a gaping black hole which led through a ladder to another cave. The cave area was said to have been inhabited by Shamans who worshipped nature. The Black Jade river flowing deep below the cave borrows its name from the black jade that is found in abundance in the area.

We find mention by Xuanzang[6] of a somewhat similar cave: 'South-east of the city 300 li or so, there is a great rock like a stone wall with two stone chambers in it, in each of which sits an arhat in a profound state of ecstasy'.

It is said that since this part of the country was the closest to India there were many *arhats* who dwelt in the mountains of southern Xinjiang. In his memoirs Xuanzang mentions[7] niches found in a mountain to the south of Cha-kiu-kia or Yarkiang where several monks from India who had attained spiritual power found shelter and some even attained 'nirvana' in these niches. Xuanzang also talks of three *arhats* who lived in the mountain caverns and had amnesia. They had reached such a state of forgetfulness that they stayed unkempt and unshaven for days and local priests came infrequently to give them the much-needed shave. At Khotan, he mentioned[8] hundred monasteries and about five thousand priests who mostly studied the 'Great Vehicle'. While the king claimed to be a descendant of Vaisravana, a Buddhist deity of northern India, the monk traced the lineage of the kings to Kunal, the eldest son of Emperor Asoka who reigned over Taxila[9]. Local legend has it that Khotan was colonised by Indian immigrants from Taxila who were banished from their kingdom for blinding Kunal.

Xuanzang also saw[10] a seven feet high bejewelled image of the sitting Buddha in a temple on the borders of Khotan. This image, he said had come from Kashmir. The famous twenty feet high sandalwood image of the standing Buddha was found by the pilgrim outside Khotan at Pima which came all the way from Kausambi near Allahabad. As the story goes, King Udyayana commissioned the image while Buddha was still alive and kept it in his palace.[11]

At a Silk Weaver's Village

Silk is the most precious commodity in Khotan and there are thousands of families weaving the best quality Atles silk. It is said that when Xuanzang visited Khotan he saw the monastery that had been built to commemorate the successful and secret introduction of sericulture from China. The art of sericulture was introduced by China but for centuries they guarded the secret zealously. But the king of Khotan was eager to know the art; he was so enamoured by the beautiful fabric that he was ready to try any trick to get the silkworms into his kingdom. As the story goes, he requested the Chinese emperor for the hand of the princess. Before the marriage was solemnised he sent an envoy to the princess urging her to secretly bring the silkworms so that he could always drape her porcelain skin in yards of silk. In 140 BC, when the Chinese princess was headed to Khotan her maids topped her tresses in a huge bouffant into which they hid silk cocoons and mulberry seeds. Who would have thought that the secret of sericulture that the Chinese had guarded so obsessively for centuries would be slipped out stealthily in a bouffant and that too by the princess herself![12]

All along the Silk Road I had heard incredible tales of silk weaving and wanted to see how it was actually done. We headed to a silk weavers' village near Jiaxiang town where the world-famous Atles silk is woven on looms. It was a dusty village, dotted with mud houses arranged symmetrically in tidy rows. We stepped into Karim's house who was playing with his grandson in the afternoon sun while his daughter-in-law was dressing a chicken for lunch.

In a corner two elderly women sat spinning silk yarn from pale brown cocoons immersed in hot water. The thread was uncoiled and pulled to a wooden spinning wheel and turned into spindles. There was smart division of labour—while some turned thread into yarn, others weaved Atles silk on horizontal wooden looms. Karim was enterprising, he does not sell the yarn; he turned them into exquisite fabric and sold them in the showroom that occupied one corner of his house. Various kinds of silk weaves, dress material, hats and scarves were on display in the not-so-fancy showroom.

The courtyard was replete with countless bunches of ripe grapes. Several sacks full of cocoons were kept in a corner that would last the entire season. The women had a routine to follow, after meals they boiled the cocoons and sat for hours spinning yarn. The silk was beautiful and I made a small purchase.

Jiaxiang is a traditional centre of Atles silk. There were hundreds of silk-weaving units where young women are the main task force. With nimble fingers they weaved on wooden frames hanging from the ceiling. The silk is first spun, dyed in vegetable colours and woven on traditional looms. No synthetic dye is used and colours are procured from nature – yellow from *Tohomak*, black from walnut skin, maroon from *ordan*, red from pomegranate.

Famous Face of Shahrukh Khan

It was my last evening in Xinjiang and I decided to spend it at the vibrant Sunday market of Khotan. The market was bustling and again, the most famous face here is of actor Shahrukh Khan (pronounced Shahru Han here). At the Gillan bazaar, I partook in the commotion and the fun. I bought some chicken tikkas with green chutney. The tikkas were pulled straight out of burning charcoal and they melted in the mouth. I took photographs of Yasin who was roasting sheesh kebabs over fire. He was indeed photogenic. He chopped a large chunk of flesh off the hanging sheep carcass, sliced it into small pieces, sprinkled hot spices and salt, pasted them with lard, skewered them in an iron rod and left them on the slow charcoal fire to be first smoked. As the kebabs turned golden, more spices and oil were sprinkled until they turned brown and were ready to melt in the mouth. Not too far away, a shop was selling different kinds of *naan*, and hot permudas. Here people seldom bake *naan* at home. They buy them by the dozen in the market bakery and store them for the week wrapped in a dry cloth. Naan is usually eaten with soup alongwith mutton and vegetable gravy. Women generally cook finely chopped mutton or beef with lots of onions, tomatoes and eggplant. They use a lot of oil, hot spices and dried red chillies for flavour. Interestingly, the naans are never heated before eating; they are eaten cold.

However, Gillan bazaar was not the only one; there were other markets like the Dopa market and animal market which were centres for selling *Atles* silk, carpets, garments, bakeries, mutton, beef, vegetables and fruits. The animal market was much like the Kashgar market where sheep, goat, horses and donkeys are traded.

From the bazaar I found my way to the City Square where I saw a sculpture of former Chinese chairman Mao Tse Tung shaking hands with Uighur tribal leader Kurban Turum. This sculpture was unusual, says Gorbustan; it was the only known public sculpture in which Mao was depicted with another figure. Gorbustan tells me about Kurban Turum (b. 1883), an Uighur electrical worker from Khotan, who set out on a donkey to Beijing in order to present raisins to Mao in 1959. On arriving in Urumqi, party officials sent him on a flight to Beijing where he was received by Mao himself. The meeting has been celebrated in many works of art and the statue at Khotan's Square is one of them. It was installed here to mark the fiftieth anniversary of the establishment of the Xinjiang Uighur Autonomous Region.

I strolled around leisurely and captured the monumental statue from all angles in my camera. The Square was swarming with hundreds of men, women and children who were there to spend some lazy and unhurried moments. Neon lights falling from fancy chandeliers lit up the granite floor which had been scrubbed so clean that it served as a mirror. Flower beds had been arranged neatly. Hawkers were peddling eatables from their motorcycles parked at the edge of the square. I saw huge bunches of bananas hanging near the motorcycle's tyres. Some even had mud ovens fixed on their bikes and used a prong to fish out roasted potatoes, sweet buns and stuffed bread. I bought steamed corncobs from a hawker for a yuan and plonked myself on a wooden bench. I intended to spend the entire evening at the square watching young mothers playing with chubby toddlers, little boys struggling to learn cycling, old men flying luminous kites and couples strolling holding hands.

The second leg of my journey on the Silk Road from Urumqi to Khotan was over. I was not far from the borders of India. Not long ago the trade routes from Khotan met at Leh in Ladakh through Yarkand, a journey of about seven hundred kilometres across the Karakoram passes to the borders of India. In the olden times, this journey must have taken frenzied days and shuddering nights, with many succumbing to the vagaries of Nature and the pain of jaded feet. But how times have changed. Today, this would barely take a day!

The magnificent Maitreya Buddha, the world's largest, at Leshan sitting between two mountain cliffs. Set against the sapphire sky at the convergence of the three rivers, Min, Dadu and Qinggi, the seventy-one metre high stone-carved Maitreya was built in AD 713. The giant Buddha is a UNESCO World Heritage site.

13

To Chengdu— The City of Poets

Home of the Leshan Buddha

The first two laps of my journey along Highway 312 and its branches 313, 314 and 315 from Xian along the north-western regions of the Silk Road up to Kashgar and Khotan had concluded. From mountains, high peaks, lush valleys and immense rivers to the barren lands of the Gobi and the Taklamakan deserts, so many days over thousands of kilometres, such varying landscapes, so many memories, so many unusual experiences and so many different faces. I failed to translate all into words; even my camera could not capture it all. The Silk Road was just too beautiful to translate into words or canvas. The journey had come full circle. The eventful journey had started in Xian and I was now back there. From Xian to Xian, the map read.

But now I was headed in another direction. The 600 miles-long journey to the city of Chengdu, on National Highway 108 that ran south-west from Xian passed through lush forests and beautiful sceneries. Alas! with thousands of kilometres of road journey already behind me I decided to take the flight to Chengdu. I was received at the airport by a young Chinese girl Zhu Ya who preferred to call herself Juliet. She took me to Luoman Hotel.

After the parched desert of the Gobi and the Taklamakan, the luxuriant Chengdu with its spectacular beauty, was such a welcome change—the picturesque red hills emerged from the cluster of rain clouds, their slopes adorned by green carpets of tea plantations and thick bamboo forests, the myriad lakes where pink and purple lotus bloomed and water fowls gambolled and where a strange luminescence settled over everything.

Besides living the reputation of being a paradise, Chengdu is also the gateway to Tibet. Once upon a time it was a thriving city on the south-western trade route to Lhasa where trade routes from India met. It was through this route that many art and sculptural styles from India are believed to have passed onto the caves in Dazu (Sichuan), Majishan, Binglingsi and Dunhuang (Gansu).

Assamese Silk in Chengdu

It might sound far-fetched now, but in those ancient times Chengdu was in direct contact with the north-east regions of India along the river Brahmaputra especially Assam from where it procured lac for its lacquer industry and non-mulberry muga silk for its high-fashion clothing. In the production of silk, the weavers of Assam were reputed all over the world. Export of unbleached Assamese silk (called Muga silk) from Assam villages to Lhasa and onwards to Chengdu is a recorded fact. It was considered to be the most popular and fashionable silk in China.

We have an account of the clothing fashions of China in *The Land of the Lamas* (by Wiliam Woodville Rockhill): 'The well to do people wear shirts of coarse unbleached silk of Indian manufacture, with high red collar and half rupee pieces as buttons in the case of men and elaborate gold buckles and coral buttons mounted with gold or silver for women'.[1]

It is believed that the silk trade in Assam dates back to the pre-Christian era. Chinese envoy and explorer Zhang Qian who was sent to the Western Regions on a mission traced his country's trade links with India probably via Yunan, Burma or Assam as far back as in 100 BC.[2]

Sualkuchi village, forty kilometres from Guwahati was on the international map even before Xuanzang visited Pragjyotishpur (modern Guwahati) in the seventh century. It is said that the ancient trade route from China passing through Tibet crossed into Assam touching the renowned silk villages of Sualkuchi, Amguri, Lakhimpur, Phukuakhana, Sibsagar and Golaghat where the silk trade flourished. It was just a day's caravan trek from the banks of the Brahmaputra river for a trader who could then pick a variety of Muga silk from any Sualkuchi family at a very low price.

The village has known only silk work and hundreds of generations of weavers have gone by picking thread from a muga cocoon and weaving exquisite silk on wooden looms accompanied by the singing of the melodious Bihu geet.

The traditional designs of Banaras, Haziranga, Phulkari and Diamond and others inspired by birds and animals like peacocks, elephants, parrots and horses were the stuff that dreams were made of. At times the weavers weaved Indian ornaments like the *jhumka, haar* and *jhumar* or the banana tree, creepers and ferns into the fabric. There was nothing to beat Assamese silk anywhere in the world and the Chinese were simply besotted by it. The Assamese had learnt to rear non-mulberry cocoons or 'leta' on *soom* trees that flourished in the dense jungles. Exports from Assam also included elephant tusks, stick lac, cotton, pepper, mustard seeds.

There was extensive external trade and the merchants of Kamarupa traded with distant countries going by boat. They had trade relations with China both by land and sea. Tamralipti was an important sea-port and under the control of king Bhaskaravarmana.[3]

The route from Assam passed along the Brahmaputra valley crossed into Tibet, thence to Lhasa and onwards east to Chengdu from where it joined several routes going to Chongqing, Wuhan, Shanghai, Xian, Beijing etc. It is said that on being invited by king Bhaskaravarmana, Xuanzang came to Kamarupa (Assam) and lived there for more than a month. Writing about Kamarupa the monk said:[4] 'Their frontiers therefore are contiguous to the barbarians of the south-west(of China)....I ascertained that after a two months journey we reach the south-western frontiers of the province of Sz'chuen (Sichuan)'.

In fact, according to the great monk, people from Assam were travelling to Sichuan covering the long journey in two months. People undertook the travel inspite of the fact that the 'mountains and rivers presented obstacles, and the pestilential air, the poisonous vapours, the fatal snakes, the destructive vegetation, all these causes of death prevail.'

There are references of Buddhist scholars of ancient Kamarupa going to Tibet.[5] King Rudra Singha (AD 1696-1714) is also known to have built trade links with Tibet.[6] The great Tibetan river Yarlong Tsangpo or the Brahmaputra also gave gold to the Assamese which was collected by washing the sands of the river. Ten to twelve thousand people were engaged in this work.[7] They paid to the king one tola of gold per head per year for extracting gold from the river. In Tibet too gold washing was one of the most common occupation as every stream seemed to contain gold in its sand particles. Interestingly we learn from the author of *The Land of the Lamas* and traveler to Tibet, William Woodville Rockhill[8] that upto Ta-chien-lu, Chinese silver bullion was not accepted and only the Indian rupee was prevailing.

The more I learnt about Chengdu, the more sobriquets I found for it. After I had heard about it being a paradise and a gateway, I was told that during its 2,500 years of recorded existence, it was proudly known as the 'Brocade City',[9] the name coming from its flourishing silk industry. Juliet, my guide, told me that even as early as third century BC, Chengdu was producing the finest brocades. By the first century, brocade workers of Chengdu were working on the foot-driven looms.

Celebrities Lived in Chengdu

Chengdu was not without its share of celebrities–Xuanzang, the great monk, spent a few years of his life here studying the different schools of Buddhism. It is said that while the monk and his brother were living at the Pure Land Monastery in Luoyang, the eastern capital of the Sui dynasty his studies were interrupted in AD 618 when the Sui dynasty collapsed. The great monk and his brother fled to Changan (Xian) but not finding any safe shelter there, they made their way to Chengdu in Sichuan province[10]. He was not alone; a number of monks came with him. Xuanzang stayed for four years up to AD 622 in the Chengdu Daci temple.

Chengdu was a poet's delight. When the famous eighth century Chinese poet, Du Fu wrote about the dark clouds in the wide sky, sailing over mountains and boundless forests, the endless waves of surging rivers, the wind so swift and the beach so white,[11] he was perhaps describing the beauty of Chengdu. His thatched cottage overlooking the Huanghua river has been preserved over the centuries as a garden. It is said that Chengdu had such heavenly beauty that made the great poets like Li Bai tipsy—not only with sparkling wine, but also with the iridescence of the silver river and the gleaming moonshine, the floating clouds and the green mountains, gushing streams and the azure sky.[12] Chengdu became the home of several great poets and writers and most composed their best works here.

Xue Tao (AD 758-832), the poetess is said to have written five hundred poems, many of them at the Riverview Pavilion park by the side of the Fuhe river. She drew water from a well, now named Xue Tao well, to dye and design her own paper on which she would write her poems. She greatly revered the bamboo plant and more than 120 species of bamboo have been planted in her memory at the pavilion where stood her marble statue. That the lovely ambience of the beautiful river bank, the blooming flowers and bamboo forests at the time spring could stirr up melancholy in the heart of the poetess was a bit touching. She once wrote:

'We don't enjoy together blooming flowers,
Nor at their fall together shed our tears.
Oh why am I lovesick from hour to hour

To see flowers appear or disappear!'

('Spring View' Trans. Yuanchong, Xu; *300 Gems of Chinese Classical Poetry*)

To Leshan Mountains

Even age has not withered the beauty of Chengdu, I was absolutely delighted to be in the land of writers and poets. But I had a bigger motivation to be here, I wanted to see the world's biggest Maitreya Buddha in Leshan, which was 120 kilometres from Chengdu. The lovely drive to Leshan mountains ran through tea plantations sprawled over thousands of acres. All along the air was laden with the whiff of the fragrance of large white flowers that burdened the freshly pruned bushes. The hills were decked with silvery streams that looked like white lace trim on the green sheath. I have seen tea estates in Assam and Darjeeling (West Bengal) but they are no match to the aroma or the deep colour of the Chengdu plantations.

This region is all about tea and to know more we stopped at the tea museum in the suburbs near the Jugao Yang tea gardens. Here we were welcomed by a statue of the third century special officer Jugao (of the Sui Kingdom) standing in his splendid robes and waving a branch of the tea leaves as if beckoning the passersby to stop for a while and relax over a cup of tea in the shaded tea house within his estate. It is said that Jugao owned a huge tea plantation in Chengdu and did everything to grow and popularise several varieties of tea and their products. Around him was a beautiful pond full of blooming lotuses. On a mound stood two bullocks in black stone pulling a cart full of tea bags and driven by two men. The statue looked very real and was testimony to the age when tea processing was done manually–there were no machines to pick or dry leaves; neither were there speeding vehicles to transport the dried leaves or granules from one end of the world to another. Inside the tea museum we learnt about different kinds of tea grown in Chengdu. In the tea house were stacked various by-products like tea toffees and tea snacks.

Tea Road

Ta-chien-Lu is the western-most sub-prefecture in the province of Sichuan. Its chief importance was as a trading center and it is said to be the emporium between China and Tibet. According to Rockhill (*The Land of the Lamas*) tea was the most important product exported to Tibet from Sichuan province of China. It is estimated that several million pounds were sent to the Tibetan market for sale and consumption. This tea was brought from the tea gardens of Sichuan by porters on their backs. At Ta-chien-Lu the tea was sent to the packing houses where they were pressed into bricks and packed and sewn in raw hide[13] ready for export to Tibet on the backs of yak. A road ran from Chegdu to Lhasa via Ta chien Lu and was called the Tea Route along which tea caravans moved to Lhasa.

The tea also went upto upper Assam. When the first tea gardens were opened in Assam at Lakhimpur in 1835 the first seed is said to have been brought from China and skilled Chinese tea manufacturers were imported. Possibly the seeds came from Chengdu tea estates that flourished on the low hills.

Saffron from Kasmir, soap from South India, unbleached silk from Assam and medicinal herbs from Garhwal Himalayas and the north-eastern states were sent to Ta-chien-Lu through Tibet.[14] The people were also fond of the Indian tobacco coming usually from Sikkim. The volume of trade with India was so high that the Indian rupee (in which the payments were usually made) brought to Ta-chien–Lu was melted in eight forges. These were kept going for melting the rupees into silver ingots which was in use all over western Sichuan.[15]

By the time Juliet and I reached the Leshan mountains it was lunch time. We walked into a mountain restaurant by the side of the road. I was in the mood for some fire on my palate and picked some spicy chicken, maize bread and chilli king prawns from the Sichuanese menu. There was no immediate lavish spread; the food arrived gradually in courses. First, there was a huge plate of boneless chicken with capsicum, black mushrooms, a large dose of red chillies with a fair sprinkling of peppercorns cooked in Sichuanese spicy sauce. I got heady with the scent and wanted to dig in.From amidst a bed of spring onion juliennes sat the steamed king prawns topped with chilly sauce. I was stuffed to the gills but there was still more to come and I was ready—a plate of boiled and shredded duck with a bowl of uncooked tofu that was flipped with a dash of soya sauce. I washed down all this with ladles full of jasmine and chrysanthemum tea that calmed the fire of the chillies that had singed my insides! I was told the punch comes from peppercorns and red chilles that were grown in this area.

Giant Buddha at Leshan

After the sumptuous meal we headed to the jetty and hired a speed boat to the turbulent river flowing at the foot of the holy mountains facing the Leshan city. The mountains are joined and shaped like the body of the Sleeping Buddha. Between two cliffs sat the world's largest Maitreya Buddha. Set against the sapphire sky at the convergence of the three rivers, Min, Dadu and Qinggi, the seventy-one-metre high stone-carved Maitreya was built in AD 713.

Like every other Buddha, even this one has a story. Juliet told me that each summer Min, Dadu and Qinggi—the three rivers—threw tantrums; they became turbulent and livid. The irate sea would wreak havoc, taking many within its folds. Boats capsised, boatmen vanished and the villagers dreaded the onset of summer. Along the angry rivers lived Haitong, a Buddhist monk who had made Linggun Hill his home. He was a kind soul; perturbed by the wails of the villagers he decided to resolve the problem, he wanted to calm the sea and bring back its serenity. He invoked the Buddha. He knew only the Buddha had an answer. But this Buddha he would create himself—he would carve the Buddha off a cliff, hoping that the Buddha's presence would subdue the lashing waves and protect the boatmen. Haitong set out on a mission; he travelled along the rivers in a bid to collect funds for the mammoth Buddha.

The world's largest Maitreya was completed in AD 803. The Buddha faces the river and watches the rolling waves in solemn stillness. Though He sits at the confluence of three rivers, the Buddha remains safe from severe winds and fatal soil erosion because the image has been carved into a cliff.

There were dangers on the way, but Haitong was not daunted. He fended them all, even an evil official who tried to pilfer the money that the monk had collected. The monk was vehement in his protests, he said, 'I would rather gouge out my eyes than give a penny to you.' The official retorted, 'Gouge your eyes out now.' Haitong honoured his word; he dug out one of his eyes.

The story of the resolute monk spread like wild fire, encouraging sculptors and other construction workers to chip the cliff more diligently, more quickly. Unfortunately, Haitong would not live to see the Buddha readied on the cliff, he died much before the last curl was carved on his deity. But Haitong's earnestness did not wither with his death, the work continued. It took hundreds of men, cartloads of patience and ninety years.

The world's largest Maitreya Buddha was completed in AD 803. The Buddha faced the river and watched the rolling waves in solemn stillness. And for thousands of years he has kept an eye on the three rivers that no longer intimidated people with their wrath. Boats now float happily on the river, smug in the thought that the Buddha would care for them.

As we got closer to the mountains we found some scattered holes around the Buddha, said to be the remains of the so-called Giant Buddha Pavilion. The nine-storied building that was set up during the Tang Dynasty to shelter the Buddha was renamed the Linggun Pavilion during the Song dynasty. After the Pavilion was destroyed in a war, the Buddha remained outside, without a roof over his head. Despite incessant rains and bouts of dry weather, the Giant Buddha is well preserved. Scholars would have you believe that the intact Buddha enjoys topographical advantages. It lies on the southern side of the hill, where verdant trees grow and protect rocks and slope from erosion. Add to it the fact that though the Buddha sits on the confluence of the three rivers, it remains safe from severe winds and fatal soil erosion because it has been carved into the cliff. The natural advantages are buffered by the water-drainage system that remains hidden from view. The system starts with 1021 fastened buns or channels which appear like the matted hair of Buddha which connect one another at the back of the head. The end of the channels interlinks the shoulders and the robe pleats carved on the body. The hair, shoulders and pleats together form a complete system that carries away the entire surface water on the body and disappears underground. This system keeps the inner part of the stone structure dry and plays an important part in the preservation of the statue.

By the river stood a beautiful house that was built for the emperor to have a view of the river and mountains along with the Giant Buddha which is now included in the UNESCO World Natural Heritage list. The Holy Mount Emei on the other side of the river is a favourite pilgrimage site with more than thirty temples. Of these the most famous is the bronze statue of Bodhisattva Samantabhadra who lived and preached here.

A Stroll Along the Qin Tai Street

I was headed away from the Leshan mountains but I could not forget the Buddha smiling solemnly from a cliff, the image etched in my mind. It was time to head back to the hotel but I changed my mind. I did not want another precious hour spent insipidly in the hotel room, instead Juliet and I headed to the famous Qin Tai Street. Juliet filled me with interesting details; she said the street had been designed to recreate and restore the architecture and culture of ancient China. From the paved boulevard we watched the city in all its extravaganza. At the end of the street a large bronze chariot, perhaps excavated out of one of the royal mausoleums, was on display. A rider astride a bronze horse seemed to be in a hurry; so was the horse, its mane flying, its hooves hoisted in the air. In the glittering street light the metal sparkled like gold.

In another part of the street two young men clad in yellow robes were sparring with glistening swords. Many evening strollers had gathered around them to hear the clank of the clashing swords and admire the agility of the two men as they soared in defence. The boulevard was lined with shops stacked with Chinese handicrafts and tea from the region of Chengdu. I loved the scent of jasmine and bought some jasmine tea for friends in India. Piled by the roadside were paintings of Chengdu's beautiful landscapes made by local artists, some hunched over huge canvases on the sidewalk adding that stroke of scarlet to complete the setting sun. I walked into an antique shop selling the famous satin and brocade of Chengdu, where in one dusty corner sat a woman embroidering a floral pattern on silk that was stretched on wooden frames.

Silk was not the only item that had innumerable takers, there was a store selling sex toys. The sex shop looked anomalous but Juliet said that such shops were very popular!

Qin Tai Street has too many things within its narrow lanes; however, what was most famous were the hotpot restaurants. A narrow lane led us into Shi Zi Lou, a crowded restaurant, where people were tapping their feet to the beat of a live gig. The crooner, a young woman in a figure-hugging sequined dress, had whipped up quite a sensation. The fast song had youngsters tapping and jiving. They were like a perfect accompaniment to the woman with a guttural voice; together they set a boisterous mood amidst which elders wined and dined. There were other singers, each adding to the evening's crescendo with their music. When the music ended, out of nowhere came dancers wearing demonic masks. They jumped and turned and twisted and somersaulted and changed their masks so quickly that I was amazed at their nimbleness.

I loved the music, and stayed on and ordered a hotpot, the restaurant's specialty. Before the meal arrived a waitress poured some rose tea out of a silver kettle with a long snout. In the typical Chinese style, for several cups of tea hot water is poured over the same flowers, herbs and spices till the colour and flavour runs out. Interestingly, no extra money is charged and one can taste the best jasmine, rose, guava or unroasted green tea. Near the entrance large glass jars were spilling with live snails, prawns, snakes and all kinds of fish.

Soon a small wok of boiling liquid sitting on a stove was placed on my table. I looked at the broth—it was oily, red and bubbling like a fiery volcano. The liquid was a mixture of oil, vinegar and native spices, especially lots of red chillies and peppercorns. Along with the broth arrived a plate full of assorted and sliced vegetables, fish, chicken and mutton. These shredded and julienned vegetables and meat were slowly immersed in the boiling liquid and left to become tender and spicy. Red chilli sauce adds to the fire of this hot, straight from the fire, lip-smacking Sichuanese cuisine. To douse the fire of the tiny but deadly peppercorns are lots of fruits like watermelon, muskmelon and a variety of flavoured tea served with bowls of raisin. Trust me, that oily, red broth can burn your stomach, but it is so good that it is worth every burn, every hiss.

ABOVE: *The Daci Temple where the great monk Xuanzang lived and studied. The monk stayed at this famous Buddhist Academia of the Tang Dynasty to study Buddhist sutras before he left for India. The 'precious hall' was later constructed as a befitting memorial to him.*

BELOW: *A golden lion roars by the side of the Wenshu pagoda in Chengdu. It is believed that stroking the lion brings good luck.*

Xuanzang's Stay at Daci Temple

Situated in the downtown centre of Chengdu, Daci temple has been known since ancient times as the first monastery of China. According to the temple literature the long history, large size and rich cultural deposits of the temple date back to the third century AD. The eminent Indian monk, Baozhang is said to have journeyed east to China in the Western Jin period (AD 265-316) and stayed in Daci temple to pay his respect to Bodhisattva Samantabhadra. A pavilion was built in the memory of the bodhisattva where eminent monks were invited to give lectures on Buddhist philosophy.

According to the temple brochure, Daci was a famous Buddhist Academia in Tang Dynasty and Xuanzang stayed here to learn Buddhist sutras from teachers. In the spring of AD 622, this was his retreat to study Vinaya in the College of Commandments at the Daci temple. He sojourned here before leaving for India to fetch Buddhist scriptures.

Under immense royal patronage, famous artists gathered here to produce works of great fame and over a thousand frescoes covered the walls of the great temple. In its prime Daci temple is said to have occupied nearly half of the eastern downtown area of Chengdu. It became a major tourist destination with seasonal markets and fairs being held regularly. The markets sold special goods—there was the lantern market, markets for flowers, silkworms, medicines, linen and seven-treasure market at the temple while evening markets were set up along both sides of Jie Yu brook flowing at the front of the temple.

A huge hall was constructed as a befitting memorial to the great monk, where hangs a huge map showing Xuanzang's route to India. Murals on the wall depict the journey of the monk on an elephant back to western lands and his return with huge loads of Buddhist scriptures. There is an artist's rendition of the monk holding a yak tail in his right hand and a sutra book in his left shaded by an umbrella with the yak's back loaded with sutra books. There are other halls, the Hall of Maitreya, Hall of Avalokitesvara, Lecture Hall and the Sutra Library.

It is said that the Daci temple was so esteemed as an academy because of its association with the great monk and other eminent Buddhist scholars and so rich in Buddhist sutras and exquisite paintings that even during Emperor Wuzong's destruction of Buddhism[16], the temple was 'exempted from the temples to be destroyed'.

Buddha's Relics at Baoguangsi

Baoguangsi or Jewel Light Monastery—the well-known ancient temple is the largest extant temple in Sichuan. It was first built in the Eastern Han dynasty (AD 25 to 220).

It consisted of a pagoda soaring high in the sky and marks the place from where the holy relics of the Buddha were dug out. It is said that in AD 811 when Changan—the capital of the Tang Empire was conquered by Huang Chao's uprising army, Emperor Xizong retreated to Sichuan and stayed here. One night he saw a purple glow coming from the bottom of the pagoda. Immediately he ordered his followers to dig the ground. A stone case was dug out, with thirteen pieces of Buddha's relics inside. The emperor regarded them as a good omen for the nation's destiny. A thirteen-storied pagoda was then built to pay homage to the relics and the temple was extended with many more halls and rooms for 3000 monks. In AD 1851 the Hall of Arhats was completed with five hundred gilded statues of saints and seventy-six statues of Buddha and Bodhisattvas. There are splendid halls and beautiful statues of Buddha. More than 1,300 precious cultural antiques dating from the seventh century AD are kept here.

Morning Walk at Wenshu

Before retiring for the night Juliet, asked me if I wanted to have a close contact with the great monk Xuanzang. 'Closer than Daci?' I asked, 'where I had walked the ground where Xuanzang had lived, studied and lectured?' 'Yes, closer'.

That night in sleep I went back to my childhood in Kushinagara where Xuanzang had once wandered like me, in search of the Buddha.

Early next morning we walked into the sprawling monastery of the Wenshu temple. So many gardens, so many people. It seemed as if all morning walkers of Chengdu had descended on this monastery. I could hear soft music and men and women were exercising. In front of the main temple stood the Wenshu pagoda like a beacon tower. The eleven-storied slender pagoda has been built over the skull

The Jewel Light pagoda at Chengdu. It is located inside the ancient temple of Baoguangsi, built in the Eastern Han Dynasty (AD 25-220). It is the largest extant temple in Sichuan. The soaring pagoda is built over the holy relics of Buddha. In the early ninth century, a stone case was dug out from here with thirteen pieces of Buddha's relics inside.

FACING PAGE:
A painting of the great monk Xuanzang at the Master's Hall of the Daci temple in Chengdu. He has a chhatra *over his head and carries a whisk or* chavar *in his right hand while on his back he carries a load of Buddhist scriptures from India. Many more paintings and carved panels showing the route taken by the monk in India and his return with elephant loads of* sutras, *adorn the walls.*

The Wenshu temple inside the sprawling monastery of the Wenshuyuan at Chengdu. Inside the huge prayer hall several hundred monks and nuns gather to chant 'Namo Amitabho' every morning.

fragments of Xuanzang. The guide informed that the golden structure inside the front opening of the pagoda was the receptacle in which the skull had been interred. I stood in complete awe and silence with my hands folded. Behind it there was a drone of a loud chorus emanating from the huge prayer hall where several hundred monks had assembled. I joined the procession of nuns slowly circumambulating with candles in their hands singing praises of the Buddha *Namo Amitabho*. The walls of the hall depicted huge murals of bodhisattva Samantabhadra on a white elephant surrounded by deities and another had bodhisattva Manjusri sitting on a lion. In the centre lay the blissful paradise of the Buddha Amitabha–the sukhavati, a picture of heaven–the 'Pure Land' devoid of evil and suffering.

The prayer session ended and we went into the monastery dining hall for breakfast. The chief monk had deputed a junior monk to attend to us; he had heard that I was from the land of Buddha's Mahaparinirvana in Kushinagara. The monk had travelled several times to the land of Buddha and was elated to have Indian visitors.

ABOVE: The Jade Buddha at Wenshuyuan temple in Chengdu. The image carved out of a single piece of creamy jade is said to have been brought from Burma.
RIGHT: The walls of the prayer hall of the Wenshu temple depict huge murals of the blissful paradise of the Buddha Amitabha—the sukhavati*. On both sides of the* sukhavati *are murals depicting bodhisattva Samantabhadra on a white elephant surrounded by deities and of bodhisattva Manjusri sitting on a lion.*

The Vegetarian's Hall, a dining hall that can seat six hundred, is the largest in south-west China. Visitors can enjoy delicious vegetarian dishes here or in the Great Hall of Wisdom which specially arranges private gatherings. The monastery kitchen is run by the monks themselves. Among the large store of cultural antiques kept in the temple are the rare treasures of the great monk Xuan Zang's skull, the Kasaya with thousand Buddhas, the Goddess of Mercy statue, the White Jade statue of Buddha from Burma and Sanskrit sutras from India.

As I bade goodbye to the kind monk I did feel a strange bond with him, perhaps a bond between my hometown and Chengdu. Looking at the photographs of Kushinagara pasted on the picture board in his office I was reminded of old and decrepit China baba (a Chinese priest from Kushinagara) who not only made the long journey to the small town in eastern Uttar Pradesh but made the Ramabhar stupa in Kushinagara his home. In his devotion to Buddha he spent his life time at the stupa reading the scriptures and learning Sanskrit, Hindi and Bhojpuri, the local dialect spoken in the small suburban town.

The preaching Avalokitesvara 'the personification of kindness and knowledge', at Baodingshan grottoes in Chongqing. The Avalokitesvara is the most popular deity because of his compassionate nature and concern for the suffering humanity.

(14)

A Cliff Theatre at Chongqing

Hotpot in a Loquat Orchard

It was raining when Juliet and I started for the next destination—270 kms south-east of Chengdu—the Dazu grottoes acclaimed as 'the gallery of Avalokitesvaras' because of the numerous statues of bodhisattvas Amitabha, Avalokitesvara and Ksitigarbha. The weather was gorgeous. We broke journey several times to get a view of the tea gardens and orchards.

It was close to lunch by the time we reached Dazu county. We stopped at a loquat orchard deep inside which was hidden an unusual restaurant —the Pipa. It conjured up visions of beautiful apsaras, dancing and singing in the grottoes of Kuqa and playing the four stringed lute, also called the pipa, their diaphanous skirts hanging low and silky ribbons wrapping their slender bodies, billowing and streaming through the air and soft music wafting through the dark caves. I was in Baoding town where The Pipa has earned a reputation for its fish 'hot pot' and rice. The fish comes fresh from the nearby fish farm and we do not have to wait too long for our order.

I learnt that three enterprising young girls had pooled in money to start The Pipa and were doing brisk business. The Pipa was not made of concrete; it was a three-storied structure built of thatched bamboo with upturned roofs and hanging eaves, a poet's resort, really. I ran up to the top floor to get a good look at the dense loquat forest and banana fields. The dense foliage of the evergreen shrub set like a dark green, glossy crown on a stump. I was the only visitor that day and the girls didn't have much work on hand. Juliet told me that not many knew of this loquat restaurant and the owners took special care of those who walked in for a meal.

Some pavilions were set in the heart of the forest and food and drinks were being served right inside the orchard. I trekked to the pavilion and sat down for a refreshing cup of coffee. Tiny green birds were flitting from one bough to another. Bees and butterflies were sucking honey from the wild flowers that were blooming on the low hills. Never before had I seen such a dense loquat growth and I relished every moment of it.

By the time I finished my coffee and returned to the restaurant, lunch was ready. I sat on a delicate wrought iron chair and waited impatiently for the meal. Soon there arrived steaming rice and a big pan in which six small fish were dunked in spicy, boiling gravy. The hot pot was simmering on a stove. The fish tasted fabulous with the peppercorns and red chillies. That day it was not just about the tender fish, the ambience added to the enjoyment. So quiet, calm and peaceful. Just the right kind of locale to forget the woes of the world.

It was raining and I could see tiny drops of rains dripping languorously from the thatched roof. It was just beautiful and I wanted to stay on. I liked the unhurried pace of this world and enjoyed the bliss that came leisurely with unpacked hours. A slight drizzle caressed my skin. I walked back to the coach, my shoes a little squelchy, my heart a little jubilant at the thought of meeting the Avalokitesvara at the famous Baodingshan and the Beishan grottoes of Dazu.

It is said that although grotto art originated in India it flourished in China along the Silk Road[1] oasis towns on the fringe of the Gobi and the Taklamakan and along the regions of the Yellow and the Yangzi rivers. The grotto sites of Dazu are said to rival Dunhuang, Majishan and Binglingsi but were later additions in the eighth upto the nineteenth century AD (beginning from Tang through the Song and continuing upto the Ming and the Qing dynasties).

According to the Art Museum of Dazu Park Carvings in Chongqing, the carvings in Dazu form a large ritual site of tantric or mystic Buddhism also called *Vajrayana*. In 1961 the State Council of China designated the Dazu cliff carvings as national protected monument for their historical and cultural value as 'a complete system of Buddhist doctrine'. In 1999 the grottoes were on the list of UNESCO World Cultural Heritage site.

What led to the carvings at Dazu was the transfer of Chinese political power from north to the south following the An Lushan rebellion which almost overthrew the Tang dynasty in the mid-eighth century.[2] According to historical records[3] by AD 750 An Lushan, an able general of emperor Xuanzong (r. 712-56) had become very powerful. After acquiring control of the north-eastern frontiers he invaded Hebei in AD 755 and took Luoyang and in 756 he took Changan. The Tang emperor fled to the south in Sichuan. This also caused the cultural and the religious scene to shift to the south. The Yangzi river areas in Sichuan now became the centre of grotto art. The province was comparatively more peaceful and stabler than the Central China plain.[2] It is said that when Tang rulers fled to Sichuan to take refuge in the years of war, they were accompanied by many artistes, scholars and Buddhist teachers. As a result grottoes were dug on the hillsides and embellished with stone sculptures comprising Buddhist, Taoist and Confucian figures and themes.[4]

A Paradise Carved on Hills

I arrived first at the Baodingshan grottoes situated deep within thick forests of bamboos, palm and loquat. These were said to have been dug under the supervision of the famous monk Zhao Zhifeng who was a native of Baodingshan in the Southern Song dynasty in more than seventy years from AD 1174 to 1252. More than 50,000 pieces of carved rock figures are scattered at statutuaries spread over eleven locations mainly in Beishan (North Hill), the Baodingshan (Precious Peak Hill) and Nanshan (South Hill).

I was awestruck at the superb carvings and the colour schemes on the sculpted rocks - the shades of blue and green used by the painter, all gave life to the dull grey stones. The artist's ingenuity in creating the 'Paradise of Buddha' out of a rough hill was visible in every crevice. In making pagodas that stood for thousand years without falling from the hands of the gods; in creating a water body inside a cave so that the Avalokitesvara could gaze at the moon; in chipping a cliff into a peacock and moulding the tail to support the roof; with a simple chisel the artiste has breathed life into the rocks that became a mass of clay in his small hands. He also created the colours of the rainbow by crushing stones in a simple mortar. The finely chiselled images captured the different moods and ambience of deities and the depiction of religious and secular stories ran like the pages of a picture book.

The 'Three Saints' cave at Baodingshan grottoes depicts the perfectly enlightened Vairocana Buddha in the centre flanked by bodhisattva Samantabhadra on his left and bodhisattva Manjusri on his right. They hold pagodas two metres high weighing 500 kilograms each.

Some of the Best and Spectacular Carvings

The Goddess of Mercy spreads her wings like a dancing peacock illuminating the world with love and compassion. Her one thousand hands occupied eighty-eight square metres of the rock face. She appeared to be a blend of the animal and the human world, of the male and the female, of Saraswati and Siva, of Buddha and Indra. Like the Goddess Saraswati she wore golden robes and held the store of knowledge in the form of books and the repertoire of music in the form of the conch shell. Like the Buddha she held the Dhamma or the Law in the form of pagodas, had a third eye on the forehead like Siva and an eye in the hands like the Indra. A pair of hands held the lotus and another, the gem with which she removed all sufferings and sorrows.

According to the guide the Buddhist deity Avalokitesvara is represented here as the female goddess, the Guanyin Buddha whose head wears a huge two-tier crown bearing a small Buddha. A pair of central hands held the image of the meditating Buddha, while two hands, one on the right and another on the left held pagodas. The entire composition also appeared to convey the idea of triratna—the Buddha—

The gilded Mercy Buddha carved on rocks at the Baodingshan grottoes at Dazu in Chongqing. The goddess or the Guanyin Buddha spreads her wings like a dancing peacock illuminating the world with love and compassion.

represented by the central image, the pagoda representing the Dhamma or the Law and the thousand hands representing the Sangha. Two other figures on either side wearing long gowns appeared to be disciples. A touch of blue in gold gave a magical effect to the image.

A huge Wheel of Life was cut into another cliff. It expressed the basic doctrine of Buddhism that all living beings will be reincarnated according to their actions in their former life. Nobody can escape the result of his actions. It is a reminder of the predicaments of human beings and their liberation symbolised by the great Buddha sitting inside the central temple. It is believed that Buddha himself had made the first of these drawings. The cycle of life is depicted as a wheel with a hub, spokes and ring gripped between the jaws of the Lord of Death or the *Mahakaal*.

The Bodhisattva cave was adorned with the image of Manjusri—the symbol of wisdom, having a soft feminine face and a protuberance marked with vermillion on the forehead. He sat within a lotus on the back of a lion and wore a solemn expression. A pair of hands were folded in front while another pair held the holy sutras. Like a scholar he imparts perfect wisdom and enlightenment. Like goddess Durga, the symbol of *sakti*, Manjusri sits calmly on the lion who is roaring and thundering, his fierce eyes bulging out and his tongue hanging from the mouth, ready to devour his prey. But the fierce animal symbolising desires and passions has been subjugated by the fearless and calm bodhisattva. Another deity sitting on a sheep also holds sutra books and has a pagoda on the head.

The 'Three saints of Buddhism' cave depicts the perfectly enlightened and unsurpassed, Vairocana Buddha in the middle, flanked by the most tranquil bodhisattva Samantabhadra on the left and the wise bodhisattva Manjusri on the right. Wearing jewelled crowns and holding high pagodas they are carrying the 'dhamma' to its ultimate goal of salvation for all beings. It is said that the pagodas about two metres in height and weighing about 500 kgs each, have been standing in the hands of the Buddhist deities for thousand years and have never fallen off. The seven metre high images standing on double lotus wear heavy, long and flowing robes and lean forward at the top in order to avoid visual distortion. The wall at the back has the engraving of Thousand Buddhas.

The Buddha in deep meditation. A rock carving at the Baodingshan grottoes in Dazu.

Artistes' Skill Turn Cliff into Theatre

Skilfull artistes have turned the face of a huge cliff into a cinematic portrayal of Chinese culture and religion with engravings of the Buddha and bodhisattvas depicted in different *mudras* (postures). While the bodhisattvas are blessing, meditating and preaching, their actions are in essence an intermingling of the Confucian ideal of filial piety, Hindu concept of 'Karma' and Buddhist stories where Sakyamuni is carrying his father's coffin on his shoulders. Another scene showed him carrying his blind parents in hanging baskets. The carvings depicted love of parents for their children and anxiety and fear for their well being. A

FACING PAGE:
The Buddha delivers a sermon.

joyful mother is in close embrace with her child while another is suffering the pangs of labour.

Bad actions bring dreadful results. The carvings present horrifying images of hell. The sinner lies on a hot iron bed; he is being sawed, being devoured by snakes, his tongue is being pulled out, he is pushed in a cauldron of boiling oil or made to climb a hill of knives.

The thirty-one-metres long Nirvana Buddha, one would think comes straight out of the Mahaparinirvana temple at Kushinagara, except that the artiste has sculpted only the upper part of Buddha's body on the rock leaving the rest to our imagination. Heavenly deities, emperors and laymen are mourning the 'Great Decease'. Beautiful patterns have been carved on Buddha's robes and on the halo around his head. A narrow channel cut into the rock to drain out rain water or mountain streams appears as though it is the flowing river Hiranyawati on whose banks Buddha spent his last moments before attaining Nirvana. The great architectural skill in carving the giant Reclining Buddha sleeping in perfect bliss under an overhanging cliff lends a magnificent superhuman effect while those of the kings and disciples, inspite of their crown and robes, appear ordinary. As in other caves the judicious use of the different shades of the blue pigment gave an ethereal quality to the carvings.

The 'Paradise of Amitabha' depicted a happy world of 'Buddhist Pure Land', the *Sukhavati*, where there is profound happiness. Darkness and ignorance have been banished by the radiance of Amitabha. Devas bow in obeisance; there is end to suffering and affliction. Here all beings are equal with the potential of attaining salvation. Three large images painted in cobalt blue and copper green are those of three sages of the 'Pure Land'. The Amitabha dwells in the centre of the Paradise and illuminates it with his radiance. He is flanked by the crowned Bodhisattvas Avalokitesvara on the left and Mahasthamaprapta on the right. Other Buddhist deities and apsaras are also present. We see happy joyful children playing the flute or climbing the ladder leading to the paradise.

Carvings at Baodingshan depict horrifying images of Hell. Bad actions bring dreadful results. The sinner lies on a hot iron bed; he is sawed, devoured by snakes or pushed in a cauldron of boiling oil. Here he is made to climb a hill of knives.

FACING PAGE:
The thirty-one metre long Nirvana Buddha sleeps eternally at the Baodingshan. Heavenly deities, emperors and laymen are mourning the 'Great Decease' at Kusinara. In a first of its kind, the artiste has sculpted only the upper half of the Buddha's body leaving the rest to our imagination.

The 'Cave of Enlightenment' is a huge cave six metres high and twelve metres deep into the mountains. Three Buddhas of the past, present and future are sitting against the back wall in a grave meditating posture with their eyes half closed. They also bring to mind the three bodies of the Buddha or the 'Trikaya' doctrine of the Mahayana.[5] According to the *Buddhanusmrti* (p.203) the three aspects are the 'dharmakaya' or the Law or the doctrine; the 'sambhogkaya' or the body that exists in the celestial spheres like the Amitabha in his Pure Land the Sukhavati; the 'nirmankaya' or the incarnation of Sakyamuni. Resting against the side walls sit half a dozen enlightened Bodhisattvas. Marvellous robes have been carved on the statues which appear to have the sheen and fall of real silk. Behind the Buddha statue falls a thin stream from the mountains. One can only hear the sound but the water escapes from behind the rocks.

Splendid Hall of Avalokitesvara

After driving for about an hour we reached the Beishan grottoes – the splendid gallery of the Avalokitesvara in his numerous manifestation and adorning thousands of niches that were as dense as beehives. The deity was a picture of magnificence and beauty. The face was round with soft features and dreamy eyes; the posture was serene. The deity wore heavy jewels in the ears, around the neck and hands. Even the fabulous gowns were studded with precious gems and embroidered with flowery creepers. On the forehead was a protruding round vermillion mark and on the head an elaborate multi-tiered crown with a small image of Buddha in the centre.

The different manifestations of the bodhisattva were depicted by the holy objects held by the deity: sun and the moon, a jade seal, a pearl or a rosary. Lovely lotus flowers bloomed under the feet of the deity who exuded feminine beauty and seemed to rise from a bed of flowers. An engraved halo round the head and a disarming smile on the lips; the deity stood a little inclined holding his right wrist with the left hand. He

FACING PAGE:
The paradise of Buddha depicted on the rocks of the Baodingshan grottoes at Dazu portrays the happy world of Sukhavati "*the Buddhist Pure Land where there is profound bliss.*

wore flowing robes and the silk ribbons on his dress fluttered in the breeze.

In the most prized 'Hall of Avalokitesvara' the most compassionate, the 'iswara' who is 'avalokita' or the lord who looks down with compassion,[6] was seated on the lotus. The great bodhisattva wearing a decorated crown looked splendid. Holding the universe in his hands the deity has the miraculous power of saving all beings from danger.

'He is the Lord and Sovereign of the world. From his eyes come the Sun and the Moon, from his mouth the winds, from his feet the Earth. In all these aspects Avalokitesvara resembles the Hindu God Brahma'. (Edward Conze; *Buddhism Its Essence and Development*; p.147)

In the numerous caves forming the 'Exhibition Hall' of the Avalokitesvara and his incarnations the sculptor depicts the deity in different moods. In one cave Avalokitesvara stood gazing at the moon's reflection in water. A pool was created inside the cave at such an angle that water from a thin stream collecting in its depths actually caught the moon's reflection. The face of the deity shines in the radiance of the moonlight and a blissful smile escapes his lips. The magic of the pool, the flowing rivulet from somewhere behind the rocks and the heavenly face of the deity together with the richness of the gem studded robes, ornately carved jewellery and elaborate head gears made one wonder if some divine hand was behind the rock carvings. The hand that turned

The gilded thousand-armed Mercy Buddha, the Avalokitesvara or the Guanyin at the Longhua, the oldest and most famous temple in Shanghai. The Guayin Buddha is female in appearance and is widely worshipped all over China. It is believed that the Guayin Buddha blesses barren women and saves people from misery.

FACING PAGE:
The Beishan grottoes in Dazu county of Chongqing depict the splendid gallery of Avalokitesvara in his numerous manifestations.

the rocky hills into the abode of the great Avalokitesvara.

Bodhisattva Manjusri appeared similar to the Hindu goddess Durga seated on a lion. The idea of Shakti represented by Manjusri is said to have been borrowed from Hindu mythology. Maitreya Buddha sat on a double lotus pedestal surrounded by lay disciples listening to his sermon. The roof of the cave had been ornately carved and a heavenly crown hung over the Buddha's head. Another stunning example of craftsmanhip was the cave of the 'Peacock King' called the *Mayurasana raja* wearing a crown of flowers and an ornamented robe. He sat on the back of a peacock whose tail turned up to support the ceiling. The walls depicted the Thousand Buddhas.

By the time I reached the stone engraving of the 'Book of Filial Piety' by Confucious, it became dark. There was thunder and lightning. The drizzle that started at The Pipa and stayed with us throughout our journey to Dazu threatened to turn into a rainstorm. I retraced my steps through the gallery of Avalokitesvara and with great difficulty managed to take a few shots of the crowned Avalokitesvara in his flowing robes and various *mudras*.

A narrow path in the dense foliage led to the main road. The thought of never seeing Dazu again in my life saddened me. I took a last look at the towering image of the crowned bodhisattva sitting under the high cliff. He raised a hand in blessing and I bade him goodbye. Thousands of generations will come and go but Avalokitesvara will continue to live in his paradise at Dazu.

To Eling Park at Chongqing

Taking Highway 319 we passed through Yongchuan and going through a dark tunnel near Qingang and onwards through Zouma town we arrived at Chongqing about 160 kms south-east from Dazu. It was late evening when I arrived at the Dongfang Garden hotel tired and worn out. After the next day's itinerary was confirmed with the guide, I had a quick meal and quietly settled in my room.

Chongqing is a hilly city and a busy riverport in the eastern part of Sichuan province. Built on the hills at the point of confluence of the Yangzi with the Jialing river it is said to be a major point of embarkation and disembarkation for the Yangzi cruise. Yangzi is the largest river in China and the third longest in the world after the Nile and the Amazon. It flows over six thousand kilometres from its source in western Qinghai province, north of Tibet, to the East China sea at Shanghai.

The most favourite holiday cruise from Chaotianmen port in the city is on the Three Gorges on the Yangzi river. One can depart from Chongqing by boat in order to pass through the Gorges. My guide told me that it was also possible to go up to the Leshan Buddha by boat. Before the arrival of the trains and airplanes all of Sichuan's trade flowed through Chongqing to the port of Shanghai.

We drove up the Loquat Hill and visited the famous Eling Park. Here we climbed up the six storey pagoda to get a view of the entire city and the river below. There were plenty of flowers at the park and a dense forest of loquat and other trees. Once upon a time the park was the private garden of Chiang Kai Shek. It is said that Chiang Kai Shek stayed in Chongquing, the capital of the Koumintang for some months before moving to Taiwan until he lost to the Communist forces.

The scenery from the top of the pagoda was beautiful. Innumerable ships had docked in the yard. There was a crowd of workers at the jetty. At least two bridges were visible over the Jailing and the Yangzi rivers. The rest were lost in the thick mist that enveloped the river and the dockyard. I learnt that there are atleast twenty-two bridges over the rivers in Chongqing. The third leg of my journey on the Silk Road was about to end. On the way to the airport to catch a flight to Shanghai the following day, I stopped briefly at the red Arhat temple. Built about a thousand years ago the temple has hundreds of monks living in the temple monastery. The main attraction is the hall of 500 Arhats or Buddhist saints. The life-sized images appear real and surround the central image of Buddha in obesience.

I bade a tearfull farewel to Buddha. Prostrating myself in the dark room lit up by a dim red flickering bulb a short prayer of gratitude escaped my lips.

A Stroll on the Shanghai Bund

I planned to spend a couple of days in Shanghai before taking the flight back to India. I could not have returned home without a stroll on the Bund–the water front boulevard on the Yangzi River.

This was the place where the heart of Shanghai beats to the tune of lilting Chinese music. For both tourists and local residents this was the place to be in–both at dawn and dusk. Just after dawn people gathered here for a host of activities like aerobics, kungfu, *kaitai* by the young and the old alike. In the evening the river was bathed in the neon lights and glittering architectural wonders of the Pudong area across the river.

The day was spent walking through the labyrinth of the Yu gardens in the heart of the Old Town. Here apart from natural beauty one can find the finest collection of pearls. While providing a fascinating landscape, the ponds on all sides of the garden running like a channel, also brought in cool air. It was the perfect place for a visitor to peacefully meditate. The famous King of Noodles at the Yu Garden serves excellent vegetarian food and the best Chinese tea poured out of a three feet long spout of a silver kettle.

However, things turned rather frightening at the Bird's Nest restaurant near Nanking Road, where chiefly non-vegetarian meals were served. Here I did not have the heart to put even a morsel of food in my mouth. I was simply transfixed by the scene of people chomping live shrimps and prawns and digging their chopsticks into roasted cobra–considered to be the most venomous snake in India. Near the entrance, massive glass cases filled with water enclosed fresh turtles, molluscs, prawns, shrimps and fish of all kind. There was also a heap of caterpillars in one corner. One of the glass cases had a dozen live spotted cobras that hissed and spread their hoods and flicked their forked tongues.

The fearless chef pushed his gloved hands inside to pull out one of them for cooking. After nabbing a fat cobra he weighed it on a machine and then took it to a corner of the glass kitchen to sever its head. The body was then roasted on a slow fire. The twisted rope-like baked snake was then devoured by the guests.

Another glass case had about half a dozen pythons. It is believed that the more poisonous the snake, the more delicious it tastes and the more

The Reclining Buddha of Yufo Si or the Jade Buddha temple at Shanghai is a rare treasure brought to the temple by Abbot Weiken from Burma. The Buddha carved from a single piece of creamy white jade wears robe of precious gems and represents the 'Dying Buddha' at Kusinara in India.

The sitting Buddha of Yufo Si.

its aphrodisiacal potency. Some others ordered live shrimps and pincerless prawns which were wriggling on their plate. But they were soon caught between the chopsticks and chewed up.

I then headed for the famous Jade Buddha temple – the busiest and the most famous of Shanghai's temples. The two Jade Buddhas are said to have been brought from Burma (now Myanmar) and carved from a single piece of creamy white jade and housed separately. The first is the thirteen feet long Reclining Buddha and the second is the six and a half feet sitting Buddha said to weigh over 2000 pounds. They wore robes encrusted with precious gems. The rush at the temple was so great that no one could stand in front of the Jade Buddha for more than a second. Visitors have to just keep moving to avoid a stampede.

Every evening, before I take the China Eastern MU 563 to Delhi, I returned to the Bund, still the most fascinating place in Shanghai. I loved to sit through the dark hours, listening to the grumbling ferries and the singing river, watching the crowds waving from the festival boats and youths waltzing on the sparkling boulevard. Everyone was there to enjoy, to forget, to muse, to recreate. What else is life about!

Breathtaking scenery on the Tibet-Sichuan Highway 318. The highway dotted with poplars meanders along the bank of the Niyang river. On both sides lie emerald fields of paddy and orchards of apples, peaches and pears.

(15)

Routes into Tibet

For centuries the borderlands between India and Tibet and the adjoining territories of Nepal, Bhutan, Bangladesh and Myanmar formed a colossal corridor through which the Southern Silk Route passed on its way from Beijing to Kashmir and onwards to Central Asia.

Although Tibet was little known to the outside world until the seventh century AD due to mountain barriers that surrounded the plateau, there was regular Indo-Tibetan contact since ancient times. Indian and Tibetan traders, scholars and pilgrims crossed into neighbouring territories on foot, horseback and mules through much beaten trade routes that were said to be branches of the main southern silk route. These included routes[1] along rivers that rose in Tibet and ran westwards into India and southwards into India, Nepal and Bhutan, reaching the mouth of the Ganges.

The Brahmaputra flows eastwards through southern Tibet till it turns in its course and flows through the gorges of Dihang into upper Assam. The Lohit river and other tributaries of the Brahmaputra stretch directly into Tibet from the Assam valley.

The Sutlej and the Indus flow westwards into India. The Indus rises on the slopes of the mount Kailash and flows northwest through gigantic mountains for about five hundred kilometres before it plunges into the gorge and enters the Ladakh area at Demchok. The Sutlej rises on

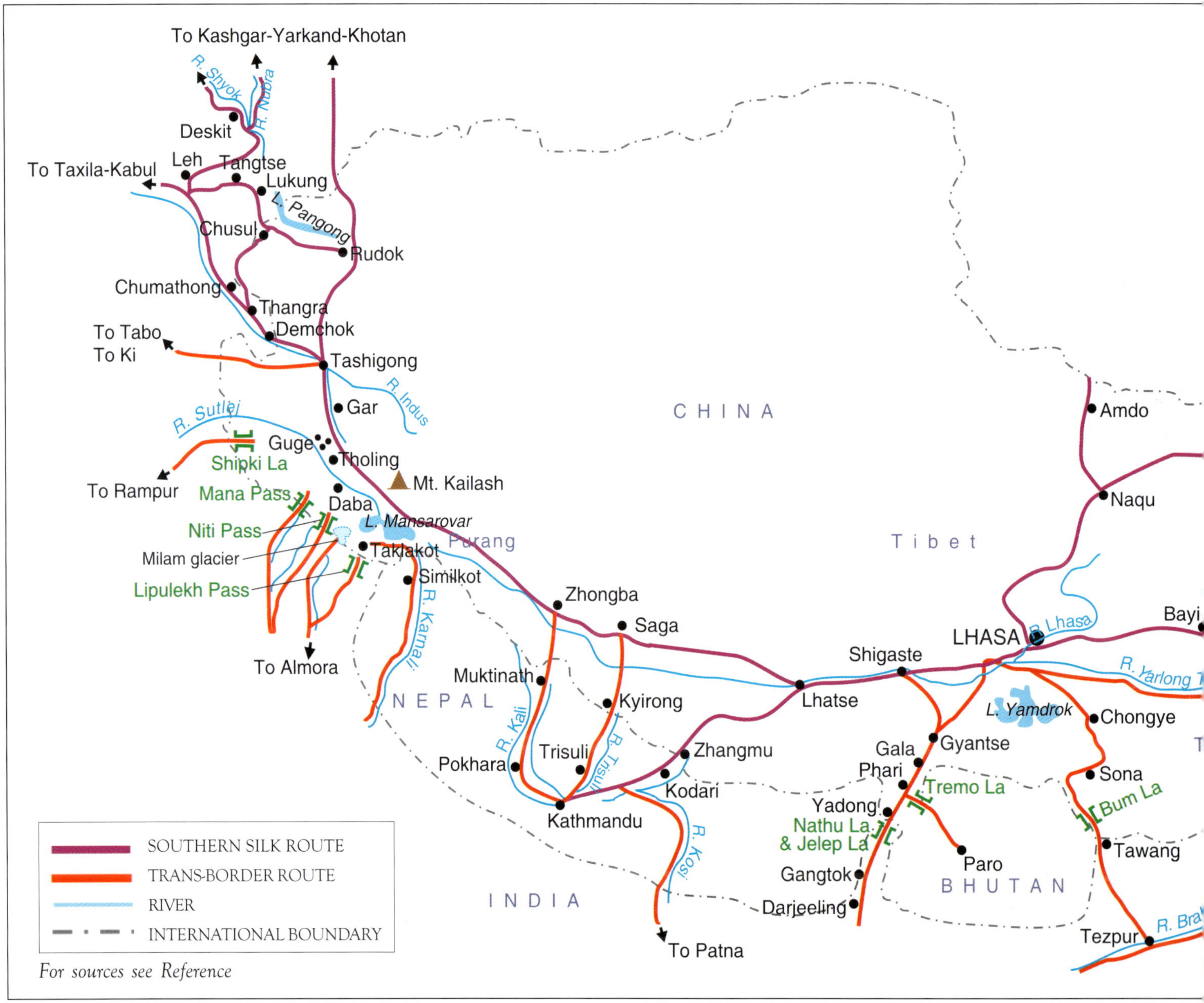
To Kashgar-Yarkand-Khotan
R. Shyok
R. Nubra
Deskit
To Taxila-Kabul
Leh
Tangtse
Lukung
L. Pangong
Chusul
Rudok
Chumathong
Thangra
Demchok
To Tabo
To Ki
Tashigong
R. Indus
Gar
R. Sutlej
Guge
Shipki La
Tholing
Mt. Kailash
To Rampur
Mana Pass
Daba
Niti Pass
L. Mansarovar
Purang
Milam glacier
Taklakot
Lipulekh Pass
Simikot
R. Karnali
To Almora
Zhongba
Saga
CHINA
Tibet
Amdo
Naqu
LHASA
R. Lhasa
Bayi
Shigaste
R. Yarlong
Lhatse
Muktinath
NEPAL
Kyirong
R. Kali
R. Trisuli
Trisuli
Pokhara
Zhangmu
Kodari
Kathmandu
R. Kosi
L. Yamdrok
Chongye
Gyantse
Gala
Phari
Sona
Tremo La
Bum La
Yadong
Nathu La
& Jelep La
Paro
Tawang
Gangtok
BHUTAN
Darjeeling
INDIA
To Patna
Tezpur
SOUTHERN SILK ROUTE
TRANS-BORDER ROUTE
RIVER
INTERNATIONAL BOUNDARY
For sources see Reference

THE SOUTHERN SILK ROUTE VIA TIBET AND KASHMIR

Map not to scale
Disclaimer: Despite the best efforts of the author the hand drawn map may have inaccuracies. The international boundaries, trading routes and places marked on the map are only approximate and not to scale.

the southern slopes of Mount Kailash, travels westwards piercing the Himalayas and entering Himachal Pradesh in the Shipki la region. Besides the sources of the Indus and the Brahmaputra, the Karnali, Bhote Kosi and Trisuli rivers flow through the Himalayas into Nepal. The Amu Chhu flows from Tibet's Chumbi Valley across the south-western corner of Bhutan. The Kuri Chhu, a tributary of the Manas rises in Tibet and crosses into Bhutan. The rivers flowing through Bhutan eventually join the Brahmaputra. It is believed that the Manas river valley provided an easy access through the Himalayas and formed the migration route from India into Tibet.

The main southern trade route ran from Xian through the province of Szechuan into Tibet and thence through several river tracks and mountain passes along the Tibetan border stretching from east to west into India, Nepal, Sikkim, Bhutan and Myanmar. These were the routes through which ponies, salt, borax, gold dust, wool, musk, furs, yak tails, medicinal herbs and carpets were said to be traded for rice, spices, silk, cotton, tea, brass utensils, silver, lac and rubber. Important trade marts lay at Gyantse, Rima, Kibithoo, Yadong, Nathu La, Sherathang, Renguingang, Taklakot, Chaprang, Tholing, Shipki La, Lipulekh where Indian and Tibetan goods were exchanged in barter trade. Marts also operated at Kyirong, Simikot, Kodari at the Nepal-Tibet border and near Tremo La and Phari at the Bhutan-Tibet border.

A traveller who wished to enter Tibet had a considerable choice of routes. He could arrive at Lhasa from the East, West, North or South.

The following routes were generally taken by the travellers:

Kashmir-Beijing route

A remarkable trade route, the Kashmir-Beijing route,[2] the most elevated '*Junglam*' connected Kashmir with Beijing. From Leh it ran south-easterly along the Pangong lake to Rudok, the western frontier town of Tibet and crossed the breadth of the Changtang region till it touched the upper Yarlong Tsangpo (Brahmaputra) at Mariom la. Crossing the river it passed through the town of Shigatse and Gyangtse and ran upto Lhasa. East of Lhasa it ran to Chamdo, the capital of Kham and thence to Batang, Litang and Ta-chien-lu on the border of Sichuan province. At Chengdu the road joined the one coming from Beijing through Xian.

The route westwards from Leh ran through Srinagar and joined the main Uttarapath or the Northern Highroad going to Taxila upto Kabul, Bamiyan and Balkh in Afghanistan. From here it ran west through Turkmenistan, crossed the Caspian Sea to join the route to the Mediterranean.

The *Junglam* was the thus longest Asian Highway connecting the Mediteranean with the Pacific through Tibet. According to Thomas H. Holdich, writing in 1906 (*Tibet The Mysterious*, p.34) the Junglam 'was the official post road between Kashmir and Peking (Beijing) traversable at all seasons of the year by mounted men and is probably the most remarkable postal highway in the world'.

From Leh to Lhasa the *Junglam* stretched over a distance of about two thousand kilometres. Presently this route is represented by the National Highway 219. Towards the north this route was extended through Yarkand and the plains of Kashgar linking Central Asia with Tibet. Now an extension of the Highway 219, this route is said to have been exploited by the famous explorers Prjevalski, Sven Hedin and Aurel Stein. Beyond Lhasa the Highway 219 joins 318 going to Sichuan where it meets 108 coming from Beijing through Xian.

Alexander Cunningham in *Ladak-Physical, Statistical and Historical* mentions seven roads leading from or to Leh on all sides: the western road from Kabul and the Punjab through Kashmir; the south-western road from central Punjab through Zanskar; the southern road from Lahore and Amritsar through Kullu and Lahaul joined by a road from Spiti; the south-eastern road from Lhasa to Garo where it was joined by a road coming from India via the Niti Pass and thence along the river Indus to Leh; the eastern road from Chinese Tartary through Rudok and Chusul to Leh; the northern road from Yarkand and Khotan over the Karakorum mountains and down the Shyok and Nubra rivers to

Leh; the north-western road from Balti, via the Shyok and Indus rivers to Leh.

C.Wessels, S.J. (Notes to Introduction – *An Account of Tibet – The Travels Of Ippolito Desideri* says that the people traveling from Leh to Tashigong instead of taking the direct route could also take the Tankse-Shushal route (via Lukung along the Pangong lake) and reach the Indus at Thangra.

Himachal Routes

Charles A. Sherring in *Western Tibet And The British Borderland*, (Chapter XVII. p340) mentions a route from Spiti through Shangrang Pass by means of a coolie track; He also mentions a route that corresponds with the present Hindustan Tibet Road NH-22 from Simla along the Sutlej over the Shipki and Sirang passes; Another route from Lahaul ran through a pass between Hanle and Demchok to Rudok.

The Spiti river valley was the main connection for trade coming from west Tibet via the Shipki pass to Kulu in Himachal Pradesh. The old caravan route approximated to the present Hindustan-Tibet Highway running through Kalpa and Pooh to Khab and onwards to Sipki Pass and into western Tibet. Important trade connections existed between the Spiti valley and the Guge kingdom of western Tibet. It is said that local monks traveled to Guje for their religious education.[3] Two passes have been traced from Spiti valley into Guje—the Parang pass and Tunglung pass.[4]

The long route from Simla to Khab and onwards to Tabo, Ki and Kibber monasteries runs along the river Sutlej and Spiti. Kibber, the highest permanently inhabited village not long ago acted as a base for trek into Tibet. Trade caravans travelled along old routes through high mountain passes into western Tibet. These were traversed by nomads who carried goods across the border on horses and mules. The route into Tibet through Shipki La is said to have been one of the four most prominent trade routes along the entire Indo-Tibet border for centuries.

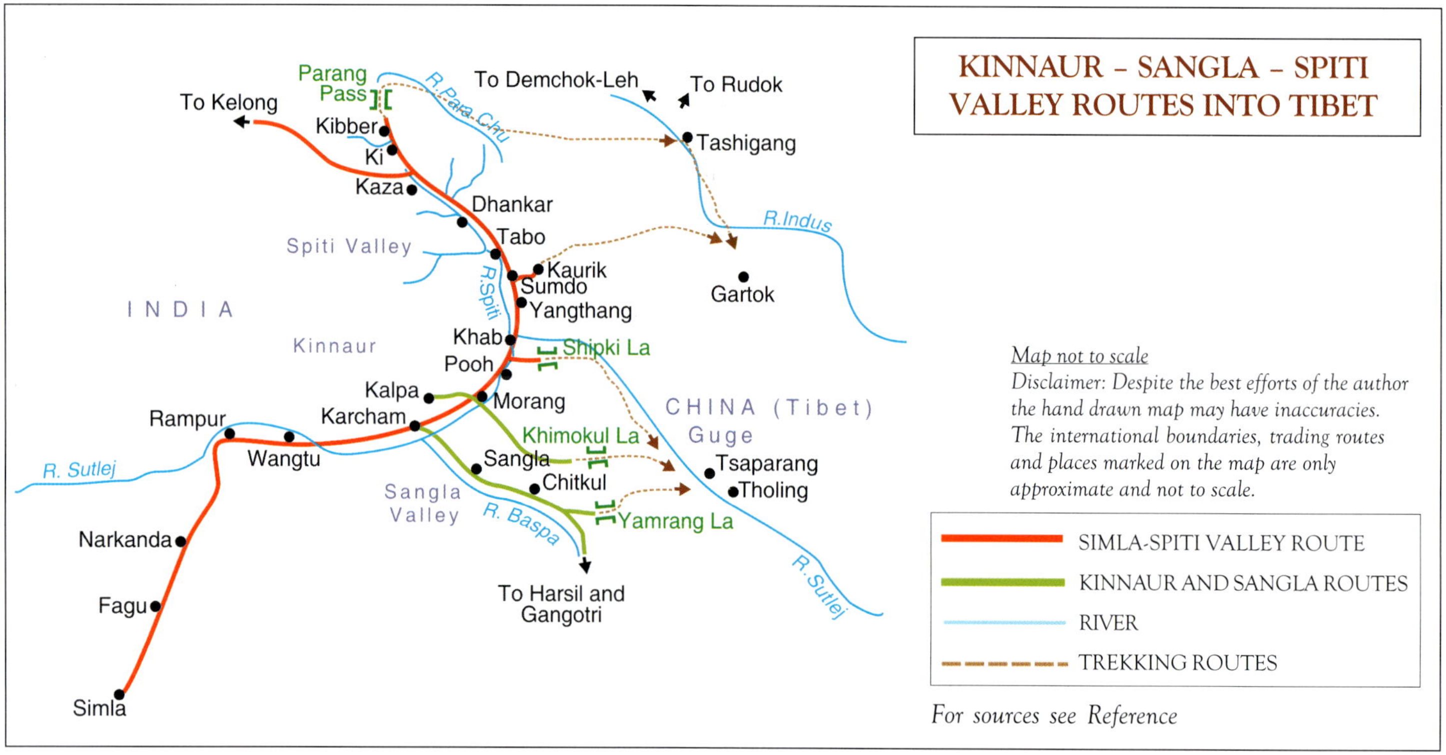

Many monasteries along this Indo-Tibet highway are recorded to have been built by Tibetan kings during the temple building movement by Richen Zangpo (Tibetan Buddhist scholar known as the Great Lotsaba, AD 958-1055). One such monastery is the famous Heritage site of Tabo, said to be the 'Ajanta of the Himalayas', was built by the king of Guje, Lha-chen Yeshes-O (AD 967-1040). Being close to the border of Tibet the monasteries served as a meeting place for scholars of both countries. R. Bhattacharji's *Of People and Land Routes to China* mentions routes from the Kalpa and Sangla valley via Moirang and Chitkul through the passes of Khimokul La and Yamrang La to Tsaparang and Gartok. He also mentions the Kalpa-Pooh-Sumdo-Kaurik route to Tashigong and Gartok which was used for local trading.

Routes From Garhwal and Kumaon

Southern Tibet is approached by a group of passes viz the Mana and Niti passes[5] leading from Garhwal and Kumaon in the State of Uttranchal in North India. A branch of the ancient trade route is said to have passed through the last Indian village of Mana on the border with Tibet near Badrinath in Garhwal district. Known in Hindu scriptures as Manibhadrapam, Mana is four kilometres north of Badrinath and is the last Indian village situated at the confluence of the Alaknanda and the Saraswati rivers. From here a path led to the Mt Kailash.

ROUTES INTO TIBET FROM UTTRANCHAL

Map not to scale

Disclaimer: Despite the best efforts of the author the hand drawn map may have inaccuracies. The international boundaries, trading routes and places marked on the map are only approximate and not to scale.

ROUTE

RIVER

For sources see Reference

According to the *Gazetteer of Garhwal*, there are two routes from Niti into Tibet, one through Hoti and the other through Chorhoti. The Niti village lies in pargana Painkhada thirteen miles to the south of the Niti pass and is only forty-five miles from Joshimath. Both passes lead towards Gartok in western Tibet.

Other routes, the Milam[6] and the Lipulekh route that are followed to this day for entry into Tibet at Taklakot by *yatris* going to Mansarovar go through the Pithoragarh district of Kumaon in Uttranchal. Pithoragarh borders both Tibet and Nepal. From here a motorable road runs north to Munsiyari and then heads for the Milam village right on the border with Tibet. The trek passes east of Nanda Devi following the gorge of the Ghori Ganga river and reaches Milam village. From here the Milam glacier on the Tibetan border is only five kilometres away. The Dharchula-Taklakot route goes through Tawaghat, Gala, Budhi, Gunji through Lipulekh pass into Tibet. Charles A. Sherring in *Western Tibet And The British Borderland*, mentions routes from Tehri Garhwal and British Garhwal through the Lilang, Mana and Niti passes to Chaprang and Daba.

He writes about three passes of Untadhura, Janti and Kungri-Bingri situated in a line one after the other and the Darma Pass to Gyanema;

Two other passes that he mentions are the Lankpya Lekh and LipuLekh.

Nathu La, Tremo La and Bum La Routes

In the south-east of Tibet several tracks led to the states of Bhutan and North-east India. These tracks had been used for centuries by Tibetan and Bhutanese traders. From Lhasa across the Yarlong Tsangpo (Brahmaputra river), a south-westerly route passed into India via the Nathu La and the Jelep La leading to Gangtok in Sikkim and further down to Darjeeling through the Teesta valley. Nathu la and the Jelep La, seperated only by a few kilometres are the most significant passes leading from Sikkim into Tibet connecting the Teesta basin and Ammu

Chu with the valley of the Yarlong Tsangpo or the Brahmaputra river. The route goes via Yadong, Phari, Gyantse and joins the Friendship Highway to Lhasa. Only 56 kilometres from Gangtok, Nathu La was the main route for trade between Sikkim and Tibet and formed a branch of the Silk Road.

In Bhutan, fourteen kilometres from Paro, the westerly road reaches the ruins of Drukgyel Dzong sitting at a point where the trail from Tibet enters the Paro Valley via the Tremo La, the 5000 metres pass. This is said to have been a major trade route between Bhutan and the Tibetan town of Phari joining the route coming from Sikkim and leading to Gyantse and Lhasa.

One of the greatest pioneering travelers, Sarat Chandra Das' *A Journey To Lhasa And Central Tibet* (edited by W.W. Rockhill) describes his journey in disguise through Darjeeling, Sikkim and southern Tibet before reaching the Tashi Lhunpo.

Another south-easterly route from Lhasa to Tawang went via the Che La or the 'Sandy Pass'[7] across the Brahmaputra to Zhanang,

ROUTES INTO TIBET FROM NORTH-EAST INDIA AND BHUTAN

Map not to scale

Disclaimer: Despite the best efforts of the author the hand drawn map may have inaccuracies. The international boundaries, trading routes and places marked on the map are only approximate and not to scale.

ROUTE

RIVER

For sources see Reference

Mindroling, Chongye, Karpo La, Sona and thence through the Bum La to Tawang. Both the Tawang and the Gangtok routes running southwards from Lhasa joined the main highway to the mouth of the Ganges making this the shortest and the most important route from Lhasa to the Bay of Bengal. The route along the Lohit river ran along Tezu, Walong, Kibithoo and Kahao into the Tibetan town of Rima. The route called the Rima (Zayul) route was open till recent times when an Indian agent was posted in Rima and a Chinese agent at Tezu, the headquarters of the Lohit district which borders both Myanmar and China and is the point of tri-junction.

Romesh Bhattacharji in *Of People and Land Routes to China-Kibithoo to Karakorum* mentions the following nine routes from Arunachal Pradesh into Tibet and marks the nearest dwellings in Tibet: Dibrugarh-Tezu-Walong-Kibithoo-Kahao along the Lohit river; Dibrugarh-Ledo-Pangsau Pass-Mytkina (Burma)-Kunming (Yunan, China) route; Dibrugarh-Roing-Anini-Mipi-Yongop La to Shuden Gompa (in Tibet); North Lakhimpur-Along (or directly from Assam via Pasighat)-Yingkiong-Tuting-Gelling -TungLa or Shouka La or Lamb La to Kemteng-Gye Dzong (in Tibet); North Lakhimpur-Along-Mechuka-NeparLa or NyugLa to Kyim Dzong (in Tibet); North Lakhimpur-Dapporijo-Nacho-Taksing-Limeking to Lhontse Dzong (in Tibet); Tezpur-Bomdila-Tawang-Bum La-Tsona Dzong (in Tibet).

Route Through Nepal

It is learnt that passes from Nepal into Tibet were the connecting link between India and Tibet and were the routes through which travelled celebrated Indian scholars and Buddhist monks on their way to Kailash–Mansarovar and the Tholing monastery in Guge.

The Kathmandu-Lhasa route[8] went north-eastwards through Bhaktapur, Sanga Pass and continued through Dhulikhel, Dholaghat, Lamosangu and Barabise along the road (presently covered by the Arniko Highway) to the Chinese border at Kodari. Here the road over the Bhote

ROUTES INTO TIBET FROM NEPAL

Map not to scale

Disclaimer: Despite the best efforts of the author the hand drawn map may have inaccuracies. The international boundaries, trading routes and places marked on the map are only approximate and not to scale.

ROUTE

RIVER

TREKKING ROUTES

For sources see Reference

Kosi River crossed into the Tibetan town of Khasa. Inside Tibet the route passed through Zhangmu, Nyalam, Tingri, Lhatze, Shigatse and finally to Lhasa.

Another route went through the Kyirong valley along the Trisuli River. The old Kyirong town is only 150 kilometres from Kathmandu. The founder of Lamaism in Tibet, Guru Padmasambhava, renowned as the 'wizard–priest' of the Indian monastery of Nalanda arrived at Samye in Tibet by way of Kathmandu and Kyirong in the year AD 747.[9]

The Muktinath route to Mansarovar is said to be the ancient trading route. Atisa Dipamkara, the great Buddhist *acharya* from Bengal and the high priest of the ancient Vikramsila Vihar who was invited by the rulers of Western Tibet in the eleventh century AD is said to have taken the old pilgrim route from Patna to Kathmandu, and through Pokhara and Muktinath to Taklakot in Tibet.[10]

Sherring mentions a pass in the extreme north-west corner of Nepal (probably from Simikot) to Taklakot in Tibet.

Breathtaking scenery all the way from the Gonggar airport to Lhasa running along the Yarlong Tsangpo or the Brahmaputra River. The unending expanse of verdant fields forms the 'food bowl' of Tibet and produces all kinds of fruits, vegetables and grains.

16

Beyond the Himalayas to Lhasa

On several occasions during my travels along the Indus river on the Leh-Kargil route and along the Sutlej on the Hindustan–Tibet road (NH 22) to Tabo in Himachal Pradesh, I had been quite close to the borders of western Tibet. My sojourn in the North–eastern monasteries of Rumtek and Tawang brought me close to the borders of southern Tibet. Passing along the Indo-Chinese border I had always yearned to cross over into the Tibetan territory–the land of mystic beauty, about which I had read with such interest in the accounts of Sarat Chandra Das (*A Journay To Lhasa and Central Tibet*), H. Thomas Holdich (*Tibet The Mysterious*) and William Woodville Rockhill (*The Land of the Lamas*).

One day there actually landed an invitation to head to Tibet as part of a press delegation. I could not have asked for more. On 11 June 2005, I was accompanying a delegation led by Prof C. Raja Mohan of the Jawaharlal Nehru University to Tibet. First the Chinese Eastern MU 564 carrier flew into Beijing and from there via Lanzhou to Chengdu and onwards to Lhasa. We covered the journey in two days including a short stopover at Beijing. The reason being that there is no direct air or road link to Lhasa only 500 kilometres from Gangtok and about 1000 kilometres from Kolkata.

As I slouched on the cushy seat of Chinese Airline to Lhasa I went back into history and an era gone by when Tibet was the 'Land in a Veil of Mystery'. For centuries the lofty land of Tibet was inaccessible and unknown. Few westerners could lay eyes on this mysterious kingdom called the 'land of the snow and the roof of the world'.[1] Spies in disguise were sent to study the geography of the land. Many risked their lives to just get a glimpse of this enchanting and matchless 'Shangrila'. The stunning views of the snow-clad mountains, gushing milky streams, the long rivers and crystal lakes seemed to have descended from the heaven itself. There was a mad race by explorers to reach Lhasa, even though danger to life was great.

It is said that nothing much was known about the 'shadowy land beyond the Himalayas' until the fourteenth century when a traveller, Friar Odoric's description of Tibet reached the West and set others onto the trail of the enchanting 'Shangrila'.[2] At first there was no attempt to keep away travellers from entering Lhasa, but as the two warring giants Russia and Britain began the 'Great Game' of extending their empires in the neighbouring Pamir region, the 'Tibetans took fright fearing for their way of life and religion...'.[3] Since then Tibet became a closed and forbidden land.

Peter Hopkirk's *Tresspassers On The Roof Of The World–The Race For Lhasa* and *The Great Game* provide an interesting account of the intense rivalry between Britain and Russia for the control of Tibet. It is said that by the end of the nineteenth century the focus of the great rivalry had shifted from the Pamir region directly to Tibet. We learn this happened when it became known to the British in India that twice within a year an emissary of the Dalai Lama had visited St. Petersburg and had been warmly received by the Tsar.[4] Although Russia insisted that the visits were purely religious, the British viceroy in India, Lord Curzon was certain that Dorjief, the emissary, 'far from being a simple Buddhist monk, was working on behalf of the Tsar Nicholas against Britain's interest in Asia'.[5]

As a befitting answer to the dealings between Russia and Tibet, Curzon dispatched a mission in July 1903 under the famous Capt Francis Younghusband and then a second mission in December 1903 under him accompanied by 'one thousand strong military escort'. In the summer of 1904 Younghusband 'rode unopposed into Lhasa'. But not before a fierce battle at the 'Karo Pass' and the fortress of Gyantse on the road to Lhasa in which hundreds lost their life.[6]

The closure of Tibet did not deter travellers who had set their hearts on the mystery land. Armed with sextants, modern rifles and gold and in disguise as traders or monks, Indians and Westerners stealthily sneaked into the forbidden land and many of them never returned.

I remember having read of one Maurice Wilson whose frozen body was found on the slopes of Everest. Another traveller Dutreuil de Rhins was attacked and tossed into the river. Still another, Henry Savage Landor, was seized and tortured by the Tibetans when he refused to turn back.[7]

Flying over 'Tea Route'

The territory of Sichuan province that we were flying over was hidden under fluffy clouds. It was once known as the 'Tea Route' to Lhasa. Even now the best tea comes through this route from Chengdu in Sichuan. As we stopped for a short while at the Chengdu airport the weather seemed to be pretty fine. As we hit the tarmac at Gonggar airport near Lhasa the intense cold took us by complete surprise. But when I saw the gorgeous purple mountains over which hung a sheet of translucent blue mist, I forgot about the biting cold and basked in the beauty of this attractive land.

In the lobby, a Tibetan team was waiting to welcome us. A young lady stood with a tray full of grains heaped like a cone and lit incense. It was a traditional welcome. They put garlands and a scarf around our neck. As is the custom I dipped my fingers in the heap and sprinkled grains in the four cardinal directions and stepped forward. As I took that first step beyond the threshold I was reminded of the folk tradition in Indian villages where it is imperative to make offerings to the spirits.

A swank coach was ready to take us to Lhasa, some hundred kilometres away. It would take us two hours, at least. All along, the road was lined with thick foliage of poplars and we drove happily along the banks of the Lhasa river, a tributary of the Yarlong Tsangpo or the mighty Brahmaputra river. The scenery was breathtaking. Literally! As we hit a higher altitude I started gasping for breath, the Tibetan plateau was taking my breath away! The suburban road from the airport to the city was dotted with countless green houses. We were driving so close to habitation that I could count the stout green cabbages growing out of square fields. The vegetable fields generously gave way to rows and rows of apple, peach, pear and walnut. Herds of yak, sheep and goats were grazing on the plentiful pastures on the river bank. The landscape was not cluttered with villages; they were few and far between. I was reminded of the stone houses in Ladakh and Spiti replete with insignificant stone houses surrounded by fluttering prayer flags and white-washed stupas. The fields were trimmed with huge mounds of yak dung cakes. In the green of the fields there was a dash of red and scarlet, I could see women in long dresses tending to their fields.

Niedang Dafo Tourist village

Soon we crossed the river and turning eastwards came upon Niedang Dafo, a village where I stopped to see the cave paintings. Inside, a colossal Buddha was cut into the rocks and painted in cobalt blue and emerald green. There were frescoes of Buddhist deities. It seemed some ancient pilgrims on way to Lhasa had cut the cave and sculpted the image.

The caves opened onto a shining lake set like a crystal in the grassy meadows along a low hill surrounded by wooden huts. The white clouds descending on the surface of the lake added to the allure. Near the left bank pearly white boats made of bloated sheep skin floated without a care in the world. All along the Silk Road I had seen yak and sheep goat skin boats and had longed to cross the river sitting in their hollow. The idea of a sheep skin boat intrigued me. I wondered why there were no

Rock paintings at the tourist village of Neidang Dafo on way from Gonggar to Lhasa. A colossal image of Buddha has been cut into the rock. There are frescoes of Buddhist deities on the cave walls. Bright colours like cobalt blue and emerald green have been used to paint the images.

wooden boats. I soon found the answer. I learn that in regions where wood is scarce or forests under state protection, the people have not much option but to use the animal hides. They kill the animals, cook the meat, dry the skin and then sew them as boats that can carry two. I envisage people using thick needles to stitch the jagged end of the hide to make neat boats. Indeed a tedious task!

Half way through we reached Dinlong Deqing county, known as the Food Bowl of Lhasa. Acres and acres of green rice fields looked like an unending expanse of a green canvas that, according to the driver, belonged to the Sunshine Biology Horticulture Company. Here other passengers got down for a smoke, while I walked along the thin lanes hemming the fields. Back on the bus, meandering through a maze of hills, rich farmlands, and vegetable fields and racing along lakes and swift flowing streams we arrived at Lhasa in the afternoon.

At the Himalaya Hotel

Lhasa seems so high above the hills that you feel closer to heaven than earth. But that proximity is not without its follies—each breath seems so exacting that you can feel your lungs straining and panting for that one elusive heave of a full breath. The guide exhorted us not to head out. He said it took about a day to acclimatise and we should not move out of the hotel. There were enough preparations to keep any illness at bay; a large chest of medicine lay on the side drawer of the bed containing packets of Tibetan herbal preparation to counter high altitude sickness. I dissolved two packets in a cup of water, drank the concoction and quietly slipped out while my friends slumbered. I had defied the guide's warning, but Lhasa seemed too beautiful to idle away in a monotonous hotel room.

Outside the hotel bejewelled Tibetan women wearing long brown robes and beaded headress were selling antiques, jewellery and images of Buddhist deities in make-shift stalls. I haggled for a bronze Tara and shelled out a hundred yuans. One of them was thrilled to see an Indian; she hugged me as if we were long lost friends. I muttered that I wanted to see the Barkhor bazaar. Before I could blink she had hailed a rickshaw and off the two of us went to see the famous bazaar.

The rickshaw-puller was frail but he pedalled furiously through a maze of paved streets behind the Lhasa stadium and onto the famous Barkhor Street. I stopped to frame a few pictures of traditional architecture in

The glittering Barkhor Street facing the Jokhang temple is an interesting confluence of religion and trade. The wide quadrangular space in front of the temple is a hub of activity. The Jokhang temple, the oldest structure and the spiritual centre of Lhasa dates back nearly 1,400 years. It is in this temple that the most precious gold image of Child Buddha brought by Chinese princess Wencheng in seventh century is kept.

my camera and then turned towards the Potala. One look and I was captivated. The Potala, the largest palace on the highest altitude in the world, was stunning. I walked up and down the huge front square of the palace and shot an entire roll. Happy with my shots, I put my feet forward to hop back into the rickshaw. But the old man seemed irked, the man who until a few moments ago was humming happily, suddenly turned brusque. In a gruff voice he asked for fifty yuans. But we had hardly done two kilometres I retorted. My Tibetan friend tried drilling sense into him, reminding him that he had agreed at ten yuan for a two-way fare. But the man was incensed. I was in no mood to get into a scrap

with anyone and tried to wriggle into another rickshaw. Before we could escape into the Barkhor Street the rickshawpuller spat at us. I was aghast. But in the land of Buddha I forgave him. I did not want him to spoil my stay in Lhasa which had barely begun.

Barkhor Area

The glittering Barkhor Street is an interesting confluence of religion and trade. A broad street ran through the large stretch that sat right in front of the Jokhang monastery. All of it is forever droning with activity; however, the wide quadrangular space at the entrance of the monastery was the best place to be at all times of the day. Here you can sit by the sidewalk and watch men and women offering oil lamps to the Buddha and burning incense and branches of juniper in an a earthen receptacle. It is believed that evil spirits disappear in the thick column of smoke and good fortune descends. Monks and nuns chanting Buddhist mantras *om mani padme hum* circumambulated the monastery with prayer wheels in their hands. Devotees kissed the ground and prostrated. Just outside the square in the lanes and bylanes of the Barkhor Street, women were selling antique jewellery, statues and Buddhist deities. Like an oddity the statues of Chairman Mao Tse Tung stood out. However, the most popular item off the street was CDs of Indian movies that sold like hot cakes. Almost everyone knows film actors Shahrukh Khan, Preity Zinta and Kajol. They seemed to be everywhere, staring out of flat television screens in the bazaar. I walked past the filmy stuff and wanted to buy stone bead necklaces that are handmade by Tibetan women; they say it is the best souvenir from Barkhor Street.

After an hour of loitering in the Barkhor area my Tibetan friend and I were back at the hotel in another rickshaw. She went back to her antique handicrafts stall while I slipped into my room.

The Lhasa River is a major tributary of the Yarlong Tsangpo (Brahmaputra River). It originates in the Qinghai–Tibet plateau and is cold and crystal clear.

Lhasa River Front

My evenings in Lhasa were spent strolling along the fascinating river front not very far from the hotel. A major tributary of the Yarlong Tsangpo (Brahmaputra), the Lhasa river, originates in the Qinghai–Tibet plateau and is cold and crystal clear like the Ganges at Haridwar. It is called the Mother River of the Tibetans. The cobbled boulevard along the river stretches for miles on the outskirts of the Lhasa city. In the glow of the evening sun young couples strolled hand in hand along the river, some sit by quietly watching the sun glide down the horizon. Far away boats could be seen carrying sand from the river bank.

The river front reminded me of the Shanghai Bund, the famous water front boulevard at Shanghai. While the Lhasa river flowed past the city in complete silence against a backdrop of high mountains and snow clad peaks, the Bund at Shanghai showcases the recently constructed and busy Pudong area. The former flows in thoughtful meditation, silently and peacefully; the latter was noisy and exuberant.

However, there was no lilting music, no dancing or acrobatics on the boulevard of the Lhasa river. No music band and no waltzing couples as on the Shanghai Bund. But the quiet river plays its own music. The birds twitter and swoop on the surface of the water while white ducks dive and frolic, flapping their wings, looking for fish and snails. There are willow and poplar trees along the bank, their branches bending as if trying to caress the water. A beautiful Tibetan resort sat in the curve of the river on the east boulevard. Surrounded by lush lawns and beds of flowers, the resort is the favourite haunt of foreigners who flock to Lhasa. In the evening, a soft light swathes the landscape and the mountain and the river seem to be out on a rendezvous. However, this solitude is broken in July during the Bathing Festival, also known as *Gamariji*, another name for Venus.

Evening Opera

In the hotel, the demonic masks of animals and demons and striking costumes of the opera artistes added an eerie touch. The masks appeared heavy but were actually carved out of light wood or made of mashed paper and painted. Every evening after dinner, guests gathered in the opera hall to watch dance-drama, a unique part of the Tibetan culture. It is said that the Tibetan opera began as early as the fourteenth century and was recently declared as the *Oral and Intangible Heritage of Humanity* by UNESCO. In modern times the opera is performed in hotels but historically it was held in public places like courtyards, fields and in monasteries.

I found a seat for myself in the hall. I could not understand the spoken words, but could appreciate the facial expressions of the artistes, their costumes and masks and their dance moves. A woman wearing a long red satin gown, a thick coating of powder on her face and kohl in her eyes that had been stretched obliquely to meet her earlobes, appeared before the audience waving a magic wand. There soon appeared a young monk who, I was sure, said something very offensive to the honourable lady and even tried to embrace her. At this the woman pranced about wildly delivering long dialogues as if shrieking. Then came the kicks and fisticuffs. The woman seemed to excell and soon she had the monk pinned down. Was it the story of the monk who did not observe the 'sila' of the monastic order? It is on record that some monks did not observe discipline and had to be admonished. Eminent director of the Dunhuang Academy, Duan Wenjie wrote in 'Dunhuang Art During Sixteen Kingdoms and the Northern Dynasties', (*Dunhuang Art Through The Eyes of Duan Wenjie*) that 'in North China, a large number of monks and nuns often observed the 'sila' of the monastic order in contravention'. Among these we learn of two greatly respected and renowned monks Kumarjiva and Dharmaksema who are said to have led irregular lives.

Soon another monk appears on the stage holding a monkey by a rope. The monkey jumped about frolicking and dancing. The artiste appeared to have a difficult time holding his animal mask in place while rolling on the stage. Whether he was the wise monkey of the Jataka who saved his entire tribe from being killed I cannot tell. The dances and songs to the beat of cymbals and drum by artistes wearing masks of animals was definitey entertaining but their dialogues were incomprehensible. The theme appeared to revolve around popular folk tales, perhaps a Buddhist story, ending in the victory of good over evil.

It was similar to the monastic dances at the Himalayan monasteries and I was reminded of the tribal dance drama I had seen during the Buddha Mahotsava celebrations at Tawang monastery in Arunachal Pradesh. The Monpa dance, the Adi tribal dance, the Shoy masked dance and the Nishi *janjati* dance were performed by young artistes wearing elaborate headgears and masks of animals, birds and demons. Some favourite dances are the Yak dance celebrating the discovery of yaks hundreds of years ago; the lion and the peacock dance depicting a strange friendship between man and animal. It is the story of a monk who meditates in the Himalayas. Two snow lions that lived there witnessed the severe austerities of the monk and offer him milk.

In monasteries the dance dramas are usually dedicated to Guru Padmasambhava depicting significant events from his life. A popular dance-drama during festivals represents the assassination of the anti-Buddhist Tibetan king, Lang Darma at the hands of a monk. The monks wearing gowns of brocade and masks of animals, birds or humans dance in rhythmic movements to the loud beat of drums.

Legend has it that in eighth century AD when Guru Padmasambhava or 'the lotus born' arrived in Tibet from India to build the Samye monastery he organised a tantric dance. The magical dance at the consecration ceremony was performed to subdue evil spirits believed to be obstructing the construction of the monastery. With the passage of time folk tales and religious stories were added to the dance movements and the opera was thus created.

It is said that the Tibetan King Thi-Srong De-tsan's endeavours to build the monastery were frustrated by earthquakes which were attributed to demons. On the advice of the Indian Buddhist monk Shantarakshita, the latter sent to the great Indian monastery of Nalanda for the 'wizard-priest' Padma Sambhava of the Yogacharya School, who was a famous sorcerer. A native of Udyana, or Ghazni, a region famed for sorcery, Padmasambhava promptly responded to the Tibetan King's request and arrived at Samye, by way of Kathmandu and Kyirong in Nepal, in the year AD 747. With the 'dorje' (Sansk. Vajra) or thunderbolt and spells he vanquished the devils, built the monastery in AD 749, and established the first community of lamas.[8]

At the Buddha Hall in Jokhang

The Buddha hall is the essence of the Jokhang the oldest structure and the spiritual centre of Lhasa dating back nearly 1,400 years. It is in this hall that the most precious gold image of Child Buddha brought by the Chinese princess Wencheng in the seventh century AD was kept. It was here that all visitors converged to offer prayers. In this holiest of holy halls is brought the portrait of the goddess, the 'Heavenly Maid' from the Moru Monastery and worshipped by devotees to mark the *Fairy Festival* every year. The goddess is said to be the protector of the Buddhist doctrine.

It is said that when the Tubo rulers first moved their capital to Lhasa in AD 647 the Tang dynasty Emperor Taizong married his daughter Princess Wencheng to King Songtsan Gambo (AD 617-97). She brought with her a 1.5 metre tall life size gold statue of a twelve-year old Buddha. The image was initially placed inside the Ramoche monastery built in honour of the Chinese princess, but was later shifted to the Jokhang temple. According to legend the rare image made of five precious metals–gold, silver, iron, zinc and copper and set with precious stones like diamond, rubies, emeralds and lapis lazuli was actually made in India at Magadh. It had been gifted to the Chinese emperor Taizong in return for his help against foreign invaders (*Yavanas*) from the west. When the princess, his daughter married the King of Tibet she brought the image as a part of her dowry.[9]

Through several renovations the temple has expanded into a large group of buildings covering an area of over 25,000 sq meters. Tens of thousands of monks gather at the Jokhang Monastery to pray and recite Buddhist sutras to mark the Grand Summons Ceremony held on the eighth day of the first month of Tibetan calendar.

I found myself in the crowd that had entered the Jokhang. A huge image of Padmasambhava adorned the Buddha hall. There were murals on the walls painted in gold and coloured dust from precious stones. The hall, resplendent in the gold of the paintings and thangkas hanging from the ceiling, added a surreal touch to the ambience. In the centre was a small enclosure where the precious image of Child Buddha was enshrined. A crushing crowd of devotees was inching forward to circumambulate inside the shrine. I joined the crowd as I could not have gone without a picture of the Buddha; I trained my camera at the gilded image while pushing forward but I was rebuked by the guards who asked me to switch off the camera.

There were so many devotees in the shrine that I was pushed and jostled even before I could kneel in front of the deity. But I persevered, I held on to the ground, bowed to the Buddha to thank him for this opportunity. In the chambers surrounding the hall, monks were reading the scriptures. In one chamber there was a huge thangka of the Buddhist tantra deities in an embrace or the 'yub-yum' posture called the *Chakrasamvara*. The deity with four faces and a dark body was in union with his consort, who clings to him in an eternal embrace. She was coloured red and has only one face. The pair is inseparable and interlocked. According to some this represents *Shakti* like the *Shivling*.

Another famous thangka was that of the Yamantaka embroidered in coloured silk. In this chamber of the precious thangka sat an old lama beating a small metal drum. He appeared to be in a trance with eyes tightly shut. But the moment I pressed the video button he opened his eyes and shouted. I quickly retraced my steps out of the ante-chamber and got lost in the crowd of devotees.

Even in Ladakh the temples of the fearful Yamantaka are completely covered and kept in darkness. May be because the terrible deity denotes Yama, the Lord of Death. One such temple of Yamantaka founded by Lama Lawang Lotus in the fourteenth century lies at the Spituk gompa in Leh. The temple is completely shut off from sunlight and is dark inside. The lama led me with a torch into the tunnel like temple where ancient animal masks were hung from the side walls. A towering thirty-five-feet image of a veiled Yamantaka surrounded by other Vajrayana deities stood in complete darkness. I pleaded with the lama to lift the veil but he got angry and started to shut the door, telling me that the image was unveiled only at the time of the monastery festival.

The Buddha Hall also houses various incarnations of the Sakyamuni. There is an image of Avalokitesvara, the most celebrated image of the Jokhang after the 'Child Buddha'. According to legend, the image was created with a branch of the sacred Bodhi tree from Bodhgaya, sand from the River Nairanjana, soil from the eight sacred places of India and many other rare and valuable substances.[10]

In another hall there were images of King Songtsan Gambo and his two Buddhist wives, the Chinese and the Nepalese princesses who are considered as incarnations of goddess Tara. The king's Nepalese wife was worshipped as the Green Tara or 'Dolma–the Saviouress' of the Tibetans and Chinese wife was believed to be an incarnation of the White Tara or the 'Dolma' of the Chinese.

The white Tara is seated like a Buddha, and has seven eyes, one being on the forehead in addition to the ordinary facial pair, and one in each palm and in the sole of each foot. The green Tara is usually represented in the form of a bejeweled young woman of a green complexion seated on a lotus.[11]

The corridor walls are decorated with splendid murals of Buddhist stories and this lends it the name, the Thousand Buddha Corridor. There are huge frescoes of the Chinese princess Wencheng journeying towards

Tibet and filling up the lake to build the Jokhang temple.

According to Catalogue of Jokhang Monastery by the Fifth Dalai Lama, the first Tangka in Tibetan history was the image of dpal-lha-mo (Auspicious goddess) painted by King Songtsen Gampo with blood from his nose. The goddess also called Sridevi is the special protector of Lhasa and is said to be the female counterpart of Mahakala. The deity has a terrifying face and her image is always kept veiled.

The goddess is believed to have her origin in the Hindu goddess Kali. Like Kali dpal-lhamo is dark in colour and wears tiger skin and earrings of serpants. She wears a string of skulls and carries a skull full of blood and a club. There is a corpse in her mouth. She rides a chestnut coloured mule believed to be an 'offspring of a red ass and a winged mare'. The saddle is made of the skin of an ogre and poisonous vipers are the bridle. In this dreadful attire she wages a war against the enemies of Buddhism.[12]

The genesis of the Tibetan fresco also goes back to the reign of King Songtsen Gampo (AD 617-97) when they were used to explain Buddhist doctrines. The earliest extant fresco is preserved in the aisle on the second storey of Jokhang Monastery. The fresco depicts Buddha, Bodhisattvas, disciples and patrons and stories from the Buddha's life.

There are priceless treasures in Jokhang including the golden urn used for drawing the lot to choose the Dalai Lama and the Panchen Lama, fifty-four boxes of the Tripitaka and the embroidered tangkhas of deities *Chakrasamarava* and the *Yamantaka*.

I climbed to the top of the Jokhang through narrow corridors and dark staircases. Here I found that the top was decorated with golden tiles and the gilded 'Wheel of the First Sermon' of the Buddha, the Chakrapravartana. The golden tiled roofs are said to be an exclusive feature of the Tibetan temples. The decorations are usually made of bronze with a plating of gold to give a grand and magnificent look to the holy structures. But when the king built the Jokhang in honour of his Nepalese wife princess Bribhuti, the roof of the holy temple was decorated with pure gold tiles.

It was with great difficulty that I spotted the Tang-Tubo Alliance (also called the Lhasa Alliance) tablet in front of the Jokhang that was erected in AD 823 during the Tang dynasty. The almost six-metre high stele is capped like a palace roof having a ridge of lotus flower, its base carried by a giant tortoise. It read that the 'Tang emperor Muzong and the Tubo Tsampo Tritso Detsan (AD 742-97) discussed the unity of the nation, signed the alliance agreement and became uncle and nephew'.[13] However, the tablet was in a shambles, covered in dust and soot from the construction work. Outside on Barkhor Street, Tibetans played the traditional Tibetan music, burned juniper leaves in huge receptacles and chanted prayers. There were hundreds of monks and nuns circumambulating the Jokhang.

I headed to the back of the monastery through a lane and found it cluttered with shops and houses on both sides. Black and brown gowns made of woollen fabric and animal hide hung from wooden hangers. There were hats of different styles for both men and women and a variety of adornments for the head, neck, ears, waist and arms. High leather boots made of sheep skin dangled from the low roof of shops. Some big shops displayed expensive brocade gowns and heavy gold, silver and coral jewellery for the head that could fall like a veil over the face. Huge earrings that could reach the shoulders were inlaid with all kinds of coloured gems. The yellow and white jade multi-stringed necklaces were long enough to reach the knees. But I bought only shoes and caps and headed to the hotel.

TOP AND ABOVE: *Faces of modern Lhasa. High glistening sky scrapers and beautiful road crossings. Foreign tourists abound in Lhasa.*

Visit to the Potala

At the Potala groups of men and women were singing to the beat of the hammer while levelling the roof of a newly discovered structure. Many visitors were gasping for breath and unable to negotiate the steep climb from the eastern gate; they stayed behind in the front square of the palace or loitered at the Barkhor Square. Others climbed through the gate and onto the entry point where hundreds of people were engaged

The gigantic Potala Palace stands proudly on the Red Hills of Lhasa. The massive red and white complex with its golden roof covers nearly 1.5 lakh square metres of land. It has been listed as a World Heritage Site by UNESCO.

in the renovation work. As renovation progressed, more and more underground rooms were being discovered.

Standing in front of the Potala I was overawed by its beauty and magnificence. The gigantic white and red complex with its golden roof on the Red hills of Lhasa cover nearly 1.5 lakh sq metres of land. Together with the encircled city in front and the Dragon's Pool behind, the Potala covers an incredible 3.60 lac sq metres. In 1994, it was tagged a World Heritage Site by UNESCO.

The grand entrance leading to the top of the hill is a steep climb making many a climber dizzy. In hundreds of halls that sit within red and white walls live beautiful images of the Buddha, Buddhist deities and the exquisite thrones and stupas of the Dalai Lamas. It is said that the construction of the grand palace began with King Songston Gambo of Tubo when he moved his capital to Lhasa in the seventh century. The Potala Palace we see today was built gradually on the ruins of the ancient palace built by this Tubo king.

As I climbed into the Lima Lakhang that appears to be a huge and dark cave cut into the mountains, I noticed several statues of Buddha and Buddhist deities and that of the Dalai Lama, all cast in alloys of silver, copper and gold. They smile beatifically and I felt they were welcoming me in this holy land. Here the Buddha was flanked by Avalokitesvara and the Fifth Dalai Lama.

Through another hall called the Kunsung Zedro Llakhang I entered the cave of the Raja Dharma which is said to have survived centuries of inclement weather and other intrusions.

Cave of Prince Dharma

I entered the dark and narrow caves marked 07 and 08, known as Chogyal Drubphuk or the Cave for Prince of Dharma, another name for Sakyamuni Buddha. Originally, the dark cave is said to have been excavated in the mountain top but was later enlarged into a hall. It was in this cave that King Songtsan Gambo once meditated. The cave has images of Songstsan Gambo and his two wives, preserved since the days of the Tubo reign. Other objects preserved in the cave include stone mortar, stove, stone pot that was used by the king while he lived in the cave. It is considered one of the most holy places in the palace and thousands were milling to make offerings here.

I passed through innumerable halls embellished with the stories of Buddha's life on their walls and where heavenly deities sit in deep meditation. The ornate thrones and stupas of the previous Dalai Lamas remind one of the high spiritual importance the palace once commanded.

Hall of Avalokitesvara

Avalokitesvara literally means, 'the Lord who looks down' with infinite pity on all living-beings. According to the *Buddhanusmrti*:[14] 'Avalokitesvara is the deity of the Pure Land School of the Mahayana Buddhism. He is a Bodhisattva, one amongst the Pure Land sages, the other two being Buddha Amitabha, and the Bodhisattva Mahasthamaprapta. Avalokitesvara arose from the spirit of the Adi-Buddha, that is, the first Buddha. He is a cosmic being. All gods have come out of his body. Avalokitesvara attained enlightenment through the faculty of hearing'.

We read further that in the early iconography 'Avalokitesvara is represented in the male form. He bears the head of a horse, sometimes a horse-head crown, eleven heads, a thousand eyes and a thousand arms'.[15]

I reached the most sacred Hall of Avalokitesvara (marked 015), also known as Phakpa lakhang. In front of the hall lamas chanted sutras, dispensed holy water and greeted the visitors. A flight of steps led me inside the hall. Here there was a long queue waiting to have a look at the Avalokitesvara and seek his blessings. I was last in the queue but the High Lama on hearing that a team from India was visiting beckoned me and other delegation members quietly inside. We circumambulated inside the small precincts of the hall and reached the image of Avalokitesvara who stood in superb glory. There was a whiff of sandalwood and roses. The High Lama threw a silken scarf around my neck and blessed me by chanting prayers. At the feet of Avalokitesvara, I felt blessed. Above the door hung a board inscribed with the words *Futian miao guo* (Profound Fruits in the Fields of Fortune) said to be written by Emperor Tongzhi of the Qing Dynasty.

The guide informed me that the image of Avalokitesvara had been carved out of a single piece of sandalwood. The memorial halls of the Dalai Lamas and the Hall of Avalokitesvara have golden roofs and form the gilded top of the Potala Palace. The murals inside the palace are painted with gold, silver and dust of precious stones. There are 10,000 tangkha paintings and about 100 scrolls of Buddhist scriptures written on pattra leaves from ancient India make a rich library collection. Some of the oldest scriptures are said to date back several thousand years.

Largest Repair on Potala

After taking a round of the study and living rooms of the 13th and the 14th Dalai Lama we reached the courtyard of the White Palace and take photos. It was here that the Dalai Lamas lived and conducted political activities. Here we meet the director in-charge of the Potala Palace who is currently overseeing the renovation of the grand structure.

According to the Director, this is the largest repair work of the Potala undertaken since 1989 and more than 200 million yuan have been spent. The renovation is not superficial, deft workers were going down to a depth of seventeen metres to reach the foundation of the palace structure in order to repair the fissures in the walls. Because of the undulating hills, new rooms were being discovered during the process of renovation. Nobody can count the rooms that comprise the palace; some say a hundred of them are hidden in the knotty hill.

Extensive restoration work is underway also at the Norbulingka to protect the monument. Many other cultural and historical monuments and religious institutions are being restored. I was told that China has allocated more than 380 million yuan for the repair and restoration of monasteries including the Potala Palace, Jokhang, Samye, Sera, Tashilhunpo, Gandain monasteries. Nearly twenty sites known for their cultural relics have been opened to public and work is on to open thirty more.

History has it that when the Fifth Dalai Lama ordered the reconstruction of the Potala Palace and the building of the Red Palace and the Holy stupa, more than 7,000 craftsmen of Han, Manchu and Nepalese nationalities were pressed into the project costing 66,154 kgs of gold. The majority of the Red Palace which was the religious centre of the Dalai Lamas is occupied by numerous halls and eight holy stupas. The stupas contain the remains of the Dalai Lamas. The stupa of the Fifth Dalai Lama is said to be encased in 110,000 taels of gold and inlaid in gem stones and pearls. The stupa also contains the holy relics of Buddha.

The 'Lion Throne' of the God kings

Inside the largest hall of the Potala called the Western Hall is the holy throne of the Dalai Lama named the 'Fearless Lion Throne' supported by carved lions. Here the hangings are of the richest brocade and golden weaves. Behind the throne are exquisite tapestries forming a canopy over the throne. '*Sitringasol*' or the Enthronement ceremony of the Dalai Lamas or the God kings were held in this Lion Throne. The ceremony was held after consultation with state astrologers and the holy date was intimated to the neighbouring countries. In 1940 when the 14th Dalai Lama was enthroned, the Indian representative is said to have been present along with those from China, Nepal, Bhutan and Sikkim.

Sarat Chandra Das, the secret British agent from Bengal in his fascinating narrative (*A Journey To Lhasa And Central Tibet*) describes his audience in 1882 with the Grand Lama (the 13th) sitting in this very throne as an eight year old child with 'bright and fair complexion and rosy cheeks'.

Sarat Chandra on meeting the Dalai Lama, placed in his lap a piece of gold weighing a *tola*. Interestingly the vessels in which His Holiness was offered saffron water, perfumed tea and rice were all made of gold. 'Two gold lamps, made in the shape of flower vases, burnt on either side of the throne'.[16] Much earlier in 1866 another secret British agent Nain Singh met the thirteen-year-old 12th Dalai Lama seated in the 'Lion Throne'.

It was the 5th Dalai Lama who first moved into the White Palace of the Potala from the Zhaibung Monastery. All later Dalai Lamas lived in the Potala Palace from where they excercised political power. The Potala is known for its huge collection of cultural relics including 10,000 statues of the Buddha and one thousand Buddhist pagodas, Buddhist doctrines written in Sanskrit in ink prepared with gold, silver, coral, iron and white conch shell and pearl dust.

Debating Monks at Sera

Next day I headed to the Sera Monastery. Built by Sagya Yeshes in 1419, it is considered one of the three most famous monasteries of Lhasa. The grand monastic complex comprises Buddha halls, Buddhist colleges and residences for over 5,000 monks and Living Buddhas. The walls of the monastery are covered with superb frescoes portraying Buddhist stories.

Here hundreds of monks had gathered in the huge pebbled courtyard for a monastic debate. Along with the local Lhasa people there were crowds of foreigners ready to shoot this strange style of debate that uses physical as well as sound energy. This is the most interesting spectacle at the monastery. It involves intellectual as well as physical exercise as monks jump in the air, twist their bodies, stamp their feet and swing their hands while loudly debating with their colleagues.

Sera monastery is one of the three most famous monasteries of Tibet. It has a rich collection of cultural relics. The scriptures enshrined in the temple and the paintings on the walls of the monastery are the most precious.

RIGHT: Hundred of monks gather in the pebbled courtyard of the Sera Monastery for a monastic debate. The debate uses intellectual, physical and sound energy. The monks jump in the air, twist their bodies, stamp their feet and swing their hands while loudly debating.
BELOW: Frescoes are an indispensable part of traditional Tibetan painting and are used to explain Buddhist doctrines and stories. Apart from gold dust, precious stones and rocks were ground to give rich natural colours that were used by monks to paint the frescoes.

We visited the main prayer hall. Hundreds of ancient thangka paintings hang from the ceiling and the hall is replete with images of the Sakyamuni Buddha, Avalokitesvara, Maitreya, Guru Atisa, White Tara and other Buddhist deities. The right corner of the main hall led into the inner chamber where lay a huge chorten around which were images of Buddhist gurus.

The monastery is known for its rich collection of the Buddha statues, scriptures written in gold powder ink and sandalwood statues of arhats and the most important 108-volume Gangyur (Tripitaka) printed in cinnabar in AD 1410 and bestowed by the Ming emperor Yongle.

The steep climb to the Drepung monastery made me breathless. It is the largest monastery in Tibet and home to all the Dalai Lamas. It was founded in 1416 by Jamyang Qoigyi Zhaxi Bendain, a favourite disciple of Zongkapa, founder of the Gelug sect of Tibetan Buddhism. It has numerous mansions, lanes and huge courtyards and once upon a time over 10,000 monks lived here. From the top of the monastery hill, I could see the entire Lhasa city below in all its splendour. When I walked into the huge central plaza of the monastery a dozen monks were holding a conference. I waited for their meeting to end so that I could be shown around. A junior monk led me up a narrow ladder to the four-storey structure where there were numerous worshipping halls with images of Buddhist deities. Each storey had ancient ladders leading to the upper storey. A faint light entered the rooms. One room that held the image of the Avalokitesvara was completely dark, but the monk's torch came handy, throwing a beam at the deity. Inside, I felt a little scared of the darkness and of the furious-looking deities who seemed to stare right into my eyes.

There was a maze of lanes and bylanes connecting one structure to another. One could spend hours walking inside the monastery. I saw monks drawing water from the handpumps installed by the side of the lanes while passing through the ancient monk quarters surrounded by trees. Before the 5th Dalai Lama moved into the Potala Palace he lived at the Gandain Phodrang section of this monastery.

Just below the Drepung, amidst a huge forest, lies the Nechung monastery smaller but set beautifully among the hills of Lhasa.

In the evening I set off to see the Ramoche monastery that was constructed in the AD seventh century. The monastery itself lies in the old part of the city and is undergoing renovation on a massive scale. A corridor on the left leads one to the main prayer hall. Here generous lamas let me shoot a video film. From the walls and the ceiling hang hundreds of ancient thangkas. Inside this hall was once enshrined the image of Child Buddha brought by Princess Wencheng.

A beautiful wall painting inside the verandah of the Sera monastery.

On the Tibet – Sichuan Highway 318

One can travel anywhere in Tibet through the wide network of national highways and provincial roads connecting every major town and almost every village. Even in remotest destinations one can find Internet cafes; one can never go hungry, the best meals are available in wayside restaurants. You can sniff progress everywhere, even in something as

insignificant as the hand tractor which has replaced the traditional ploughs. Travelling on the Tibet-Sichuan highway 318 one can see power cables all along the mighty mountains. Not even for a second does the mobile phone service go off on the long highway that passes through some of the most difficult terrains of Tibet and Sichuan provinces. The signs of development are plenty.

China has accomplished an incredible task of constructing railways, airways and roads networks in Tibet. Four national highways–Sichuan-Tibet, Qinghai-Tibet, China-Nepal, Nagqu-Qamdo–and Zetang-Gonggar Airport Highways have connected all of Tibet with the neighbouring provinces.

The mobile telecom business has developed at a rapid pace. For the first time on the roof of the world optical fibre telecommunication cable has been installed from Lhasa to Xigaze which extends for 340 kilometres through the mountain peaks on an elevation of 4000 metres.

We had the opportunity of travelling on the highway leading into Sichuan. It had rained all night in Lhasa and the earth was soggy and frosty. From the mountains a pleasant breeze blew as we drove towards Nyingchi on the Tibet-Sichuan Highway. Our destination: the famous Lamaling temple and the confluence of the Brahmaputra, known as the Yarlong Tsangpo in Tibet, and its tributary, the Niyang river.

The highway ran between paddy fields along the bank of the Niyang. Small villages lay in the foothills of the high mountains rising on either side of the river like sentinels. Smoky clouds nestled on the hills. Rows of plastic green houses had been pitched along the road for the cultivation of a special variety of dwarfed tomatoes.

Along the river banks are huts for tourists who want to spend the night there. Light canoes and yak skin boats sit patiently by the river bank waiting for tourists. Out of nowhere, milky streams seem to gush forth from the mountains only to mingle with the river. I saw Tibetan women drawing water from the streams in large bamboo baskets to irrigate their fields.

Dazi county is a big town. The mountains here are grassy and green. Afforestation has been done on a large-scale to provide dense foliage along the highway. The scenery is picturesque, with herds of black yak wandering on the hill slopes and tourist huts occupying the base of the hills. Villages with stone walls and prayer flags fluttering in the wind looked straight out of history books.

The Gandan temple town appears to have been recently built with new structures surrounded by vast fields. The gompa on top of the hill can be reached by a circuitous route lined by prayer flags and Mani stones.

As we neared the Moshu Gongka county the mighty river appeared swollen from the rain and exuberant streams. For several kilometres on both sides of the banks there lay green meadows.

A huge gate proclaimed that it was the birthplace of the King Songtzen Gampo, the famous Tibetan emperor. Here, women holding long poles were clearing a stream, others were herding their horses. Black leather yak skin tents belonging to nomads had been set up in the meadows.

The nomadic tribes subsist on animal husbandry. They usually pitch their tents by the river where they can find fodder for their animals and dry wood from the forest. They spend hours in the forest collecting produce, specially the medicinal caterpillar fungus which is coveted as an aphrodisiac. As soon as I stopped in the Riduo township a bunch of women hustled me to buy a handful of fungus. At the Kongpo Gyamda township lazy men played chess by the roadside while women sat picking fat caterpillar fungus to make a quick buck.

Soon we came upon the Mihla mountain entrance to Nyingchi where we stopped for an enchanting view of the mountains with snow-clad peaks. A thick growth of wild purple flowers with an intoxicating fragrance covered the low hills.

At the Song and Jiaxing townships the river calmly flowed at the road level with a wide embankment and clear blue waters. At several places there were deep valleys and the river swirled and gushed as if in fury. Innumerable streams emptied into the river and caused it to swell like an endless blue sheet.

The River Niyang flows along the Tibet-Sichuan Highway 318. Along the road there are huts for tourists who may like to spend a day on the banks of the river. The scenery is picturesque with herds of black yak grazing on the grassy river side and nomadic yurts dotting the landscape.

The Highway 318 to Sichuan takes a detour through the magnificent Boksom lake. In the centre of the lake arises an island where Guru Padmasambhava is said to have meditated. A stone pathway through lush forest pine leads to the ancient Tsodzong monastery.

At Zhong, a row of small houses with red roofs stand out in the meadows. We stopped at the Bahe countryside restaurant for a light meal.

Near the Kong bu Jianda county bridge we leave the highway and turn right to take the detour to Bayi town. On the way is the stunning Boksom lake and the famous Island monastery where Guru Padmasambhava is said to have meditated. The lake is called the bright pearl of Tibet. The wonderful landscape formed by high mountains and dense forests is reflected in the clear blue waters of the lake. Black and orange fish swim in gay abandon. A stone pathway on the island in the middle of the lake leads to the ancient Tsodzong monastery. Built in the mid-thirteenth century, the monastery's presiding deity is Guru Padmasambhava.

Model Village of Gongzhong

The highway continues further to touch the Bayi town. Here in the suburbs, just next to the river, is the model village of Gongzhong on the main Tibet–Sichuan highway. Interestingly, under the leadership of the village committee it has been developed into a 'telephone village' and a 'car village'. It is a sparse village with barely nineteen households with a total population of ninety people and a farming area of just over seventeen hectares. However, the village boasts of eleven Dongfeng-brand trucks used as transport vehicles and of the nineteen homes, seventeen have telephones. The school enrollment is 100 percent.

Along the way, at some places the road teases the river, at others it runs through a winding maze of hills. Beautiful villages lie interspersed with splendid landscape and ancient Buddha temples. There are wild fungus, mushrooms, medicinal herbs and wild pawpaw trees in the jungle. The Pawpaw King, said to be a thousand years old, is revered because the villagers believe that the village god lives in this tree. They burn joss sticks and offer sacrifices on auspicious days. Pawpaw usually grows at low altitude and in the Bayi township, it is a rarity. Other than hosting the village god, the pawpaw is also said to cure inflammation and internal fever.

In some villages, one can see the waterwheel sutra bucket driven by water revolving clockwise which symbolises sutra chanting for good fortune and safety of the village. Ancient water mills are still in existence and some of them have been preserved well as a testimony to the days gone by.

We walked into a huge park of wild lilies with wild peach and mulberries growing along the river and streams and at the foot of the mountains. Wild parrots swarm the region to feast on mulberries while squirrels fatten on succulent peaches. I was intrigued by the pierced trunks of the walnut tree only to learn later that it is done to discharge unnecessary moisture. People believe that such an exercise leads to a better bloom.

The village is seeped in superstition. People worship trees and stones and the most revered spot is the Holy Seat in the model village where the guardian angel is said to have rested when he crossed the village. Today, it is a treasured seat; people believe that sitting on the Holy Seat can ward off disasters and exorcise evil spirits.

At Bayi

We spent a couple of days in Bayi at the Nyingchi Hotel resort located in the heart of the town. In Tibet, the altitude of Bayi (2900 metres from sea level) is said to be the lowest, as such its topography is very distinct; there is a dense forest on all sides giving it a very verdant look. The climate is more like Sichuan. Here we met Tibetan officials and learnt about the prefecture of Nyingchi. The hotel was surrounded by immense gardens and orchards and the dining hall was covered with creepers of pink roses. A blue mist perpetually hung over the far away mountains that could be seen from the window of my room. At the hotel I met a Tibetan girl who was happy to see an Indian. She folded her hands in a gracious *namaste* and invited me to her house in a lane where she lived with her sister. In her home, she regaled me with Hindi songs as I sipped tea that she had prepared with so much love.

Indian Tradition of Tibetan Medicine

Many traditions in Tibet appear to have something in common with India and one of these happens to be in the field of Tibetan medicine. A visit to a Tibetan hospital in Lhasa and a pharmaceutical factory at Nyingchi province brought amazing facts before us. The legacy of traditional herbal medicines in Tibet owes its origin to India. I was surprised to see several Sanskrit texts like the *Charak-Samhita* in the library of the Tibetan Institute and Hospital. It is said that Lhatori Nyitsang, the 28th Tsenpo of Tubo kingdom of ancient Tibet married his daughter Yidki Rolcha to a physician from India called Biji Gajed. Their son Dungi

FACING PAGE:
A forest of oaks in village Gongzhong in Bayi. The trees are ancient and the village folk believe that worshipping them will exorcise the evil spirits.

Thorchok learned medicine from his parents and another Indian physician Biga Lhaze, becoming a renowned physician in time.[17]

During the reign of Songtsan Ganbo one Indian physician called Bhardvaj (granted the title of Big Immortal) was hired by the king in AD 650. He along with two others from Arabia and China wrote a seven volume comprehensive medical book *A Fearless Weapon*.

During the reign of King me-Agtson (Tri De Tsotsang) physicians from India were invited and one of them, Shanti Garhwa, presented Tara Medicinal herbs to the Tsenpo as a tribute at the beginning of the eighth century AD .

The Tibetan Hospital conducts research on Tibetan medicine and also collects recipes of ancient Tibetan medicines. The hospital is also promoting green therapy for preserving people's health and environment and laying more emphasis on traditional medicines to heal both body and mind.

It is believed that the traditional Tibetan medicine has a remarkable effect on difficult and complicated cases of illness. The system professes to have a profoud understanding of human physiological anatomy and a large part of medicine includes minerals, herbs and plant secretions. The typical ingredients used in medicine are the commonly found Chinese caterpillar fungus also used as a potent aphro, the bulb of fritillary and other plants, snow lotus or Brahmkamal which also grows in the snow lakes above Kedarath and Tungnath in India, musk, pilose antler etc. A.Bor, Solamwn Muicatnm, Rhodiola sachalinensis. The caterpillar shaped fungus is very small and hard to find and is said to be one of the most expensive medicines in Tibet selling at 40,000 yuan for a kilo.

I was curious about Tibetan medicines and visited the Cheezheng Pharmacy Company at Nyingchi where tradition mixes well with modernity–traditional medicines from herbs and minerals are prepared with state-of-the-art equipment. Here I was informed that the Qinghai–Tibet plateau is home to many rare medicinal herbs with unique qualities. There are atleast 2000 species of plants and fungi that grow on the plateau and are used as ingredients in Tibetan medicine. In addition

The caterpillar fungus grows abundantly in Tibet. It is sold as a traditional medicine for its potent aphrodisiacal and healing properties. It forms an important ingredient in many Tibetan medicines.

Beautiful paintings adorn the walls of the Lamaling temple and a huge image of Padmasambhava sits inside the main hall. A wall painting inside the temple depicts Buddha surrounded by snakes. He appears like the Hindu god Shiva.

159 species of animal and 50 kinds of mineral are also used as ingredients. Tibetan medicines are also said to contain rare materials like turqoise, coral, pearls, carnelian, gold, silver, bronze and iron.

I learnt of the 2,000 kinds of plants and fungi that grow on the Qinghai–Tibet plateau. These are used as basic ingredients in Tibetan medicine along with 159 species of animal products and 50 kinds of minerals. These are not all, though. In some concoctions even rare materials like turquoise, coral, pearl, carnelian, gold, silver, bronze and iron are used.

There are curious legends about the herbs of immortality or the '*sanjeevani buti*' growing in the Tibetan plateau. It is believed that when the Hindu god Hanuman had to fetch the '*sanjeevani buti*' for the wounded Lakshman, brother of Lord Rama, he searched for the herb in the Tibetan plateau and brought back on his palms a mountain covered with herbs.

On the Banks of Yarlong Tsangpo or Brahmaputra

In Bayi town is the ancient temple of Lamaling; octagonal in shape it rises up to four storeys. Here beautiful wall paintings adorn the temple and a huge image of Padmasambhava sits inside the main hall on the first floor. The upper hall has an image of the Avalokitesvara. To the right of the temple is a hall where religious ceremonies are held each month before an immense statue of Sakyamuni. In the park around the temple are huge mud receptacles where visitors burn juniper leaves and incense. Thick column of smoke billows continuously from the receptacle.

We left Bayi and drove another fifty kilometres to the confluence of the Niyang and Yarlong Tsangpo. I was mesmerised by majesty and grandeur of the mighty river that is said to be the son of Brahma, hence the name Brahmaputra. Devouts believe that India's only male river descends not from a mountain but from the heavens. But in Tibet it is the mother river that cradles the Tibetan people. Together with its five main tributaries the river is the main fascination for tourists to Tibet.

The high mountains screen the sunlight and a peculiar glow falls on the waves. The clear, shining waters of the Yarlong Tsangpo reflects the green mountains and the blue sky interspersed with grey clouds. It seems bathed in some heavenly light. Gulls flit over the surface looking for a tender catch. I climb up a high mound to get a good view of the river which enters the Indian border just about 300 km down south after taking a huge U-turn.

The mighty Yarlong Tsangpo river or the Brahmaputra flowing past Nyingchi. Originating near Mt. Kailash it flows east across southern Tibet until it bends south around Mt. Namche Barwa to form the grand canyon. It enters India as the Dihang, sweeps gracefully through Assam as the Brahmaputra and cuts through Bangladesh as the Jamuna. It merges with the Ganga to form a vast delta at the Bay of Bengal.

Originating from the Gyima Yangzoin glacier on the northern slopes of the Himalayas the river is the biggest in Tibet and on the highest altitude among the world's large rivers. Flowing west to east for over 2000 kms in Tibet it crosses Xigaze, Lhasa, Shanan, Nyingchi and twenty-three counties that fall within these cities. But as if on a whim the river stops moving eastwards between the counties of Mainling and Medog. The giant Gyala Pelri and the Namchebarwa peaks of the Himalayas stand in the way of the river forcing it to take a U-turn. This is the Grand Canyon of the Brahmaputra, sweeping over a length of over 500 kms, with a depth ranging between 2000 and 6000 metres, said to be the world's biggest canyon.

It was at one time thought that the Yarlong Tsangpo might be identical with Irrawaddy, the great river of Burma. Needham, in 1885-86, marched from Sadiya up the Brahmaputra to Rima, a village east of Sama in the Zayul valley and proved that the river at Rima and the river that flowed past Sadiya were the same. The Yarlong Tsangpo having no outlet towards Burma in any direction, leaves little room for doubt with regards to its identity with the Brahmaputra. And it was also found that the channel by which it makes its way through the Himalayas is the Dihang which is the largest river that falls into the Brahmaputra from the north.[18]

The river crosses the border at Medong county and enters India where, fed by a hundred tributaries flowing down the hills of Arunachal Pradesh, the magnificent river sweeps gracefully through Assam and meets the Ganges beyond Meghalaya and flowing through Bangladesh falls into the Bay of Bengal. On a casual visit to Guwahati I had seen devotees worshipping the river with offerings of milk and honey amidst a crescendo of chants of '*joi mahadeb, joi krishna*'. But here at the confluence of the Yarlong Tsangpo and Niyang there are no pundits, no chantings, no steamers or ferries. Only blissful peace and tranquility.

The driver disturbed my reverie with a loud honk, it was time to head back. I snatched a few last moments for myself and relished my good fortune of being by the river. Another shrill honk and I scampered into the bus.

Devotees burn juniper leaves and incense in mud ovens and make offerings to gods and goddesses by bellowing smoke. With prayers and chants they propitiate the deities for blessings.

On our way to a picnic by the side of the Tsangpo river we sat on the meadows where large yellow and pink dandelions were nodding in the breeze. Beyond the river were the green rocky hills covered with pine. This was the end of our journey but the highway continues to run for over 2000 kilometres through Chamdo, Derge and Ganzi and cutting the boundary of Tibet at Ta-chien-lu (Darchendo) before joining Chengdu in Sichuan province. It goes up to Shanghai through Wuhan covering a journey of over 5000 kilometres from Lhasa, forming a part of the prestigious Highway Number 318. From Shanghai the national highway goes up to Beijing connecting it with Lhasa. It is said to be one of the greatest Asiatic trade routes like the Grand Trunk Road of India.

The Sichuan–Tibet highway is only one of the major national highways in the Tibet Autonomous Region of China; others being the famous the 920 kms China–Nepal Friendship Highway connecting Kathmandu (Nepal) through the border town of Zhangmu; the 1115 km Qinghai–Tibet highway connecting Golmud to Lhasa; the 1350 km Xinjiang–Tibet Highway connecting Kashgar with Ali in western Tibet. and the Yunnan–Tibet Highway. These form a network in and around Lhasa and approximate to the ancient trade routes that ran through the length and breadth of Tibet.[19]

Train to Tibet

Before another night melted into morning and another road took me to another destination, I sat back and caught a heavy breath that I had forgotten in the gorgeous Lhasa. I remembered the angst that I was riddled with before the Tibet invitation fell into my lap as a blessing. Call it coincidence or a quirk of Fate, but I was so grateful to that square white matte paper that invited me to Lhasa. If I had not seen Lhasa I would not have known what possibly is the closest approximation to heavens.

A year after I returned to India the most elevated Qinghai–Tibet railroad from Beijing to Lhasa was launched bringing the Chinese

Railways within barely 600 kilometres of the Indian Railways at Darjeeling.

On 1 July 2006 train T 28 to the 'Roof of the World' from Beijing to Lhasa started on its 4000-kilometre maiden run through Xinning and Golmud covering hundreds of kilometres of permanently frozen ground.[20] Believed to be a miracle in the world's railroad history it was yet another engineering feat accomplished by China. Another train

On 1 July 2006 the first train –T 28 took the 4000 kilometre journey from Beijing to Lhasa through Xinning and Golmud, covering hundreds of kilometres of permanently frozen ground.

'T 27' meanwhile pulled out of its stations at Lhasa for its maiden journey in the opposite direction to Beijing through Golmud and Xinning. At the Tanggula mountain pass at 5,072 metres above sea level the trains passed the highest point of world's railway.

Close on the heels of the Qinghai–Tibet railroad came another historic event–the opening of the Nathu la Pass on the borders with India on 6 July 2006. Nathu la is the most significant pass leading from Sikkim in India into Tibet connecting the Teesta basin and Ammu Chu with the valley of the Brahmaputra river near Lhasa.

Wired fences were dismantled and replaced by a twenty metre long stone walled passage to connect once again a major artery of the Silk Road that historically linked India and China. The Pass is a mere fifty-six kilometres from Gangtok on one of the highest motorable roads with the scenic beauty of alpine flora and fauna. It was closed in the aftermath of the 1962 war and the border dispute that ravaged the 2000-year-old friendship shared by India and China. Before sealing of the border merchants on both sides had traded silk, tea, jewellery, spices in and out of Nathu la accounting for eighty percent of the trade between the two countries.[21]

This coupled with the Chinese plan to launch a Gangtok–Lhasa bus service[22] and an airport and better tourist facilities at Kailash-Mansarovar[23] will be good news for millions of Indian tourists who have never seen the most revered places in the Himalayas.

The magnificent bodhisattva Avalokitesvara, towering above all bodhisattvas, looks down with infinite compassion at all sentient beings. He holds the blooming lotus of the 'True Law', wears a gem-laden crown with the image of 'Amitabha in dhyan mudra' and holds a jug of sweet nectar which only the immortal gods drink. With his third eye he can see the past, present and future. (From Dunhuang, tenth century, painting on silk)

(17)

Gallery of 'Avalokitesvara'

In describing the attributes of Avalokitesvara I have drawn mainly from the works of eminent scholars, Lokesh Chandra viz. *Transcendental Art of Tibet*; P. Banerji viz. *New Light on Central Asian Art and Iconography* and *Central Asian Art – New Revelations From Xinjiang*; Kala Acharya viz. *Buddhanusmrti;* B.N. Puri viz. *Buddhism in Central Asia;* Sir Charles Eliot viz. *Hinduism and Buddhism*; Edward Conze viz *Buddhism–Its Essence and Development.*

While taking a round of the Magao grottoes at Dunhuang I was least aware that some of the best paintings of the Buddha and bodhisattvas, especially of 'Avalokitesvara' were lying at the National Museum, Delhi. And it was only after I returned from the Silk Road that I started looking for the myriad Buddhas and bodhisattvas that the British-Hungarian explorer Aurel Stein had brought to India from his expeditions of 1906-8 and 1913-16 to the Silk Road section passing through Chinese Turkestan.

The collection of more than 13,000 antiquities by Stein, the world's largest after Chinese, included of some of the most marvellous paintings from Dunhuang on silk and paper of the bodhisattva Avalokitesvara and Amitabha's Paradise, silk banners, sculptures in wood, stucco and terracotta, ancient documents, written on paper and wood in seventeen languages and twenty-four scripts. Of these about 1300 objects dated to the first millennium of the Christian era, now form an important and fascinating section of the Museum on its first floor.

According to S.P Gupta (Edited: *Masterpieces From National Museum Collection Central Asian Antiquities*),[1] the main source of the antiquities were Buddhist stupas, monasteries and temples which were richly decorated with wall paintings, stucco figures and votive banners. The monastic libraries had texts written in a variety of scripts, including Brahmi, Kharosthi, Uighurian and Chinese. Another source of the antiquities was the cemetery at Astana near Turfan.

The most beautiful collections at the Museum comprise paintings of bodhisattva Avalokitesvara in his various attributes on both silk and paper. The bodhisattva attained the highest popularity because of his compassionate nature and concern for the suffering humanity. The deity has been depicted sitting or standing on a blooming lotus, and wearing a gem laden crown with the image of 'Amitabha in Dhyana mudra'. He holds a jug of sweet nectar, perhaps the bliss giving heavenly 'Som-rasa' which only the immortal gods drinks. He holds aloft the thunderbolt or Vajra of Indra and the Lotus of the 'True Law'. Like the Siva he holds the trident and has a third eye in his forehead.

In many paintings Avalokitesvara has been shown having more than one head (he may have upto eight or eleven). The most magnificent painting has a thousand hands and a thousand eyes, one in every palm. This means that 'Avalokitesvara sees every object, destroys every evil and bestows benedication on all living beings', writes S.P. Gupta (Edited: *Masterpieces From National Museum Collection Central Asian Antiquities*).

Ekdasa-mukha Avalokitesvara or the Eleven-headed Avalokitesvara has eleven heads arranged in a pyramidal sequence. The top most head is that of Amitabha.

According to Lokesh Chandra, the legend behind the eleven heads is that once the bodhisattva descended into hell, converted the wicked, liberated them, and conducted them to the Sukhavati of his spiritual father, Amitabha. But for every wicked person thus converted another sprang up to take his place. The legend goes that in grief at the extent of

An unadorned Buddha sits cross-legged on a lotus seat lost in deep meditation. (From Dunhuang)

The beautiful eleven-headed or the Ekadasa-mukha Avalokitesvara has a third eye in the forehead and in his hands holds the sun and the moon. He looks splendid in his gem-studded necklace from which hang huge pendants. Bangles adorn his wrists and earrings or kundals *hang from his earlobes. (From Dunhuang, tenth century, painting on paper)*

wickedness in the world Avalokitesvara's head split into ten pieces. Amitabha turned each piece into a head and placed them on the body of Avalokitesvara in three tiers of three each with the tenth head on top and his own image above them all.

Chandra further elaborates that the eleven heads symbolize the 'synthesis of space' and explains that 'the spatial emanance goes back as early as the Saddharma- pundarika (Lotus sutra) where Avalokitesvara has been termed *samanta-mukha* which means facing all directions'.

At another instance he explains that the ten heads represent the ten paramitas (perfections) and the eleventh head is the attainment of Enlightenment.

Says the noted art historian, P. Banerji (*New Light on Central Asian Art and Iconography* that Avalokitesvara is 'an all embracing reality with many forms and function'. This composite figure combines in himself both Buddhist and Hindu elements, says Banerji. The art historian has traced affinities of the attributes of Hindu god Siva with the 'blue-necked' Nilankantha Avalokitesvara as well as Vaishnava elements (of Krishna and Visnu) in the 'Visvarupi' aspect of the Avalokitesvara. In some paintings Avalokitesvara is accompanied by divinities such as the Surya (sun) and Chandra (moon) and like 'Vishwadeva', the god of the universe he controls the 'eternal pair of day and night'. At his command the sun rises and sets and the glorious moon appears in the night sky.

Lokesh Chandra (Theophany, p.39) writing about *Cittavisramana Avalokitesvara* who 'casts his compassionate look on suffering beings' says: 'He is the deification of the action of the Tathagata. ...He transmits positive energy and calms the restless mind with pure thoughts.'

The most compassionate Avalokitesvara,[2] the 'personification of kindness and knowledge', is the 'iswara' who is 'avalokita' or the lord who looks down with infinite pity on all living beings. He has many names and is also known as Lokeswara, Lokanatha and Padampani.[3] He is eulogised in the *Saddharma Pundarika Sutra* and the *Karanda Vyuha Sutra.*[4] A deity of the 'Pure Land' school of the Mahayana Buddhism, he is a bodhisattva along with two other Pure Land sages, the Buddha Amitabha and Mahasthamaprapta.[5]

Through countless existences Avalokita, the 'personification of divine mercy and pity', has come to be regarded as the son of the original 'Adi-Buddha' produced through meditation.[6] He has the appearance of a 'heavenly deva' and towers above all bodhisattvas.

The beautiful deity is seated on the lotus. Wearing a decorated crown he looks splendid. Holding the universe in his hands–the sun, moon, the miraculous thunderbolt and carrying the effigy of the Dhyani Buddha Amitabha in the front of his crown, it is in him that all beings take refuge from danger.

According to Edward Conze, Avalokitesvara 'is the Lord and Sovereign of the world. From his eyes come the Sun and the Moon, from his mouth the winds, from his feet the Earth. In all these aspects Avalokitesvara resembles the Hindu God Brahma'.[7]

Avalokitesvara has the appearance of a 'heavenly deva' and towers above all bodhisattvas. He is the personification of kindness and knowledge. He is the 'iswara' who is 'avalokita' or the lord who looks down with infinite pity. (From Dunhuang, tenth century, painting on silk)

The bejewelled, eleven-headed or Ekadasamukh Avalokitesvara is the protector of the suffering humanity. He is a composite figure and designed as a god having all attributes of Siva, the god of the Hindu pantheon. Here he is holding tridents in both his hands and seems to be in the act of showering flowers. (From Dunhuang, tenth century, painting on paper)

FACING PAGE:

LEFT: *The thousand-armed Avalokitesvara with an eye in every hand and a third eye in the forehead like Hindu god Shiva. He wears a crown of jewels, dwells on a mountain of flowers and holds the 'cintamani' gem with which he wipes out the sufferings of the humanity. (From Dunhuang, ninth-tenth century, painting on paper)*

RIGHT: *Here the bodhisattva Avalokitesvara wears a moustache. He has Mongoloid features with small eyes and a flat face. Apart from the heavy earrings and bangles he wears the multi-stringed 'moti lata' which covers his entire upper body. (From Dunhuang, tenth century, painting on silk)*

Says P. Banerji, 'several features of Surya belong to Aalokiteswara, who is a composite figure and designed by the Buddhists as an all god' His attributes indicate his affinity to various Hindu deities such as Brahma, Visnu, Siva, Indra, Varuna and Surya.[8]

The beautiful eleven-headed Avalokitesvara or the 'Ekadasamukh-Avalokitesvara' with the richness of his gem-studded and ornately carved jewellery and elaborate head gear looks splendid. Strings of heavy necklaces with huge pendants hang on his bare chest. From his long ears hang heavy rings or 'kundals' and bangles adorn his wrists. The only clothing on his upper body is a red sash which winds across his shoulders and flutters as if in motion. According to Dr Kala Acharya[9] in early iconography Avalokitesvara is represented as having the head of a horse or a crown of horse-head. Sometimes he has eleven heads, a thousand eyes and a thousand arms. He dwells on a mountain of white flowers and holds the 'cintamani' gem with which he removes the sorrows of all beings.

Another eleven-headed Avalokitesvara has a ring of flames around his head and a thin moustache on his upperlip. From his hands fall a stream of flowers. He is heavily adorned in jewelled strings and red fluttering ribbons. Instead of holding the sun and the moon he holds the trishul or the trident and has a third eye, like Lord Siva, in his forehead. His long lustrous hair falls over his shoulders.

The Avalokitesvara has a thousand arms with an eye in every palm. On his forehead is a third eye. A pair of upper hands hold a double-edged trishul or a trident. A lower hand on the left holds a pot of sweet nectar while another holds a lasso. In the right he holds the chakra or the wheel. A ring of orange flames surround his body. A halo of blue rays emanate like cones from his head. He wears scarcely any clothing on the upper half of his body except for the multi-stringed jewellery that falls in several rows over his chest. Huge lotus like earrings adorn his ears.

The Avalokitesvara sits on a huge blue lotus with folded hands. Guardian deities are seated in the northern corners of his heavenly realm while four-armed deities are singing and dancing in the southern realm. Among his worshippers is a scantily dressed sadhu or a yogi. Lotus flowers decorate his head gear.

Another thousand-armed Avalokitesvara wears a crown of eight heads from which emanate rays of light. There is a third eye on his forehead and a thin moustache adorns his upper lips. He is embellished with gems and wears a necklace of 'rudraksh' beads and a red garment like a dhoti. He holds the sun and the moon discs in his hands. A pair of

The painting depicts the 'sukhavati' or the paradise of the Buddha Amitabha where there is 'boundless light' and blissful happiness. Buddha Amitabha at the centre of his paradise is flanked by Avalokitesvara and Mahasampraptha. They are draped only in a sash that wraps around their upper body while their lower half is draped in the Indian 'dhoti'. (From Dunhuang, eigth-ninth century, painting on silk)

A painting of Buddha from Khadalik. Here the Buddha appears with his face slightly turned to the left. There is a protuberance on his forehead and traces of jewels around his neck. A halo designed with flowers and creepers surrounds his head and a jewel that resembles a small chhatra or flowery lamp hangs over his head. (From Khadalik)

tridents can be seen in his upper hands. Seated on a row of lotuses, he is surrounded by worshippers.

Says Lokesh Chandra (Theophany) The Sun disc cures blindness (or destroys the veil of ignorance) and the Moon disc gives soothing coolness and cures illness. The remaining arms depicted as an aureole in the background of the figure are symbolic of his measureless skillful means.

Sukhavati is the 'world of Amitabha'.[10] It is called Sukhavati because it is full of happiness. The inhabitants of this world are free from all disease and dangers and 'enjoy the bliss of nirvana'. Amitabha illumines it with his radiance and 'infinite light.' Any sentient being who sincerely calls his name.and constantly contemplates on the Amitabha is born in this Sukhavati.[11]

'The Heaven of Amitabha has been conceived as a pure land of heavenly bliss which every Buddhist desires to achieve. It is very much similar to 'Heaven' or 'Svarga' of different religions'.[12]

The silk banners exhibiting the Paradise of Amitabha were recovered from Dunhuang in 1907 by Aurel Stein from the Caves of Thousand Buddhas. These banners, dated AD ninth and tenth century, portray Buddhist themes.[13] Besides the central image of Buddha Amitabha, the paintings depict bodhisattvas, such as Avalokitesvara, Ksitigarbha and Samantabhadra esconced in a heaven of their own.

A mystical world of 'Buddhist paradise' is sought to be created. The bejewelled deities are scantily clad with their lower bodies covered in a diaphanous clothing that resembles the Indian dhoti. The naked upper half is draped carelessly in fluttering ribbons or sash painted in a combination of red, green, black and brown and trimmed with gold. Their crowns are embedded with gems, layers of stringed pearls and armlets adorn their arms and huge necklaces with colossal pendants cover their bare chest. They wear large *kangan* or bangles on their wrist; their hair tied in a chignon. The deities are bathed in the fragrance of flowers falling from heaven and lute wielding devas play heavenly music.

According to Chandra (Theophany, p13), Sukhavati is the 'Buddha-ksetra' of Amitabha, a 'place of unparalleled magnificence and splendour.' He describes it as the celestial city of Amitabha having seven enclosures of gold, silver, beryl, crystals, ruby, coral and one of all jewels. Says Chandra, in the North-west of India, the triad of Sakyamuni, Brahma and Indra was replaced by Amitabha, Avalokitesvara and Mahasthamprata.

According to B.N.Puri[14] the main principle connected with the paradise of Amitabha is that there is a 'paradise of light belonging to a benevolent deity and those good men invoking his name would be led to that region'. The highest heaven is called 'boundless light' or 'endless light'. Puri points out reference to the Zoroastrian deity Ahuramazda who is constantly spoken of as being full of radiance and glory. It is also a land of song and music and pleasant sounds.

Reference to Visnu worship along with that of Siva have been traced by scholars in some of the paintings and banners depicting Buddha..

Vaisnavite influences have been traced in a Buddha image from Balawaste in the Domoko region on the southern silk route. The painting now in the National Museum, Delhi, as part of the Stein collection of wall paintings, has been assigned about eighth century AD. The body and arm of the figure are covered with mystic symbols depicting, according to historian B.N. Puri, the influence of Mahayana Buddhism.[15]

Among the mystic symbols that we see decorating the body of the Buddha are the Sun and the Moon believed to symbolize the light of knowledge; book or manuscript in the likeness of flaming jewels on lotus flower believed to symbolize the Lotus Sutra or the *Saddharmapundariks sutra*; the Vajra or the thunderbolt, a Vajrayana symbol (*Buddhanusmrti*, p. 217) on the forearm stressing the 'resolve for enlightenment'; the 'Triratna'—the three jewels of the Buddha, the Dhamma and the Sangha (*Buddhanusmrti* p.207) and the 'Wheel of Law', 'Dhammachakra' represented by triangle and circle respectively depicted on the body of the Buddha; There is a splendid chain around the neck.

Avalokitesvara smiles as he daintily holds a blooming lotus in his left hand, which seems to be raised in 'gyan mudra'. His head is tilted a bit to the left as he gazes lovingly with warmth and compassion. The painting resembles that of bodhisattva Padampani on the walls of Ajanta. The elaborate crown on the head and jewels impart beauty and grace. (From Dunhuang, tenth century)

The Universal or Vairochana Buddha 'the manifestation of all gods'. Wall painting depicting Buddha covered with several mystic symbols on the body and arm and has reference to 'Vaisnavite' influences on the paintings and banners of Buddhist deities. Among the symbols seen here are the Sun and the Moon, a Sutra book on the Lotus, the Vajra or thunderbolt, the Wheel symbolising elements of Hindu and Buddhist worship. (From Balawaste, sixth-seventh century)

Most importantly, P. Banerji draws our attention to the symbols of 'Srivatsa', the 'Mandara' and the galloping horse marked on the chest of the Buddha. This, in his opinion, represents the theme of 'Samudramanthan' or the churning of the ocean of milk, a famous episode in the Puranas. The story goes that once the Devas formed an alliance with the Asuras to jointly churn the ocean for the nectar of immortality. The mount Mandara became the churning rod and the king of serpents became the churning rope. Among the gems churned out was Uchhaishravas, the divine horse.

According to P. Banerji[16] 'the artist has portrayed the universal or Vairochana Buddha, conceived by the Buddhists as an all embracing reality'. The representation of the symbols go to show that 'all other gods were in essence nothing but the manifestations of him'—the Buddha.

Lokesh Chandra writing about 'MahaVairochana' says 'as the Sun shines in all times, in the same manner MahaVairochana 'Great Sun' as the 'Supreme Buddha' eliminates untruth and errors by the light of his wisdom. Vairochana symbolises 'germinal luminosity'... 'Everything emanates from him'... He is pure knowledge as the central sub-stratum of being.'

The guardians of all the four cardinal directions of the Buddhist heaven, the Lokapalas, figure on silk banners and sutra manuscripts. They are gorgeously attired and heavily armoured. Vaisravana, the guardian of the north, is identified by a spear, a flag and a small stupa, in his different hands. Virudhaka, the guardian of the south, is shown by a club. Dhratarastra, the guardian of the east, is shown holding a bow and an arrow. Virupaksa, the guardian of the west, is shown with a sword. The Lokpalas, originally Hindu deities, were absorbed in the Buddhist pantheon, says Banerji.

According to Lokesh Chandra (Scroll, p.46) Lokpalas are defenders of the faith and inspire mankind to act in accord with Dharma. The four Lokpalas are also known as *caturmaharajika* , the four great kings who defend the four points of the compass against evil and protect the faithful from all odds..

Says Chandra, 'Vaisravana has two predominant functions, one as the dispensor of riches and the other as the king of yaksas. In accordance with his position he is richly dressed in flowing garments of silk and wears a diadem and ornaments of gold'.

A painting with an inscription showing Tibetan Lamas worshipping the Buddha. The lamas with long pleated hair and wearing cap and cloak are seen kneeling before an image, probably that of the Buddha.

The famous painting depicts the Buddha with six monks. The Buddha appears to be standing in a grove with his disciples whose heads are shaven. One of them holds the whisk over the Buddha's head while another is about to shower flowers.

A painting from Khadalik shows a beautiful, unadorned image of Buddha against a picturesque background. His head is turned slightly to the left and is surrounded by a halo that has a green creeper designed on its border.

A painting from Karakhojo having an inscription, depicts two Tibetan Lamas with long pleated hair and wearing cap and cloak, kneeling. Their hands are folded in supplication before an image (probably of Buddha).

'Buddha with six monks' from Miran portrays the theme of conversion of Sakyan princes. It shows the Buddha standing in a grove with his disciples, unadorned with large eyes, hair done up in a top knot, sporting a small moustache and wearing a simple robe of dark brown colour. The halo is partly broken and the right hand raised in 'abhaya mudra'. His left hand supports his robe. To the Buddha's left are six monks or arhats ranged in two rows and wearing robes in brown and orange. Their heads are shaven. One monk in the upper row carries a yak or a horse tail or a chavar which he fans over the Buddha. To the extreme left stands a dark green tree studded with red and white flowers. A right hand is shown grasping a handful of flowers and is just about to shower them on Buddha. (See Puri, *Buddhism in Central Asia* p. 261).

According to P. Banerji, on close examination these are not flowers but a mass of beads or jewels. He explains[17] the hand belonging to that

Painting probably depicts the dream of Queen Mayadevi. Baby Buddha is seen flying across the sky seated on the back of an animal which appears to be a lion or an elephant. On the ground below sleeps the queen in her Hamsavati palace at Kapilvastu dreaming of the white elephant entering her womb. (From Dunhuang)

FACING PAGE:
Painting depicts a bodhisattva, identified by B.N. Puri and P. Banerji as Hindu god Indra from the eyes on his body. The deity is magnificently decorated and shown as a dreamy-eyed worshipper supplicating, probably before an image of the Buddha. (From Balawaste)

of Upali who received the jewels from the Sakyan princes and hung them on the branch of a tree. The panel, according to Banerji depicts the conversion of the six Sakyan princes. The scene is laid in a garden or grove and relates to the conversion of the six princes Bhadiya, Anuruddha, Ananda, Bhagu, Kimbila and Devadutta. They wore valuable jewellery and since they were proceeding to be ordained as monks they thought it fit to take them off and give it to Upali.

Some of the other famous paintings from the caves of Chinese Turkestan include the Nativity scene from Dunhuang in which the 'Baby Buddha' sitting on a flying animal (which appears like a lion or an elephant) is flying across the sky. There is a halo around the baby's head and the face appears like a cherub. On the ground below is a sleeping figure, possibly of Queen Mayadevi in the Hamsavati palace at Kapilvastu.

A beautiful, magnificently decorated and dreamy-eyed worshipper shown supplicating (probably before an image of the Buddha) has been identified by B.N. Puri and P. Banerji as Indra, god of the Hindu pantheon. Here the god is shown as subservient and subordinate to the Buddha.

Banerji draws our attention to the eyes depicted on the body of the worshipper, the ornamented cap like crown and the holy thread 'yajnopavita' decorating the upper body.

The beautiful paintings on paper of Bodhisattva Vajrapani and Padmapani are from Dunhuang. They are seated on lotus. The former is holding the *vajra* or the thunderbolt. According to E. Conze[18] vajra is identified with 'dharma and enlightenment'. According to P. Banerji[19] it symbolises the law which is eternal and indestructible.

Says Lokesh Chandra, 'Vajrapani is revered for his efficacy in protecting from losses besides being 'protector of the nagas against garuda, Vajrapani is the implacable enemy of the demons...'

Bodhisattva Padmapani holds the lotus symbolising the Lotus Sutra. The deity is elaborately draped in the Indian style embroidered blouse and dhoti with beautiful motifs on the border. Long scarves wrap around his upper half. He wears precious jewels—earrings, garlands, bangles and armlets. There is a vermillion mark on his forehead. The crown on the head is decorated with Dhyani Buddhas. From the halo round his body brown and orange flames are emanating and below his seat two snakes with glittering gems on their head are hissing.

The painting depicts the bejewelled bodhisattva Padampani seated on a lotus flower and holding a lotus. The deity is elaborately draped in Indian style embroidered blouse and dhoti with beautiful motifs on the border. Below the lotus seat two snakes with glittering gems on their head are hissing. (From Dunhuang)

Epilogue—
How Many Buddhas! How Many Miles!

Even though I bade farewell to the Child Buddha at Jokhang and the Avalokitesvara at the Potala, my heart continued to dwell on the meandering shores of the mighty Brahmaputra and the Yellow River, on the snowy cliffs of the Pamirs and in the mysterious deserts of the Gobi. I continued to meet the Buddha on the ancient thoroughfare. The memories of beautiful deities sailing on misty clouds, of fairies dancing by the mountain streams and singing celestial songs followed me like a shadow; the chants of '*namo amitabho*' and '*om mani padme hum*' resonated in my ears much after the din had died down; I continued to feel swathed in the fragrance of the joss sticks before the Maitrya. I wanted to live with these memories as long as I had the last breath in me.

But somewhere deep inside I was saddened by the empty caves and gaping holes in the ancient grottoes of the Taklamakan and the Gobi deserts. Whole walls alongwith murals had been cut away, Buddha statues in the central pillar of the caves had been snatched from their niches, sacred relinquaries with the remains of Buddhist holy men had been whisked away. In the name of research and exploration frescoes had been literally gouged out from their walls with axes and knives, Buddha images hacked away from their heavenly paradise and precious and rare manuscripts had been exchanged for a few pieces of silver. What nature had preserved for over a thousand years the treasure hunters had made short work with deadly tools.

During my safari on the Silk Road I came across information in both Chinese and English that paintings, stucco images and statues had been stolen by Stein, by Peliot, by le Coq. Many questions were also put to the guides belonging to research Institutes at Kizil, Dunhuang, Bezeklik by visitors and pilgrims about what China was doing to get back the lost treasures of the Silk Road.

In the caves of Kuqa and Turfan many foreigners hung their head in shame as guides recounted how cruelly Buddhist images had been cut away and stolen. Suddenly from among the European crowd a chorus of 'shame shame' went up at Bezeklik as cave after cave was found to be ravaged under the garb of exploration. Angry tourists at Kizil wanted to know what China was doing to get back its stolen wealth. It was sad to see enlarged photos of murals (believed to have been taken away to Germany) being displayed in front of the Bezeklik caves from where it had been stolen.

On my return to India I asked many Central Asian scholars what they thought about the ravaged caves of Xinjiang. Many said that these mistakes of history could not be set right. 'We can only go forward not backwards in history'. Others wanted the dissemination and sharing of knowledge by the countries who had participated in the 'great loot'. Still others questioned the silence of China while the desert cities were dug out one by one by foreigners who held proper Chinese visa, employed Chinese labour and enrolled Chinese translators. Afterall it was the Chinese monk, Wang who handed out the sutra manuscripts from the Library Cave at Dunhuang!

I was concerned about the poor facilities that a developing nation like India could provide for the upkeep of the 13,000 antiquities brought by Stein under the instructions of his British masters. The lack of proper power for air conditioned halls and regular restoration work.

One fine day I ventured to meet Prof S.P. Gupta, president of Indian Achaeological Society to ascertain his views on the return of antiquities that were lying in the closed boxes of the Indian museums to their rightful owners. He was aghast. 'Can antiquarian remains belong to one country?' he asked. 'They belong to the whole humanity at one level and at the other level to the country of its origin.' For this reason, he said, bodies like the UNESCO have come up with the World Heritage Site project for maintaining important sites.

According to him the pages of human history are not the endeavours of one country but of the whole world, being a product of culture. All have a right to share its aesthetics and message. 'History cannot be reversed particularly in matters of antiquarian remains.'

I gathered courage to remind him that the antiquarian remains of Sanchi were returned to India. That, he said that was largely due to religious sentiments attached to the relics.

The relics of Sariputra and Maudgalyayana, the two foremost disciples of Buddha, were found by Cunningham in Stupa 'three' at Sanchi dated to second century BC. Cunningham found the relics enshrined at the centre of its dome. According to Bhadant, Dr Anand Kaushalyayana, the relics along with those discovered from the Satdhara stupa in a village near Sanchi in year 1815 were taken away to London.

However, the relics were returned to the Buddhist world following intense efforts by the Mahabodhi Society. In 1947 the relics reached Colombo where they were received and worshipped with great fervour after which they arrived in Calcuta at the famous Dharamarajika Vihar. From where they were taken to Bihar, Uttar Pradesh, Ladakh, Assam, Sikkim, Tibet, Burma and Nepal. Finally in 1953, the relics were housed in the modern Chetiyagiri Vihar built on the Sanchi hills.

While this debate about antiquities went on endlessly in my mind I had two things on my wishlist: a photographic exhibition on the Silk Road sites and a short film on the journey. But none happened. No, I was not being lazy, just that in mid-2007 I had packed my bag and was back on the Silk Road dreaming of another land, another destination.

This time I wanted to pick up the trail of the Chinese highway A 312 at Jarkent near Korgas on the Sino-Kazakh border and travel through Central Asia on the International highway M-39.

M-39 is no ordinary highway. It has real history behind it. It approximates to the route taken by Tamerlane over 600 years ago when he marched from Samarkand to Delhi in 1398 to subdue the Sultan. As many as 128 years later he was followed by another conqueror Zaheeruddin Mohammad Babur in 1526 who took much the same direction from Samarkand to Kabul to Delhi where he laid the foundations of the Moghul dynasty. Called the lifeline of Central Asia the highway also approximates the path of the ancient caravans to and from India. At Termez the M-39 is joined by the Balkh-Bamiyan-Taxila route that ran across Afghanistan and entered through the Khyber Pass into north-west India (now Pakistan). At the Pass the great route met the Grand Trunk Road running through Delhi upto Calcutta.

My drive through vast steppelands from Jarkent near Korgas on the Kazakh-China border south-west to Almaty was both exciting and adventurous. In the company of my archaeologist friend Alisher and Russian guide Anastasia I came several times face to face with wild asses and gazelles roaming the steppelands in large groups. With the aid of shepherds we also looked for new trails along mountain streams in the Altyn—Emel region. That the ancient caravans going to China took the route along the Ili river was indicated by a group of six striking Buddha figures with Sanskrit like inscriptions carved on the rock faces near lake Kapshagay.

Through Bishkek and Tashkent my route lay over a thousand kilometres west to Urgench, the capital of the province of Khorezm. My purpose of coming here was to see the beautiful Heritage township of Ichon Kala at Khiva and the desert settlement of Toprak kala across the river Oxus. This was the branch of the silk road that went westwards from Tashkent through Otrar following the river Oxus and along the northern shores of the Caspian and the Black Sea onwards to the Mediterranean.

My journey southwards from Tashkent along M-39 wound through the picturesque Amankutan mountains through dense orchards and nature reserves of wild animals like the Asian bear and the quick footed deer and many species of birds. This path, the shortest through the Amankutan, is believed to have been used since time immemorial by the invading armies coming through Sogdiana and Bactria and across the Indus into India. It is believed that those coming from China also preferred this route instead of the difficult route through the Pamirs.

Strange though it may seem the close proximity between the regions of Central Asia and India has for millennia defied the barriers of high mountains, glacial peaks and torrentous rivers of the Hindukush and the Himalayan ranges. As a proof of the ancient ties between the two regions stand majestic monuments of rock engravings showing scenes of sun worship and fertility rites at Karabastau near Almaty, Buddhist petroglyphs near the Ili river, monasteries and stupas at Termez and splendid statues and paintings of Hindu gods and goddesses in the museums of Central Asia.

The journey ended in Termez at the Friendship Bridge on the Afghan border. Firstly because I had no documents to enter Afghanistan and secondly I lacked courage to step into a highly volatile region where every road, I feared, was a landmine. Whether I like it or not I would have to give up the stretch onwards from Termez through Balkh, Bamiyan upto the Khyber Pass. But in order to trace the entire route of the ancient Indian caravan through Central Asia I would have to pick up the trail from the Khyber Pass through Taxila into India to complete the circuit from India to India.

The account of this journey will have to wait for another time, for another book.

References

Introduction – A Safari on the Silk Road

1. Yiping, Zhang; *Story of the Silk Road,* 2005, China Inter Continental Press, China.pp17. Tucker, Jonathan; *The Silk Road Art and History*, 2003, Timeless Books. Whitfield, Susan; *Life along the Silk Road,* first published: 1999, reissued: 2004, John Murray Hodder Headline, London Man, John; *Attila The Hun,* 2005, Bantam Books Transworld Publishers, London; Needham, Joseph; *Science and Civilisation in China,* first published: 1954, reprint: 1979, Cambridge University Press, London. Beal, Samuel; Trans. from Chinese by Xuanzang *Si-Yu-Ki Buddhist Records of the Western World,* first published:1884, reprinted:1995, Low Price Publications, Delhi Butler, David and Miles, Keith; *Marco Polo,* 1982, Futura Publications, MacDonald & Co. (Publishers) Ltd, London; Marozzi, Justin; *Tamerlane,* first published: 2004, reprint: 2005, Harper Perennial, London Chien, Szuma; *Selections from Records of the Historian,* 1979, Foreign Languages Press, Peking, China; pp.91. Liu, Xinru; *Silk and Religion,* 1996, Oxford University Press, Bombay, Calcutta, Madras.Man, John; *Kublai Khan,* 2006, Bantam Press, Transworld Publishers, London. Davids, T. W. Rhys; *Buddhist India,* First published:1903, reprint: 2002, Low Price Publications, Delhi. Gibb, H. A. R; *IbnBattuta: Travels in Asia & Africa*; first published:1929, reprinted: 2001 and 2006, Manohar Publishers & Distributors, New Delhi; Puri, B. N; *Buddhism In Central Asia,* first edition: 1987, reprint: 1993, 1996 and 2000, Motilal Banarsidass Publishers Pvt. Ltd., Delhi. Lixin, Zheng; *Guide to Chinese Buddhism,* 2004, Foreign Language Press, Beijing,China. Beal, Samuel; Shaman Hwui Li *The Life of Hiuen-Tsiang,* first published: 1911, reprinted: 2001, Low Price Publications, Delhi. Hopkirk, Peter; *Foreign Devils on the Silk Road,* first published: 1980, first issued in 1984 and reissued in 2001, Oxford University Press, Oxford, Great Britain. Lansdel, Henry, D.D; *Chinese Central Asia,* 1887, Harell, Watson and Viney Ltd, London and Aylesbury. Information office of Xinjiang Uygur Autonomous Region of China; *Footprints of Foreign Explorers on the Silk Road,* 2005, China Intercontinental Press, China.
2. Sobhan, Rehman; *Re-discovering the Southern Silk Route,* 2000, Mohiuddin Ahmed at The University Press Limited, Dhaka, Bangaldesh, p.2. Verghese, B.G; *India's North East Resurgent,* 1998, Konark Publishers, New Delhi, p.368. Singh, Upinder; *A History of Ancient and Early Medieval India-from Stone Age to the12th Century*; 2008, Pearson Longman, New Delhi; p.290.
3. Allen, B.C; Gait, E.A; Howard H.F; Allen, C.G.H; *Gazetteer of Bengal and North- East India,* reproduced: 1979, again in 1982, 1986, 1989, 1993, 1996, 2001 and 2005, Mittal Publications, Mohan Garden, New Delhi; pp.26, 87. Dutta, Debabrata; *Histroy of Assam,* re-issued fourth edition: 1989, reprint:1995, Sribhumi Publishing Company, Calcutta, p.3.
4. Hindustan Times, March 22, 2007; '*India-China to revive part of old Silk Route*' by Anirban Choudhary, p.19.
5. Sobhan, Rehman; *Re-discovering the Southern Silk Route,* 2000, Mohiuddin Ahmed at The University Press Limited, Dhaka, Bangaldesh, pp.1, 2, 85.
6. Yiping, Zhang; *Story of the Silk Road,* 2005, China Inter Continental Press, China, p.9.
7. Liu, Xinru; *Silk and Religion,* 1996, Oxford University Press, Bombay, Calcutta, Madras; pp.17,49. Beal, Samuel; Shaman Hwui Li *The Life of Hiuen-Tsiang,* first published: 1911, reprinted: 2001, Low Price Publications, Delhi, p.42. Butler, David and Miles, Keith; *Marco Polo,* 1982, Futura Publications, MacDonald & Co. (Publishers) Ltd, London; pp.171, 195. Marozzi, Justin; *Tamerlane,* first published: 2004, reprint: 2005, Harper Perennial, London; pp.213. Whitfield, Susan; *Life along the Silk Road,* first published: 1999, reissued: 2004, John Murray Hodder Headline, London; pp.41.
8. Butler, David and Miles, Keith; *Marco Polo,* 1982, Futura Publications, MacDonald & Co. (Publishers) Ltd, London;

pp.171, 195. Beal, Samuel; Shaman Hwui Li *The Life of Hiuen-Tsiang,* first published: 1911, reprinted: 2001, Low Price Publications, Delhi, pp.42.
9. Marozzi, Justin; *Tamerlane,* first published: 2004, reprint: 2005, Harper Perennial, London; p.213.
10. Whitfield, Susan; *Life along the Silk Road*, first published: 1999, reissued: 2004, John Murray Hodder Headline, London; pp.41. Beal, Samuel; Trans. from Chinese by Xuanzang *Si-Yu-Ki Buddhist Records of the Western World,* first published:1884, reprinted:1995, Low Price Publications, Delhi, p.22.
11. Johnston, E.H. Trans. *Asvaghosh's Buddhacharita or Acts of the Buddha*, Trans. 1995, first published in Lahore, 1936; Munshiram Manoharlal Publishers Pvt. Ltd; p.89, 90.
12. Yiping, Zhang; *Story of the Silk Road,* 2005, China Inter Continental Press, China. pp.12.
13. Wriggins, Sally Hovey; *The Silk Road Journey with Xuanzang,* 2004, Westview Press, USA, p.176.
14. Yiping, Zhang; *Story of the Silk Road,* 2005, China Inter Continental Press, China, pp.15.
15. Liu, Xinru; *Silk and Religion*, 1996, Oxford University Press, Bombay, Calcutta, Madras; p.62.
16. Man, John; *Kublai Khan,* 2006, Bantam Press, Transworld Publishers, London; p.242.
17. Yiping, Zhang; *Story of the Silk Road,* 2005, China Inter Continental Press, China, p.14.
18. Vincent, William; *The Commerce and Navigation of the Ancient in the Indian Ocean,* Vol I &II;1998; Asian Educational Services, New Delhi. Singh, Upinder; *A History of Ancient and Early Medieval India- from Stone Age to the 12th Century*; 2008, Pearson Longman; NewDelhi; pp.408. Davids, T. W. Rhys; *Buddhist India,* First published:1903, reprint: 2002, Low Price Publications, Delhi; pp.104, 116. Beal, Samuel; Shaman Hwui Li *The Life of Hiuen-Tsiang,* first published: 1911, reprinted: 2001, Low Price Publications, Delhi, p. xli. Needham, Joseph; *Science and Civilisation in China,* first published: 1954, reprint: 1979, Cambridge University Press, London; pp.177-180. Gibb, H. A. R; *IbnBattuta: Travels in Asia & Africa*; first published: 1929, reprinted: 2001 and 2006, Manohar Publishers & Distributors, New Delhi; Yiping, Zhang; *Story of the Silk Road,* 2005, China Inter Continental Press, China. pp.66, 95.
19. Needham, Joseph; *Science and Civilisation in China,* first published: 1954, reprint: 1979, Cambridge University Press, London; pp.182.
20. Hook, Brian; editor, *The Cambridge Encyclopedia of China*, first edition: 1982, second edition: 1991, Press Syndicate of the University of Cambridge; Cambridge, Great Britain. pp.46.
21. Hook, Brian; editor, *The Cambridge Encyclopedia of China*, first edition: 1982, second edition: 1991, Press Syndicate of the University of Cambridge; Cambridge, Great Britain. pp.46.
22. Yiping, Zhang; *Story of the Silk Road,* 2005, China Inter Continental Press, China; pp.94-95. Tucker, Jonathan; *The Silk Road Art and History*, 2003, Timeless; pp.90. Hook, Brian; editor, *The Cambridge Encyclopedia of China*, first edition: 1982, second edition: 1991, Press Syndicate of the University of Cambridge; Cambridge, Great Britain. pp.46.
23. Beal, Samuel; Shaman Hwui Li *The Life of Hiuen-Tsiang,* first published: 1911, reprinted: 2001, Low Price Publications, Delhi. pp.xxv-xli.
24. Davids, T. W. Rhys; *Buddhist India*, First published:1903, reprint: 2002, Low Price Publications, Delhi; pp.104, 115.
25. Davids, T. W. Rhys; *Buddhist India*, First published:1903, reprint: 2002, Low Price Publications, Delhi; pp.104.
26. Gibb, H. A. R; *IbnBattuta: Travels in Asia & Africa*; first published:1929, reprinted: 2001 and 2006, Manohar Publishers & Distributors, New Delhi.
27. Tucker, Jonathan; *The Silk Road Art and History*, 2003, Timeless; pp.366 See also Hook, Brian; editor, *The Cambridge Encyclopedia of China*, first edition: 1982, second edition: 1991, Press Syndicate of the University of Cambridge; Cambridge, Great Britain. pp.46, 198 (map).
28. Rockhill, William Woodville; *The Land of the Lamas*, first published: 1891, reprint: 2004, Sri Satguru Publications, Indological and Oriental Publishers- a Division of Indian Books Centre, Delhi.pp.277, 282. Whitfield, Susan; *Life along the Silk Road*, first published: 1999, reissued: 2004, John Murray Hodder Headline, London;. pp.7, 22. China's Tibet; published by China's Tibet; Beijing;Vol. 16, No.4, 2005; pp.46-49;
29. Needham, Joseph; *Science and Civilisation in China,* first

published: 1954, reprint: 1979, Cambridge University Press, London; pp.212, 204.

30. Bagci, P.C; *India and China,* first Saraswat edition: 1981, Saraswat Press, Delhi, pp.97. Sachau C.Edward; *Alberuni's India* first published by Trubner and Co. Ludgate Hill, 1888, Rupa and Co. first published 2002, fourth impression 2005, New Delhi, pp.176-179 Beal, Samuel; Shaman Hwui Li *The Life of Hiuen- Tsiang,* first published: 1911, reprinted: 2001, Low Price Publications, Delhi. pp.xxviii Hartog, Leo De; *Genghis Khan: Conqueror of the World,* first published: 1989, paperback edition: 1999, I.B. Tauris & Co. Ltd., London; pp.124. Chien, Szuma; *Selections from Records of the Historian,* 1979, Foreign Languages Press, Peking, China; pp.173. Thapar,Romila; *The Penguin History of Early India,*Penguin Group, 2002, New Delhi, pp.177. Leonardo Olschki, *Marco Polo's Asia,* University of California Press, Berkeley and Los Angeles, California; Cambridge University Press, London, England, 1960. pp.415- 424.
31. Butler, David and Miles, Keith; *Marco Polo,* 1982, Futura Publications, MacDonald & Co. (Publishers) Ltd, London; pp.203.
32. Gibb, H. A. R; *IbnBattuta: Travels in Asia & Africa*; first published:1929, reprinted: 2001and 2006, Manohar Publishers & Distributors, New Delhi; pp.214.
33. Historical dates taken from: Wriggins, Sally Hovey; *The Silk Road Journey with Xuanzang,* 2004, Westview Press, USA. Tucker, Jonathan; *The Silk Road Art and History*, 2003, Timeless Books. Yiping, Zhang; *Story of the Silk Road,* 2005, China Inter Continental Press, China. pp. Needham, Joseph; *Science and Civilisation in China,* first published: 1954, reprint: 1979, Cambridge University Press, London; pp.128. Holden, Edward, S; *The Moghul Emperors of Hindustan*, 2004, Asian Educational Services, New Delhi. Hartog, Leo De; *Genghis Khan: Conqueror of the World,* first published: 1989, paperback edition: 1999, I.B. Tauris & Co. Ltd., London; Beal, Samuel; Shaman Hwui Li *The Life of Hiuen-Tsiang,* first published: 1911, reprinted: 2001, Low Price Publications, Delhi. Gibb, H. A. R; *IbnBattuta: Travels in Asia & Africa*; first published:1929, reprinted: 2001 and 2006, Manohar Publishers & Distributors, New Delhi; Butler, David and Miles, Keith; *Marco Polo,* 1982, Futura Publications, MacDonald & Co. (Publishers) Ltd, London; Wikipedia, the Free Encyclopaedia.
34. Puri, B. N; *Buddhism In Central Asia*, first edition: 1987, reprint: 1993, 1996 and 2000, Motilal Banarsidass Publishers Pvt. Ltd., Delhi. pp.vii, 90, 318-319. Bagci, P.C; *India and China,* first Saraswat edition: 1981,Saraswat Press, Delhi, pp.8-9.
35. Yiping, Zhang; *Story of the Silk Road,* 2005, China Inter Continental Press, China; pp.127-128. Tucker, Jonathan; *The Silk Road Art and History*, 2003, Timeless Books. pp.90. Needham, Joseph; *Science and Civilisation in China,* first published: 1954, reprint: 1979, Cambridge University Press, London; pp.128.
36. Yiping, Zhang; *Story of the Silk Road,* 2005, China Inter Continental Press, China; pp.130-131 see also Tucker, Jonathan; *The Silk Road Art and History*, 2003, Timeless Books. pp.90. Needham, Joseph; *Science and Civilisation in China,* first published: 1954, reprint: 1979, Cambridge University Press, London; pp.128.
37. Yiping, Zhang; *Story of the Silk Road,* 2005, China Inter Continental Press, China; pp.129-130 see also Tucker, Jonathan; *The Silk Road Art and History*, 2003, Timeless Books. pp.89.
38. Yiping, Zhang; *Story of the Silk Road,* 2005, China Inter Continental Press, China. pp.132-133 See also Tucker, Jonathan; *The Silk Road Art and History*, 2003, Timeless Books. pp.90-91.
39. Hopkirk, Peter; *Foreign Devils on the Silk Road*, first published: 1980, first issued in 1984 and reissued in 2001, Oxford University Press, Oxford, Great Britain.

Map: Land and Sea Routes Connecting Asia and Europe
Bo, Jin; *China in Diagrams,* 2003 , China Intercontinental Press, Beijing, China; 20, 116. Fengjun, Jin & Jinkai, Qian; *A Social and Economic Atlas of Western China,* 2003, China Intercontinental Press , China; p.16. Tucker, Jonathan; *The Silk Road Art and History*, 2003, Timeless Books, New Delhi; pp.12-13. Singh, Upinder: *A History Of Ancient And Early Medieval India-From Stone Age to the 12th Century*; 2008; Pearson Longman; New Delhi; pp. 290, 410. Bidari, Basanta; *Lumbini: A Haven of Sacred Refuge*, first Published: 2002, reprinted: 2003

and 2004, Hill Side Press (P) Ltd., Kathmandu, Nepal; p.9. Sobhan, Rehman; *Re-discovering the Southern Silk Route,* 2000, Mohiuddin Ahmed at The University Press Limited, Dhaka, Bangaldesh. p.2.

Chapter One – My Journey begins from Xian

1. Sobhan, Rehman; *Re-discovering the Southern Silk Route,* 2000, Mohiuddin Ahmed at The University Press Limited, Dhaka, Bangaldesh. pp.2.
2. Ahir, D.C; *Ashoka The Great*, 1995, B. R. Publishing Corporation, Delhi. pp.200. 'Manshera Text' a major rock edict of Asoka translated by D.C. Sarkar in "Inscriptions of Asoka" published by the Govt. of India, Ministry of Information and Broadcasting, Publications Division, Delhi, 1957.
3. Ahir, D.C; *Ashoka The Great*, 1995, B. R. Publishing Corporation, Delhi. pp.54, 89, 90, 206. Medhankar, Dr. Bhadant Sawangi; *The Great Buddhist Emperors of Asia*, 1997, Kashinath Meshram Buddha Bhoomi Prakashan, Nagpur, Maharashtra. pp.27-28. Radhakumud Mookerji; *Asoka,* First edition, London, 1928; Third revised edition, Delhi, 1962; Reprint Delhi, 1972, 1989, 1995, 2002, 2007; Motilal Banarsidass, Delhi. pp.29-32.
4. Medhankar, Dr. Bhadant Sawangi; *The Great Buddhist Emperors of Asia*, 1997, Kashinath Meshram Buddha Bhoomi Prakashan, Nagpur, Maharashtra. pp.27-28. Ahir, D.C; *Ashoka The Great*, 1995, B. R. Publishing Corporation, Delhi. pp.89, 90 Chattopadhyaya, Alaka; Trans, Taranath's *History of Buddhism in India,* first edition (Simla):1970, reprint: Delhi 1990, 1997 and 2004, Motilal Banarsidass, Delhi. pp.60.
5. Beal, Samuel; Trans. from Chinese by Xuanzang *Si-Yu-Ki Buddhist Records of the Western World,* first published:1884, reprinted: 1995, Low Price Publications, Delhi. pp27. Bk. vi. Ahir, D.C; *Ashoka The Great*, 1995, B. R. Publishing Corporation, Delhi. pp.110.
6. Chattopadhyaya, Alaka; Trans, Taranath's *History of Buddhism in India,* first edition (Simla):1970, reprint: Delhi 1990, 1997 and 2004, Motilal Banarsidass, Delhi. pp.61.
7. Liu, Xinru; *Silk and Religion*, 1996, Oxford University Press, Bombay, Calcutta, Madras; pp.47.
8. Liu, Xinru; *Silk and Religion*, 1996, Oxford University Press, Bombay, Calcutta, Madras; pp.47.
9. Beal, Samuel; Shaman Hwui Li *The Life of Hiuen-Tsiang,* first published: 1911, reprinted: 2001, Low Price Publications, Delhi. pp.60.
10. Beal, Samuel; Shaman Hwui Li *The Life of Hiuen-Tsiang,* first published: 1911, reprinted: 2001, Low Price Publications, Delhi. pp.213-214.
11. Beal, Samuel; Shaman Hwui Li *The Life of Hiuen-Tsiang,* first published: 1911, reprinted: 2001, Low Price Publications, Delhi. pp.213-214.
12. Wriggins, Sally Hovey; *The Silk Road Journey with Xuanzang,* 2004, Westview Press, USA.pp.186. Beal, Samuel; Shaman Hwui Li *The Life of Hiuen-Tsiang,* first published: 1911, reprinted: 2001, Low Price Publications, Delhi. pp.212.
13. Hook, Brian; editor, *The Cambridge Encyclopedia of China*, first edition: 1982, second edition: 1991, Press Syndicate of the University of Cambridge; Cambridge, Great Britain. pp.309.
14. Puri, B. N; *Buddhism In Central Asia*, first edition: 1987, reprint: 1993, 1996 and 2000, Motilal Banarsidass Publishers Pvt. Ltd., Delhi.pp.123. Bagci,P.C; *India and China,* first Saraswat edition: 1981, Saraswat Press, Delhi, pp.45-50, 58.
15. Bagci, P.C; *India and China,* first Saraswat edition: 1981, Saraswat Press, Delhi, pp.45.
16. Luo Xiaofei and Yao Xuefeng Trans Qin yuyin, Wei Lingcha and Lu Zuben. *Xian: Places on Interest-Memories of Changan*, World Publishing Corporation, Xian First edition. pp.46
17. Hook, Brian; editor, *The Cambridge Encyclopedia of China*, first edition: 1982, second edition: 1991, Press Syndicate of the University of Cambridge; Cambridge, Great Britain. pp.309.
18. Hook, Brian; editor, *The Cambridge Encyclopedia of China*, first edition: 1982, second edition: 1991, Press Syndicate of the University of Cambridge; Cambridge, Great Britain. pp.309.
19. Acharya, Kala; *Buddhanusmriti* (A Glossary of Buddhist Terms), 2002, Somaiya Publications Pvt. Ltd; Mumbai, New Delhi. pp. 215.
20. Luo Xiaofei and Yao Xuefeng Trans Qin yuyin, Wei Lingcha and Lu Zuben. *Xian: Places on Interest-Memories of Changan*, World

Publishing Corporation, Xian First edition. pp.46.

21. Puri, B. N; *Buddhism In Central Asia*, first edition: 1987, reprint: 1993, 1996 and 2000, Motilal Banarsidass Publishers Pvt. Ltd., Delhi. pp.117-128, 327.
22. Bagci, P.C; *India and China*, first Saraswat edition: 1981, Saraswat Press, Delhi, pp.255. Luo Xiaofei and Yao Xuefeng Trans Qin yuyin, Wei Lingcha and Lu Zuben. *Xian: Places on Interest- Memories of Changan*, World Publishing Corporation, Xian First edition. pg.44-45.
23. Bagci, P.C; *India and China*, first Saraswat edition: 1981, Saraswat Press, Delhi, pp.140-141.
24. Bagci, P.C; *India and China*, first Saraswat edition: 1981, Saraswat Press, Delhi, pp.256. Acharya, Kala; *Buddhanusmriti* (A Glossary of Buddhist Terms), 2002, Somaiya Publications Pvt. Ltd; Mumbai, New Delhi. pp. 217-218.
25. Acharya, Kala; *Buddhanusmriti* (A Glossary of Buddhist Terms), 2002, Somaiya Publications Pvt. Ltd; Mumbai, New Delhi. pp. 217-218.
26 Edward, Conze; *Buddhism- its Essence and Development*, 2001, Munshiram Manoharlal Publishers Pvt. Ltd. New Delhi. pp.174-197.
27. Tucker, Jonathan; *The Silk Road Art and History*, 2003, Timeless Books, New Delhi, pp. 88.
28. Sachau C.Edward; *Alberuni's India* first published by Trubner and Co. Ludgate Hill, 1888, Rupa and Co. first published 2002, fourth impression 2005, New Delhi, pp.176- 179.
29. Needham, Joseph; *Science and Civilisation in China*, first published: 1954, reprint: 1979, Cambridge University Press, London; pp.212.
30. Bagci, P.C; *India and China*, first Saraswat edition: 1981, Saraswat Press, Delhi, pp.97.
31. Needham, Joseph; *Science and Civilisation in China*, first published: 1954, reprint: 979, Cambridge University Press, London; pp.212.
32. Beal, Samuel; Shaman Hwui Li *The Life of Hiuen-Tsiang*, first published: 1911, reprinted: 2001, Low Price Publications, Delhi. pp.xxviii.
33. Bagci, P.C; *India and China*, first Saraswat edition: 1981, Saraswat Press, Delhi, pp.99.
34. Hartog, Leo De; *Genghis Khan: Conqueror of the World*, first published: 1989, paperback edition: 1999, I.B. Tauris & Co. Ltd., London; pp.124-126.
35. Tucker, Jonathan; *The Silk Road Art and History*, 2003, Timeless Books, New Delhi, pp.80.
36. Hook, Brian; editor, *The Cambridge Encyclopedia of China*, first edition: 1982, second edition: 1991, Press Syndicate of the University of Cambridge; Cambridge, Great Britain. pp.296.
37. Olschki, Leonardo; *Marco Polo's Asia*, 1960,University of California Press, Berkeley and Los Angeles, California; Cambridge University Press, London, England, pp.424.
38. Xiaocong Wu & Youmin Guo; *The First Emperor of China*, 2000, China Photographic Publishing House, pp. 83.
39. Xiaocong Wu & Youmin Guo; *The First Emperor of China*, 2000, China Photographic Publishing House, pp. 78. Chien, Szuma; *Selections from Records of the Historian*, 1979, Foreign Languages Press, Peking, China. pp.181.
40. Xiaocong Wu & Youmin Guo; *The First Emperor of China*, 2000, China Photographic Publishing House, pp. 94-95 Chien, Szuma; *Selections from Records of the Historian*, 1979, Foreign Languages Press, Peking, China. pp.179.
41. Xiaocong Wu & Youmin Guo; *The First Emperor of China*, 2000, China Photographic Publishing House, pp. 94-95 Chien, Szuma; *Selections from Records of the Historian*, 1979, Foreign Languages Press, Peking, China. pp.186.
42. Luo Xiaofei and Yao Xuefeng Trans Qin yuyin, Wei Lingcha and Lu Zuben. *Xian: Places of Interest-Memories of Changan*, World Publishing Corporation, Xian, First edition. pg.32-35, 39. Tucker, Jonathan; *The Silk Road Art and History*, 2003, Timeless Books, New Delhi, pp. 97.
43. Luo Xiaofei and Yao Xuefeng Trans Qin yuyin, Wei Lingcha and Lu Zuben. *Xian: Places of Interest-Memories of Changan*, World Publishing Corporation, Xian, First edition. pg.32-35, 39. Tucker, Jonathan; *The Silk Road Art and History*, 2003, Timeless Books, New Delhi, pp. 97.

Chapter Two – To the Pavilion of Buddha at Majishan

1. Tucker, Jonathan; *The Silk Road Art and History*, 2003, Timeless Books. pp.112

2. Lixin, Zheng; *Guide to Chinese Buddhism,* 2004, Foreign Language Press, Beijing,China. pp.3.
3. Hook, Brian; editor, *The Cambridge Encyclopedia of China*, first edition: 1982, second edition: 991, Press Syndicate of the University of Cambridge; Cambridge, Great Britain. pp.305-306.

Chapter Four – To Dafosi at Zhangye

1. Tucker, Jonathan; *The Silk Road Art and History*, 2003, Timeless Books. pp.117-118.
2. Yiping, Zhang; Trans. Jiazongyi; *Story of the Silk Road*, 2005, China Intercontinental Press, China. pp. 80. Tucker, Jonathan; *The Silk Road Art and History*, 2003, Timeless Books. pp.117-118.
3. Henry Yule, Henri Cordier *The Book of Ser* Marco *Polo* Vol I, first edition 1871, first Indian edition 1993; Munshiram Manohar Lal Publisher Pvt. Ltd. Chapter XLIV-Of the city of Campichu. City of Kanchau. pg. 219- 220.
4. Butler, David and Miles, Keith; *Marco Polo,* 1982, Futura Publications, MacDonald & Co. (Publishers) Ltd, London; p.78.
5. Bagci, P.C; *India and China,* first Saraswat edition: 1981, Saraswat Press, Delhi, pp.44.
6. Puri, B. N; *Buddhism In Central Asia*, first edition: 1987, reprint: 1993, 1996 and 2000, Motilal Banarsidass Publishers Pvt. Ltd., Delhi. pp.120.
7. Puri, B. N; *Buddhism In Central Asia*, first edition: 1987, reprint: 1993, 1996 and 2000, Motilal Banarsidass Publishers Pvt. Ltd., Delhi. pp.116-125. Bagci, P.C; *India and China,* first Saraswat edition: 1981, Saraswat Press, Delhi, pp.42-44.
8. Tucker, Jonathan; *The Silk Road Art and History*, 2003, Timeless Books. pp.119.
9. Henry Yule, Henri Cordier *The Book of Ser* Marco *Polo* Vol I, first edition 1871, first Indian edition 1993; Munshiram Manohar Lal Publisher Pvt. Ltd. Chapter XLIV-Of the city of Campichu. City of Kanchau. pg. 219- 220.
10. Man, John; *Kublai Khan,* 2006, Bantam Press, Transworld Publishers, London. pp.203.
11. Man, John; *Kublai Khan,* 2006, Bantam Press, Transworld Publishers, London. pp.203.
12. Man, John; *Kublai Khan,* 2006, Bantam Press, Transworld Publishers, London. pp.203.
13. Man, John; *Kublai Khan,* 2006, Bantam Press, Transworld Publishers, London. pp.39.

Chapter Five – To the Great Wall at Jiayuguan

1. Beal, Samuel; Shaman Hwui Li *The Life of Hiuen-Tsiang,* first published: 1911, reprinted: 2001, Low Price Publications, Delhi. pp.16.

Chapter Six – To Yulin Grottoes at Anxi

1. Jianshan, Zhang; Trans, Li Yuming, *The Anxi Yulin Grottoes*, 2000, Gansu People's Fine Arts Publishing House. pp.8.
2. Tucker, Jonathan; *The Silk Road Art and History*, 2003, Timeless Books. pp.124.
3. Tucker, Jonathan; *The Silk Road Art and History*, 2003, Timeless Books. pp.124.
4. Lixin, Zheng; *Guide to Chinese Buddhism,* 2004, Foreign Language Press, Beijing, China. pp.88.

Chapter Seven – Highway 313 to Dunhuang

1. Yiping, Zhang; Trans. Jia Zongyi *Story of the Silk Road,* 2005, China Inter Continental Press, China. pp.75. p.79.
2. Hopkirk, Peter; *Foreign Devils on the Silk Road*, first published: 1980, first issued in 1984 and reissued in 2001, Oxford University Press: Oxford, Great Britain. pp.157. Dexiang, Gao; Trans Zhu Fuming, *Dunhuang & The Silk Road,* 2000, China Intercontinental Press, Gansu People's Fine Art. pp.2. Tucker, Jonathan; *The Silk Road Art and History*, 2003, Timeless Books. pp.125 Yiping, Zhang; Trans. Jia Zongyi *Story of the Silk Road,* 2005, China Inter Continental Press, China. pp.79.
3. Wenjie, Duan; *Dunhuang Art Through The Eyes Of Duan Wenjei*, Edited, Tan Chung, 1994, Indira Gandhi National Centre For Arts, New Delhi, pp.34. (Introduction-Tan Chung).
4. Yiping, Zhang; Trans. Jia Zongyi *Story of the Silk Road,* 2005, China Inter Continental Press, China. pp.170-173. Hopkirk, Peter; *Foreign Devils on the Silk Road*, first published: 1980, first issued

in 1984 and reissued in 2001, Oxford Dexiang, Gao; Trans Zhu Fuming, *Dunhuang & The Silk Road,* 2000, China Intercontinental Press, Gansu People's Fine Art. pp.222.

5. Dexiang, Gao; Trans Zhu Fuming, *Dunhuang & The Silk Road,* 2000, China Intercontinental Press, Gansu People's Fine Art. pp.223.
6. Hopkirk, Peter; *Foreign Devils on the Silk Road*, first published: 1980, first issued in 1984 and reissued in 2001, Oxford University Press: Oxford, Great Britain. pp.174.
7. Yiping, Zhang; Trans. Jia Zongyi *Story of the Silk Road,* 2005, China Inter Continental Press, China. pp.75.
8. Rhysdavids, T.W. and Oldenberg, Hermann; Translated from Pali; Vinaya Texts, Part I, The Kullavagga IV-XII Khandaka; Motilal Banarsidass Publishers; Delhi; First published by Oxford University Press, 1882; Reprinted: Delhi, 1965, 1968, 1974, 1982, 1990; pp.120.
9. Hopkirk, Peter; *Foreign Devils on the Silk Road*, first published: 1980, first issued in 1984 and reissued in 2001, Oxford University Press: Oxford, Great Britain. pp.220-221.
10. Wenjie, Duan; *Dunhuang Art Through The Eyes Of Duan Wenjei,* Edited, Tan Chung, 1994, Indira Gandhi National Centre For Arts, New Delhi, pp.100
11. Wenjie, Duan; *Dunhuang Art Through The Eyes Of Duan Wenjei,* Edited, Tan Chung, 1994, Indira Gandhi National Centre For Arts, New Delhi, pp.106.
12. Yuanchong, Xu; *300 Gems of Chinese Classical Poetry,* 2004, Peking University Press, China. pp.189.

Chapter Eight – To the Grape Valley at Turfan

1. Yunfei, Cen, Turfan Museum; Edit. *Turfan Museum*, 1992, Xinjiang Fine Arts & Photo Publishing House, Urumqi, China. pp.9.
2. Yunfei, Cen, Turfan Museum; Edit. *Turfan Museum*, 1992, Xinjiang Fine Arts & Photo Publishing House, Urumqi, China. pp.10.
3. CIP; *Comprehensive Survey of 1400 Year History of famous city on the Silk Road-'The Ancient City of Gaochang'* 2001, Xinjiang Fine Arts Photographers Press Publications, pp.2.
4. CIP; *Comprehensive Survey of 1400 Year History of famous city on the Silk Road-'The Ancient City of Gaochang'* 2001, Xinjiang Fine Arts Photographers Press Publications, pp.11.
5. Beal, Samuel; Shaman Hwui Li *The Life of Hiuen-Tsiang,* first published: 1911, reprinted: 2001, Low Price Publications, Delhi. pp.25-30.
6. Hopkirk, Peter; *Foreign Devils on the Silk Road*, first published: 1980, first issued in 1984 and reissued in 2001, Oxford University Press: Oxford, Great Britain. pp.129.
7. Banerji, P; *New Light on Central Asian Art And Iconography*, 1992, Abha Prakashan, Noida, UP. pp.108-109.
8. Johnston, E.H. Trans. *Asvaghosh's Buddhacharita or Acts of the Buddha*, Trans. 1995, first published in Lahore, 1936; Munshiram Manoharlal Publishers Pvt. Ltd; Canto xxii.8-14 pp. 64-65. Misra, Swati; Editor and publisher:*Walking With The Buddha-Buddhist Pilgrimages in India*; Eicher Guide, 1999, New Delhi; Eicher Good Earth Publication; pp. 129.
9. Hopkirk, Peter; *Foreign Devils on the Silk Road*, first published: 1980, first issued in 1984 and reissued in 2001, Oxford University Press: Oxford, Great Britain. pp.126-127.
10. Hopkirk, Peter; *Foreign Devils on the Silk Road*, first published: 1980, first issued in 1984 and reissued in 2001, Oxford University Press: Oxford, Great Britain. pp.208.

Chapter Nine – To Korla on Desert Express

1. Beal, Samuel; Trans. from Chinese by Xuanzang *Si-Yu-Ki Buddhist Records of the Western World,* first published:1884, reprinted:1995, Low Price Publications, Delhi. pp.18.
2. Beal, Samuel; Trans. from Chinese by Xuanzang *Si-Yu-Ki Buddhist Records of the Western World,* first published:1884, reprinted:1995, Low Price Publications, Delhi. pp.18.
3. Younghusband, Captain Frank E; *The Heart of A Continent,* 1994, Book Faith India, Delhi. pp.148.

Chapter Ten – Kuqa—the City of Kumarjiva

1. Chaudhuri, Saroj Kumar; *Lives of Early Buddhist Monks*;2008, Abha Prakashan, New Delhi; pp.101-104.
2. Chaudhuri, Saroj Kumar; *Lives of Early Buddhist Monks*;2008, Abha Prakashan, New Delhi; pp.99.

3. Chaudhuri, Saroj Kumar; *Lives of Early Buddhist Monks*; 2008, Abha Prakashan, New Delhi; p.100.
4. Sir Eliot, Charles; *Hinduism and Buddhism-An Historical Sketch*; First edition 1921, London; Reprint 1988, sri Satguru Publication, Delhi; Vol.III, p.203.
5. Chaudhuri, Saroj Kumar; *Lives of Early Buddhist Monks*;2008, Abha Prakashan, New Delhi; pp.99.
6. Puri, B. N; *Buddhism In Central Asia*, first edition: 1987, reprint: 1993, 1996 and 2000, Motilal Banarsidass Publishers Pvt. Ltd., Delhi. pp.38.
7. Sir Eliot, Charles; *Hinduism and Buddhism-An Historical Sketch*; First edition 1921, London; Reprint 1988, sri Satguru Publication, Delhi; Vol. III, pp. 203.
8. Sir Eliot, Charles; *Hinduism and Buddhism- An Historical Sketch*; First edition 1921,London; Reprint 1988, sri Satguru Publication, Delhi; Vol.III, pp.205.
9. Beal, Samuel; Shaman Hwui Li *The Life of Hiuen-Tsiang*, first published: 1911, reprinted: 2001, Low Price Publications, Delhi. pp.38. Beal, Samuel; Trans. from Chinese by Hieun-Tsiang Si-Yu-ki Buddhist Records of the western world, first published: 1884, reprinted: 1995, L pp, Delhi, pp.19.
10. Tucker, Jonathan; *The Silk Road Art and History*, 2003, Timeless Books, New Delhi. pp.154-156.
11. Beal, Samuel; Trans. from Chinese by Xuanzang *Si-Yu-Ki Buddhist Records of the Western World,* first published:1884, reprinted: 1995, Low Price Publications, Delhi. pp.10.
12. Sir Eliot, Charles; *Hinduism and Buddhism-An Historical Sketch*; First edition 1921, London; Reprint 1988, Sri Satguru Publication, Delhi; Vol.I, pp.140.
13. Burlington, Eugene Watson; *Buddhist Legends*; Translated from original Pali text of the Dhammapada Commentary; Munshiram Manoharlal Publishers Pvt. Ltd. 1999; First published 1921; pp.41-56-'*The Twin Miracles*' Misra, Swati; Editor and publisher:*Walking With The Buddha-Buddhist Pilgrimages in India*; Eicher Guide, 1999, New Delhi; Eicher Good Earth Publication; pp.124.
14. Cowell, E.B; Edit; and Chalmers, Robert, B.A; Trans; *The Jataka or Stories of The Buddha's Former Births*; First published, 1895-1907; Reprinted in LPP, 1990, 1993, 1997, 2001, D.K. Publishers and Distributors Pvt. Ltd. New Delhi; VolIV-VI, No.514.
15. Nelson, Walter Henry; Buddha- His Life and Teaching; 1996; Jeremy P. Thatcher/ Putnam member Penguin Putnam Inc; New York; pp.68-69.
16. Ahir, D.C: *The Influence of Jatakas on Art and Literature*; 2000; B.R. Publishing Corporation; New Delhi; pp. 8.
17. Medhankar, Bhadant Sawangi; *The Great Buddhist Emperors of India*; 1997; Buddha Bhoomi Prakashan, Nagpur; pp.41-55.
18. Medhankar, Bhadant Sawangi; *The Great Buddhist Emperors of India*; 1997; Buddha Bhoomi Prakashan, Nagpur; pp.46.
19. Acharya, Kala; *Buddhanusmriti* (A Glossary of Buddhist Terms), 2002, Somaiya Publications Pvt. Ltd; Mumbai, New Delhi. pp.57. Medhankar, Bhadant Sawangi; *The Great Buddhist Emperors of India*; 1997; Buddha Bhoomi Prakashan, Nagpur; pp.48.
20. Johnston, E.H; Trans, *Asvaghosh's Buddhacharita or Acts of the Buddha*, 1995, first published in Lahore, 1936; Munshiram Manoharlal Publishers Pvt. Ltd, New Delhi; Canto xxvii, 72-73, pp.113.
21. Rhysdavids, T.W. and Oldenberg, Hermann; Translated from Pali; Vinaya Texts, Part III, The Kullavagga IV-XII Khandaka; Motilal Banarsidass Publishers; Delhi; First published by Oxford University Press, 1882; Reprinted: Delhi, 1965, 1968, 1974, 1982, 1990; pp.247.
22. Rhysdavids, T.W. and Oldenberg, Hermann; Translated from Pali; Vinaya Texts, Part III, The Kullavagga IV-XII Khandaka; Motilal Banarsidass Publishers; Delhi;First published by Oxford University Press, 1882; Reprinted: Delhi, 1965, 1968, 1974, 1982, 1990; pp.245.
23. Sir Eliot, Charles; *Hinduism and Buddhism-An Historical Sketch*; First edition 1921, London; Reprint 1988, Sri Satguru Publication, Delhi; Vol.III, pp.204.
24. Whitfield, Susan; *Life along the Silk Road*, first published: 1999, reissued: 2004, John Murray Hodder Headline, London; pp.138.
25. Whitfield, Susan; *Life along the Silk Road*, first published: 1999, reissued: 2004, John Murray Hodder Headline, London; pp.139.
26 Cowell, E.B; Edit; and Chalmers, Robert, B.A; Trans; *The Jataka or Stories of The Buddha's Former Births;* First published, 1895-

1907; Reprinted in LPP, 1990, 1993, 1997, 2001, D.K. Publishers and Distributors Pvt. Ltd. New Delhi; Part II, Vol.IV-VI, No.485.
27. Cowell, E.B; Edit; and Chalmers, Robert, B.A; Trans; *The Jataka or Stories of The Buddha's Former Births*; First published, 1895-1907; Reprinted in LPP, 1990, 1993, 1997, 2001, D.K. Publishers and Distributors Pvt. Ltd. New Delhi; Part II, Vol.IV-VI, No.407.
28. Fei, Feng; *The Nude Art Of The Qiuci Grottoes*, 1992, China Photographic Publishers, China. pp.18-26.
29. Beal, Samuel; Trans. from Chinese by Xuanzang *Si-Yu-Ki Buddhist Records of the Western World*, first published:1884, reprinted:1995, Low Price Publications, Delhi. pp.19-24. Beal, Samuel; Shaman Hwui Li *The Life of Hiuen-Tsiang*, first published: 1911, reprinted: 2001, Low Price Publications, Delhi. pp.37-38.
30. Tucker, Jonathan; *The Silk Road Art and History*, 2003, Timeless Books, New Delhi. pp.159.

Chapter Eleven – Kashgar—A Heady Mix of Old and New

1. Tucker, Jonathan; *The Silk Road Art and History*, 2003, Timeless Books, New Delhi. pp.163.
2. Beal, Samuel; Trans. from Chinese by Xuanzang *Si-Yu-Ki Buddhist Records of the Western World*, first published: 1884, reprinted: 1995, Low Price Publications, Delhi. pp.307.
3. Tucker, Jonathan; *The Silk Road Art and History*, 2003, Timeless Books, New Delhi. pp.164.
Puri, B. N; *Buddhism In Central Asia*, first edition: 1987, reprint: 1993, 1996 and 2000, Motilal Banarsidass Publishers Pvt. Ltd., Delhi. pp38.
4. Hopkirk, Peter; *The Great Game- The Struggle for Empire in Central Asia*, 1994 Kodansha International, New York, Tokyo, London.
5. Hook, Brian; editor, *The Cambridge Encyclopedia of China*, first edition: 1982, second edition: 991, Press Syndicate of the University of Cambridge; Cambridge, Great Britain; pp.222.
6. Kadian, Rajesh; *Tibet : India & China*, 1999, Vision Books Pvt. Ltd, New Delhi. pp.39- 69.
7. Hopkirk, Peter; *The Great Game-The Struggle for Empire in Central Asia*, 1994 Kodansha International, New York, Tokyo, London. pp.502.
8. Hopkirk, Peter; *The Great Game-The Struggle for Empire in Central Asia*, 1994 Kodansha International, New York, Tokyo, London. pp.503. Mayhew, Bradley; Bloom, Greg; Noble, John; Starnes, Dean; *Central Asia*; 2007; Lonely Planet Publications; Australia, USA, UK; pp.44.
9. Hopkirk, Peter; *The Great Game- The Struggle for Empire in Central Asia*, 1994 Kodansha International, New York, Tokyo, London. pp.503.
10. Tucker, Jonathan; *The Silk Road Art and History*, 2003, Timeless Books, New Delhi. pp.165.
11. Bo, Wang; Xuchu, Huo; Trans. Liu,Wensuo, *A Collection of Important Historical Sites and Relics in the Western Regions*, 1999, China Intercontinental Press, Xinjiang Peoples' Publishing Press,China. pp.70.

Chapter Twelve – Inside Taklamakan at Khotan

1. Hedin, Sven; *Central Asia and Tibet* (Vol.I), first published: 1903, first reprint in Nepal:1991, Tiwari's Pilgrim Book House, Kathmandu, Nepal in association with Classics India Publication, Delhi. D.K. Fine Art Press, Delhi, pp.90-98, 272. Hedin, Sven; *Through Asia* (Vol.I and Vol.II), first published: 1898, first reprint in India:1993, Book Faith India, Delhi. pp.788-805.
2. Stein, M.A; *Archaeological and Topographical exploration in Chinese Turkestan*,1985, Anmol, Delhi. pp.40.
3. Antique Administration of Hetian Area. Trans.Liu Chang, *Yutian; Xinjiang History and Culture Series*, 2004,Xinjiang Fine Art and Photograph Publisher. pp.130-135.
4. Stein, M.A; *Archaeological and Topographical exploration in Chinese Turkestan*,1985, Anmol, Delhi. pp.62.
5. Xinjiang Institute of Archaeology, Xinjiang Uygur Autonomous Region Museum; *Sampula in Xinjiang of China*; 2001; Xinjiang Peoples's Publishing House. pp.4.
6. Beal, Samuel; Shaman Trans. Hwui Li *The Life of Hiuen-Tsiang*, first published: 1911, reprinted: 2001, LPP, Delhi. pp.199.
7. Beal, Samuel; Trans. from Chinese by Xuanzang *Si-Yu-Ki Buddhist Records of the Western World*, first published:1884, reprinted:1995, Low Price Publications, Delhi. pp.308.

8. Beal, Samuel; Shaman Hwui Li *The Life of Hiuen-Tsiang,* first published: 1911, reprinted: 2001, Low Price Publications, Delhi. pp.203.
9. Beal, Samuel; Shaman Hwui Li *The Life of Hiuen-Tsiang,* first published: 1911, reprinted: 2001, Low Price Publications, Delhi. pp.203.
10. Beal, Samuel; Shaman Hwui Li *The Life of Hiuen-Tsiang,* first published: 1911, reprinted: 2001, Low Price Publications, Delhi. pp.204.
11. Beal, Samuel; Trans. from Chinese by Xuanzang *Si-Yu-Ki Buddhist Records of the Western World,* first published:1884, reprinted:1995, Low Price Publications, Delhi. pp.322.
12. Beal, Samuel; Trans. from Chinese by Xuanzang *Si-Yu-Ki Buddhist Records of the Western World,* first published:1884, reprinted: 1995, Low Price Publications, Delhi. pp.319.

Chapter Thirteen – To Chengdu—The City of Poets

1. Rockhill, William Woodville; *The Land of the Lamas*, first published: 1891, reprint: 2004, Sri Satguru Publications, Indological and Oriental Publishers- a Division of Indian Books Centre, Delhi. pp.244.
2. Needham, Joseph; *Science and Civilisation in China,* first published: 1954, reprint: 1979, Cambridge University Press, London. pp.174.
3. Dutta, Debabrata; *Histroy of Assam,* re-issued fourth edition: 1989, reprint:1995, Sribhumi Publishing Company, Calcutta. pp.37.
4. Beal, Samuel; Trans. from Chinese by Xuanzang *Si-Yu-Ki Buddhist Records of the Western World,* first published:1884, reprinted:1995, Low Price Publications, Delhi. pp.198.Bk vi.
5. Dutta, Debabrata; *Histroy of Assam,* re-issued fourth edition: 1989, reprint:1995, Sribhumi Publishing Company, Calcutta. pp.35.
6. Honan, Mark; Bindloss, Joseph; Conolly, Joyce; Greenway Paul; Ham, Anthony; Murphy, Allen; Singh, Sarina; *North India,* 2001, Lonely planet Publications Pvt. Ltd,. Australia. pp.644.
7. Dutta, Debabrata; *Histroy of Assam,* re-issued fourth edition: 1989, reprint: 1995, Sribhumi Publishing Company, Calcutta. pp.83.
8. Rockhill, William Woodville; *The Land of the Lamas*, first published: 1891, reprint: 2004, Sri Satguru Publications, Indological and Oriental Publishers- a Division of Indian Books Centre, Delhi. pp.208.
9. Itallie, Nancy van; Ed. *Fodor's China*, 1998, Fodor's Travel Publication,1998, US. pp.346.
10. Beal, Samuel; Shaman Hwui Li *The Life of Hiuen-Tsiang,* first published: 1911, reprinted: 2001, Low Price Publications, Delhi. pp.6.
11. Yuanchong, Xu; Translated; *300 Gems of Chinese Classical Poetry,* 2004, Peking University Press,China.'On The Height' pp.227.
12. Yuanchong, Xu; Translated;*300 Gems of Chinese Classical Poetry,* 2004, Peking University Press, China. pp191-203.
13. Rockhill, William Woodville; *The Land of the Lamas*, first published: 1891, reprint: 2004, Sri Satguru Publications, Indological and Oriental Publishers- a Division of Indian Books Centre, Delhi. pp.278.
14. Rockhill, William Woodville; *The Land of the Lamas*, first published: 1891, reprint: 2004, Sri Satguru Publications, Indological and Oriental Publishers- a Division of Indian Books Centre, Delhi. pp.282.
15. Rockhill, William Woodville; *The Land of the Lamas*, first published: 1891, reprint: 2004, Sri Satguru Publications, Indological and Oriental Publishers – a Division of Indian Books Centre, Delhi. pp.282.
16. Lixin, Zheng; *Guide to Chinese Buddhism,* 2004, Foreign Language Press, Beijing,China. pp.23.

Chapter Fourteen – A Cliff Theatre at Chongqing

1. Jian, Go Xing (Editor); *DAZU: Rock Carvings of China*; 1993, Sichuan Art Publishing House, Chongqing. pp.6,7.
2. Jian, Go Xing (Editor); *DAZU: Rock Carvings of China*; 1993, Sichuan Art Publishing House, Chongqing. pp.6,7.
3. Hook, Brian; editor, *The Cambridge Encyclopedia of China,* first edition: 1982, secondedition: 1991, Press Syndicate of the University of Cambridge; Cambridge, Great Britain. pp.171.
4. Lixin, Zheng; *Guide to Chinese Buddhism,* 2004, Foreign Language Press, Beijing, China. pp.140.
Jian, Go Xing (Editor); *DAZU: Rock Carvings of China*; 1993, Sichuan Art Publishing House, Chongqing. pp.7.

5. Acharya, Kala; *Buddhanusmriti* (A Glossary of Buddhist Terms), 2002, Somaiya Publications Pvt Ltd; Mumbai, New Delhi. pp. 203.

6. Edward, Conze; *Buddhism – its Essence and Development,* 2001, Munshiram Manoharlal Publishers Pvt. Ltd. New Delhi. pp.147.

Chapter Fifteen – Routes into Tibet

1. Holdich, H. Thomas; *Tibet The Mysterious,* 2005, Rupa & Co, New Delhi. pp.10-11. Cunningham, Alexander: *Ladak Physical, Staistical And Historical,* first published 1854, Wm.H.Allen and Co., London; 1998 Asian Educational Services, New Delhi, Madras. pp.146-166. Bhattacharji, Romesh; *Lands Of Early Dawn-North-East India;* 2002; Rupa and Co; New Delhi; *Of People and Land Routes to China* 2002; *Road To Progress;* Frontline; Vol 26, Issue 4, Feb 14-27, 2009. Shering, A.Charles: *Western Tibet and Indian Borderland,* CA (Vol 37); first published 1974;1987;Cosmo Publications; Delhi (Indian Historical Researches p.340 chpt xvii.

2. Holdich, H. Thomas; *Tibet The Mysterious,* 2005, Rupa & Co, New Delhi. p.33.

3. Klimburg-Salter, Deborah. E; *TABO: A Lamp for the Kingdom,* first published: 1989, reprint: 1997, Skira Editore, Milan, Italy. p.31.

4. Klimburg-Salter, Deborah.E; *TABO: A Lamp for the Kingdom,* first published: 1989, reprint: 1997, Skira Editore, Milan, Italy. p.31.

5. Walton, H.G; *Gazetteer of Garhwal Himalaya,* first published: 1910, reprint: 1989, Upendra Arora for Natraj Publishers, Dehra Dun. pp.182,192.

6. Honan, Mark; Bindloss, Joseph; Conolly, Joyce; Greenway Paul; Ham, Anthony; Murphy, Allen; Singh, Sarina; *North India,* 2001, Lonely planet Publications Pvt. Ltd,.Australia. p.475. See map

7. Lama, Dalai; *My Land and My People-Memoirs of His Holiness the Dalai Lama,* first Published: 1977, paperback: 1999, Srishti Publishers & Distributors, New Delhi. pp.202-216.

8. Prakash A. Jha; *Kathmandu & the Kingdom of Nepal*, Lonely Planet, 13th edition, 2000, Nabeen Publications, Kathmandu, Nepal. pp.127-129.

9. Risley, H.H; Introduced; *The Gazetteer of Sikkim*; first published 1928, reprinted 1993, 1995, 1999, 2001; D.K. Publishers Distributors P. Ltd. New Delhi; p.244.

10. Chattopadhyaya, Alaka; *Atisa and Tibet,* First Edition: Calcutta 1967, Reprint: Delhi 1981, 1996 and 1999, Narendra Prakash Jain for Motilal Banarsidass Publishers Pvt. Ltd, Delhi.

Map: The Southern Silk Road via Tibet and Kashmir
Map of 'Tibet And Adjacent Countries'; REG. No. 433x.D.D. 1938-1,000; Compiled 1919. Courtesy Romesh Bhattacharji. Cunningham, Alexander: *Ladak Physical, Statistical And Historical,* first published 1854, Wm.H.Allen and Co., London; 1998 Asian Educational Services, New Delhi, Madras.pp.146-166. Klimburg-Salter, Deborah.E; *TABO: A Lamp for the Kingdom,* first published: 1989, reprint: 1997, Skira Editore, Milan, Italy. p.31-33. Bhattacharji, Romesh; *Lands Of Early Dawn-North-East India;*2002; Rupa and Co; New Delhi; *Of People and Land Routes to China* 2002; Rupa and Co; New Delhi; Prakash.A.Jha; *Kathmandu & the Kingdom of Nepal,* 13th edition, 2000, Nabeen Publications, Kathmandu, Nepal.pp.127-129. Allen, B.C; Gait, E.A; Howard H.F; Allen, C.G.H; *Gazetteer of Bengal and North-East India,* reproduced: 1979, again in 1982, 1986, 1989, 1993, 1996, 2001 and 2005, Mittal Publications, Mohan Garden, New Delhi; map of Eastern Bengal and Assam with Bhutan.

Map: Kinnaur-Sangla- Spiti Valley Routes Into Tibet
Map of 'Tibet And Adjacent Countries'; REG. No. 433x.D.D. 1938-1,000; Compiled 1919. Courtesy Romesh Bhattacharji. Bhattacharji, Romesh; *Of People and Land Routes to China* 2002; Rupa and Co; New Delhi. Klimburg-Salter, Deborah.E; *TABO: A Lamp for the Kingdom,* first published: 1989, reprint: 1997, Skira Editore, Milan, Italy. pp 31-33. Honan, Mark; Bindloss, Joseph; Conolly, Joyce; Greenway Paul; Ham, Anthony; Murphy, Allen; Singh, Sarina; *North India*, 2001, Lonely Planet Publications Pvt. Ltd, Australia. p.475.

Map: Routes Into Tibet From Uttranchal
Map of 'Tibet And Adjacent Countries'; REG. No. 433x.D.D. 1938-1,000; Compiled 1919. Courtesy Romesh Bhattacharji. Walton, H.G; *Gazetteer of Garhwal Himalaya,* first published: 1910, reprint: 1989, Upendra Arora for Natraj Publishers, Dehra Dun.pp.182, 192. Kumaon Tourism Department, Govt.

Of India, New Delhi. Kumaon Tourism; Tourism Department; Govt of India; Janpath, New Delhi.

Map: Routes Into Tibet From North-East India and Bhutan
Map of 'Tibet And Adjacent Countries'; REG. No. 433x.D.D. 1938-1,000; Compiled 1919. Courtesy Romesh Bhattacharji. Bhattacharji, Romesh; *Lands Of Early Dawn-North-East India*; 2002; Rupa and Co; New Delhi; *Of People and Land Routes to China* 2002; Rupa and Co; New Delhi; *Road To Progress*; Frontline; Vol 26, Issue 4, Feb 14-27, 2009; Rupa and Co; New Delhi. Allen, B.C; Gait, E.A; Howard H.F; Allen, C.G.H; *Gazetteer of Bengal and North- EastIndia*, reproduced: 1979, again in 1982, 1986, 1989, 1993, 1996, 2001 and 2005, Mittal Publications, Mohan Garden, New Delhi; pp.168 Sali, M.L: *India –China Border Dispute –A Case Study of the Eastern Sector; 1998; APH Publishing Corporation; New Delhi*; pp.17-30,59,110.

Map: Routes Into Tibet From Nepal
Map of 'Kathmandu To Tibet'; Mandala Maps; Mandala Publications; Mandala Graphic Art; courtesy Romesh Bhandari Prakash. A. Jha; *Kathmandu & the Kingdom of Nepal*, 13th edition, 2000, Nabeen Publications, Kathmandu, Nepal. pp17.

Chapter Sixteen – Beyond the Himalayas to Lhasa

1. Holdich, H. Thomas; *Tibet The Mysterious*, 2005, Rupa & Co, New Delhi. Hopkirk, Peter; *Trespassers on the Roof of the World*; first published: 1982, first Issued: 1983; Oxford University Press; Oxford, Great Britain.
2. Hopkirk, Peter; *Trespassers on the Roof of the World*; first published: 1982, first Issued: 1983; Oxford University Press; Oxford, Great Britain. pp1.
3. Hopkirk, Peter; *Trespassers on the Roof of the World*; first published: 1982, first Issued: 1983; Oxford University Press; Oxford, Great Britain. pp1-2.
4. Hopkirk, Peter; *The Great Game-The Struggle for Empire in Central Asia*; 1994, Kodansha America Inc.; 1990, 1992; Kodansha International Ltd; New York, Tokyo, London; first published in Great Britain in 1990 as *The Great Game: On Secret Service in High Asia*; John Murray Publishers Ltd. pp.505.
5. Hopkirk, Peter; *The Great Game-The Struggle for Empire in Central Asia*; 1994,. Kodansha America Inc.; 1990, 1992; Kodansha International Ltd; New York, Tokyo,. London; first published in Great Britain in 1990 as *The Great Game: On Secret. Service in High Asia*; John Murray Publishers Ltd. pp.505-506.
6. Hopkirk, Peter; *Trespassers on the Roof of the World*; first published: 1982, first. Issued: 1983; Oxford University Press; Oxford, Great Britain. pp.159-183.
7. Hopkirk, Peter; *Trespassers on the Roof of the World*; first published: 1982, first Issued: 1983; Oxford University Press; Oxford, Great Britain. p.3.
8. Risley, H.H, Introduced; *The Gazetteer of Sikkim*; first published 1928, reprinted 1993, 1995, 1999, 2001; D.K. Publishers Distributors P. Ltd. New Delhi; p.244.
9. Das, Sarat Chandra; *A Journey To Lhasa And Central Tibet*; Edited by W.W. Rockhill; 2007, Rupa and Co. Delhi. p.153.
10. Das, Sarat Chandra; *A Journey To Lhasa And Central Tibet*; Edited by W.W. Rockhill; 2007, Rupa and Co. Delhi. p.154.
11. Risley, H.H. Introduced The Gazetteer of Sikkim; first published 1928, reprinted 1993, 1995, 1999, 2001; D.K. Publishers Distributors P. Ltd. New Delhi; p.314.
12. Das, Sarat Chandra; *A Journey To Lhasa And Central Tibet*; Edited by W.W. Rockhill; 2007, Rupa and Co. Delhi. p.160.
13. Caidan An; *Tibet of China*, 2003, China Intercontinental Press, China. p.72.
14. Acharya, Kala; *Buddhanusmriti* (A Glossary of Buddhist Terms), 2002, Somaiya Publications Pvt. Ltd; Mumbai, New Delhi. p.112.
15. Acharya, Kala; *Buddhanusmriti* (A Glossary of Buddhist Terms),2002, Somaiya Publications Pvt. Ltd; Mumbai, New Delhi. p.112.
16. Das, Sarat Chandra; *A Journey To Lhasa And Central Tibet*; Edited by W.W. Rockhill; 2007, Rupa and Co. Delhi. pp.167-168. Hopkirk, Peter; Trespassers on the *Roof of the world*; first published: 1982, first Issued: 1983, Oxford University Press, Oxford. Great Britani. p.33.
17. Tibetan Medicine Pharmaceutical Factory of TAR, China Intercontinental Press

18. Allen, B.C; Gait, E.A; Howard H.F; Allen, C.G.H; *Gazetteer of Bengal and North- East India*, reproduced: 1979, again in 1982, 1986, 1989, 1993, 1996, 2001 and 2005, Mittal Publications, Mohan Garden, New Delhi; pp.168.
19. Caidan An; *Tibet of China,*2003, China Intercontinental Press, China. pp.3, 159-164.
20. Yang Shuying; *News From China*, July 2006 (Vol XVIII No.7) published New Delhi. pp.11.
21. Yang Shuying; *News From China*, July 2006 (Vol XVIII No.7) published New Delhi. pp.12.
22. Yang Shuying; *News From China*, July 2006 (Vol XVIII No.7) published New Delhi. pp.12. China's Tibet, Vol.17, *Qinghai-Tibet Railway 'Train Ready to Climb toLhasa,'* 2006, Beijing. pp.30.
23. Disclosed by Mr Thondrup, Director of Tourism Bureau of the Tibet Autonomous Region of China while meeting an Indian delegation of which the author was a part.

Chapter Seventeen – Gallery of 'Avalokitesvara'

1. Gupta, S.P; Edit. *Masterpieces from the National Museum Collection, Central Asian Antiquities*, National Museum, New Delhi. Catalogue- Chaya Haesner
2. For description of Avalokitesvara see: Chandra, Lokesh; *Transcendental Art Of Tibet; Indo-Asian Literatures Vol* 385, first published 1996 International Academy of Indian Culture and Aditya Prakashan, New Delhi. Lixin, Zheng; *Guide to Chinese Buddhism,* 2004, Foreign Language Press, Beijing, China. pp.78. Banerji, P; *Central Asian Art-New Revelations from Xinjiang,* 2001, Abha Prakashan, Noida, UP, pp.101. Acharya, Kala; *Buddhanusmriti* (A Glossary of Buddhist Terms), 2002, Somaiya Publications Pvt. Ltd; Mumbai, New Delhi. pp.36, 67, 69, 112. Edward, Conze; *Buddhism-its Essence and Development,* 2001, Munshiram Manoharlal Publishers Pvt. Ltd. New Delhi. pp.146, 147. Banerji, P. *New Light on Central Asian Art and Iconography,* 1992, Abha Prakashan, Noida, UP, pp.162-164. Puri, B. N; *Buddhism In Central Asia*, first edition: 1987, reprint: 1993, 1996 and 2000, Motilal Banarsidass Publishers Pvt. Ltd., Delhi. pp.142. Sir Eliot, Charles; *Hinduism and Buddhism- An Historical Sketch*; First edition 1921, London; Reprint 1988, Sri Satguru Publication, Delhi; Vol.II, pp.7-25.
3. Sir Eliot, Charles; *Hinduism and Buddhism-An Historical Sketch*; First edition1921, London; Reprint 1988, Sri Satguru Publication, Delhi; Vol.II, pp.15.
4. Acharya, Kala; *Buddhanusmrti* (A Glossary of Buddhist Terms), 2002, Somaiya Publications Pvt. Ltd; Mumbai, New Delhi. pp.112.
5. Acharya, Kala; *Buddhanusmrti* (A Glossary of Buddhist Terms), 2002, Somaiya Publications Pvt. Ltd; Mumbai, New Delhi. pp.112.
6. Sir Eliot, Charles; *Hinduism and Buddhism-An Historical Sketch*; First edition1921, London; Reprint 1988, Sri Satguru Publication, Delhi; Vol.II, pp.15.
7. Edward, Conze; *Buddhism- its Essence and Development,* 2001, Munshiram Manoharlal Publishers Pvt. Ltd. New Delhi. pp.147.
8. Banerji, P; *Central Asian Art-New Revelations from Xinjiang*, 2001, Abha Prakashan, Noida, UP. pp.101.
9. Acharya, Kala; *Buddhanusmrti* (A Glossary of Buddhist Terms), 2002, Somaiya Publications Pvt. Ltd; Mumbai, New Delhi. pp.112.
10. Acharya, Kala; *Buddhanusmrti* (A Glossary of Buddhist Terms), 2002, Somaiya Publications Pvt. Ltd; Mumbai, New Delhi. pp.200.
11. Acharya, Kala; *Buddhanusmrti* (A Glossary of Buddhist Terms), 2002, Somaiya Publications Pvt. Ltd; Mumbai, New Delhi. pp.94.
12. Gupta, S.P; Edit. *Masterpieces from the National Museum Collection,Central Asian Antiquities*, National Museum, New Delhi. pp.182-306. Catalogue- Chaya Haesner.
13. Gupta, S.P; Edit. *Masterpieces from the National Museum Collection, Central Asian Antiquities*, National Museum, New Delhi. pp.182-306. Catalogue-Chaya Haesner.
14. Puri, B. N; *Buddhism In Central Asia*, first edition: 1987, reprint: 1993, 1996 and 2000, Motilal Banarsidass Publishers Pvt. Ltd., New Delhi. pp.38.
15. Puri, B. N; *Buddhism In Central Asia*, first edition: 1987, reprint: 1993, 1996 and 2000, Motilal Banarsidass Publishers Pvt. Ltd., New Delhi. pp.271.

16. Banerji, P; *New Light on Central Asian Art And Iconography*, 1992, Abha Prakashan, Noida, UP. pp.17 and 20. See also: Gupta, S.P; Edit. *Masterpieces from the National Museum Collection, Central Asian Antiquities*, National Museum, New Delhi. pp.182-306. Catalogue-Chaya Haesner.
17. Banerji, P; *New Light on Central Asian Art And Iconography*, 1992, Abha Prakashan, Noida, UP. pp.40).
18. Edward, Conze; *Buddhism- its Essence and Development*, 2001, Munshiram Manoharlal Publishers Pvt. Ltd. New Delhi. pp178.
19. Banerji, P; *Central Asian Art- New Revelations from Xinjiang*, 2001, Abha Prakashan, Noida, UP. pp.190).

Photo Credits

Special thanks to **The Government and the Ministry of Culture of the Peoples' Republic of China** and the **Chinese Embassy** at New Delhi for permitting the author to travel and photograph the sites along the Silk Road through the provinces of Shaanxi, Gansu, Xinjiang, Sichuan and Tibet Autonomous Region.

All photos by Sunita Dwivedi except the following mentioned under photo credit:

World Heritage; Patrimoine Mundial, China Intercontinental Press, photo by Wang Baoping, p.21, photo by Xia Juxian and Guo Yan, p.22.

Wu Zhengke: *Probing Into the History of Dafosi Temple*, photo by Xue Qinxue, Zhang Minlin, People's Publishing House of Gansu, p.69.

Jianshan Zhang, Yunshi Liu, *The Anxi Yulin Grottoes*, 2000 Gansu People's Fine Arts Publishing House and Anxi Yulin grottoes ticket office, China, p.86 and p.87.

Dunhuang Research Academy and **Dunhuang Slides Publishing Company**, Dunhuang, China, p.96.
Beijing Slides Publishing Company, Lan Peijin, photo by Wang Guanmin, p.101, p.102.
Magao Grottoes Ticket office, p.104-105.
Dunhuang Museum, p.109. Western Thousand Buddha Caves Ticket Office, p.112.
Xinjiang Kucha Institute of Caves, Xinjiang, China, p.165, p.166, p.168, p.170-171.

Chinese Embassy, New Delhi, Li Hubing, p.308.

Lokesh Chandra: p.xii, xxi.

National Museum, New Delhi, p.xxxi, xxxii, xxxiii, xxxiv, xxxvi, xliv, p.95, p.138, p.145 (extreme left, middle, extreme right). p.310, p.312-316, p.318-326.

Index